Community

 McMaster Divinity College Press
**McMaster Biblical Studies Series,
Volume 9**

Community

*Biblical and Theological Reflections
in Honor of August H. Konkel*

Edited by
RICK WADHOLM JR. *and* MEGHAN D. MUSY

☙PICKWICK *Publications* · Eugene, Oregon

COMMUNITY

Biblical and Theological Reflections in Honor of August H. Konkel

McMaster Biblical Studies Series, Volume 9
McMaster Divinity College Press

ISSN 2564-4343 (Print)
ISSN 2564-4351 (Ebook)

Copyright © 2022 Wipf and Stock Publishers. All rights reserved. Except for brief quotations in critical publications or reviews, no part of this book may be reproduced in any manner without prior written permission from the publisher. Write: Permissions, Wipf and Stock Publishers, 199 W. 8th Ave., Suite 3, Eugene, OR 97401.

Pickwick Publications
An Imprint of Wipf and Stock Publishers
199 W. 8th Ave., Suite 3
Eugene, OR 97401

McMaster Divinity College Press
1280 Main Street West
Hamilton, Ontario, Canada
L8S 4K1

www.wipfandstock.com

PAPERBACK ISBN: 978-1-5326-3928-9
HARDCOVER ISBN: 978-1-5326-3929-6
EBOOK ISBN: 978-1-5326-3930-2

Cataloguing-in-Publication data:

Names: Wadholm, Rick Jr., editor| Musy, Meghan D., editor

Title: Community : biblical and theological reflections in honor of August H. Konkel / Rick Wadholm Jr. and Meghan D. Musy, editors.

Description: Eugene, OR: Pickwick Publications, 2022 | McMaster Biblical Studies Series | Includes bibliographical references and index.

Identifiers: ISBN 978-1-5326-3928-9 (paperback) | ISBN 978-1-5326-3929-6 (hardcover) | ISBN 978-1-5326-3930-2 (ebook)

Subjects: LCSH: Konkel, August H. | Bible. Criticism, interpretation, etc.

Classification: BS2361.3 W23 2022 (paperback) | BS2361.3 (ebook)

04/08/22

In honor of his 70th birthday, this volume is dedicated to the tireless commitment of August "Gus" H. Konkel for the Lord on behalf of the Church and World.

Contents

Contributors | viii

Abbreviations | x

Introduction—Rick Wadholm Jr. | xvi

1 A Cord of Three Strands is Not Quickly Broken: The Deterioration of Unity and Community in Judges —*Mary L. Conway* / 1

2 An Evil Spirit from God? The Role of (the) (S/s)pirit(s) of God in Judges, Samuel, and Kings—*Mark J. Boda* / 24

3 Prophetic Testimony for the Community: Reflections from 1 Kings 13 for the Church Today—*Rick Wadholm Jr.* / 43

4 The Community of Israel in 1 Chronicles 1–9 —*Gary V. Smith* / 57

5 All in the Family of David: The Chronicler's Change from the Ammonite (2 Sam 17:25) to the Davidic Zeruiah (1 Chr 2:16)—*Paul S. Evans* / 74

6 Job Breaks Bad: When God Weighs In—*Randall Holm* / 93

7 Babylon in the Book of Isaiah—*H. G. M. Williamson* / 103

8 Where is the Study of the Septuagint Going, and Should It? —*Stanley E. Porter* / 126

9 Lexicographical Notes on the Septuagint of Zechariah —*Al Wolters* / 144

10 The Congregation of the Poor: Poverty as a Self-Designation in the Dead Sea Scrolls—*Daniel K. Falk* / 170

11 Reading Luke-Acts as a Mennocostal: Pentecostals, Mennonites, and the Prophethood of All Believers —*Martin W. Mittelstadt* / 194

12 The Word of God and Christian Community —*David Johnson* / 212

13 Destruction and Restoration of Genuine Human Community in Dietrich Bonhoeffer's *Creation and Fall* —*Patrick S. Franklin* / 226

Ancient Documents Index | 255

Authors Index | 269

Contributors

Mark J. Boda is Professor of Old Testament at McMaster Divinity College, Hamilton, ON, Canada.

Mary L. Conway is Assistant Professor of Old Testament at McMaster Divinity College, Hamilton, ON, Canada.

Paul S. Evans is Associate Professor of Old Testament at McMaster Divinity College, Hamilton, ON, Canada.

Daniel K. Falk is Professor of Classics and Ancient Mediterranean Studies, and Head, Department of Classics and Ancient Mediterranean Studies at The Pennsylvania State University, State College, PA.

Patrick Franklin is Associate Professor of Theology at Tyndale Seminary, Toronto, ON, Canada.

Randall Holm is Professor of Spiritual Formation at Providence University College, Otterburne, MB, Canada.

David H. Johnson is President of Providence University College and Seminary, Otterburne, MB, Canada.

Martin Mittelstadt is Professor of New Testament at Evangel University, Springfield, MO.

Meghan D. Musy is Assistant Professor of Old Testament at the Assemblies of God Theological Seminary at Evangel University, Springfield, MO.

Stanley E. Porter is President and Dean, Professor of New Testament, and Roy A. Hope Chair in Christian Worldview at McMaster Divinity College, Hamilton, ON, Canada.

Contributors

Gary V. Smith is retired from Union University, Jackson, TN.

Rick Wadholm Jr. is Associate Professor of Old Testament the Assemblies of God Theological Seminary at Evangel University, Springfield, MO.

H. G. M. Williamson, OBE, FBA, is Regius Professor of Hebrew Emeritus at University of Oxford and Emeritus Student of Christ Church.

Al Wolters is Emeritus Professor of Religion at Redeemer University College, Ancaster, ON, Canada.

Abbreviations

AB	Anchor Bible
ABD	Freedman, David Noel, ed. *Anchor Bible Dictionary*. 6 vols. New York: Doubleday, 1992
AG	Assemblies of God
AnBib	Analecta Biblica
ANET	Pritchard, James B., ed. *Ancient Near Eastern Texts Relating to the Old Testament*. 3rd ed. Princeton: Princeton University Press, 1969
AOAT	Alter Orient und Altes Testament
ApOTC	Apollos Old Testament Commentary
ARTA	*Achaemenid Research on Texts and Archaeology*
ATDan	Acta Theologica Danica
BA	*La Bible de'Alexandrie*
BCBC	Believers Church Bible Commentary
BDB	Brown, Francis, et al. *A Hebrew and English Lexicon of the Old Testament*. Oxford: Clarendon, 1907.
BEATAJ	Beiträge zur Erforschung des Alten Testaments und des antiken Judentum
BETL	Bibliotheca Ephemeridum Theologicarum Lovaniensium
BG	*Libros proféticos*. Vol. 4 of *La Biblia Griega Septuaginta*. Translated by María Victoria Spottorno et al. Biblioteca de Estudios Bíblicos 128. Salamanca: Sígueme, 2015
Bib	*Biblica*
BibInt	*Biblical Interpretation*

Abbreviations

BibInt	Biblical Interpretation Series
BJSUCSD	Biblical and Judaic Studies from the University of California, San Diego
BKAT	Biblischer Kommentar, Altes Testament
Brenton	*The Septuagint with Apocrypha: Greek and English.* Translated by Lancelot C. L. Brenton. London: Bagster & Sons, 1851. Repr., Peabody, MA: Hendrickson, 1986
BSac	*Bibliotheca Sacra*
BWANT	Beitrage zur Wissenschaft vom Alten und Neuen Testament
BZAW	Beihefte zur Zeitschrift fur die alttestamentliche Wissenschaft
BZNW	Beihefte zur Zeitschrift für die neutestamentliche Wissenschaft
CBC	Cambridge Bible Commentary
CBET	Contributions to Biblical Exegesis and Theology
CBQ	*Catholic Biblical Quarterly*
CC	Continental Commentaries
CCSL	Corpus Christianorum: Series Latina
CD	Cairo Genizah copy of the Damascus Document
CNRS	Centre National de la Recherche Scientifique
ConBOT	Coniectanea Biblica: Old Testament Series
CP	*Sacra Biblia ad LXX: interpretum fidem diligentissime translata.* Translated by Juan de Vergara. Alcalá de Henares: de Brocar, 1514–1517. Repr., Basel: A. Cratander, 1526
CurBR	*Currents in Biblical Research*
DJD	Discoveries in the Judaean Desert
Doutreleau	*Didyme l'Aveugle Sur Zacharie: Text inédit d'après un papyrus de Toura.* Introduction, critical text, translation, and notes by Louis Doutreleau. 3 vol. SC 83–85. Paris: Cerf, 1962
DSD	*Dead Sea Discoveries*

Abbreviations

EB	Echter Bibel
Ebib	*Etudes bibliques*
EJL	Early Judaism and Its Literature
FAT	Forschungen zum Alten Testament
FRLANT	Forschungen zur Religion und Literatur des Alten und Neuen Testaments
GE	Montanari, Franco. *The Brill Dictionary of Ancient Greek.* English edition edited by Madeleine Goh and Chad Schroeder. Leiden: Brill, 2015
GELS	Muraoka, Takamitsu. *A Greek-English Lexicon of the Septuagint.* Leuven: Peeters, 2009
Giguet	*Job–Malchie.* Vol. 3 of *La Sainte Bible: Traduction de l' Ancien Testament d' après les Septante.* Translated by P. Giguet. Paris: Librairie Poussielgue Frères, 1872
HAL	Koehler, Ludwig, et al. *Hebraisches und aramaisches Lexikon zum Alten Testament.* 3rd ed. Leiden: Brill, 1995, 2004
HALOT	Koehler, Ludwig, et al. *The Hebrew and Aramaic Lexicon of the Old Testament.* Translated and edited under the supervision of Mervyn E. J. Richardson. 4 vols. Leiden: Brill, 1994–1999
HAT	Handbuch zum Alten Testament
HBM	Hebrew Bible Monographs
HCOT	Historical Commentary on the Old Testament
HKAT	Handkommentar zum Alten Testament
HSM	Harvard Semitic Monographs
IBC	Interpretation: A Bible Commentary for Teaching and Preaching
ICC	International Critical Commentary
IEJ	*Israel Exploration Journal*
Int	*Interpretation*
JAOS	*Journal of the American Oriental Society*
JBL	*Journal of Biblical Literature*

Abbreviations

JBQ	*Jewish Bible Quarterly*
JCS	*Journal of Cuneiform Studies*
Jerome	Jerome. *Commentarii in Prophetas Minores.* Vol. 1.6 of *S. Hieronymi Presbyteri Opera.* Edited by Marcus Adriaen. CCSL 76A. Turnholt: Brepols, 1970
JETS	*Journal of the Evangelical Theological Society*
JHebS	*Journal of Hebrew Scriptures*
JSOT	*Journal for the Study of the Old Testament*
JSOTSup	Journal for the Study of the Old Testament Supplement Series
KHC	Kurzer Hand-Commentar zum Alten Testament
LEH	Lust, Johan, et al., eds. *Greek-English Lexicon of the Septuagint.* Rev. ed. Stuttgart: Deutsche Bibelgesellschaft, 2003
LHBOTS	The Library of Hebrew Bible/Old Testament Studies
LSAWS	*Linguistic Studies in Ancient West Semitic*
LSJ	Liddell, Henry George, and Robert Scott. *A Greek-English Lexicon.* 9th ed. Oxford: Oxford University Press, 1940
LSJ1996	Liddell, Henry George et al. *A Greek-English Lexicon.* 9th ed. with revised supplement. Edited by P. G. W. Glare with A. Thompson. Oxford: Clarendon, 1996
LSTS	The Library of Second Temple Studies
MDS	Mennonite Disaster Service
NAC	New American Commentary
NCB	New Century Bible
NETS	*A New English Translation of the Septuagint.* Edited by Albert Pietersma and Benjamin G. Wright. New York: Oxford University Press, 2007
NIBCOT	New International Biblical Commentary on the Old Testament
NICOT	New International Commentary on the Old Testament
NIVAC	New International Version Application Commentary

Abbreviations

NSKAT	Neuer Stuttgarter Kommentar, Altes Testament
OBO	Orbis Biblicus et Orientalis
OED	*Oxford English Dictionary*. Edited by J. A. Simpson and E. S. C. Weiner. 2nd ed. 10 vols. Oxford: Oxford University Press, 1989.
OTG	Old Testament Guides
OTL	Old Testament Library
OTS	Old Testament Studies
PIBA	Proceedings of the Irish Biblical Association
PIHANS	Publications de l'Institut historique-archeologique neerlandais de Stamboul
Prob.	*Quod omnis probus liber sit*
ProEccl	*Pro Ecclesia*
RelSoc	Religion and Society
SBLDS	Society of Biblical Literature Dissertation Series
SBLSCS	SBL Septuagint and Cognate Studies
SC	Sources chretiennes
Schleusner	Schleusner, J. F. *Novus thesaurus philologico-criticus, sive lexicon in LXX et reliquos interpretes graecos ac scriptores apocryphos Veteris Testamenti.* 3 vols. Leipzig: Weidmann, 1822
SEÅ	*Svensk exegetisk årsbok*
SGLG	Sammlung griechischer und lateinischer Grammatiker
SJT	*Scottish Journal of Theology*
SNTSMS	Society for New Testament Studies Monograph Series
SOG	The Story of God Bible Commentary
SPCK	Society for Promoting Christian Knowledge
STDJ	Studies on the Texts of the Desert of Judah
SV	Rehkopf, Friedrich. *Septuaginta-Vokabular.* Göttingen: Vandenhoeck & Ruprecht, 1989
SymS	Symposium Series

Abbreviations

Thomson	*The Old Covenant, Commonly Called the Old Testament: Translated from the Septuagint*. Translated by Charles Thomson. Vol. 2. London: Skeffington & Son, 1904
ThWAT	*Theologisches Wörterbuch zum Alten Testament*. Edited by G. Johannes Botterweck and Helmer Ringgren. Stuttgart: Kohlhammer, 1970–
TLG	*Thesaurus Linguae Graecae: Canon of Greek Authors and Works*. Edited by Luci Berkowitz and Karl A. Squitier. 3rd ed. New York: Oxford University Press, 1990
TJ	*Trinity Journal*
TOTC	Tyndale Old Testament Commentaries
UBCS	Understanding the Bible Commentary Series
VT	*Vetus Testamentum*
VTSup	Supplements to Vetus Testamentum
WBC	Word Biblical Commentary
WLAW	Wisdom Literature from the Ancient World
YNER	Yale Near Eastern Researches
ZAW	*Zeitschrift für die alttestamentliche Wissenschaft*

Introduction

A SHORT BIOGRAPHY OF AUGUST H. KONKEL

For his first year of pastoral ministry (1969–1970), August "Gus" H. Konkel took a small Associated Gospel Church, Kelfield Gospel Church, in Kelfield, Saskatchewan, right after graduating from Briercrest Bible Institute at the age of 20. From Kelfield, he entered Winnipeg Bible College (now Providence University College and Theological Seminary), Otterburne, Manitoba to earn a Bachelors of Religious Education (1971). From 1971 to 1982, Gus pastored Bethel Bergthaler Mennonite Church in Winkler, Manitoba, from which he would commute to Winnipeg Theological Seminary to finish an MDiv (1977). Gus was ordained a minister by the General Conference Mennonite Church, which is now the Mennonite Church Canada, in 1972. In May of that same year, Gus married Esther Andres and over the coming years welcomed their four children: Melanie, Blythe, Theodore (Ted), and Tessa all while Gus continued pursuing his master's degree and PhD. While pastoring in Winkler, he also taught at Winkler Bible Institute (1978–1982) until entering Westminster Theological Seminary (Glenside, PA) to earn a PhD. under the supervision of Raymond Dillard. While writing his dissertation, Gus returned to his alma mater, Providence Theological Seminary, in 1984 as a professor of Old Testament. Gus completed his dissertation, titled, "Hezekiah in Biblical Tradition," in 1987. After In 2001, after over 15 years of serving as a faculty member, Gus became the president of Providence and held this post until he retired in 2012. He was appointed President Emeritus at Providence. However, Gus's passion for the church and academia

xvii

Introduction

drew him back into teaching at McMaster Divinity College, Hamilton, Ontario. as Professor of Old Testament. Gus remains a widely sought preacher—preaching an average of thirty Sundays a year since 1984—and has annually traveled internationally to teach.

PERSONAL REFLECTIONS: ON GUS AND COMMUNITY

I (Rick) took a number of graduate courses with Gus during my time at Providence Theological Seminary. As a pastor of a rural church in Minnesota who was seeking eventually to pursue a PhD in Old Testament, I had found an ideal mentor in Gus. At once both pastoral and scholarly, he offered a fine example of that noble and rare admixture. Three short stories exemplify my experience of Gus and why this volume is a fitting collection of essays broadly addressing "Community."

I had already taken a couple of courses with Gus, but one semester I took Hermeneutics with him. One of the assignments he required was to write an original lexical entry on a Hebrew/Aramaic/Greek term in the vein of the theological lexicons. Because I was intending to do my master's thesis on Gen 1, I determined to write on בהו//תהו and informed Gus of my decision. I knew these terms did not occur often in the OT, so I would not have many texts to work through in my study. I had begun work with Gus doing an independent study in Ugaritic (briefly also discussing Aramaic through the course) and expanded my work on the OT to include cognates. I felt proud of my work; after I had read and analyzed original texts, I sifted a host of lexicons as well to fill out my work with other proposals and references. I, then, worked through numerous critical commentaries on the passages covered. I finally turned in my paper with the pride. Gus wrote a simple response on the paper: "See NIDOTTE." To be honest, I had considered checking the *New International Dictionary of Old Testament Theology and Exegesis* (NIDOTTE) but not until I was nearly completed with the paper. I had done my homework . . . or so I thought. I went straight to the library to check the NIDOTTE. When I found the entry and read the (very helpful) article, I noticed the author: "A. H. Konkel." Gus, in his typical graciousness, had allowed me, as his student, to pursue a topic he had written on without any indication beforehand (and I still received a decent grade).

Introduction

That same semester in Hermeneutics, Gus required his students to consider an issue within their respective church traditions—particularly a doctrine or practice distinctive from other traditions—in light of Scripture and interpretive methodologies. He took time during the class sessions to ask individual students to speak about those distinctions. When he came to me, my reply concerned the initial physical evidence of the baptism in the Holy Spirit, a distinct Classical Pentecostal doctrine. He was not intent on forcing students to reject their distinctions but to help us to work through the exegetical issues involved. This assignment helped me to process my own tradition's distinction in light of Scripture, other church traditions, and the hermeneutical processes involved in wrestling with this tradition. This assignment invited me to tease out issues in a safe space and to deepen and widen my own community's engagement with Scriptures in relation to one of our distinguishing contributions (and challenge) to the broader church.

Finally, there was an academic year when I wanted to study Ugaritic as a poetical prerequisite for doctoral studies, but there was not enough student interest to offer the course formally. Gus made space in his calendar, which serving as president and teaching courses, to me with me one-on-one to study Ugaritic. I spent many hours in his office, discussing text-critical and lexical issues, Semitics, ancient Near Eastern culture, history, and religion. More importantly, to the benefit of my own well-being, each time we met he asked about my family, my church, and my health (remembering I had suffered a debilitation during seminary). With the tenderness of a pastor, he asked questions and offered care; he listened and spoke life. I had needed not only a linguistic tutor but also a pastor; Gus was both, with the wit, charity, and insightfulness only he could offer.

ON THE CONTRIBUTIONS TO COMMUNITY

The essays in this volume engage the idea of community biblically and theologically. The tone and content of the individual chapters reflect the diversity of its contributors, because this is the nature of a *Festschrift*, a collection of essays in honor of a scholar. These chapters were written to honor Gus, as a former student, professor, scholar, colleague, and friend; they reflect a diversity of aims, overall, and writing styles.

Introduction

These contributing scholars have known Gus from different chapters in his life, some are former professors or students of Gus and others are colleagues and friends; all have found themselves enriched by Gus' life and work.

The eclectic nature of the chapters that follow represent many of the research interests Gus has pursued through his scholarship. They all some perspective on community, something Gus has fostered both in academia and in ecclesial settings. Mary L. Conway's contribution sheds light on some of the fractures of the Israelite community in the book of Judges. Mark. J. Boda examines the language of an "evil spirit from God" as encountered in the books of Judges, Samuel, and Kings. My essay offers a prophetic testimony for community drawing upon his reading of 1 Kgs 13. Gary V. Smith reexamines Israel's self-understanding in light of 1 Chr 1–9. Paul S. Evans works toward a resolution of Zeruiah's identification as Ammonite in 2 Sam and as a relative of David's in 1 Chr. Randall Holm provides a creative juxtaposition of Job and Walter White, the lead character from the television series "Breaking Bad." H. G. M. Williamson investigates the shifting portrayal of Babylon in the book of Isaiah. Stanley E. Porter reconsiders the movements of Septuagintal studies. Al Wolters offers fresh lexicographical notes on the Septuagint of Zechariah. Daniel Falk pursues the ways in which the Dead Sea Scrolls portrays the constructs of poverty. Martin W. Mittelstadt's essay stands at the intersection of Pentecostal and Mennonite understandings of the prophethood of all believers. David Johnson works toward a biblical theology of the Word of God and Christian community. Finally, Patrick S. Franklin provides a theological engagement of Bonhoeffer's work on genuine human community.

These essays represent eclectic biblical and theological concerns, reflecting the variety of Gus' own research interests. Some of these chapters engage texts that Gus has also studied and written on, like Job, Kings, Chronicles, and Isaiah. Gus's own trajectory of work is reflected by the essays engaging semantic range, lexicography, the Septuagint, and Dead Sea Scrolls. His consideration of ecclesiological matters is also embodied by these essays, particularly in the ways communities have received and responded to Scripture theologically. It is our hope that this volume blesses Gus for his astute work on behalf of the

Introduction

Christian community, blesses that community, and, above all, blesses the Lord, the center of this community.

Rick Wadholm Jr.

AUGUST H. KONKEL BIBLIOGRAPHY
Books

Konkel, August H. *1 & 2 Chronicles*. Believers Church Bible Commentary. Harrisonburg, VA: Herald, 2016.

———. *1 and 2 Kings*. NIV Application Commentary. Grand Rapids: Zondervan Academic, 2006.

Konkel, August H., and Tremper Longman III. *Job, Ecclesiastes, Song of Songs*. Cornerstone Biblical Commentary. Tyndale, 2006.

Translation

Job, The New Living Translation, Tyndale 1996; second edition 2004.

Dictionary Articles

Three articles in Ryken, Leland et al. *Dictionary of Biblical Imagery*. 2 vols. Downers Grove, IL: IVP Academic, 1998.

Articles in VanGemeren, Willem A., ed. *New International Dictionary of Old Testament Theology and Exegesis*. 5 vols. Grand Rapids, MI: Zondervan Academic, 1997:

אֱוִיל 1:309; אֶזְרָח 1:344–45; אָח 1: 354–58; אֶמֶשׁ 1:449–50; אנה 1:451–53; אֲנָךְ 1:460–62; אסר 1:472–73; ארב 1:490–91; בְּדִיל 1:602–3; בֹּהוּ 1:606–9; בקק 1:705–6; בֹּקֶר 1:710–20; בַּרְזֶל 1:741–43; גוּר 1:836–39; גלל 1:867–68; זעק 1:869; דאב 1:906; דמה 1:967–70; דמם 1:973–74; דמע 1:975–77; גלם 1:1131–32; זָר 1:1142–43; חטף 2:106; חֶלְאָה 2:135; יצר 2:503–6; כּוֹל 2:614–15; כלא 2:638–39; כֶּסֶף 2:683–84; לכד 2:800–801; מָחַר 2:922–23; מִסְגֵּר 2:995–96; מִסְגֶּרֶת 2:996–97; מַעֲבֶה 2:1010; מְצָד 2:1064; מָצוֹד 2:1069–70; מקק 2:1092–93; מָשׁוֹשׁ 2:1115; נהה 3:43; נֵכָר 3:108–9; נְקֻדָּה 3:151–52; עצר 3:501–3; סהר 3:228–29; סִיג 3:244–45; עטה 3:380–81; עֹפֶרֶת 3:473–74; צוּר 3:743–44; צְדִיָּה 3:619–20; פלשׁ 3:630–31; צדה 3:742–43; פְּלָדוֹת 3; 3:792–93; צֶעַע 3:826–27; צעק 3:827–30; צפה 3:832–33; קָלָל 3:927–28; רמם 3:936–37; קפד 3:953 (co-authored with Terence E. Fretheim); קמט שׁאה 3:1125–26; רקב 3:1193–94; שׂכה 3:1241–42; שׂנא 3:1256–70; 4:2–4; שָׁבוּעַ 4:20–24; שחט 4:80; תּוֹשָׁב 4:284–85; תמד 4:305–6[1]; תפשׂ 4:326–27; and "Isaac" 4:723–24.

---

1. This is improperly labeled as article "9458" that should read "9461" in the

Introduction

Articles & Essays

"What is the Future of Israel in Romans 9–11?" In *The Letter to the Romans: Exegesis and Application*, edited by Stanley E. Porter and Francis G. H. Pang, 115–127. McMaster New Testament Studies Series 7. Eugene, OR: Pickwick, 2018.

"In Defense of Human Values: The Good Life under Divine Covenant." *Didaskalia* 24 (2015) 25–39.

"Job 38–42." *McMaster Journal of Theology and Ministry* 15 (2013) 1–5.

"The Elihu Speeches in the Greek Translation of Job." In *"Translation Is Required": The Septuagint in Retrospect and Prospect*, edited by Robert J. V. Hiebert. SBL Septuagint and Cognate Studies 56. Atlanta: Society of Biblical Literature, 2010.

"Biblical Wisdom for Tending the Garden." *Didaskalia* 20 (2009) 97–104.

"The Bible and Archaeology." *Didaskalia* 5.2 (1994) 56–65.

"The Sources of the Story of Hezekiah in the Book of Isaiah." *Vetus Testamentum* XLIII (1993) 462–82.

"Wisdom as the Way to Knowing God." *Didaskalia* 4.1 (1992) 15–25.

"Male and Female as the Image of God." *Didaskalia* 3.2 (1992) 1–8.

"The Sacrifice of Obedience." *Didaskalia* 2.2 (1991) 2–11.

"The Apostolic Preaching of the Resurrection." *Didaskalia* 2.1 (1990) 12–22.

"Resist or Surrender." *Journal for Case Teaching* 1 (1989) 16–21.

"The Exaltation of the Eternal King." *Didaskalia* 1.2 (1989) 14–22.

Book Reviews

Review of *Jesaja 1—Eine Exegese der Eröffnung des Jesaja-Buches: Die Präsentation Jesajas, JHWHs, Israels und der Tochter Zion*, by Joachim Eck. *BBR* 27.3 (2017) 401–2.

Review of *The Lost World of Adam and Eve: Genesis 2–3 and the Human Origins Debate*, by John H. Walton. *Perspectives on Science & Christian Faith* 68.1 (March 2016) 67–68.

Review of *A Chorus of Prophetic Voices: Introducing the Prophetic Literature of Ancient Israel*, by Mark Harold McEntire. *JETS* 59.3 (2016) 618–20.

Review of *Die Stadtfrau Zion im Zentrum der Welt: Exegese und Theologie von Jes 60–62*, by Andrea Spans. *BBR* 26.4 (2016) 569–71.

Review of *Hoffnung in Bethlehem: Innerbiblische Querbezüge als Deutungshorizonte im Ruthbuch*, by Andrea Beyer. *BBR* 25.4 (2015) 566–67.

"Index of *NIDOTTE* Contributors" found in 5:840.

Introduction

Review of *Sennacherib at the Gates of Jerusalem: Story, History and Historiography*, by Isaac Kalimi and Seth Richardson, eds. BBR 25.4 (2015) 567–70.

Review of *Status, Tod und Ritual: Stadt-und-Sozialstruktur Assurs in neuassyrischer Zeit*, Harrassowitz, by Stefan R. Hauser. BBR 24.4 (2014) 548–50.

Review of *Impeccable Solomon? A Study on Solomon's Faults in Chronicles*, by Yong Ho Jeon. JETS 57.1 (2014) 157–58.

Review of *Exodus 1–15*, by Helmut Utzschneider and Wolfgang Oswald. BBR 24.3 (2014) 410–12.

Review of *Gottes Herrlichkeit: Bedeutung und Verwendung des Begriffs* kābôd *im Alten Testament*, by Thomas Wagner. BBR 24.1 (2014) 101–3.

Review of *Ecclesiastes*, by Douglas B. Miller. Direction 41.1 (2012) 184–85.

Review of *Human Consciousness of God in the Book of Job: A Theological and Psychological Commentary*, by Jeffrey Boss. JHS 13 (2013).

Review of *Im Himmel und auf Erden: Dimensionen von Königsherrschaft im Alten Testament*, by Rüdiger Jungbluth. BBR 23.3 (2013) 424–26.

Review of *Text and Canon of the Hebrew Bible*, by Shemaryahu Talmon. RBL 1 (2012).

Review of *Rumors of Wisdom: Job 28 as Poetry*, by Scott C. Jones. JHS 11 (2011).

Review of *Textual Criticism of the Hebrew Bible*, by Emmanuel Tov. RBL 12 2012.

Review of *Ecclesiastes*, by Craig Bartholemew. JETS 53 (2010) 389–91.

Review of *Introduction to the Hebrew Bible: A Thematic Approach*, by Sandra L. Gravett. JETS 52 (2009) 587–89.

Review of *Reshaping of Ancient Israelite History in Chronicles*, by Isaac Kalimi. JETS 49 (2006) 404–5.

Review of *The Politics of Ancient Israel*, by Norman Gottwald. Didaskalia 15.1 (2003) 86–88.

Review of *Windows into Old Testament History: Evidence, Argument, and the Crisis of "Biblical Israel,"* by V. Philips Long, et al. Didaskalia 14:1 (2002) 103–5.

Review of *Eerdmans Dictionary of the Bible*, by David Noel Freedman et al., eds. JBL 4 (2002) 67–9.

Review of *The Apocalyptic Imagination: An Introduction to Jewish Apocalyptic Literature*, by John J. Collins. Didaskalia 12:2 (2001) 129–31.

Review of *Invitation to the Septuagint*, by Karen H. Jobes and Moisés Silva. Didaskalia 12.2 (2001) 131–32.

Review of *Micah*, by Ehud Ben Zvi, and *Minor Prophets*, by Michal H. Floyd. Didaskalia 12.2 (2001) 133–35.

Introduction

Review of *The Book of Ecclesiastes*, by Tremper Longman III. *Didaskalia* 12.1 (2000) 109–14.

Review of *The Dead Sea Scrolls and Christian Origins*, by Joseph A. Fitzmyer. *Didaskalia* 12.1 (2000) 114–16.

Review of *Beyond the Essene Hypothesis: The Parting of the Ways between Qumran and Enochic Judaism*, by Gabriele Boccaccini. *Didaskalia* 11.2 (2000) 115–18.

Review of *The Dead Sea Scrolls and the Origins of the Bible*, by Eugene Ulrich. *Didaskalia* 11.2 (2000) 122–24.

Review of *Isaiah 1–39; Isaiah 40–66*, by Walter Brueggemann. *Didaskalia* 10.2 (1999) 109–11.

Review of *Old Testament Wisdom: An Introduction*, by James L. Crenshaw. *Didaskalia* 10.2 (1999) 111–12.

Review of *The Theology of the Prophetic Books: The Death and Resurrection of Israel*, by Donald E. Gowan. *Didaskalia* 10.2 (1999) 112–14.

Review of *The Book of Amos: A Commentary*, by Jörg Jeremias. *Didaskalia* 10.1 (1998) 98–100.

Review of *Preaching from the Minor Prophets: Texts and Sermon Suggestions*, by Elizabeth Achtemeier. *Didaskalia* 10.1 (1998) 101–2.

Review of *The Book of Ezekiel*, by Daniel I. Block. *Didaskalia* 10.1 (1998) 102–4.

Review of *Old Testament Survey: The Message, Form, and Background of the Old Testament*, by William S. LaSor, et al. *Didaskalia* 9.2 (1998) 91–93.

Review of *Leviticus: A Commentary*, by Erhard S. Gerstenberger. *Didaskalia* 9.2 (1998) 100–101.

Review of *Jewish Wisdom in the Hellenistic Age*, by John J. Collins. *Didaskalia* 9.2 (1998) 118–200.

Review of *Theological Dictionary of the Old Testament*, by Johannes Botterweck, et al. *Didaskalia* 8.2 (1997) 81–83.

Review of *Deep Things out of Darkness: The Book of Job*, by David Wolfers. *Didaskalia* 8.2 (1997) 83–87.

Review of *The Task of Old Testament Theology: Substance, Method, and Cases*, by Rolph P. Knierim. *Didaskalia* 8.2 (1997) 88–91.

Review of *Canon and Theology: Overtures to an Old Testament Theology*, by Rolf Rendtorff. *JETS* 39 (1996) 518–19.

Review of *The Book of Genesis Chapters 18–50*, by Victor P. Hamilton. *Didaskalia* 7.2 (1996) 88–89.

Review of *The Politics of Jesus*, by John Howard Yoder. *Didaskalia* 6.2 (1995) 90–91.

Review of *I & II Chronicles: A Commentary*, by Sara Japhet. *WTJ* 57 (1995) 257–59.

Review of *Job*, by Robert L. Alden. *WTJ* 57 (1995) 259–60.

Introduction

Review of *An Introduction to the Old Testament Historical Books*, by David M. Howard Jr. *Didaskalia* 6.1 (1994) 70–72.

Review of *The Book of Numbers*, by Timothy R. Ashley. *Didaskalia* 5.2 (1994) 98–99.

Review of *Abraham and all the Families of the Earth: Genesis 12–50*, by J. Gerald Janzen. *Didaskalia* 5.2 (1994) 99–101.

Review of *God's People in God's Land: Family, Land, and Property in the Old Testament*, by Christopher J. H. Wright. *Didaskalia* 5.1 (1993) 108–9.

Review of *Let us be Like the Nations: 1 & 2 Samuel*, by Gnana Robinson. *Didaskalia* 5.1 (1993) 110–11.

Review of *Song of Songs*, by John G. Snaith. *Didaskalia* 5.1 (1993) 112–13.

Review of *Reason for Being: A Meditation on Ecclesiastes*, by Jacques Ellul. *Didaskalia* 3.1 (1991) 45–46.

Review of *1 & 2 Chronicles*, by Simon J. DeVries. *WTJ* 53 (1991) 357–9.

Review of *Portraits of Creation: Biblical and Scientific Perspectives on the World's Formation*, by Howard J. Van Till, ed. *Didaskalia* 2.1 (1990) 46–48.

Review of *Psalms: The Divine Journey*, by Mark S. Smith. *RST* 10 (1990) 92–93.

Review of *Amos: A Commentary*, by Gary V. Smith. *Didaskalia* 1.1 (1989) 45–46.

1

A Cord of Three Strands is Not Quickly Broken
The Deterioration of Unity and Community in Judges

Mary L. Conway[1]

INTRODUCTION

THE PEOPLE OF ISRAEL experienced Yahweh's grace in the exodus under the leadership of Moses, and advanced into their promised land under the direction of Joshua. The book of Judges opens with the death of their erstwhile leader, and the twelve tribes set out to establish themselves in their new territory. Up until now, in spite of episodes of stumbling and discord, Israel has nevertheless adhered as a unit, a federation of tribes with a common identity and purpose as the people of Yahweh, led and motivated by strong charismatic leaders. The

---

1. I have enjoyed working with Dr. Gus Konkel in the Old Testament department of McMaster Divinity College for the past few years and I appreciate his insight into Scripture, which is very broad and deep indeed. One of my key areas of interest is the book of Judges, which has much to say on the topic of community. I have written this chapter in appreciation of Gus's own interest and work in this core area in the hope that it will encourage more reflection on the value of community today.

writer of Ecclesiastes has wisdom to offer about the value of unity and community:

> Two are better than one,
> because they have a good return for their labor:
> If either of them falls down,
> one can help the other up.
> But pity anyone who falls
> and has no one to help them up.
> Also, if two lie down together, they will keep warm.
> But how can one keep warm alone?
> Though one may be overpowered,
> two can defend themselves.
> A cord of three strands is not quickly broken. (Eccl 4:9–12 NIV2011).

That is, it is not quickly broken if the cords remain entwined. The book of Judges, however, recounts the deterioration of the community of Israel in a downward spiral that ends in fragmentation and internecine warfare. This story, although tragic, has much wisdom to offer the contemporary church.

Although all the tribes play a role in the descent of Israel to its nadir in the second conclusion, the trajectories of three tribes in particular exemplify the transition of Israel from a united community to a fragmented mosaic of disparate groups pursuing their own agendas.[2] The seeming unity of most tribes in Judg 19–21 is an illusion, for they unite only against Benjamin. The adventures of three strands in the Israelite cord—Judah, Ephraim, and Benjamin—exemplify the swinging of the pendulum in Israel between unity and cooperation on the one hand and isolation and betrayal on the other.

---

2. This, of course, is not to imply that the author of Ecclesiastes had the Judges narrative in mind when the text above was composed, or that the three strands apply specifically to these three tribes. However, Qoholeth's metaphor can be usefully applied to the community situation in Judges as a heuristic device.

JUDAH: LEADERSHIP > BETRAYAL AND APATHY > LEADERSHIP

Judah as Leader of the Community

After Joshua—the last charismatic leader over all Israel—dies, the Israelites inquire of Yahweh as to who should lead them in occupying the land. Yahweh responds, "Judah should go up. Take note, I hereby give the land into its power" (Judg 1:1).[3] Although no specific leader within the tribe is designated, Judah as a community accepts the responsibility to lead the other tribes in following Yahweh's instructions to settle their new territory. Judah immediately cooperates with its brother tribe Simeon to do battle with the Canaanites. The rest of Judg 1 is an account of the various tribes working independently, yet in cooperation, to take control of their allotments within the land God had promised them. The metaphorical cord is strong and sound.

Some tribes, however, prove to be more successful than others. In Judg 1:11 Judah attacks Debir, but there is no immediate notice of victory over the town in spite of Judah's leadership role and early successes (see Judg 1:4–9). In v. 12, Caleb appears, a warrior who seemingly holds a position of leadership. Caleb was the second faithful spy, along with Joshua, who earlier encouraged the Israelites to trust Yahweh and follow his instructions to move into the promised land when the other ten spies proved reluctant and discouraging (see Num 13). The failure to take Debir must have disappointed Caleb; after all, Yahweh had promised to give Israel the land. In this situation he acts in a less trusting manner than when he was scouting out the new territory; he does not inquire of Yahweh and seek his advice, as his fellow spy and Israel's previous leader, Joshua, did in the case of the failure to defeat Ai (see Josh 7). When Joshua inquired of Yahweh as to the reason for this failure, it was revealed to him that there was sin in the camp, and he proceeded to correct the situation that led to the defeat. Caleb, however, brashly offers his daughter, Achsah, in marriage as a bribe to any warrior who can successfully take the town. His relative, Othniel, is the successful conqueror, and Caleb gives his daughter a

---

3. Unless specified otherwise, translations are taken from Boda and Conway, *Judges*.

dowry of land.[4] Unfortunately, the gift disappoints Achsah, since the land is too dry to be productive. Nevertheless, although she is disappointed, Achsah does not resort to bribery to get what she wants, as did Caleb. Instead, she goes directly to her father, who has long supported her and with whom she has a trusting relationship, and inquires of him, laying out her situation and asking for what she needs to make the land a productive home. In so doing she effectually rebukes her father for not going and inquiring of Yahweh—who has long supported him and with whom he had a trusting relationship—when he is in a similarly disappointing situation.[5]

It is significant that Caleb disappears from the narrative of Judges a few verses later in Judg 1:20; he is obviously not the new leader that Israel needs to replace Joshua. Cooperation and mutual support within the community are of great value. However, dependence on one's own community must never replace dependence on, and obedience to, Yahweh. Leaders, and indeed the Israelite people in general, were called on to model and exemplify covenant loyalty and trust in Israel's God. Similarly, in the church today, leaders and members form a community of support and fellowship. We are encouraged to look after each other's needs, providing emotional, social, physical, and spiritual assistance (Matt 25:31–46; Luke 10:25–37). In loving and helping others we are gratefully responding to the love of God for us and the deliverance that he alone can provide (1 John 4:19). It is tempting, however, for a church community to become a social support group, depending exclusively on each other and our own wisdom. If there is "sin in the camp," we need to deal with it, inquiring of Yahweh as to his will and obediently following his directions as revealed in his word and by his Spirit.

It is also worth noting that although Caleb, Othniel, and Achsah seem to be associated with Judah, they are also identified as Kennizites. Caleb is described as being from the tribe of Judah (Num 13:6; 34:19), but he is also termed a "Kenizzite" in Num 32:12 and Josh 14:6, 14. In Judg 1:13 and 3:9, Othniel is called the "son of Kenaz," another way of

---

4. This act foreshadows Jephthah's attempt to bribe Yahweh by offering to sacrifice his daughter in order to ensure victory over the Ammonites in Judg 11.

5. For a more detailed analysis of this episode, see the chapter on the First Introduction in Boda and Conway, *Judges*.

designating his ethnic background, although he is also described as Caleb's younger brother (Judg 3:9; Josh 15:17) and therefore has Judahite connections.[6] It is possible that the family was not of purely "Israelite" descent but members of a different ethnic group that had been grafted into Judah over time. Indeed, tribal membership in the ancient Near East (ANE) was not entirely a biological matter, exclusively based on natural descent; it could also be attained by political or economic affiliation, settlement within a group, or shared religious conviction.[7]

It is thus possible that Caleb and Othniel were in some sense "foreigners"; however, they were, to all intents and purposes, completely integrated into Israel in general, and Judah in particular, and their ethnic origin, although acknowledged, had become a non-issue. In the contemporary church we have many people that join our communities. Some are from non-Christian upbringings. Others are from different ethnic, racial, cultural, or socioeconomic backgrounds. Nevertheless, all of us are "adopted" into the household of God (Eph 1:5) and "born again" into his family (John 3:5–8; 1 Pet 1:23). While acknowledging and honoring a variety of social, cultural, and ethnic expressions, we need to accept everyone who comes into the church as a fully integrated member of the church universal and the local church community.

Just as the church lives within a secular world, however, Israel lived among nations who did not recognize Yahweh as their God. "The people of Israel dwelled in the midst of the Canaanites, Hittites, Amorites, Perizzites, Hivites, and Jebusites. And they took their daughters for themselves as wives and they gave their daughters to their sons and they served their gods" (Judg 3:5–6). This led to a repeating cycle of

---

6. The syntax is actually unclear as to whether it was Othniel or Kenaz who was the brother of Caleb, therefore Othniel could have been either Caleb's brother or nephew. Kenaz is the immediate antecedent of "younger brother," but it is also possible to treat "Othniel son of Kenaz" as a unit which forms the antecedent.

7. See Younger, *Judges and Ruth*, 66n17. See also Miller and Hayes, *A History of Ancient Israel and Judah*, 103; Fretz and Panitz, "Caleb (Person)," 1:809–10; and Kuntz, "Kenaz (Person)," 4:17, who states: "Toward the close of the LB Age and the onset of the Iron Age (ca. 1300–1100 B.C.E.), the S portion of Palestine's central hill country was occupied by diverse tribal groups. These included the Judahites, the Calebites, the Othnielites, the Simeonites, the Korahites, the Jerahmeelites, the Kenites, as well as the Kenizzites . . . These S tribes were eventually subsumed under the category of 'Greater Judah.'"

increasing apostasy and sin, as described in Judg 2:10–19. Discipline followed, in the form of oppression by their enemies, until Yahweh raised up judges through whom he delivered his people and gave them a fresh start (2:18). The first of these judges, the paradigmatic judge who will set the standard of leadership for all the judges that follow, is Othniel, the Judahite/Kennizite. Othniel proves to be a better leader than Caleb. He is endowed with the spirit of Yahweh (3:10) and during his tenure there is no sign of apostasy within Israel; only after his death do the people once again do "the evil thing." The effectiveness of leaders, who serve as role models for the community, is a significant factor in maintaining community character and avoiding religious syncretism.

Judah Undermines Community

Interestingly, after the tenure of Othniel, Judah virtually disappears from the narrative of Judges for the entire central part of the book.[8] The interaction of various tribes and their leaders with Ephraim takes central stage; this strand will be examined in the next section. It is not until the Samson narrative that Judah finally reappears. Samson is a striking contrast to Othniel; although the text mentions twice that Samson judged Israel for twenty years (15:20; 16:31), the reader is hard put to find any evidence of his actual "judging." Samson spends much more time consorting with Israel's Philistine enemies than he does with his own tribe of Dan, which is scarcely mentioned, even though Israel is once again doing the evil thing in the eyes of Yahweh. He apparently feels little or no identity with, or concern for, his own community; he is too involved in pursuing his own appetites and goals. Ironically, Yahweh is able to use Samson's weaknesses to provoke confrontations with the Philistines in the hope of delivering Israel from their oppression; ultimately, however, Samson is only able to "begin" to deliver his people from the Philistines (13:5). It is after one of these confrontational incidents—that of the foxes and torches which resulted in the destruction of important Philistine crops (15:4–5)—that "the Philistines went up and they camped in Judah, and they overran Lehi" (15:9). They were looking for the destructive Samson in order to gain revenge. Although

---

8. Except for one brief mention in Judg 10:9, which makes a passing comment about Judah, Benjamin, and Ephraim.

the exact location of Lehi is unknown, it must have been somewhere within Judahite territory.

Since readers have been informed that Yahweh was specifically looking for "an opportunity against the Philistines" (14:4), they might expect Judah, the erstwhile leader of Israel against the Canaanites, to rise to Samson's defense and fight off the oppressive Philistine troops. No such courageous action ensues, however; the Judahites have apparently become apathetic and docile and would rather live a quiet, if degraded, life under the subjection of their overlords than stand up for their fellow Israelite. They do worse than nothing: they blame Samson for stirring up trouble—"Do you not know that the Philistines are ruling over us? And what is this that you have done to us?" (15:11)—and set out to betray him into the power of the enemy. Samson, for all his idiosyncrasies, is part of the Israelite community, one of their own. They share a faith in Yahweh, they share a history of oppression and release to their new home, and they share a hope of freedom and a future. Nevertheless, they are willing to betray one of their own people in exchange for submissive security. In ancient Mediterranean societies, acting "dishonorably" against an outsider or enemy, an "out-group," was actually considered honorable; however, acting in a dishonorable way against members of one's own clan or tribe, one's "in-group," was condemned.[9] Judah, in betraying a fellow Israelite, has sunk from courageous, faithful leadership to cowardly, treacherous subservience.

It is also the responsibility of Christians to act in חֶסֶד, "covenant loyalty," towards Yahweh and their fellow Christians. Compromising our behavior and beliefs in order to attain an easy life or avoid conflict with secular society is just as unacceptable as Judah turning in Samson to avoid conflict with the Philistines that would disrupt their complacent, submissive lives. Of course, there are many occasions when "a gentle answer turns away wrath" (Prov 15:1) or when cooperation and even compromise provides an authentic option in dealing with dispute. Jesus advised his followers to turn the other cheek (Matt 5:38–40); the

---

9. Bartusch, *Understanding Dan*, 147; Lambert, "Tribal Influences in Old Testament Tradition," 46; Chalcraft, "Deviance and Legitimate Action," 197: "In the view of the narrator of the book of Judges, deviance is constituted by transferring certain action patterns legitimate in dealings with the out-group to dealings with the social group. This most often occurs when societal goals are replaced by individual ends."

motive should not be cowardice or self-interest, and compromise and submission should not necessarily be the church community's default position.

Judah Returns as Leader of the Community

In Judg 20:2, the narrator reports that "the leaders of all the army, all the tribes of Israel, presented themselves at the assembly of the army of God." After carrying out their more or less independent activities throughout the narrative of Judges, the Israelites assemble as one united community . . . with one exception. The atrocity committed by Benjamin on the Levite's concubine at Gibeah (Judg 19) has set this tribe apart from the people of Yahweh, and the other tribes unite to deal with them: "All the men of Israel gathered to the city in unity as companions" (20:11) . . . all except Benjamin, that is.[10] One strand of the cord is clearly unravelling. At the very beginning of Judges, Israel inquired of Yahweh: "Who should go up for us to the Canaanites at first in order to make war against them?" (1:1). Yahweh answered, "Judah should go up" (v. 2). Now, at the very end of Judges, they ask again: "Who shall go up for us at first into battle against the people of Benjamin?" Yahweh responds, "Judah at first" (20:18). Their inquiry of God seems commendable, but closer examination shows that it is deeply flawed. In Judg 1, the enemy is the Canaanites; here in Judg 20, the enemy is their fellow Israelite tribe, Benjamin. There, the Israelite community had received clear instructions from Yahweh to possess the land and drive out the Canaanites; here, Yahweh has given them no instructions as to whether or how to discipline Benjamin. There, Yahweh gives them assurance of success; here there is none. Israel makes a number of assumptions, or rather presumptions, that prove to be incorrect when they lose the first battle and twenty-two units of soldiers are annihilated (20:21). The second inquiry shows more sensitivity to the situation when Israel asks, "Shall I continue to advance into battle against Benjamin, *my brother*?" (v. 23, emphasis added). The united tribes begin to realize that they have turned inward against themselves,

---

10. For a much more detailed analysis of this episode, see the Second Conclusion chapter in Boda and Conway, *Judges*.

and that the Israelite community is fragmenting. Once again, they are defeated by Benjamin.

It is only on the third inquiry that Israel asks, "Shall I continue to go out into war against the people of Benjamin my brother, or should I quit?" (20:28). The people are finally willing to admit that the entire venture might have been ill-conceived. This time, the Israelite coalition is victorious but goes so far as to destroy most of the tribe of Benjamin, only to suddenly realize the extent of the tragedy they have caused (21:1–3). Their attempts to undo the damage that they have precipitated and preserve the future of Benjamin involve the slaughter of even more Israelites at Jabesh Gilead (vv. 8–14) and the abduction and rape of Israelite women at Shiloh (vv. 18–23). Judah's leadership at the end of Judges is as even more equivocal than that at the beginning of the narrative. The occupation of the promised land, which was intended to drive out the Canaanites and establish a home for Yahweh's people in which they could live in covenant loyalty to their God and each other, has devolved into a situation in which the Israelite community has turned in on itself, indulging in distrust, disrespect, and violence, and has degenerated into internecine warfare.

It is easy for New Testament Christians to condemn the behavior of Old Testament Israelites in Judg 20, but is the record of the church any better? It is important to stand up against injustice, but historical violence between segments of the church on less justifiable grounds is well known, as evidenced by events as diverse as the St. Bartholomew's Day Massacre and the sectarian conflict in Northern Ireland. The mere existence of many denominations within Protestantism reflects inner conflicts which have sometimes become antagonistic or even violent. At a less physical level, differences of theology or praxis among contemporary evangelical groups have too often become verbally hostile. Numerous individual churches have split over issues that might have been handled with more generosity and less rancor. Just as Israel presented a divided front to a world in which they were supposed to exemplify the *shalom* of God's chosen people, so Christians today often discredit the gospel of Christ by their hostility to each other. Nor can we always blame weak leadership; a community holds some responsibility for whom it chooses to follow. It is interesting that although Judah is chosen to lead in Judg 20:18, a specific leader is not mentioned, and the tribe of Judah is not specifically mentioned subsequently. Most of the blunders were enthusiastically undertaken by the community as a whole (e.g., 20:12, 22, 26; 21:5. 10, 13 etc.). In a democratic society, there is even more onus on the community members to accept responsibility for decisions made by leaders they have chosen, inside and outside the church.

EPHRAIM: COOPERATION > DISPUTE > CONFLICT

Cooperation involving Ehud and Deborah

The former charismatic leader of Israel, Joshua, was an Ephraimite, and he is generally commended for leading Israel effectively. In the book of Judges, Ephraim starts out with a positive and cooperative reputation. Ehud, the second judge, is a Benjaminite, at a time when Israel is once again being disciplined for apostasy. In assassinating Eglon, the Moabite oppressor of Israel, he acts alone (3:18–26), except perhaps for a few fellow tribesmen who carry the tribute but are later dismissed. There is no mention of any other Benjaminites taking any part in the covert operation. This is not surprising, since Ehud's plan is to sneak into the Moabite court and attack from within; however, it is somewhat unexpected when, after dispensing with King Eglon, he calls on the Ephraimites to back him up in dealing with the now leaderless Moabite troops (3:27): "It came about when he arrived, that then he blew the ram's horn in the hill country of Ephraim. Then the people of Israel went down with him from the hill country."[11] It is perhaps possible that there are other Israelite troops mustered and waiting with the Ephraimites, but if so, they are not specifically mentioned. Ehud cooperates with Ephraim to defeat the Moabite army, and the Ephraimites are willing participants in capturing the fords of the Jordan (v. 28)—a crossing place that the Moabite army could use to escape to their own country—thus ensuring the success of Ehud's venture.

The next time Ephraim takes center stage involves the prophet-judge Deborah, who pronounces judgment "between Ramah and Bethel in the hill region of Ephraim" (4:5). Here, the situation is reversed.

---

11. This may be due to factors such as proximity and the relative strength and size of the Benjaminite and Ephraimite armies.

Whereas the Benjaminite Ehud cooperates with and leads the tribe of Ephraim, Deborah, an Ephraimite, cooperates with and leads the other tribes. The Israelites are again suffering disciplinary oppression, this time by Sisera, the general of Jabin, a Canaanite king. Deborah summons Barak, from the tribe of Naphtali, to lead his tribesmen and those of Zebulun in battle against Sisera. It is only Deborah's reproof and encouragement that convinces the reluctant Barak to undertake this task (4:6–9). He manages to win the battle but is shamed when a foreign woman, Jael, is honored for destroying the fleeing Sisera.

Although Deborah and Barak eventually bring victory and rest to Israel, her confrontation of Barak is the first sign of disagreement among the tribes in the Judges narrative. The Song of Deborah (Judg 5), the victory song that follows the prose account, shows deeper divisions in Israel, however. Deborah arises "as a mother in Israel," encouraging cooperation among the tribes, but some of her "children" are rebellious. Some tribes are willing volunteers—Naphtali, Benjamin, Ephraim, Machir (a clan of Manasseh), Zebulun, and Issachar—but some, for unclear reasons, do not participate to support their fellow Israelites—Reuben, Gilead (another clan of Manasseh), Dan, and Asher. At this point, however, Ephraim itself remains a positive and contributing part of the community of Israel.

The church has much to learn from the narratives of Ehud and Deborah about interdenominational cooperation. Although they hail from different tribes, these two leaders take the reputation of Yahweh and the interests of Yahweh's people as a whole to heart. Ehud is willing to cooperate with and use the resources of other tribes to work for their common interests under Yahweh. Deborah summons, encourages, and promotes cooperation among the leaders and people of the various tribes in order to attain the same goal; she also reproves those who fail to participate in shared interests (Judg 4:6–9; 5:9, 13–18). Christians, in spite of some differences in theology and praxis, would do well to cooperate more fully in working toward God's kingdom and against the forces of evil, and in promoting human flourishing wherever they can.

Community

Dispute with Gideon

Later in the narrative, however, trouble arises between Ephraim and the rest of Israel. The judge Gideon comes from the tribe of Manasseh, which has been influenced by the surrounding culture to build an altar of Baal in its midst. As a result of such practices, Israel is being disciplined by Yahweh through their enemies, the Midianites, and is suffering considerable oppression. Israel is not abandoned by its God, however. Yahweh gradually builds up Gideon's confidence and trust until he is willing to act on Israel's behalf. Initially, Gideon runs into conflict with his own people when he tears down the altar of Baal, but eventually he leads a combined army from Manasseh, Asher, Zebulun, and Naphtali against the Midianite oppressors. At some point, Gideon summons the tribe of Ephraim to join the battle, although there is some doubt as to when since the *qatal* verb can be translated as an English perfect or pluperfect depending on the context: "Gideon sent/had sent messengers into all the hill country of Ephraim, saying, "Go down to encounter Midian . . . " (7:24). Ephraim responds and helps to win victory in the battle, capturing the fords of the Jordan and killing the enemy leaders Oreb and Zeeb (7:24–25).

Ephraim later complains, however, and accuses Gideon for not calling them soon enough: "'What is this thing you have done to us, by not calling for us when you went into battle against Midian?' And they quarreled with him passionately" (8:1). Their anger may be caused by missing out on their full share of booty as the prize of war. In an ANE context, however, the tribe may well be concerned about their reputation among the other tribes in a society based on honor and shame.[12] Gideon is deeply involved in a difficult situation and might be tempted to dismiss their complaints as inappropriate and petty—and perhaps they are. Instead, he makes a concerted effort to placate his fellow Israelites. He praises their contribution to the battle highly and makes

---

12. Ephraim may have been concerned about both loss of plunder and honor. See the detailed analysis by Kirkpatrick, "Questions of Honor in the Book of Judges," 19–40. See also Boda, "Judges," 1160; Matthews, *Judges and Ruth*, 94; Niditch, *Judges: A Commentary*, 103. Stone ("Judges," 289) blames Ephraim for delaying the capture of the two chieftains and for disobeying Gideon's orders to guard the crossing of the Jordan. He accuses them of striving for the very honor and credit that Yahweh warned against earlier in the narrative.

it clear that his own efforts were as nothing compared to Ephraim's significant role (vv. 2–3). He reaffirms their place and value in the community, strengthening the cord of three strands, and working toward Israelite unity. Gideon does not allow his personal pride and reputation to interfere with the unity of his people. His handling of the conflict successfully placates Ephraim and avoids a rupture in the community of Israel. The church could learn much from this approach to conflict solving. As Phil 2:3 advises, "Do nothing from selfish ambition or conceit, but in humility regard others as better than yourselves."

Gideon, however, does not always act appropriately and out of consideration for his companions. Shortly after this, he sets out to pursue what turns out to be a very personal vendetta against Zebah and Zalmunna, the kings of Midian. It might seem that Gideon is chasing the two kings because they are enemies of all Israel. The narrator informs the reader that both he and the three hundred men that accompany him are וְרֹדְפִים עֲיֵפִים, "exhausted yet pursuing" (Judg 8:4). The participles here are plural, indicating that Gideon and his men are viewed as a group, acting with a common purpose. At Succoth, he asks for provisions for his hungry men. His phrasing here echoes the narrator's phrase above, yet significantly departs from it: כִּי־עֲיֵפִים הֵם וְאָנֹכִי רֹדֵף, "for *they* are exhausted, and *I* am pursuing" (v. 5). Gideon is clearly differentiating between himself and his companions, a situation stressed by the pleonastic pronouns הֵם ("they") and אָנֹכִי ("I") and the differentiation between the plural participle עֲיֵפִים ("exhausted") and the singular participle רֹדֵף ("pursuing").[13] The reader eventually learns that Gideon's single-minded pursuit of the kings is actually due to the fact that they were responsible for the death of some of his brothers at Mount Tabor (vv. 18–19). Thus, Gideon abandons the corporate purpose of the Israelite community against their common enemy and pursues, doggedly and alone, revenge for a personal loss. Along the way he even manages to alienate two communities, Succoth and Penuel, across the Jordan in the territory of Gad. These towns are Israelite, but in the current unstable political situation they are holding back before committing their loyalty, unsure of who the victors in the battle might

---

13. See the Gideon chapter in Boda and Conway, *Judges*, for more on this incident.

be (vv. 5–8). Instead of reassuring the elders of the towns and giving them reasons to remain loyal to him as he had previously done with Ephraim, Gideon threatens them and later exacts violent retribution for their lack of cooperation (vv. 15–17). This is a turning point in Gideon's leadership of Israel. It is after this that he leads the people back into syncretism. A narrative that begins in Ophrah with an altar to Baal ends back in Ophrah with an illegitimate shrine that leads his people to "prostitute themselves" to it in apostasy (vv. 27–28). After Gideon's death, there is division and violence in his family and division and conflict in Israel as his son Abimelech seizes power.

Gideon's wise and subtle handling of the Ephraimite crisis that restored unity stands in contrast with his single-minded pursuit of personal revenge that destroyed unity. He fails to live up to his own previous example. In contemporary society it is possible for church leaders and pastors to also lose touch with the purposes that initially led them into ministry—a desire to humbly teach, nurture, and support their congregations—and be led astray by a sense of their own power and importance, especially in a culture permeated by media. We need to remind ourselves constantly: "Do nothing from selfish ambition or conceit, but in humility regard others as better than yourselves" (Phil 2:3).

Conflict with Jephthah

Although Ephraim cooperates with Ehud and argues with Gideon, in both cases unity within Israel is maintained and the oppressors are finally driven off. Unfortunately, the third encounter between the Ephraimites and the rest of Israel does not have the expected happy ending. The judge in this case is Jephthah and the action takes place in Gilead, in Transjordan. Jephthah is a man on the margins of Israel and becomes an outsider. He is the son of Gilead, an Israelite, and a זֹנָה, a "prostitute" (11:1), someone without even the status of a concubine or secondary wife.[14] Eventually, the legitimate sons of Gilead, probably

---

14. Jephthah's parentage is uncertain. He may have been an Israelite or of mixed parentage. Nothing is said about his mother's ancestry, and his father is listed as "Gilead," which seems to refer to a person in the context. However, it is also a geographical location and may be interpreted as a gentilic. See Block, *Judges*, 163–64,

fearful that he might be given—or take, since he is described as a "valiant warrior" (חַיִל גִּבּוֹר)—part of their inheritance, drive him out. He flees to Tov and gathers around himself a group of "empty men," אֲנָשִׁים רֵיקִים (v. 3), marginalized and resentful men who fend for themselves.

As an outcast, without the support of a family and a community, Jephthah has learned to maneuver, entice, and manipulate others in order to survive, and he considers himself a born negotiator. As an intrepid warrior he is also capable of fighting for what he needs and may have hired himself out as a mercenary, a stateless fighter who sells his skills to those who need them most. When Israel is attacked by the Ammonites, however, they discover that there is no suitable leader for their army, and the elders of Gilead are anxious to bring back Jephthah and ask him to serve as their general. In the following scenes, Jephthah *thinks* that he has negotiated an excellent deal for himself that will result in him becoming not only a military general but also the administrative governor over all of Gilead.[15] He does not realize, however, that the elders have actually conceded to him no more than they were willing to offer at the very beginning of the debate. Next, he tries to negotiate a settlement with the king of Ammon that will result in him giving up any claim to Israelite land without the need for battle. His argument, however, offers Ammon no way to save face, and his long, brash justification of Israel's entitlement to Gilead has no impact on a king who will not allow himself to be shamed. When forced to resort to battle at last, Jephthah makes his infamous bargain with Yahweh, bribing him with an offer to sacrifice his daughter—which he hopes he can ultimately avoid—in exchange for victory.[16] His self-promotion with the elders was not as successful as he thinks, his self-confident negotiation with the King of Ammon has failed, and now his presumptuous and unnecessary negotiation with Yahweh costs him his only daughter's life.

It is after this that Ephraim enters the narrative once more. The narrator reports, "Then the men of Ephraim were mustered, and they

---

167. See also Block, *Judges, Ruth*, 353.

15. For a detailed explanation of this negotiating process, see the Jephthah chapter in Boda and Conway, *Judges*.

16. It is impossible to do justice to this fascinating episode here. Refer to Boda and Conway, *Judges*, for a much comprehensive analysis.

crossed over" (12:1). It is unclear who mustered them, but they have come *en masse* to confront Jephthah. Ephraim accuses Jephthah of not summoning them to the battle, just as they had accused Gideon of similar disregard. Whether it was a issue of shame or material loss, this time Ephraim does not simply quarrel with the judge; they threaten to burn down Jephthah's house (v. 1). The cord of three strands is becoming frayed. Unlike Gideon, Jephthah does not attempt to placate the irate Ephraimites. Instead of stilling troubled waters he stirs them up even more, accusing the Ephraimites of negligence, claiming that he called them in his hour of need and that they did not respond. Unlike Gideon, who downplays his own efforts and praises those of disgruntled Ephraim, Jephthah aggrandizes himself. In essence, he says, "When I saw that you had let me down, I took my life in my hands and crossed over myself to confront Ammon! And I won!" (v. 3, paraphrased). He then makes the matter immeasurably worse by accusing the Ephraimites of coming to fight him, not help him. Without any attempt to defuse the dangerous situation, he summons the Gileadite forces and attacks Ephraim. In the wake of his former failed negotiations, it seems that Jephthah has decided that aggression is the only effective way to solve a dispute, even if the dispute is with his own fellow Israelites. At the fords of the Jordan once again, the men of Gilead proceed to slaughter forty-two units of Ephraimites (12:6).

Ehud cooperates with his fellow Israelites from Ephraim to successfully defeat an enemy; the Ephraimite Deborah works collaboratively with other tribes; Gideon wisely defuses a confrontation with the Ephraimites and restores unity to the people of Israel; Jephthah, however, refuses any attempt to reconcile with his alienated relatives from Ephraim and resorts to violence as the ultimate solution . . . and Israel spirals down into internecine warfare.[17] There is an important message for the church here, especially its Protestant sector, which has become subdivided into numerous sub-groups who are often more concerned about being "right" or about criticizing the theology and praxis of their fellow Christians in other denominations than they are

17. It is interesting that the Micah in Judg 17–18 and the Levite in Judg 19–21—main characters in the final two stories that typify chaos and division in Israel—are both from Ephraim.

about representing Christ to the world, loving their neighbor (whoever that may be), and working toward the kingdom of God. It is necessary to guard the faith and avoid syncretism and apostasy, but Christians would be well to remember not only Paul's admonition, "I therefore, the prisoner in the Lord, beg you to lead a life worthy of the calling to which you have been called, with all humility and gentleness, with patience, bearing with one another in love, making every effort to maintain the unity of the Spirit in the bond of peace" (Eph 4:1–3 NRSV), but also Jesus' prayer, "Holy Father, protect them in your name that you have given me, so that they may be one, as we are one" (John 17:11 NRSV).

BENJAMIN: HERO, VILLAIN

Ehud the Lone Hero

The tribe of Benjamin appears less frequently on stage in Judges, but when it does appear, it makes a powerful impact. Immediately after the paradigmatic judge, Othniel, the narrative introduces Ehud, whom Yahweh raises up to free Israel from the disciplinary oppression of Eglon, king of Moab (3:12–14). As noted above, Ehud is from the tribe of Benjamin, and is referred to as בֶּן־הַיְמִינִי, which means "son of the right hand," and yet, ironically, Ehud is "hindered in his right hand" or left-handed.[18] He stands out from the others. The narrative is full of plays on words, satirical scenes, and unexpected outcomes; humor is one effective way for a subjugated people not only to resist their oppressors but also to shame them when they are defeated.[19] As previously discussed, Ehud acts alone, with little or no mention of his fellow-Benjaminites. It is only after his successful assassination of Eglon that he calls on the Ephraimites to assist him in the clean-up operation against the Moabite army. The narrative may in fact assume the presence of Benjaminites, but the emphasis is on his cooperation with another tribe.

A number of commentators have expressed a dim view of Ehud's exploits: Wong calls him "dishonorable," Polzin considers him to be

---

18. See also Judg 20:16. For an explanation of the significance of this term see Halpern, *First Historians*, 41.

19. See the Ehud chapters in Conway, *Judgment in Judges: A Narrative Appraisal Analysis*, and Boda and Conway, *Judges*.

Community

"repugnant, deceitful, and cruel," and Webb calls him a "devious assassin."[20] However, Ehud must be judged according to the ethics of his time. It is true that in 2 Samuel the killing of Abner and Amasa by Joab with a thrust to the belly is roundly condemned by the narrative[21] and that a similar method is used here to dispense with Eglon. However, there is a significant difference in Ehud's case: Joab kills two fellow Israelites, whereas Ehud kills a foreign despot who is oppressing Israel.[22] As Bartusch argues, "While lying and deception strike the modern interpreter as always morally objectionable, they are dishonorable actions in the (ancient) Mediterranean culture only among one's kin group. It is acceptable, however, to lie for the purpose of deceiving an outsider who, it is held, has no right to the truth."[23] In addition, Lambert argues that in tribal societies "all actions are based on specific loyalties, the lines of which are structurally determined. One supports one's fellow-clansman in a dispute, regardless of moral questions. The only consideration is, 'he is my fellow clansman.'"[24] Thus, although Ehud works alone when the nature of the task calls for subtlety, he is nevertheless acting in the interests of Israel as a whole. Later, when the strength of numbers is called for, he summons the tribe of Ephraim to accomplish a task that is in their mutual interest. In terms of the ANE, there is no doubt that Ehud is a heroic figure.

Ehud lived in a theocracy, not a secular democracy, and was specifically raised up by Yahweh to deliver Israel (3:15). In our contemporary

---

20. Wong, "Ehud and Joab: Separated at Birth?," 407–10; Polzin, *Moses and the Deuteronomist*, 160; Webb, *Integrated Reading*, 132.

21. 2 Sam 3:22–34; 20:8–10. See Wong, "Ehud and Joab: Separated at Birth?," 407–10. For example, he points out that only one verse is used to describe the assassination whereas twelve describe David's negative reaction to it and that Joab is cursed by David, forced to mourn publicly, and is described as an evildoer. He points out that the author seems to share David's view (p. 407).

22. For more detail on this argument, see the Ehud chapter in Boda and Conway, *Judges*.

23. Bartusch, *Understanding Dan*, 147.

24. Lambert, "Tribal Influences in Old Testament Tradition," 46. See also Deist, "Murder in the Toilet," 269; Chalcraft, "Deviance and Legitimate Action," 183–85. On p. 184 Chalcraft notes: "Ehud's potential deviance is legitimate for the narrator because of its context. Ehud moves over to the out-group, behaves deviantly and in the process qualifies for heroic status within the in-group."

secular and democratic society, it would be unwise to ignore moral issues in supporting one's fellow citizens. Patriotism—secular community loyalty—must not be equated with, or transcend, loyalty to God, even though Rom 13:1–2 admonishes the Christian to obey the governing authorities. When secular governments conflict with God's revealed will, however, "We must obey God rather than any human authority," as Peter said (Acts 5:29 NRSV). The Israelites themselves often "did what was right in their own eyes" (Judg 17:6; 21:25) and not what was right "in the eyes of Yahweh" (Judg 2:11; 3:7, 12; 4:1; 6:1; 10:6; 13:1) and were disciplined for it. It is wise to remember Paul's words: "Do not repay anyone evil for evil, but take thought for what is noble in the sight of all. If it is possible, so far as it depends on you, live peaceably with all" (Rom 12:17–18 NRSV). The Christian today must carefully consider the nature of subversive action, especially violent action and just war, and evaluate to what extent these serve the purposes of God or of a secular government, recognizing that these purposes may, or may not, overlap.[25]

Benjamin the Lone Villain

In the beginning of Judges, the lone Benjaminite, Ehud, works alone for the good of all Israel. By the end of the narrative, however, the isolated tribe of Benjamin acts to tear apart the fabric of Israel. The cord of multiple strands that ensured the early success of Israel in their settlement of the land has now become frayed and worn and is rapidly unravelling.

At first, it is an isolated Ephraimite in Judg 19 who garners our attention. A Levite is returning home after retrieving his concubine from Bethlehem when he lodges overnight in Gibeah, an Israelite town. He considers the Benjaminites who live here to be more supportive than the "foreigners" in nearby Jebus, or Jerusalem (19:12), but they do not offer him hospitality. Instead, another Ephraimite outsider offers his group shelter. That night, however, Benjaminite "men of worthlessness" (v. 22) confront them and demand sexual relations with the Levite. When the worthless men refuse to listen to their host's protests, the Levite

---

25. This, of course, is a complex issue and it is impossible to do justice to it here. The reader is encouraged to consult works on Christian ethics for more detailed discussion.

throws his concubine outside to sate their appetites, where she is raped and murdered (vv. 25–28). Continuing his callous attitude toward his concubine, the Levite summons Israel by the grotesque method of cutting her up and sending her body parts to all the tribes,[26] who gather and decide to punish the Benjaminites when they refuse to hand over the perpetrators (20:12–15). The unity of Israel has deteriorated to the point at which it is torn apart by internecine war, Benjamin against the remaining tribes.

As noted above, the Israelites go through the motions of inquiring of Yahweh, and Judah once again takes a leadership role within Israel. This time, however, Israel's assumptions are mistaken. The result is disastrous, and many Israelites are killed. By the time that Benjamin and Gibeah are finally destroyed, after a lengthy and bloody series of battles, only six hundred Benjaminite men are left alive, in hiding at the Rock of Rimmon (v. 47), and with no wives to perpetuate the tribe. Ironically, the Israelites weep and pray, "Why, O Yahweh, God of Israel, has this happened in Israel, for one tribe to be missing from Israel today?" (21:3). Compounding their error, the tribes develop two dubious schemes to ensure the survival of Benjamin, the tribe that they themselves have virtually destroyed. Both involve further violence against their fellow Israelites. First, they destroy the inhabitants of Jabesh Gilead for failing to support the military campaign and seize the four hundred virgin women who remain to be wives for Benjamin (vv. 8–14). Then they allow the remaining Benjaminites to kidnap two hundred young women of Shiloh, arguing that because they were not given freely, the Israelites did not violate their oath to never give their daughters as wives to Benjamin (vv. 17–23). Thus, a violent and shameful action by a group of Benjaminites in Gibeah escalates into devastating internal strife, the murder of one vulnerable woman multiplies into the rape and abduction of hundreds of young women, and the eagerness to punish one group of worthless and violent Benjaminite men swells into a violent frenzy that results in the near extermination of the entire tribe.

There is no doubt that punishment is due to those who commit rape and murder and other heinous crimes; God's people cannot allow

---

26. Compare Saul in 1 Sam 11:7.

injustice and violence to corrupt their community from within. However, when judgement is reached too quickly based on unchallenged assumptions and when attempts to rectify the results of hasty and unwise decisions involve even more recklessness and violence, God's people are troubled indeed. Sadly, the church is not exempt from such inner degeneration. Internal sins and scandals do occur and are sometimes handled by self-protective attempts to deny and cover up the problem, or, conversely, by harsh judgment and schism. Church discipline is necessary but must be handled wisely and prayerfully by those who are mature in the faith so that the solution does not cause more pain and damage than the original problem. Paul's interaction with the church at Corinth is one source of guidance for handling sin within the Christian community.

CONCLUSION

By the end of the book of Judges, the cord of three strands has been shredded, largely due to errors made by Israel itself rather than as a result of oppression by their enemies. The final two verses speak of this deterioration of community. Judges 21:24 anticlimactically states, "Then the people of Israel dispersed (וַיִּתְהַלְּכוּ) from there at that time, each to his tribe and to his clan, and they went out from there, each to his inheritance." The *hithpael* of הלך indicates to "to walk about" or "to go to and fro"[27] and challenges any sense of unity of purpose, and the double reference to "each" (אִישׁ) emphasizes individual rather than unified action. The final verse, "Now in those days there was no king in Israel; each person (אִישׁ) was doing what was right in their own eyes," again stresses the disintegration of corporate function and identity. It is not until the time of King David that Israel once again—temporarily—assumes a united front. The book of Kings, however, once again presents a narrative of fraying unity. The church, under the leadership of Jesus, the son of David, once again began as a united family, but divisions erupted early on in the New Testament narrative. There is no guarantee that the church will achieve true unity this side of the eschaton, but Christian unity must nevertheless remain a primary objective

---

27. Clines et al., eds., *The Dictionary of Classical Hebrew*, 2:557.

if the church is to serve as an effective witness of the unity of the family of God. The story of Judges gives us much to ponder in this regard.

BIBLIOGRAPHY

Bartusch, Mark W. *Understanding Dan: An Exegetical Study of a Biblical City, Tribe and Ancestor.* JSOTSup 379. Sheffield: Sheffield Academic, 2003.

Block, Daniel I. *Judges, Ruth.* NAC 6. Nashville, TN: Broadman & Holman, 1999.

Boda, Mark J. "Judges." In *The Expositor's Bible Commentary, Volume 2: Numbers to Ruth,* edited by David E. Garland and Tremper Longman, 1043–1288. Rev ed. Grand Rapids: Zondervan, 2012.

Boda, Mark J., and Mary L. Conway. *Judges.* Zondervan Exegetical Commentary on the Old Testament. Grand Rapids: Zondervan, Forthcoming.

Chalcraft, D. J. "Deviance and Legitimate Action in the Book of Judges." In *The Bible in Three Dimensions: Essays in Celebration of Forty Years of Biblical Studies in the University of Sheffield,* edited by David J. A. Clines et al., 177–201. JSOTSup 87. Sheffield: Sheffield Academic, 1990.

Clines, David J. A., et al., eds. *The Dictionary of Classical Hebrew.* 8 vols. Sheffield: Sheffield Academic, 1993–2011.

Conway, Mary L. *Judging the Judges: A Narrative Appraisal Analysis.* LSAWS 15. Winona Lake, IN: Eisenbrauns, 2019.

Deist, Ferdinand. "'Murder in the Toilet' (Judges 3:12–30): Translation and Transformation." *Scriptura* (1996) 263–72.

Fretz, Mark J., and Raphael I. Panitz. "Caleb." In *ABD* 1:809–10.

Halpern, Baruch. *The First Historians: The Hebrew Bible and History.* San Francisco: Harper & Row, 1988.

Kirkpatrick, Shane. "Questions of Honor in the Book of Judges." *Koinonia* 10 (1998) 19–40.

Lambert, Frith. "Tribal Influences in Old Testament Tradition." *SEÅ* 59 (1994) 33–58.

Kuntz, J. Kenneth. "Kenaz (Person)." In *ABD* 4:17.

Matthews, Victor H. *Judges and Ruth.* New Cambridge Bible Commentary. Cambridge: Cambridge University Press, 2004.

Miller, J. Maxwell, and John H. Hayes. *A History of Ancient Israel and Judah.* 1st ed. Philadelphia: Westminster, 1986.

Niditch, Susan. *Judges: A Commentary.* OTL. Louisville: Westminster John Knox, 2008.

Polzin, Robert. *Moses and the Deuteronomist: A Literary Study of the Deuteronomic History, Pt. 1: Deuteronomy, Joshua, Judges.* Indiana

Studies in Biblical Literature. Bloomington: Indiana University Press, 1993.

Schneider, Tammi J. *Judges*. Berit Olam. Collegeville, MN: Liturgical Press, 2000.

Stone, Lawson G. "Judges." In *Joshua, Judges, Ruth*, edited by Philip Wesley Comfort, 185–494. Cornerstone Biblical Commentary 3. Carol Stream, IL: Tyndale, 2012.

Webb, Barry G. *The Book of the Judges: An Integrated Reading*. JSOTSup 46. Sheffield: JSOT, 1987.

Wong, Gregory T. K. "Ehud and Joab: Separated at Birth?" *VT* 56 (2006) 399–412.

Younger, K. Lawson. *Judges and Ruth*. NIVAC. Grand Rapids: Zondervan, 2002.

2

An Evil Spirit from God?

The Role of (the) (S/s)pirit(s) of God in Judges, Samuel, and Kings

Mark J. Boda

INTRODUCTION

THE BOOKS OF JUDGES, Samuel, and Kings regularly depict spirits from God interacting with figures in the narrative.[1] Some of the acts associated with these figures in the text often cause discomfort for modern readers and raise a question over the identity and source of these spirits, especially those traditionally translated in English versions as "evil spirit" or "lying spirit." The following analysis will review the evidence of such spirit figures in these Old Testament (OT) books with the hope that it will provide insight into the role of such spirits under Yahweh's purview and how modern readers should use such texts for theological formation and reflection.[2]

1. For overall data on the appearance of the term רוּחַ in Judges, Samuel, and Kings, see Block, "Empowered by the Spirit of God," 42–43. Block notes the challenge of telling "whether the *rûaḥ* spoken of is *the* Holy Spirit or another spirit at Yahweh's disposal" (43). On this, see further below.

2. Helpful earlier contributions on these books have been provided by Block,

SPIRITS IN JUDGES

Heavenly spirits are depicted at several key points in the accounts found in the book of Judges. Of the six major judge accounts, four (Othniel, Gideon, Jephthah, and Samson) include a depiction of an entity described as רוּחַ־יהוה (the spirit of Yahweh) exerting some form of influence on the leader. Actions associated with these entities include "being upon" (היה על; Judg 3:10; 11:29), "clothing" (לבשׁ; 6:34), "stirring up/troubling" (פעם; 13:25), "coming forcefully upon" (צלח על; 14:6, 19; 15:14). In nearly every case, the depiction of the spirit's influence is followed immediately by an activity related to a physical struggle against humans or animals, usually associated with war: whether going out to battle (Judg 3:10), journeying to the battle (11:29, 32), mustering troops for battle (6:34), tearing apart a lion (14:6), killing thirty Philistines (14:19), tearing apart bonds, or killing a thousand Philistines (15:14). Only 13:25 is not followed by a violent action, as Samson journeys to Timnah, where he sees an attractive woman.

Nearly all of these activities appear to be considered normative within the value world of the narrator of Judges, with the spirit of Yahweh indicating the deity's choice and empowerment of the leader to free the people from the oppression of a foreign entity raised up to discipline the people but now of no more use by Yahweh for discipline (3:10; 6:34; 11:29; 15:14). Other cases in Judges, however, cause difficulties. After noting that the spirit of Yahweh is upon Jephthah in 11:29, which immediately leads to his journeying through Gilead, Manasseh, and Mizpah of Gilead to Ammon, and before Jephthah engages the Ammonites in battle in 11:32, the narrator describes Jephthah making his infamous vow to Yahweh, which will lead to the death of his daughter (11:30–31). One might be tempted to see a direct connection between Jephthah's spirit-endowment and his vow.[3] However, of importance is the fact that the final phrase of 11:29 is a suffix conjugation

---

"Empowered by the Spirit of God," and Firth, "The Historical Books."

3. For example, Exum ("The Tragic Vision and Biblical Narrative," 66) states: "One could more plausibly argue that Jephthah makes his vow under the influence of the spirit of Yhwh." With thanks for this and the following argument to Mary Conway, see especially the argument and reception history traced in Conway, Judging the Judges, 163-168. Cf. Boda and Conway, Judges.

clause, signaling a paragraph break in the narrative flow and creating a disjuncture between what is described in 11:30–31 concerning the vow and the previous reception of the Spirit. The use of the same verb at the outset of v. 32, which was used at the end of v. 29 (עבר, "cross over") suggests resumptive repetition, which places the vow of vv. 30–31 separate from the present narrative flow and thus weakens the direct connection between the spirit's influence and the foolish vow. So also does the fact that the narrator makes no reference to the vow as the basis for the victory. This example reminds us that, when analyzing the book of Judges, it is uncertain whether one can firmly link all the behavior of the judges with the deity who has chosen or heavenly being who has influenced these judges.

The case of Samson, however, suggests that even inappropriate behavior may be related to a normative heavenly influence.[4] Thus, Judg 13:25 depicts the initial phase of the influence of the spirit of Yahweh on Samson, an influence which began when he was "in Maheneh-Dan, between Zorah and Eshtaol." Surprisingly, the very next event in 14:1 has Samson going down to Timnah and seeing a Philistine woman, who he wants to marry, and there is no narrative break between chs. 13 and 14 in Hebrew. At first glance, one might be tempted to argue that there is no explicit link established by the narrator between Samson's questionable action and desire in 14:1 and the influence of the spirit of Yahweh in 13:25. However, the narrator appears to resist any such argument, making clear in 14:4 that although Samson's parents disapproved of Samson's desire (14:3) Yahweh was not only using Samson's desire but, actually, was the source of his desire (מֵיהוה הִיא, "it was from Yahweh"), actively seeking an opportunity to defeat the Philistines (תֹאֲנָה הוּא־מְבַקֵּשׁ מִפְּלִשְׁתִּים). So, also, the spirit of Yahweh enables Samson to tear apart the lion in 14:9. This action not only takes place in a location which threatens Samson's Nazarite status (vineyard) but will lead to a clear violation of his Nazarite status by his contact with the lion carcass—the second step on the way to his third and final Nazarite violation (hair cutting), which will signal his demise at the hands of the Philistines (Judg 16). The case in 14:19 of Samson's killing of thirty Ashkelonites for their clothes does accomplish Yahweh's search for "an

---

4. See Merrill, "The Samson Saga."

occasion against the Philistines," even though it does seem senseless in light of its fulfillment of Samson's bargain related to his wedding riddle.

While the spirit entities reviewed so far in Judges are all identified as רוּחַ־יהוה (spirit of Yahweh), there is one case in Judges that refers to a spiritual entity using different terminology. In Judg 9:23, the narrator reveals that "God sent (שׁלח) a רוּחַ רָעָה (traditionally, 'evil spirit') between Abimelech and the lords of Shechem." The very next action described by the narrator in v. 23 is that "the lords of Shechem dealt treacherously (בגד) with Abimelech," described in v. 25 as the lords of Shechem setting ambushes in the hill country to undermine Abimelech's trade routes. It appears then that the flow of the narrative identifies the results of the influence of this רוּחַ רָעָה (traditionally "evil spirit") as reflected in the treacherous dealings of the lords of Shechem with Abimelech and by extension then the murderous response of Abimelech against the lords of Shechem.

The use of the lexeme רָעָה (fs form of רַע, traditionally translated as "evil") in connection with this spirit has caused discomfort for some readers of the OT, because this term is often used for moral evil (e.g., Prov 29:6; Jer 3:17).[5] However, this adjective is used regularly in a nonmoral way to refer to a calamity or a disaster (e.g., Deut 6:22; Ezek 5:16).[6] A similar semantic range (from moral evil to calamity/disaster) is also evident in the use of the closely associated cognates, the nominal form רָעָה (cf. 2 Kgs 22:16 with Amos 3:6) and the verbal form רעע (cf. for *hiphil* Jer 7:26 with Exod 5:22). This terminology is regularly associated with the actions of Yahweh, often appearing in contexts which regularly play on the breadth of semantic range, that is, depicting Yahweh bringing disaster (רַע, רָעָה, *hiphil* of רעע) in response to the moral evil (רַע, רָעָה, *hiphil* of רעע) of human figures (cf. 1 Kgs 21:20–21; 2 Kgs 21:11–12; Jer 18:8–12).

Returning to Judg 9, it is clear that the רוּחַ רָעָה (traditionally "evil spirit") is sent from God and, thus, should not be understood as

---

5. NASB and ESV translate רוּחַ רָעָה in Judg 9:23 as "evil spirit," NLT as "a spirit that stirred up trouble," Firth ("The Historical Books," 13) as "baleful spirit," and Merrill ("The Samson Saga," 286) as "troubling spirit."

6. So, also, Block ("Empowered by the Spirit of God," 47): "the effects of his possession are negative and destructive for the object."

a morally evil spirit but, rather, as a spirit that brings injury or has a harmful goal (an injurious spirit).[7] The sending of this רוּחַ רָעָה (injurious spirit) accomplishes the goal identified by the narrator in the closing verses of ch. 9: to repay the רָעַת אֲבִימֶלֶךְ (evil of Abimelech) and the רָעַת אַנְשֵׁי שְׁכֶם (evil of the men of Shechem).

Thus, the book of Judges depicts two types of heavenly spirits, both of which are linked to the deity. One has a positive commission, at least in relation to the Israelites (called רוּחַ־יְהוָה, spirit of Yahweh), and the other a negative commission (called רוּחַ רָעָה, injurious spirit). The one with a positive commission for the Israelites, however, is associated with individuals who perform actions that may be deemed inappropriate. In some cases, such actions may merely reflect the independent motivations of the human figure and, thus, not be necessarily linked to the influence of the heavenly spirit. But the case of Samson makes this resolution difficult to accept since even Samson's inappropriate desires and actions (e.g., seeking a wife among the Philistines, killing a lion in a vineyard that will lead to eating unclean honey) are traced to a divine source explicitly by the narrator. The other heavenly spirit with a negative commission is clearly linked to the deity who actively sends this entity to prompt the lords of Shechem and Abimelech to deal with each other treacherously and, so, to accomplish the higher divine goal of bringing down the unjust rule of Abimelech.

SPIRITS IN SAMUEL

Moving into the book of Samuel one can discern similar trends to those observed in Judges, although with some new aspects. A heavenly entity called "spirit" (רוּחַ) is closely related to the commissioning of leadership figures in 1 Samuel, first Saul and then David. At times the name of this entity is the same as that used in the book of Judges: רוּחַ יהוה (spirit of Yahweh; 1 Sam 10:6; 16:13, 14), but another also appears: רוּחַ אֱלֹהִים (spirit of God; 10:10). The action associated with this entity is the same as that found in the Samson accounts in Judges, as this spirit is

---

7. See Hamori ("The Spirit of Falsehood"), who traces the harmful spirit in the ancient Near East (ANE) and Hebrew Bible, although it is not clear from the passages that the harmful spirit must always be associated with "falsehood," especially those in 1 Samuel.

depicted as "coming forcefully upon" (צלח על) Saul in 10:6, 10; 11:6. In 16:13, a different preposition is used, so that the spirit comes forcefully "to" (צלח אל) David. In the case of Saul, at least, this spirit associated with commissioning has a similar effect to that seen in Judges. After this spirit comes forcefully upon Saul in 11:6, he performs actions associated with battle: becoming angry (וַיִּחַר אַפּוֹ מְאֹד, 11:6b), mustering an army (11:7–8), and attacking the Ammonites (11:9–11). This link between the spirit's endowment and battle can also be discerned in Samuel's prophecy of 10:6, in which the prophet tells Saul that when these signs (those related to the spirit and prophecy) occur that Saul should "do for yourself what the occasion requires, for God is with you." This is then qualified in 10:8 as "you shall go down before me to Gilgal; and behold I will come down to you to offer burnt offerings and sacrifice peace offerings. You shall wait seven days until I come to you and show you what you should do." This qualification links the spirit endowment here with Saul's military action in 1 Sam 13 (see 13:7–8). In the case of David, the immediate action depicted after the forceful coming of the spirit to him in 16:13 is his musical actions to sooth Saul's torment in 16:14–23. However, this is followed narratively by the depiction of 1 Sam 17, in which David engages the Philistine Goliath in battle, suggesting a connection if only on the narrative level between this spirit endowment and war.[8]

But the spirit of Yahweh/God related to the commissioning of these kings (or, probably better, dynasties)[9] is associated with another activity not mentioned in Judges. In Saul's case, this spirit is clearly linked to the activity of prophesying, using the *hithpael* of נבא in 10:6 and 10.[10] This prophetic activity occurs as Saul comes in contact with a

8. See, further, Firth, "The Historical Books," 18–19, on connections to battle as in Judges but emphasis on royal election.

9. Cf. Firth, "The Spirit and Leadership," 269.

10. This activity is not associated with David in 1 Samuel, but interestingly in 2 Sam 23:2 in the "last words of David" we find the declaration: "The Spirit of Yahweh spoke (דבר *piel*) by me, and his word was on my tongue. The God of Israel said (אמר), the Rock of Israel spoke (דבר *piel*) to me . . ." Block ("Empowered by the Spirit of God," 48) and Firth ("Is Saul among the Prophets?," 302–3; "The Historical Books," 20) deny that Saul's activity was verbal, yet the *hithpael* of נבא used there also appears in contexts where there is clearly verbal activity (e.g., 1 Kgs 22:8, 18; Jer 26:20; 29:27; Ezek 37:10; 2 Chr 20:37). In particular, 1 Kgs 22:10–12 shows the difficulty of

"company of prophets" (חֶבֶל נְבִיאִים; 10:6, 10). Samuel links this action in 10:6 to the fact that Saul will "be changed into another man" (הפך לְאִישׁ אַחֵר). This connection between a heavenly spirit and prophecy is found also later in Samuel in relation to Saul (1 Sam 19:20–24). As Saul seeks to capture David at Naioth in Ramah, three waves of his messengers and then Saul personally experience "the spirit of God" (רוּחַ אֱלֹהִים היה עַל) as they come in proximity to a group of prophets (לַהֲקַת הַנְּבִיאִים),[11] which prompts prophetic activity, again using the *hithpael* of נבא (to prophesy). Things get out of hand in the case of Saul as he strips off his clothes and prophesies naked before Samuel all day and night. While these events in 1 Sam 19 suggest a close association with the earlier spirit endowment in 1 Sam 10, they are also distinct in that the spirit's role here is designed to prohibit Saul from capturing David. This spirit is not described here using any negative terminology; while the immediate effect appears to be positive (prophesying in relation to a company of prophets surrounding Samuel), the ultimate purpose is to frustrate Saul's murderous intentions.

This distinction prompts further reflection on the role of other spirit entities in Samuel. First Samuel 16:14 notes how the spirit of Yahweh (רוּחַ יהוה) had departed (סור) from Saul, replaced by what is called a רוּחַ־רָעָה מֵאֵת יהוה (an injurious spirit from Yahweh). This entity is identified in the following verses as a רוּחַ־אֱלֹהִים רָעָה (injurious spirit of Yahweh; 16:15, 16) as well as just רוּחַ־אֱלֹהִים (spirit of God) and רוּחַ רָעָה (injurious spirit; 16:23); later, in 1 Sam 18:10, this entity is identified as רוּחַ אֱלֹהִים רָעָה (injurious spirit of God) and 19:9 as רוּחַ יהוה רָעָה (injurious spirit of Yahweh). This spiritual entity, whose influence is intermittent, is clearly identified with Yahweh, prompting once again this translation of "injurious spirit." Thus, as in Judges, this is a spirit that is sent from Yahweh to carry out a negative mission—here, punishment for divine purposes. This injurious spirit is depicted as terrorizing (בעת, *piel*) Saul but also being upon (היה על; 16:16; 19:9), coming

---

distinguishing between the *niphal* and *hithpael* of נבא, as Firth does in his work on 1 Sam 19:20–24.

11. Which, in light of OG, Peshitta, and targumim, may have originally read: קְהִלַּת. It could, although, refer to the root להק, which through Ethiopic may have referred to an "elder, dignitary," thus "the venerable company of prophets." See *HALOT* 521.

forcefully upon (צלח על, 18:10), and departing from (סור מעל; 16:23). The effect of this injurious spirit is also similar to the earlier depictions of the spirit of Yahweh in Samuel. This spirit prompts Saul to engage in prophetic activity (נבא *hithpael*; 1 Sam 18:10) as well as to engage in violent action akin to battle, as he throws a spear at David (1 Sam 18:10–11; 19:9–10). Of course, the irony in all of this is that David, the recipient of the royal spirit of Yahweh (1 Sam 16:13), emerges as the prescription to help Saul deal with the effects of this injurious spirit in 1 Sam 16:14–23, immediately following Saul's loss of the royal spirit of Yahweh.[12] Interestingly, the effect that David has on Saul is depicted using the vocabulary of טוֹב (good; 1 Sam 16:16, 23). The adjective טוֹב (good), the noun טוּב (goodness), and the verb טב in the *hiphil* (do well; cf. Zeph 1:12), function in Hebrew as the antonymic word pairs associated with the cognates related to the roots רעע/רעה. Thus, the effect of the spirit of Yahweh is for good, while that of the injurious spirit is for injury or harm.

What we then see in the book of Samuel is similar to the trend observed in the book of Judges, that is, two types of heavenly spirits both of which are linked to the deity. One has a positive commission, at least in relation to the Israelites and in particular their king (called רוּחַ־יהוה, spirit of Yahweh), and the other a negative commission (called רוּחַ רָעָה, injurious spirit). While the negative entity is only mentioned in one place in Judges, 1 Samuel features such entities on several occasions.

Tracking the vocabulary that is used in relation to these two types of entities reveals striking similarities.

---

12. See Howard, "Transfer of Power"; however, contrast Block, "Empowered by the Spirit of God," 52–53.

As can be readily seen, both the spirit of God/Yahweh and the injurious spirit of God/Yahweh "rushes" (צלח) to/upon people (compare 10:6, 10; 16:13, with 18:10), both come upon (היה על) people (compare 19:20, 23, with 16:16), both depart (סור) from people (compare 16:14 with 16:23), and both influence people to prophesy (נבא, hithpael; compare 10:6, 10; 19:20, 23, with 18:10).[13]

It is clear from the book of Samuel that injurious spirits are sent from Yahweh to accomplish a negative commission, that is, to bring judgment upon a human entity. This is, thus, akin to the actions of the heavenly messenger (מַלְאָךְ) sent by Yahweh to carry out the calamitous (רָעָה) punishment against Israel in 2 Sam 24:16 due to David's sin. Yahweh sending an injurious spirit to Saul and then bringing the spirit-endowed David to remedy his affliction may seem odd, but both entities carry out Yahweh's mission. What is shocking is to see how an injurious spirit from Yahweh can prompt prophetic activity as well as

---

13. See Hamori, "The Spirit of Falsehood," 19–20.

even violent activity that could threaten the life of the anointed David. One could explain this as merely a human response to the torment caused by this injurious spirit, just as the human response to the empowerment of the good spirit involves emotional turmoil and engaging in battle as seen in 1 Sam 11:6.

SPIRITS IN KINGS

The final corpus, the book of Kings, contains several references to heavenly spirit entities. The three key passages are those related to Elijah, Micaiah, and Sennacherib, which will be treated in order.

Spirit and Elijah/Elisha

A spirit of Yahweh is identified with Elijah by Ahab's official Obadiah in 1 Kgs 18:12. There, Obadiah fears for his own life because of Elijah's "disappearing" acts, which he attributes to רוּחַ יהוה. Here, we see a continuation of the connectivity between רוּחַ יהוה and prophecy established in the book of Samuel.[14] The term רוּחַ is associated with Elijah near the end of the presentation of the Elijah tradition in 2 Kgs 2 as the prophetic mantle shifts from Elijah to his disciple Elisha. When Elijah offers Elisha a parting act, Elisha asks for a double portion (פִּי־שְׁנַיִם) of "your spirit."[15] The reference to double portion points to Elisha's status as the firstborn receiving the larger portion of the inheritance and especially control of the family (Deut 21:17).[16] But the reference here to a spirit moving from a senior to junior leader as well as the reference later in the passage to the spirit resting (נוח) upon Elisha (2 Kgs 2:15) suggests a connection to the event in Num 11 (11:25–26). What is referred to as "your spirit" in 2 Kgs 2:9 and "the spirit of Elijah" in 2:15 appears to be the heavenly spirit, which is then transferred to Elisha.

---

14. Notice how the prophetic appears in Judges, but the spirit is related only to leadership and great feats of battle.

15. In Zech 13:8 this refers to two parts out of three which is also suggested by the scenario in Deut 21:15–17 where there is a son of an unloved wife alongside a son of a loved wife. Possibly the rule of the double portion relates to three portions distributed, with two reserved for the firstborn to sustain the family and the third portion apportioned to any others.

16. Although it should not be missed that Elisha doubles the number of miracles that Elijah performed during his ministry.

Community

In this context, reference is also made to רוּחַ יהוה (spirit of Yahweh), who the "sons of the prophets" see as responsible for his disappearance, bringing the tradition full circle to Obadiah's opening reference to the spirit in 1 Kgs 18:12. The heavenly spirit in the Elijah tradition appears in connection with one verb already encountered in Judges and Samuel, היה (come; 2 Kgs 2:9, followed by אל [to] as in 1 Sam 19:9) but also with others, including נוח אל (rest, 2 Kgs 2:15), נשׂא (carry, 1 Kgs 18:12; 2 Kgs 2:16), and שׁלך ב (cast on/in, 2 Kgs 2:16).

The impact of this spirit on the recipient is not always clear. First Kings 18:12 and 2 Kgs 2:16 reveal that this spirit has a spatial impact on the recipient.[17] Second Kgs 2:14 relates the parting of the Jordan to Elisha's use of the "mantle" of Elijah but does not specifically reference the spirit. This may be in view in 2:15 as the "sons of the prophets" see Elisha and conclude: "The spirit of Elijah rests on Elisha." However, it is not clear whether they conclude this from seeing the parting of the river or by some other means. This scene is followed by an account of a miracle related to unclean water (2:19–22) and, then, by the odd violent scene of 2:23–24, in which the forty-two lads are ripped to pieces by two bears.

Spirits and Micaiah

Unquestionably, the most controversial section of the book of Kings in relation to heavenly spirits is the Micaiah episode in 1 Kgs 22 (//2 Chr 18). In this passage, Ahab and Jehoshaphat plot war strategy against the Arameans and, as part of the consultation, Jehoshaphat asks Ahab to make inquiry of Yahweh for direction. Ahab gathers four hundred of his prophets together, who provide a positive reply, encouraging the kings to enter into battle since "the Lord" (אֲדֹנָי) will grant success (22:6). Jehoshaphat questions the authenticity of this prophecy, aware somehow that these four hundred prophets were not "a prophet of the Yahweh" (22:7). Ahab admits there is such a prophet, one called

---

17. See Robert B. Chisholm, "The 'Spirit of the Lord' in 2 Kings 2:16," who argues that the spirit in 2 Kgs 2:16 is a physical force (wind) which is inseparable from the "spirit" of Yahweh which "emanates from the Lord's very person and is associated with his breath" (307); for the close connection between spirit/breath/wind in relation to Yahweh see Averbeck, "Holy Spirit in the Hebrew Bible."

Micaiah ben Imlah, but Ahab does not appreciate his contributions since he prophesies (נבא *hithpael*)[18] רָע (disaster) rather than טוֹב (good/prosperity) concerning Ahab. The messenger who fetches Micaiah tries to influence the prophet of Yahweh, noting that the other prophets were speaking טוֹב (good/prosperity) and, so also, should he speak טוֹב (good/prosperity; 22:13). But Micaiah makes it clear that he will only speak what Yahweh tells him to speak (22:14). It is quite the surprise to the reader when in 22:15 Micaiah's words do indeed match those of Ahab's prophets. Ahab, however, is not surprised but is aware that Micaiah's words are not sincere, something learned from past patterns ("how many times").

Micaiah then relates two visionary experiences. The first is a scene in which Israel was scattered on the mountains as sheep without a shepherd, which prompts the divine interpretation, "These have no master," and attendant oracle of salvation (for the people), "Let each of them return to their house in peace" (22:17). Ahab understands this as depicting his demise, noting to Jehoshaphat that this confirms his view that Micaiah only prophesies רָע (disaster) and not טוֹב (good/prosperity; 22:18). This only spurs Micaiah to divulge more information through a second visionary report, which depicts a scene that took place in the divine council among "all the host of heaven" (22:19–22) followed by a divine interpretation (22:23a) and divine oracle of judgment (against Ahab; 22:23b).

The challenge of the passage relates to the proceedings which take place in the divine council visionary experience. Yahweh is depicted as asking who will "entice" Ahab to go into battle in order to be killed (22:20). Two volunteers come forward before one called הָרוּחַ (the spirit) steps forward (22:21). Yahweh then asks "how" this spirit entity intends to accomplish this mission and the spirit articulates a plan to be (היה) a deceptive spirit (רוּחַ שֶׁקֶר) in the mouth (בְּפִי) of all Ahab's prophets (22:22a).[19] Yahweh's response affirms this plan: "You are to

---

18. Notice how Ahab's prophets are depicted as "prophesying" (נבא *hithpael*) and, interestingly, later in the account their leader Zedekiah ben Chenaanah speaks of his own possession of "the Spirit of Yahweh" in 22:24.

19. Contra Block, "Empowered by the Spirit of God," 48–50, who dissociates the spirit in the divine council from this "lying spirit," the latter being a "spirit/disposition/mind set of emptiness, futility"; cf. Hamori, "The Spirit of Falsehood," 30, who

entice and also prevail. Go and do thus" (22:22b). This connection to Yahweh is then clarified by Micaiah who declares that Yahweh has put (נתן) a deceptive spirit (רוּחַ שֶׁקֶר) in the mouth (בְּפִי) of all Ahab's prophets, which was Yahweh's method to bring רָעָה (disaster) on Ahab (22:23). There is some ambiguity concerning Zedekiah's response to Micaiah in 22:24, as Zedekiah suggests sarcastically that "the spirit of Yahweh" passed from him to Micaiah. This either may mean that Zedekiah is challenging Micaiah's claim to have access to a good spirit, the spirit of Yahweh, or pointing out that Micaiah had at first spoken a word in line with the deceptive spirit and so was also implicated as a deceptive prophet.

Here, we have a scenario which provides further insight into the depiction of the function of spirit entities in the book of Kings. First, among the divine council identified as "the host of heaven," the only identified individual besides Yahweh is a being called *spirit*. This suggests that those beings that we often call *angels* (*messengers*) can be identified generically as spirits. Secondly, the one spirit entity singled out here in 1 Kgs 22 takes up the proposal of Yahweh to deceive King Ahab by influencing the speech of Ahab's prophets so that he goes to his death in battle. This spirit entity has a negative function to accomplish for Yahweh and this negative function—to deceive Ahab—is actually prompted by Yahweh; Micaiah makes clear Yahweh is responsible, since Yahweh is the subject of the verb נתן (placed) in 22:23. Interestingly, as with the earlier references to spirit in 1 Samuel, so, here, a spirit entity prompts prophetic speech.

There is no way to distance this spirit entity in 1 Kgs 22 from Yahweh, and there is no reason to see that its presence in the divine council is in any way exceptional. As with the רוח רעה (injurious spirit) in Judges and 1 Samuel, so the רוח שקר (deceptive spirit) is a spirit connected with Yahweh with a negative task to fulfil, here using a deception technique to prompt Ahab into a foolish battle, which will end his life.

---

notes that "the covert, disembodied nature of the רוח in most texts should not be assumed to indicate an impersonal force." In the case of 1 Kgs 22, the spirit in the divine council in v. 21 is most certainly the same spirit sent in v. 22. Nevertheless, Block is wise to point out the ambiguity of the message of the prophets influenced by this spiritual force. See further Chisholm, "Does God Deceive?"

Spirit and Sennacherib

Second Kings 19:7 contains one final reference to a "spirit" in the book of Kings. In this passage within Isaiah's prophetic response to Hezekiah's concern over the taunt of Sennacherib, Yahweh declares: "Behold, I will put in [נתן ב] him [Sennacherib] a spirit [רוּחַ], and he will hear a report and he will return to his land." The identical collocation is used in 1 Kgs 22:23 (cf. 2 Chr 18:22), where Micaiah declares that Yahweh has put a deceiving spirit in the mouth of all Ahab's prophets (נָתַן יהוה רוּחַ שֶׁקֶר בְּפִי). The terminology used here is similar to that found in Num 11:25, 29, where God takes of the spirit which is on Moses and distributes that spirit to the seventy elders (נתן, but there using the preposition עַל; notice in Num 11:17 how the synonym שׂים is used with עַל; cf. Isa 42:1, 5; Qoh 12:7; Ezek 11:19; 36:26; 37:6, 14; Neh 9:20).[20] This evidence suggests that this "spirit" which is put in Sennacherib is to be understood as a heavenly spirit sent from Yahweh, which prompts him to return to his land based on a report he hears concerning the Egyptians. The source of this spirit entity is clearly God; this entity enters into a foreign king who is influenced in such a way as to accomplish Yahweh's will which will have a negative outcome for the foreign king and a positive one for the people of God.

CONCLUSION

What we have discovered through this study of texts mentioning spirits in Judges, Samuel, and Kings is that various spirits are included in the presentation of the history of Israel and these spirits are all traced to Yahweh and not to any distinct evil source.[21] These spirits are presented

---

20. This collocation is also found in Isa 42:1 in reference to God's spirit upon the Servant figure. Isaiah 42:5 uses נתן ל (place into) and Qoh 12:7 uses נתן (gave) with direct object to refer to God's gift of life (רוּחַ, spirit) to all humanity. Ezekiel 11:19 and 36:26 use נתן בקרב (place into) to refer to the gift of the "new spirit" in the restoration age and Ezek 36:27 to "my [Yahweh's] spirit." Ezekiel 37:6, 14 use נתן ב (place into) to refer to the gift of "a spirit" as new life. The gift of the good spirit for interpretation of Torah in Neh 9:20 is described using נתן (gave) with the direct object.

21. Block ("Empowered by the Spirit of God," 52) presents first millennium ANE evidence that negative agents were "increasingly associated with the netherworld," which is not reflected in the OT depiction of the spirit: "the spirit's role is clearly subservient to Yahweh." Of course, being associated with the netherworld in

as accomplishing two basic functions on behalf of Yahweh: טוֹב (good) and/or רָעָה (injury).²² The spirits which are identified as accomplishing good are usually identified with the terminology of רוּחַ יהוה (spirit of Yahweh) or רוּחַ אֱלֹהִים (spirit of God) without any positive descriptor (although notice the use of טוֹב [good] with רוּחַ [spirit] in Neh 9:20; Ps 143:10; and קֹדֶשׁ [holiness] in Ps 51:13 [Eng. 11]; Isa 63:10, 11). The spirits that have a negative function are nearly always identified with a negative descriptor in Judges, Samuel, and Kings (רָעָה [injurious] or שֶׁקֶר [deceptive]) but sometimes without any descriptor, such as with the spirit that Yahweh places in Sennacherib (called just רוּחַ, spirit) or the reference to the spirit that tormented Saul in 1 Sam 16:23, which is described in this place as only רוּחַ אֱלֹהִים (spirit of God).

The precise division between these functions of טוֹב (good) and רָעָה (injury) is difficult at times to discern. Thus, the רוּחַ אֱלֹהִים (spirit of God) that frustrates Saul and his messengers in 1 Sam 19 is associated with the company of prophets gathered around Samuel and echoes the earlier reception of the spirit by Saul at the beginning of his reign. The function of this spirit is clearly negative, frustrating Saul's attempts, but the association with Samuel and the prophets suggests a positive function. In the case of the spirit that falls upon the judges or the monarchs, one can emphasize the positive function of this spirit, but that is positive for the Israelites. For the enemies of Israel, this spirit is an injurious spirit, bringing the judgment of Yahweh upon abusive foreign leaders.

Thus, the first step in dealing with texts referring to spirits in Judges, Samuel, and Kings is to understand that the spirits that are described are from Yahweh's divine cohort and function to fulfil his will either for טוֹב (good) or רָעָה (injury). Such an understanding may contribute to our understanding of the role of figures like the adversary in Job 1–2, Zech 3, and 1 Chr 21, which need not be placed necessarily on the dark side of the spirit realm.²³

---

a polytheistic context is not problematic, since that is also the realm of deity. Montague (*The Holy Spirit*, 22–23) unnecessarily refers to this as "a primitive worldview."

22. Block ("Empowered by the Spirit of God," 50) notes the distinction between "agents sent out by Yahweh, either as messengers (e.g., prophets and *malā'kîm* or agents of judgment."

23. Routledge ("An Evil Spirit from the Lord"), however, argues for the more

A second issue when dealing with these OT texts is related to the way in which human characters, who are under the influence of such spiritual entities, act. Human beings may be influenced by a spirit from God and choose to engage in actions which are not deemed ethical, but this may not be the desire of God (e.g., Jephthah). In other cases, the actions may not be deemed ethical, but God uses this fallenness to accomplish his goals (similar to Joseph and his brothers, the latter according to Joseph in Gen 50:20 intending רָעָה (injury) while God intended טוֹב (good).

A third issue arises from the evidence that God sends injurious spirits, that is, spirits who bring discipline or judgment upon human characters. This is not at odds with the presentation of OT or New Testament (NT) theology and this helps us understand the use of such spirits in relation to Saul, Abimelech/ Shechemites, and Sennacherib. The use of the injurious deceptive spirit in the Micaiah narrative may be more of a challenge to some. Some have emphasized the ambiguity of the prophecy that was actually given to Ahab or have focused on the intention of Micaiah's prophetic words as providing an opportunity for Ahab to repent. But, in the end, one cannot distance God from this spirit, and it is God who prompts the program of enticement in the first place. At issue here is the nature of deception. Yes, lying is clearly prohibited in the Torah, but, as with the prohibition concerning killing, the definition of what killing is is linked to context (thus we are talking about murder and not state execution or war). We all understand that, at times, deception can be good and need not be morally evil. I could mention Wayne Gretzky's amazingly deceptive moves on the hockey rink or more seriously Casper Ten Boom's deception of the Nazis to protect the Jewish children in his care. In a situation of war, we understand that deception is appropriate and part of the rules of engagement (it is not disallowed in the Geneva Convention). God gives strategies for Israel to cause battle diversions (see the battle of Ai in Josh 8:14, 19,

---

traditional understanding of Satan/Adversary and malevolent heavenly beings (as in 1 Samuel) as having access to and participation in the heavenly council. Even if there are good reasons to see malevolence in the Adversary figure and an adversarial tone to Yahweh's response to this figure in Job 1–2 and Zech 3, this is not necessarily connected to the injurious spirits in Judges, Samuel, and Kings; cf. Boda, *The Book of Zechariah*, 229–30.

21; and that of Jehoshaphat in 2 Chr 20:22), which are deceptive and totally appropriate. One also could mention David pretending insanity in 1 Sam 21:10–15. So, here, Yahweh can utilize deception and through this remain righteous.

And finally, Christians reading these texts are confronted with the question of how the presentation of these spirit entities relates to the Christian theology of the Holy Spirit. While no scholars have associated the injurious spirit with "the Holy Spirit," it is usually assumed in Christian scholarship that the "spirit of Yahweh" or "spirit of God" is the third person of the Trinity.[24] But these parallels suggest that just as one does not equate the injurious spirit with the deity, so also one should not assume such for spirits from God with good intentions.[25] The spirit of God/Yahweh lacking negative definition (such as רָעָה), may merely be a spiritual entity sent from the divine council to influence these humans according to their commission received from Yahweh.[26]

The presentation of spirit entities throughout Judges, Samuel, and Kings certainly prompts many questions for readers. But this prompting may be more due to mistranslations and misconceptions regarding

---

24. See Firth, "The Historical Books," 13 and 13n5, and his citation of Wood, *The Holy Spirit in the Old Testament*; Hildebrandt, *An Old Testament Theology of the Spirit of God*, 18; Wright, *Knowing the Holy Spirit through the Old Testament*. Block ("Empowered by the Spirit of God," 51) tries to make something of a distinction between spirit of Yahweh and spirit of God in 1 Samuel.

25. This is particularly noticeable in Block's presentation ("Empowered by the Spirit of God," 54): "If one must have a Trinity consisting of Father, son and Holy Spirit, based on the expressions actually found in the Old Testament, Yahweh would probably be the Father, the *rûaḥ* of Yahweh, obviously the Holy Spirit, but the son would be David and/or one of his descendants as adopted son or vassal of Yahweh." Also note this struggle in Firth's article ("The Historical Books," 13–14), which expresses the difficulty of identifying references to God's Spirit when "*ruach* is in a construct relationship with either *'elohim* or Yahweh" only because there are cases where *ruach* may refer to wind or breath. He does not appear to consider that *ruach* could refer to a spiritual entity apart from Yahweh. See, though, Merrill ("The Samson Saga," 284), who is open to the conclusion that not "every occurrence of 'spirit', even with 'God' or 'Lord', should be construed as a reference to the Holy Spirit."

26. Cf. Montague, *The Holy Spirit*, 26. Thus, it is not necessary to follow Chisholm ("Does God Deceive?," 20) in calling the spirit of Yahweh/God the deity's "personal spirit," as if other spirits from Yahweh are not so associated with the deity. Problematic also is Hamori ("The Spirit of Falsehood," 29), who distinguishes between "the spirit of falsehood" and "the divine spirit."

the spirit realm, driven by inappropriate imposition of later theological and cultural conceptions onto these Hebrew texts. Our good friend and faithful colleague Gus Konkel has spent a lifetime grappling with difficult texts just like these and has consistently displayed his commitment to guiding contemporary readers, young and old, gently but firmly, to understand more accurately the biblical texts. I, for one, am thankful for all his work in the past and in the years to come.

BIBLIOGRAPHY

Averbeck, Richard E. "The Holy Spirit in the Hebrew Bible and Its Connections to the New Testament." In *Who's Afraid of the Holy Spirit?: An Investigation into the Ministry of the Spirit of God Today*, edited by Daniel B. Wallace and M. James Sawyer, 15–36. Dallas: Biblical Studies, 2005.

Block, Daniel I. "Empowered by the Spirit of God: The Holy Spirit in the Historiographic Writings of the Old Testament." *The Southern Baptist Journal of Theology* 1 (1997) 42–61.

Boda, Mark J. *The Book of Zechariah*. NICOT. Grand Rapids: Eerdmans, 2016.

Boda, Mark J., and Mary L. Conway. *Judges*. Zondervan Exegetical Commentary on the Old Testament. Grand Rapids: Zondervan, forthcoming.

Chisholm, Robert B., Jr. "Does God Deceive?" *BSac* 155 (1998) 11–28.

Conway, Mary L. *Judging the Judges: A Narrative Appraisal Analysis*. LSAWS 15. Winona Lake, IN: Eisenbrauns, 2019.

Exum, J. Cheryl. "The Tragic Vision and Biblical Narrative: The Case of Jephthah." In *Signs and Wonders: Biblical Texts in Literary Focus*, 59–83. *Semeia* 18. Atlanta: Society of Biblical Literature, 1989.

Firth, David G. "Is Saul Also among the Prophets? Saul's Prophecy in 1 Samuel 19:23." In *Presence, Power, and Promise: The Role of the Spirit of God in the Old Testament*, edited by David G. Firth and Paul D. Wegner, 294–305. Downers Grove, IL: IVP Academic, 2011.

———. "The Historical Books." In *A Biblical Theology of the Holy Spirit*, edited by Trevor J. Burke and Keith Warrington, 12–23. London: SPCK, 2014.

———. "The Spirit and Leadership: Testimony, Empowerment and Purpose." In *Presence, Power, and Promise: The Role of the Spirit of God in the Old Testament*, edited by David G. Firth and Paul D. Wegner, 259–80. Downers Grove, IL: IVP Academic, 2011.

Hamori, Esther J. "The Spirit of Falsehood." *CBQ* 72 (2010) 15–30.

Hildebrandt, Wilf. *An Old Testament Theology of the Spirit of God.* Peabody, MA: Hendrickson, 1995.

Howard, David M. "The Transfer of Power from Saul to David in 1 Sam 16:13–14." *JETS* 32 (1989) 473–83.

Merrill, Eugene H. "The Samson Saga and Spiritual Leadership." In *Presence, Power, and Promise: The Role of the Spirit of God in the Old Testament,* edited by David G. Firth and Paul D. Wegner, 281–93. Downers Grove, IL: IVP Academic, 2011.

Montague, George T. *The Holy Spirit: Growth of a Biblical Tradition.* New York: Paulist, 1976.

Robert B. Chisholm, Jr. "The 'Spirit of the Lord' in 2 Kings 2:16." In *Presence, Power, and Promise: The Role of the Spirit of God in the Old Testament,* edited by David G. Firth and Paul D. Wegner, 306–17. Downers Grove, IL: IVP Academic, 2011.

Routledge, Robin L. "'An Evil Spirit from the Lord'—Demonic Influence or Divine Instrument." *The Evangelical Quarterly* 70 (1998) 3–22.

Wood, Leon J. *The Holy Spirit in the Old Testament.* Grand Rapids: Zondervan, 1976.

Wright, Christopher J. H. *Knowing the Holy Spirit through the Old Testament.* Downers Grove, IL: IVP Academic, 2006.

3

Prophetic Testimony for the Community

Reflections from 1 Kings 13 for the Church Today

RICK WADHOLM JR.[1]

INTRODUCTION

GUS KONKEL IS THE consummate pastor with the insight of a prophet (though I dare say he would not self-claim this latter). In his classes and personal interactions, he takes pastoral concern for students, friends, and co-workers seriously. As one of his students, I observed that he would lead classes of students to discern for themselves (in community) in what ways they might faithfully hear and obey the Scriptures within their respective church communities. This contextualization was pastoral for those communities and also provided space for prophetic witness *within* (sometimes *against*, but always ultimately *for*) those church communities. Further, he has written several volumes with just such aims: as a prophetic pastoral voice. One need only read his commentaries on Job, 1–2 Kings, and 1–2 Chronicles to witness

---

1. I would like to thank one of my administrative assistants, Emily Aguirre, for help in the research of this chapter.

this pastoral and prophetic admixture.[2] Perhaps this owes, in part, to his Mennonite background that shows deep regard for radical hearings of the word of God for the life of the community. It is this kind of concern for Christian community that drives my reflections in this chapter on the prophetic testimony for the community of Israel from 1 Kgs 13 with eyes (and voice) toward the church today.

THE COMMUNITY STORY WITH PROPHETIC CRITIQUE/S[3]

A prophet from Judah, an unnamed "man of God,"[4] explodes onto the scene in 1 Kgs 13.[5] The breakaway kingdom of Israel has gathered around their new king, Jeroboam, to carry out a new festival at a new altar at Bethel. The narrator makes clear at the outset that this prophet is "sent by Yahweh" and speaks "by the word of Yahweh" against the altar (13:1, 2, 5). The drama unfolds with the unnamed prophet of Judah arriving just as Jeroboam prepares to make sacrifice. The king believes his acts will vouchsafe his kingdom from reverting to the Davidic family.

Just as surprising as the appearance of this prophet from Judah is the prophetic naming of Josiah of the "house of David" as the one who

---

2. See the introduction to this volume for these citations.

3. This account belongs to a very particular tradition for Israel and Judah toward self-conception. Some, like J. Robinson (*The First Book of Kings*, 162–63), have argued for this account being "midrash," suggesting it "oversimplifies the issues and distorts the truth." Robinson goes on to state he believes this story is "crude in that it shows no acquaintance with the rich, many-sided understanding of the nature of God," which he believes may be found elsewhere in the Deuteronomistic History. A reading similarly viewing this account as "legendary" and "bizarre" is found in Fretheim (*First and Second Kings*, 77–78). My own suggestion is that this account offers a key insight into the overall trajectory of the Former Prophets.

4. Josephus offers the name as Yadon, in *Ant.* 8.9.1, which might point to Iddo of 2 Chr 13:22. However, for the sake of the narrative account in 1 Kings the "man of God" remains unnamed despite his burial site monument with the "old prophet from Bethel" being known in the days of Josiah (2 Kgs 23:16–18).

5. To be fair, while ch. 13 is in focus in this exposition, the literary unit of 1 Kgs 12:25—13:34 is the likelier full embedded tale. See Van Winkle, "1 Kings XII 25–XIII 34," 101–14. For one argument for the literary coherence intended to counter the historical-critical splicing of this text into many sub-texts, see Gross, "Lying Prophet," 97–135. This is counter to such a form-critical approach, attempting to wrestle with a proposed "pre-deuteronomic" version of this narrative; see Dozeman, "The Way of the Man of God," 379–93. The exposition I offer in this essay presumes some sense of a final form for a theological engagement of the text.

will destroy the altar before Jeroboam. Jeroboam points to the man of God to command his capture but finds his hand suddenly paralyzed and the altar split as prophesied. He beseeches the prophet to pray that his hand be healed, and his hand is restored. In response, Jeroboam invites the man of God to return with him to receive some gift. The man of God refuses, stating he would not eat or drink anything nor go with the king to receive even half of the kingdom because he had been given strict instructions by Yahweh.

Here, the story takes a strange twist. An old prophet from Bethel hears about the man of God and seeks him out. The old prophet convinces the man of God to return with him to his house and eat despite his confession that he was explicitly instructed by Yahweh to neither eat nor drink anything in Israel nor to return by the same path. The old prophet's tale of an angel of Yahweh giving command that the man of God should return with him is the convincing evidence for the man of God. The narrator reports for the sake of the readers, "He lied to him" (v. 18), and and the man of God returns with the old prophet. He eats bread and drinks water. As they were sitting at the table, Yahweh speaks through the old prophet concerning the violation of his command and prophesies that the man of God's "body would not be buried in the grave of" his "fathers" (v. 22).

The man of God finishes eating and drinking and rides off to Judah on the old prophet's donkey only to be killed by a lion along the way. The lion remains alongside the body and the donkey until the old prophet hears of the fulfillment of the prophetic word and finds the young man of God's body just as it had fallen. He takes the body and buries it in his own tomb with wailings of "My brother!" (13:30).[6] Then, he gives instructions to his sons to one day bury him alongside the man of God and he affirms that the words of Yahweh through the man of God against the altar at Bethel would be fulfilled.[7]

---

6. Perhaps it is noteworthy that there are plural voices crying out "My brother!" in v. 30.

7. The LXX and Vulg. traditions add that this was done according to the old prophet that "my bones may be saved with his bones" (13:31). This alternate reading is a suggestive reading of the bones not being defiled by Josiah in the future when the false priests and prophets find their bones defiled upon the altar.

The narrative of ch. 13 ends with Jeroboam failing to repent. Instead, he commences to appoint false priests and the end of his house is declared to be a bygone conclusion directly because of this. Thus, Israel (the Northern Kingdom) is already showing the signs of fracturing. The community that was formed in rebellion against the Judahite king (even justified) finds itself now shifting that rebellion toward the God of Israel. This narrative serves as a rebuking prophetic reminder toward faithfulness to Yahweh in all things. As such, there are two specific prophetic testimonies functioning within the narrative to highlight this: words and signs.[8]

WORDS OF PROPHETIC TESTIMONY

The most prominent narratival aspect of the prophetic testimony of this account is heard in the *words* of witness. These words are most prominently those attributed to Yahweh and those attributed to the prophet/s. While there is considerable overlap between these words (those of prophet/s and Yahweh), they are not synonymous and each one serves as a witness to Yahweh's intention for the community of Israel (and the community which received these texts—Judah[9] and, ultimately, the church). Konkel notes that "Deuteronomistic theology views history as a fulfillment of the will of the Lord and therefore can be announced by the prophetic word. This prophetic word is not so much predictive as declarative of the requirement of the covenant and the consequences of failing to observe it."[10] Taking this further (in light of 1 Kgs 13), these words are not simply those of Torah but also those of specific immediate obedience.

The Word of Yahweh

One refrain throughout this narrative account functions not only for the characters to know that what is spoken must be obeyed but also the

---

8. For an extended treatment of "word and sign" in the book of Acts with an eye toward Luke's use of such, drawing upon the Torah and specifically the Former Prophets (wherein our text of 1 Kgs 13 is found), see O'Reilly, *Word and Sign*.

9. Boer ("National Allegory in the Hebrew Bible," 95–116 [110–12]) describes this narrative as "political allegory" that functioned for exilic Judah as self-identifying.

10. Konkel, *1 & 2 Kings*, 29.

readers of the text to discern such. The refrain "by the word of Yahweh" (vv. 1, 2, 5, 9, 17, 18, 20, 26, 32) echoes throughout this account emphasizing the divine instruction in all these matters. The word that has been spoken not only must be obeyed but actually carries forward the action of God for and against individuals and community.

By this word the man of God is sent from Judah to Bethel (v. 1) and shouts against the altar by foretelling[11] of one Josiah of the house of David who will end this profanation with his own profanation (v. 2). The word of Yahweh is shared as a specific command to the man of God concerning his own journey's path and participation in the basics of life in Israel through eating and drinking (v. 9; reiterated in v. 17). When the man of God from Judah is persuaded by the prophet of Israel to return and eat and drink with him, the prophet receives the same word as condemnation of the man of God for disobedience and promises death and burial away from his ancestors (vv. 21–22). Finally, the account offers the words of the prophet of Israel as confirmation that the word of Yahweh spoken by the man of God from Judah would be fulfilled against the altar and shrines of Israel (v. 32). Not only are these words from Yahweh prophetic witnesses against the practices of Israel that abandoned and distorted the instructions through Moses but also personal commands to individuals calling for faithfulness toward Yahweh and the wider communities of God's people (both historically present and future). The persons entrusted with the word of Yahweh would themselves be the vessels of testimony.

The Word of the Prophet/s

The man of God from Judah is driven and determined by the word of Yahweh. He is dramatic in his delivery and emphatic in his pronouncements. That is until he is confronted by a counter revelation purported to have the support of a prophet, an angel, and Yahweh (v. 18).[12] This

---

11. It need not matter whether or not this word is *ex eventu* as it is preserved in the text with the intent that readers would hear it as foretelling.

12. Lissa M. Wray Beal (*1 & 2 Kings*, 193–94) contends that the "man of God" softens what Yahweh "commanded" (in v. 9) as he repeats it as what was "spoken" (in v. 17) when recounting to the old prophet leading to his vulnerability to deception. While Wray Beal is correct in her analysis of the shift of language, it seems to miss that these are words recited by the "man of God" to differing parties: the king and

counter word is clarified in the narrative as a lie (for the sake of the readers). Why should the narrative include that it was a lie? It functions to remind those hearing the account that while the word of Yahweh requires continuous listening followed by obedience, one must not presume that others have heard faithfully. It functions to clarify that the words spoken as if by angel and prophet were not in fact the words of Yahweh.[13] Yahweh holds each member of the community responsible for faithfulness to hear and obey. There are no trifling words from Yahweh that do not need heeding.[14] Yet, there is a discernment that is always necessary for faithful hearing and obedience. Claims of a divine source do not guarantee trustworthiness.

Further, the narrative offers the voice of the lying prophet from Israel as also trustworthy. It speaks of the faithfulness of Yahweh to give His word even to unfaithful prophets and unfaithful Israel against the seemingly faithful Judah(ite) who would be the eventual preservers of this text of the Former Prophets. To be entrusted with the word of Yahweh is not to guarantee fidelity for the messenger in every detail. It is only to know that the message of Yahweh is faithful while the messengers may not be. This offers a call for the community of Israel to hear the testimony of the word of Yahweh through (and even against) the man of God from Judah and the old prophet from Bethel. Yet Yahweh did not only give words as testimony.

SIGNS OF PROPHETIC TESTIMONY

Signs are given throughout the account as witnesses to the trustworthiness of the word of Yahweh. The signs are objects, ideas, creatures, and persons; they serve as embodied witnesses in the midst of the community: the altar, the kings, the way, the creatures, and the prophets.

---

the prophet. Neither of these are a narratorial comment and, further, the LXX has preserved the language of "command" (ἐντέταλταί) though the MT uses דבר (v. 9) over צוה (v. 17). The "prophet" (13:21–22) uses both Hebrew terms for his prophetic renouncing of the man of God to describe what Yahweh "commanded/said" to the man of God about eating and drinking.

13. Mead, "Kings and Prophets," 199–200.

14. See Deboys, "1 Kings XIII," 210–12. Van Winkle ("1 Kings XII 25–XIII 34," 31–43) proposes a "new criterion" by which one may judge between true and false prophecies drawing upon his reading of 1 Kgs 13.

The Altar

The first "sign"[15] given as witness is the splitting of the altar of Jeroboam at Bethel with the new ashes spilling out (vv. 3, 5). This sign is given as a testimony to its future destruction at the hands of Josiah of the house of David, who would defile and destroy the altar and other shrines of Israel (2 Kgs 23:15–16). This "sign which Yahweh spoke" against the altar at Bethel serves as a witness to the faithfulness of Yahweh's word and the faithfulness of Yahweh to keep covenant even while the community failed. Yahweh's word would outlast the immediate community and come to bear on future communities leading back to faithfulness. Yahweh would raise up a king to reign in righteousness and purge the land of idolatry, just as Jeroboam had been prophetically installed as king to do likewise (12:37–38).

The Kings

Peter J. Leithart notes that the very "hand" that "receives the kingdom (11:12, 31, 34–45) withers" in 13:4.[16] To receive the kingdom is not to be established with a kingdom. The arm of Yahweh will never fail, but the hand of the king can be withdrawn or crippled at any moment. Jeroboam's own hand of accusation against the man of God from Judah becomes the sign against his unfaithfulness toward Yahweh as well as the fulfillment of the word of Yahweh. Further, the name of the descendant of David (Josiah) signifies that Yahweh will not abandon His people forever over to their abandonment of Him. Disobedience would not be the last word; Yahweh will help (which is a possible sense of "Josiah" meaning Yahweh saves) and will restore, just as even the hand of Jeroboam was maimed, but made whole. This would not be on Israel's terms, but by the sheer goodness of Yahweh. While this sign to Jeroboam functioned in the immediate movement of the story to signify judgment, it bears re-telling for later generations toward potential restoration by the goodness of Yahweh. The restoration of at least part of Israel by the hand of Josiah who later cleanses the land testifies

---

15. The MT reads מופת ("sign") while the LXX reads τὸ ῥῆμα ("the word"). The former seems most likely as it is the more difficult reading, and the LXX seems to be an attempted smoothing for clarification. See Devries, *1 Kings*, 166.

16. Leithart, *1 & 2 Kings*, 98.

to this. The sign of Jeroboam's hand does not deter him from leading the Northern Kingdom into sin, which will lead to the demise of his dynasty.[17] Jeroboam will not turn back from his wayward path and turn to Yahweh.

The Way

The way had been laid for Jeroboam to walk in. He would not. The way had also been laid for the man of God from Judah. He was not to return the way he had come, yet he did. He never returned to Judah. The use of דרך ("way, road") pervades this account: 13:9, 10 (2x), 12 (2x), 17, 24 (2x), 25, 26, 28, and 33. Adding poignancy to this term is the repetition of the root שוב ("turn, return"): 13:4, 6 (2x), 9, 10, 16, 17, 18, 19, 20, 22, 23, 26, 29, and 33 (2x).[18] Such language points the way forward as a consummate sign calling for return that does not follow the same paths but always walks in faithfulness to the word of Yahweh spoken at each point. It is a faithful continuous hearing and obedience that seems to falter throughout the narrative.[19] The individuals in this pericope do not do as they should. Readers find themselves confronted by such failings. Such turning aside must not happen. Such turning aside has deathly consequences for both individuals and community. Yahweh remains faithful throughout. The word of Yahweh persists. The faithfulness of Yahweh remains. The goodness and mercy of Yahweh pursue even to the end; despite that characters of the story only experience judgment

---

17. Robert Cohn ("Literary Techniques in the Jeroboam Narrative," 23–35) moves through the nuances of this extended treatment of Jeroboam and its theological function within the larger corpus.

18. This is following the English versifications. This is noted particularly by Nelson (*First and Second Kings*, 84) and Wray Beal (*1 & 2 Kings*, 190). See Provan, *1 and 2 Kings*, 116, for a brief discussion of the literary and theological interconnection between the use of שוב and turning against Yahweh. Notably, 12:26–27 includes this term three times in Jeroboam's concern that Israel might "return" to the house of David, return to the Lord and to Rehoboam.

19. Some have suggested the restriction regarding not returning the same way might be due to the path taken being sanctified and therefore should not be retraced, see Patterson and Austel in Gaebelein, ed., *1, 2 Kings*, 119; others suggest it might have been to "avoid further contact with a cursed place and people," Wiseman, *1 and 2 Kings*, 158.

themselves, they testify to the readers that Yahweh is not finished and will at the end show grace and mercy.[20]

Jerome Walsh (who notes this broader pericope beginning in 1 Kgs 12) notes the narrative artistry, which by means of narrative inclusion frames this account with regard to the sin:[21]

A and this thing was as sin (12:30)

  B and he made the house of the high places (12:31a)

    C and he made priests from the extremities of the people (12:31b)

    C' and he made from the extremities of the people priests (13:33a)

  B' and there were priests of the high places (13:33b)

A' and this thing became as a sin (13:34a)

One might even say that "the road to Bethel is the road to exile."[22] This would not be the last word in the Former Prophets but would be a constant chord struck in the song of Israel's story. The possibility of re/turning to Yahweh might yet be open to the community by His graciousness and even this graciousness would extend to others.

The Creatures

Even the creatures of this tale—the donkey and the lion—serve as signs.[23] The calves at Dan and Bethel remind one of the disobedience of Israel at the foot of Sinai (Exod 32).[24] The donkey and the lion at the end of the account point to the providential care and direction of creation

---

20. On the development of the Deuteronomic theology through the Deuteronomistic History pointing toward "grace in the end," see McConville, *Grace in the End*.

21. Walsh, *1 Kings*, 190.

22. Leithart, *1 & 2 Kings*, 100.

23. James Mead ("Kings and Prophets," 201–5) addresses these two creatures in the narrative by pointing to their significance in representing Jeroboam (the donkey) and Yahweh (the lion).

24. On such cultural memory (though presuming faulty such memory), see Geobey, "The Jeroboam Story," 4.

itself by the hand of Yahweh.[25] Ironically, the lion does what the man of God failed to do—to refrain from eating.[26] The donkey that carried the man of God away from the word of judgment also carried him to his judgment; however, it did not itself suffer such judgment. Instead, the donkey is spared to stand alongside the lion by the road for a witness to all who pass by and would hear their story. The preserved donkey is the assurance to the old prophet that the lion was sent by Yahweh and that the words of Yahweh would indeed be fulfilled.[27] Yahweh knows both how to destroy and to save, to remove and to preserve—even faithful-faithless and faithless-faithful prophets.[28]

The Prophets

The final sign for reflection in this pericope is that of the two messengers of Yahweh: the man of God from Judah and the old prophet from Bethel. Neither is named; both are remembered. Neither appears utterly faithful; both have their memory preserved even in death. These ministers of the words of Yahweh function as seemingly poor vessels for carrying such precious contents. However, Yahweh is pleased to make use of messengers who falter even as His word never falters. Richard D. Nelson writes, "God's commands have an unconditional claim to external obedience. Any subjective feeling of guilt or innocence [or any pleading of good intentions] are ultimately beside the point." Concerning these two men, he also asserts, "Even God's agents can become God's victims if they betray their calling."[29] The community that received this account would not be sustained by any word other than the word of Yahweh. The community would remember the graves of these prophets and more specifically the words which they spoke. Konkel explains, "The prophets are not concerned with good and evil actions,

---

25. Way, "Animals in the Prophetic World," 55.

26. Also noted by Wray Beal, *1 & 2 Kings*, 194, and Konkel, *1 & 2 Kings*, 245.

27. Hayyim Angel ("When God's Will Can and Cannot Be Altered," 34) contends that the donkey in this story illustrates "the inescapability of God's Will."

28. Walsh, "The Contexts of 1 Kings XIII," 360. Placing the cause for the judgment of the man of God squarely upon the unfaithfulness of the man of God is the work of Reis ("Vindicating God").

29. Nelson, *First and Second Kings*, 89.

but with the fundamental decision on which salvation and judgment depend. In the end the nation will fall, but the work of God will not fail."[30] The word of Yahweh would outlast both men, even if only as a word to preserve each of their witnesses in death.

An analogical function for the "man of God" *as* Judah and the "prophet" *as* Israel has been noted by Werner Lemke, Jerome Walsh, Peter Leithart, and Lissa M. Wray Beal.[31] These two prophets, thus, stand as embodied witnesses of and against (and yet for) Israel and Judah. Leithart pictures it thus: "Judah remains for centuries as a prophetic witness against the Northern Kingdom, but at some point in time, Israel seduces Judah as the old prophet seduces the man of God from Judah. Eventually, the two nations will be united in death, in the grave of exile."[32]

A FEW PASTORAL PROPHETIC REFLECTIONS

This word and these signs would serve not only the immediate community context but also the later generations who would experience the goodness (and terror) of this word. The goodness of Yahweh to redeem a wayward people and persist in bearing witness against (and for) them. What could this word possibly indicate for such communities who find themselves hearing the word of Yahweh? There is a final accounting for those charged with delivering the word of Yahweh and those hearing it.

The proving test of those who claim to speak for Yahweh is, according to S. J. DeVries, "*radical obedience.* The preacher-prophet must be so committed to the transcendent truth of what he proclaims that his very own life is affected by it."[33] He goes further, saying, "Today we look for radical obedience in the way of life to which God's servants

---

30. Konkel, *1 & 2 Kings*, 26.

31. See the discussion of Lemke and Walsh in Wray Beal, "Jeremiah and the Prophets in 1 Kings 11–14," 105–24, in Boda and Wray Beal, eds, *Prophets, Prophecy, and Ancient Israelite Historiography*, 108–10.

32. Leithart, *1 & 2 Kings*, 101. See also, Walsh, "The Context of 1 Kings XIII," 368.

33. DeVries, *1 Kings*, 174, emphasis added.

commit themselves. If they stumble—and stumble they will—their very weakness may confirm the word of God which they preach."[34]

Leithart is painfully and insightfully correct in seeing in this narrative that "the church's greatest tests come not from kings who call for imprisonment and torture; Christians relish martyrdom. The great tests arise from lying prophets, from wolfish bishops and priests, pastors and preachers."[35] Indeed, such workers of wickedness are indicative of the heart of the community that receives and supports them. Such a community cannot endure. In a similar way, Dietrich Bonhoeffer made use of the sins of Jeroboam in 1 Kgs 12:25–33 with regard to the need to renounce and separate from the "heretical church" community (represented by the "German Christians" of his day).[36] He envisioned that the more subtle work of Jeroboam toward falsity (as exemplified in the story of 1 Kgs 13) would necessarily lead to outright rebellion and ultimately destruction.

A number of proposals have been suggested for the overall function of this account. Iain Provan contends that part of the point of the narrative is that "God can use even false prophets occasionally to speak the truth."[37] Devries briefly discusses the focus of this account being either "revelation" or "obedience" but settles on authentication of the prophetic authority following his sub-genre of "prophetic authorization narratives," which he describes in his work on 1 Kgs 22.[38] However, this seems to miss the overall focus of this account within the broader narratives of the Former Prophets. Terrance E. Fretheim argues, "The focus of the story must not be placed on the obedience or disobedience of the man of God or prophet. The story is not centered on these men, but on the word of God they speak about Jeroboam. The key effect of the story is a *double* prophetic witness against Jeroboam, from the leadership of *both* kingdoms."[39] Fretheim notes that such prophetic words are not *fait accompli* but are dependent upon the response—repentance

---

34. DeVries, *1 Kings*, 174.
35. Leithart, *1 & 2 Kings*, 100.
36. Bonhoeffer, "Lecture on the Path of the Young Illegal Theologians," 416–37.
37. Provan, *1 and 2 Kings*, 115.
38. DeVries, *1 Kings*, 168–69, and *Prophet against Prophet*, 55, 59–61.
39. Fretheim, *First and Second Kings*, 81, original emphasis.

and re/turning—of Israel and her kings. He asserts, "The story shows the *tenacity* of the word of God to work in and through deceptions, disobedience, and death—even of prophets—to accomplish God's purposes."[40]

This is not the end. Such a community can still be restored by re/turning to the word of Yahweh. Provan writes, "The LORD is God of history, whose word must be obeyed—even by the very prophets who deliver it—if blessing is to follow."[41] Such a community can reject the false prophets among them even as they hear the word of Yahweh in the lives of those prophets. Such a community can be restored by the hoped-for king, the son of David, who would redeem and cleanse the community even beyond their own end—even *as* their end. Such a community is attuned to the word of Yahweh in the words and signs of 1 Kgs 13. Such a community is always discerning and ever obedient by the enablement of Yahweh to walk in the ways of Yahweh.

BIBLIOGRAPHY

Angel, Hayyim. "When God's Will Can and Cannot be Altered: The Relationship Between the Balaam Narrative and 1 Kings 13." *JBQ* 33 (2005) 31–39.

Boda, Mark J., and Lissa M. Wray Beal, eds. *Prophets, Prophecy, and Ancient Israelite Historiography*. Winona Lake, IN: Eisenbrauns, 2013.

Boer, Roland. "National Allegory in the Hebrew Bible." *JSOT* 74 (1997) 95–116.

Bonhoeffer, Dietrich. *Theological Education Underground: 1937–1940*. Dietrich Bonhoeffer Works 15. Edited by V. J. Barnett. Translated by D. Schulz. Minneapolis: Fortress, 2012.

Cohn, Robert L. "Literary Technique in the Jeroboam Narrative." *ZAW* 97 (1985) 23–35.

Deboys, David G. "1 Kings XIII—A 'New Criterion' Reconsidered." *VT* 41 (1991) 210–12.

DeVries, S. J. *1 Kings*. WBC 12. Dallas: Word, 1985.

———. *Prophet against Prophet: The Role of the Micaiah Narrative (1 Kings 22) in the Development of Early Prophetic Tradition*. Grand Rapids: Eerdmans, 1978.

---

40. Fretheim, *First and Second Kings*, 81. See also, Nelson, *First and Second Kings*, 87, 89.

41. Provan, *1 and 2 Kings*, 113.

Dozeman, Thomas B. "The Way of the Man of God from Judah: True and False Prophecy in the Pre-Deuteronomic Legend of 1 Kings 13." *CBQ* 44 (1982) 379–93.

Fretheim, Terrance E. *First and Second Kings*. Westminster Bible Companion. Louisville: Westminster John Knox, 1999.

Gaebelein, Frank E., ed. *1, 2 Kings, 1, 2 Chronicles, Ezra, Nehemiah, Esther, Job*. Revised Evangelical Biblical Commentary 4. Grand Rapids: Zondervan, 1988.

Geobey, Ronald A. "The Jeroboam Story in the (Re)Formulation of Israelite Identity: Evaluating the Literary-Ideological Purposes of 1 Kings 11–14." *JHebS* 16 (2016) 1–42.

Gross, Walter. "Lying Prophet and Disobedient Man of God in 1 Kings 13: Role Analysis as an Instrument of Theological Interpretation of an OT Narrative Text." *Semeia* 15 (1979) 97–135.

Konkel, August H. *1 & 2 Kings*. NIVAC. Grand Rapids: Zondervan, 2006.

Leithart, Peter J. *1 & 2 Kings*. Grand Rapids: Brazos, 2006.

Mead, James K. "Kings and Prophets, Donkeys and Lions: Dramatic Shape and Deuteronomistic Rhetoric in 1 Kings XIII." *VT* 49 (1999) 191–205.

Nelson, Richard D. *First and Second Kings*. IBC. Louisville: Westminster John Knox, 2012.

O'Reilly, Leo. *Word and Sign in the Acts of the Apostles: A Study in Lucan Theology*. Analecta Gregoriana 243. Rome: Editrice Pontificia Universita Gregoriana, 1987.

Provan, Iain W. *1 and 2 Kings*. NIBCOT. Peabody, MA: Hendrickson, 1995.

Reis, Pamela Tamarkin. "Vindicating God: Another Look at 1 Kings XIII." *VT* 44 (1994) 376–86.

Robinson, J. *The First Book of Kings*. CBC. Cambridge: Cambridge University Press, 1976.

Rollston, Christopher A., ed. *Enemies and Friends of State: Ancient Prophecy in Context*. Winona Lake, IN: Eisenbrauns, 2018.

Van Winkle, D. W. "1 Kings XII 25–XIII 34: Jeroboam's Cultic Innovations and the Man of God from Judah." *VT* 46 (1996) 101–14.

———. "1 Kings XIII: True and False Prophecy." *VT* 29 (1989) 31–43.

Walsh, Jerome T. *1 Kings*. Berit Olam. Collegeville, MN: Liturgical, 1996.

———. "The Contexts of 1 Kings XIII." *Vetus Testamentum* 39 (1989) 355–70.

Way, Kenneth C. "Animals in the Prophetic World: Literary Reflections on Numbers 22 and 1 Kings 13." *JSOT* 34 (2009) 47–62.

Wiseman, Donald J. *1 and 2 Kings*. TOTC. Downers Grove, IL: IVP Academic, 2008.

Wray Beal, Lissa M. *1 & 2 Kings*. ApOTC. Downers Grove, IL: InterVarsity, 2014.

4

The Community of Israel in 1 Chronicles 1–9

GARY V. SMITH

INTRODUCTION

FIRST AND 2 CHRONICLES may appear to be an unending account of wars conducted by a confusing list of kings, but even more baffling is the unending list of confusing names in the genealogies that fill 1 Chr 1–9. In 2016, Dr. Konkel[1] published his interpretation of 1 and 2 Chronicles in the Believer's Church Bible Commentary[2] and provided both a detailed explanation of the relationships between the names listed in the genealogies in chs. 1–9 but also included a practical section

---

1. I knew from the very beginning of my association with Dr. Konkel, when he was one of my students at Winnipeg Theological Seminary (now Providence Theological Seminary), that I was dealing with an exceptional overachiever with an infectious laugh. His joy for studying God's word was very evident and his enthusiasm for understanding Hebrew in an intensive summer class demonstrated his determination. Some years, later after leaving that ministry, I gladly recommended that he take my teaching position, and I have marveled at how God has multiplied his ministry since that time. His commentary on Chronicles is only one excellent example of the fruit of his labors.

2. Konkel, *1 & 2 Chronicles*.

entitled, "The Text in the Life of the Church," for each literary unit. The comments in this later section connected the theological themes in Chronicles to similar themes in the New Testament and reflected on how the church should respond to these issues. Konkel's exegetical explanations of the genealogies were lengthy, quite detailed, and based on biblical evidence found in the Pentateuch and other sources covering earlier historical periods. At times, complications arose that necessitated addressing textual variants, so he suggested a way to resolve most of these problems.[3] In light of his treatment of Chronicles, this essay will: (a) investigate the nature of these genealogies; (b) explain how genealogies identify communities; (c) describe some aspects of the community of Israel; and (d) reflect on how these genealogies address issues in the life of the church.

INTRODUCTION TO THE GENEALOGIES

Anyone who has spent time on genealogical websites has probably enjoyed the fascination of discovering who his or her distant relatives are and already has a deep appreciation for the enormous difficulty of constructing a family genealogy. Figuring out one person's genealogy is hard enough, so it is even more difficult to imagine the overwhelming complexities of laying out an extended genealogy that accurately portrays the ancestors of the twelve tribes of Israel, from Adam to the exile and beyond. Although not every ancestor's name is included in 1 Chr 1–9 and the relationships between some individuals and families are not fully explained, the compiler of this list included the names that were important, that served the vital purpose of defining the community of Israel for his audience in the postexilic era. At the time the Chronicler wrote, thousands of people were living in various parts of the Persian Empire, but some had already moved to Yehud (Judah) under the leaders Sheshbazzar (538 BCE; Ezra 1–2) and Ezra (Ezra 7–8). Other Hebrews were scattered in what was formerly called Assyria (2 Kgs 15:29; 17:6, 23), in Egypt (2 Kgs 23:34; Jer 42–44), Babylon (2 Kgs 24:14–16; 25:11), Persia (Esth 2:5–7), and in some of the surrounding nations where they fled to avoid the trauma associated with the

---

3. Konkel, *1 & 2 Chronicles*, 80, 93, 109–10, 114, 115, 116.

Babylonian attack on Jerusalem (Obad 1:10–14). With this kind of dislocation from the land of Israel and Judah came the gradual erosion of traditional Israelite culture and some of the values it inherited from its sacred writings. Intermarriage with foreigners who worshipped other gods added to the decline in the people's sense of belonging to the larger Hebrew community called "Israel." So, in the postexilic period, when there was an opportunity to return to the land of Judah, restore the temple (Ezra 1:1–3), and reestablish the security of Jerusalem (Neh 1–2), it was natural to ask the question of who should be accepted and included as legitimate participants in this community. Earlier experience in the time of Zerubbabel (around 536 BCE) helped the returnees in concluding that the neighboring people in Samaria, who worshipped other gods in addition to Israel's God (Ezra 4:1–5), were not to be considered a legitimate part of the community of Israel.[4] Later, Ezra (Ezra 9:1–2, around 458 BCE) and Nehemiah (Neh 13:23–29, around 430 BCE) found that there were priests, Levites, and others who had intermarried with unbelievers from several surrounding nations, which defiled the holy nature of the Israelite community; these syncretistic actions compromised the nature of Israel's holy relationship to God. These marriages undermined the distinctive moral integrity of the community's spiritual identity, so these marriages were terminated (Ezra 10) and the foreign unbelievers were removed from the community of Israel. In light of these and other problems, the genealogies in 1 Chr 1–9 address the question: who was a legitimate member of the Israelite community? What genealogical, geographic, political, social, and religious factors united these people in community? For those already in Judah, the question was more pointedly: what do people who

---

4. Those who connect Ezra-Nehemiah closely to the author of Chronicles (e.g., C. C. Torrey) tend to characterize the community of Israel as being very anti-Samaritan, while those who focus primarily on Chronicles (Sara Japhet) do not come to this conclusion. The works by Japhet ("The Supposed Common," 330–71), Roddy L. Braun ("Chronicles, Ezra, Nehemiah," 42–64), and Hugh G. M. Williamson (*Israel in the Book of Chronicles*, 5–70) have convincingly demonstrated that the Chronicler did not write Ezra-Nehemiah, so this study will limit its focus solely on the identity of the community of Israel within Chronicles. Robert Polzin (*Late Biblical Hebrew*, 69–75) disagreed with this conclusion, arguing that the linguistic differences between Chronicles and Ezra-Nehemiah just involve different scribal practices, but this seems unlikely.

COMMUNITY

have returned to Jerusalem need to do to establish their identity as an Israelite people, so that they can be a part of the community of Israel and worship at the rebuilt temple in Jerusalem?

THE ROLE OF THE GENEALOGIES IN IDENTIFYING WHO WAS AN ISRAELITE

The first nine chapters of Chronicles contain the genealogical records of the nation of Israel from the first man, Adam (1 Chr 1:1), to a time well beyond the exile and even past the return of many Israelites to Jerusalem (1 Chr 3:15–24).[5] A new approach to understanding the biblical genealogies emerged with the publications of Robert R. Wilson, Marshal D. Johnson, and James T. Sparks on biblical and ancient Near Eastern (ANE) genealogies.[6] Wilson found that genealogies were created and maintained for domestic affairs (to define social order), for political-judicial issues (to define power and legal authority), or for religious reasons (to legitimate a cultic official). Genealogies that expressed deep kinship relationships (called linear genealogies), identified only one person in each of the following four to six previous generations (1 Chr 3:10–15). One of the purposes of these genealogies was to legitimate the status or role of the last named person and to relate that person to their kinship group.[7] Other genealogies (called segmented genealogies) displayed a wide breadth of descendants in one family, covering all the branches of a person's heirs (1 Chr 1:9–16; 2:1–4). One of the purposes of segmented genealogies was to explain the kinship relationships between the different branches of an extended tribal group. Johnson thought that the "Chronicler's genealogical survey of 'all Israel' . . . may be viewed as the attempt to assert the importance of

---

5. Peter B. Dirksen (*1 Chronicles*, 66) connected Anani to a person mentioned in an Elephantine papyri dated to 407 BCE, well after the end of the exile in 538 BCE.

6. Johnson, *The Purpose of the Biblical Genealogies*; Sparks, *Chronicler's Genealogies*; Wilson, "The Old Testament Genealogies," 169–89.

7. Johnson (*The Purpose of Biblical Genealogies*, 77–82) found nine possible uses for genealogies: (1) to relate Israel to her neighbors; (2) to piece together isolated segments of the genealogy; (3) to bridge gaps in narrative records; (4) to provide chronological connections between events and people; (5) to number people for the military; (6) to legitimate people; (7) to establish unity between groups; (8) to demonstrate continuity with the past generations; and (9) to preserve the priestly order.

the principle of the continuity of the people of God through a period of national disruption."[8]

The importance of these genealogies to the Israelite community is clear, for they take up nine chapters of Chronicles. These records were meticulously kept and highly valued in ancient Mesopotamia,[9] preexilic Israel (cf. Genesis and Numbers), as well as in the postexilic period when the Hebrews returned to Jerusalem after the Babylonian captivity (in Chronicles).[10] When the first fifty thousand exiles (Ezra 2:64–65) returned to Jerusalem with Sheshbazzar, most of them knew that they were a part of Israel; they were in possession of their genealogical history. However, a few people could not prove that they were Israelites (2:59–60) and a few who claimed to have a priestly background (2:61–63) did not have their genealogical records with them, so they were not immediately allowed to serve as priests. This implies that the vast majority of the fifty thousand people who came to Jerusalem with Sheshbazzar had valid records of their genealogical histories and were considered to be legitimate members of the community of Israel.

Although genealogies record the ancestors of a family so that descendants can be identified[11] as legitimate members of a larger Israelite family or tribal group, they also include other important identifying factors. An examination of the genealogies in 1 Chr 1–9 will show that

---

8. Johnson, *The Purpose of Biblical Genealogies*, 80.

9. Finkelstein ("The Genealogy of the Hammurapi Dynasty," 95–118), Jacobsen (*The Sumerian King List*); Malamat ("King Lists," 163–73), Hartman ("Some Thoughts," 25–32), Wilson ("The Old Testament Genealogies," 169–89), and Aufrecht ("Genealogy and History," 205–35) note that there were genealogies of kings in Mesopotamia, though no genealogies of kings in Egypt, because they needed no legitimation for they were gods.

10. Although some have viewed these genealogies as later additions, Johnson (*The Purpose of the Biblical Genealogies*, 44–47) adequately responded to some of the arguments that were used to support the idea that the genealogies were secondary (e.g., absence of the names of some high priest; Saul's genealogies do not agree; lists of sons of David do not agree, etc.), so many recent commentaries do not hold this position.

11. Jonker (*1 & 2 Chronicles*, 15) suggests, "Chronicles can also be interpreted as a bold attempt to take part in the process of social-identity negotiation." This can be applied to assessing an individual's as well as the group's identity. See also Dyck, "The Ideology of Identity in Chronicles," 89–116, and Berquist, "Constructions of Identity," 53–66.

the genealogical format often reveals much more than just the name of a person's immediate familial connection to the larger Israelite community. First and foremost, the genealogy identifies a person's father (and at times a mother, as in 2:17) or that a person was the son or daughter of a known individual (e.g., a son of Noah in 1:4). This feature enabled people to identify their immediate ancestors, connect themselves all the way back with a founding tribal leader, and justify their membership in the community of Israel. Second, some genealogies legitimate a person's role in some social structure or occupation (e.g., linen workers in 4:21; potters in 4:23; men of war in 7:9). This was particularly important for those who claimed to be temple personnel. Thus, the genealogy of the priests and Levites in 1 Chr 6:1–30 legitimated those who were named as having the right and responsibility to function in the temple. First Chronicles 6:31–46 provides an authentic list of Levitical singers, and 6:54–81 outlines where each Levitical family had the right to live. Third, the genealogies map out a person's relationship to other groups, families, or tribes. For example, the sons of Reuben in 1 Chr 5:3–10 lived next to the tribe of Gad (another Israelite group) in 5:11. Fourth, the genealogies provide a sense of corporate solidarity for those inside the community by identifying those who were outsiders (e.g., the Hagrites in 5:19 and the Assyrians in 5:26).[12] This sense of unity would be strongest at the family and clan level, but there was also considerable pride in one's tribal group and a loyalty to their nation, particularly when threatened by other nations. This unifying factor is strongly expressed in those narrative passages where "all Israel," a phrase used only once in the genealogies, decides to support some action. Fifth, the genealogies frequently identify where people lived and what territory they had dominion over, legitimating the location where returning exiles could own property. This geographic element was evident in the location of the family nations that grew out of Ham, Shem, and Japheth (in 1 Chr 1:4b–27), in the cities people started (Beersheba in 1 Chr 4:28), and the country where a person lived (the land of Edom in 1 Chr 1:43–54). Sixth, the genealogies allowed people to discover how their

---

12. A. Siedlecki ("Foreigners, Warfare and Judahite Identity," 229–66) concluded that the references to foreigners in the genealogies enabled the Israelites to identify themselves by identifying foreigners as those who were not Israelites.

historical and theological roots fit in with God's actions toward the various tribes. For example, the sins in the tribe of Manasseh resulted in their exile in 1 Chr 5:25–26, but the faith of Jabez resulted in his blessing in 1 Chr 4:9–10. Finally, these genealogies connected people to the legacy of a great spiritual forefather (i.e., Asher was the forefather of the tribe of Asher and one of the sons of Jacob/Israel in 1 Chr 2:1). If a new family wanted to move and settle in a different village in the ancient world, their identity could be established by examining their family background through a genealogy and their reputation would be evident to everyone. If their genealogical record was fully developed, it could provide the people in the village with information about this new family based on their tribal associations, their past geographic location, their occupation, their historical relationships to past events, as well as the spiritual legacy of one of their tribal ancestors.

In spelling out the genealogical information about key individuals and the tribes of Israel, the Chronicler communicates to his postexilic readers not just the names of some of the people mentioned in Genesis–Kings, but also their physical, social, political, theological, and historical connections within the larger community of Israel. The lists of the high priests, Levites, and singers who were appointed to serve the nation at the temple (1 Chr 6) were all part of an impressive legacy for a great nation made up of twelve interrelated tribes that descended from one father (Israel/Jacob in 2:1) and from one original human being, Adam (1:1). Hebrew readers in the postexilic era might have remembered a few details about how God dealt with various tribes and would have known the name of a few key individuals mentioned in these genealogies, but this genre of literature was primarily an expanded list of names; a genealogy did not retell all these detailed narrative stories or promote many theological themes.[13] The literary genre

---

13. One of the dangers of reading the genealogies would be that a reader/commentator might be tempted to imply too much and assume the author was communicating almost everything that was known about every person from the narrative portions of Scripture. By this process, some have turned a relatively bare genealogical list into a grand theological discourse and, thereby, twisted clear minimalistic statements into something much more grandiose—usually communicating what was true but blatantly adding many things (often theological points) never said or even hinted at by the Chronicler. Exegesis should comment on what is said, not on what is not said. We have no idea what popped into the mind of the reader about

of genealogy was not the same as the narrative genre which rehearsed the theological history of the Israelites (Gen 12–50). For the ancient Israelite, the genre of genealogy provides a sense of chronological order, location, occupation, and continuity between the past and the present, but it has no plot, no extended storyline, very limited character development, and relatively few theological explanations. Nevertheless, a name like Noah (1:4) might cause some readers to remember earlier biblical narrative stories. That said, relatively few people had more than a basic understanding of their sacred writings, as indicated in Ezra, Nehemiah, Haggai, and Malachi by the widespread ignorance about what God had done in the past and what he required of his covenant people.[14] From the limited information in the genealogy, people would come to understand a little bit more about the names of their ancestors, some understanding of how God used other nations to shape their own history, and perhaps a few lessons based on God's reactions towards the good or bad behavior of a few individuals. But it is impossible to know how much the average Israelite knew about the stories in Genesis through Kings. At the very least, the genealogy gave a broad overview of God's working through the family of Adam (Gen 1–11), Abraham (Gen 12–25), the twelve tribes from Jacob (Gen 49—Joshua), the kings of Israel (Samuel–Kings), and their relationships with people from other nations (e.g., Egypt, Canaan, Assyria, and Babylon).

---

each person mentioned in these genealogies, so it would be presumptuous to assume an extensive knowledge of earlier Scriptures or the ability to integrate theological themes in a manner possible today. Most people did not have a scroll of the Scriptures to study at that time.

14. Although Ezra the scribe was a student of the law of Moses (Ezra 7:10), the people and even the priests and Levites did not seem to understand that they were not to marry unbelievers (Ezra 9–10). Further evidence of a lack of knowledge of the teachings of Scripture in Nehemiah are that the wealthy charged interest (Neh 5), many people seemed to not know about the Feast of Booths (Neh 8:13–18), the High Priest Eliashab allowed his daughter to marry outside of Israel and allowed Tobiah to live in a temple storeroom (Neh 13:4–9), Nehemiah found people working—buying and selling—on the Sabbath (Neh 13:15–22), and more people intermarrying with pagans (Neh 13:23–28). Malachi found people offering unworthy sacrifices (Mal 1:6–12), not tithing (Mal 3:7–12), oppressing the poor (3:5), divorcing their wives (Mal 2:10–16), and questioning if God was just and if he really loved them (Mal 1:1–6; 2:17—3:5). This state of affairs points to the people being quite ignorant of biblical content and theology; thus, it would be quite inappropriate to assume that they were able to insert theological ideas that were not plainly stated in the text.

From a modern point of view based on a clearer understanding of all of Scripture, it is possible to see that each descendant of Adam, every family group, and all the tribes in Israel had the potential to be blessed by God, but not all were blessed in identical ways. The theological implications in the narrative stories of Scripture that lie behind this list of names reveal the many ways God graciously blessed the descendants of Jacob with many children, a large and fruitful land, and even some miraculous military victories that gave these twelve tribes dominion over the geographical areas God promised to Abram (Gen 13:14–17; 15:18–21).

After stepping back from the exegetical task of interpreting what the author meant and what the readers understood to ask further questions, one should then ask how the information in the genealogies can be integrated with the rest of the OT narrative literature. First, it is clear that these genealogies were a fundamental part of both early (Genesis) and later (Chronicles) narratives. Second, the authors of these two ancient texts did not segregate the genealogies into a separate biblical book with no theological context. Considering the use of genealogies in Chronicles may have been influenced by how genealogies found in Genesis are used, it might be helpful to compare the contexts of those in Genesis to discern how and why those in Chronicles are utilized. Some years ago, in a study of the structure and purpose of Gen 1–11, my conclusion was that one of the key theological points to be recognized in Gen 1–11 was that the genealogies record the fulfillment of God's original blessing on humanity:[15] (a) to be fruitful and multiply by having many sons and daughters; (b) to fill the earth by taking possession of different lands and establishing many cities; and (c) to have dominion over the territory God gave to each family/nation (Gen 1:26, 28). The genealogy demonstrates that people did multiply into many families and many nations over many centuries; they did spread out all

---

15. Gary V. Smith ("Structure and Purpose," 307–19) traces the theological blessing of being fruitful, multiplying, filling the earth, and having dominion over it as it was fulfilled in the proliferation of people in the genealogies of Gen 5 and 11:10–32 (fulfilling the first part of God's blessing), the spread of humanity over the face of the earth in Gen 10:1—11:9 (fulfilling the second part of filling the earth), and how humanity lost dominion over the land, animals, and other humans because of sin and violence (war).

over the earth (after the tower of Babel incident in Gen 11:1–9) with some living in southern Africa and Arabia, others in northern Israel, and some in the land that God would later give to Israel. When one of these peoples would migrate to new land or defeat their enemies in war, they claimed dominion over the territory where they settled. Therefore, to some extent, all three parts of God's original blessing were fulfilled.[16] The genealogies in Gen 5 and 11 give a brief overview of how these three aspects of God's blessing worked out over many centuries before the time of Abram. But not all people were blessed at all times, for the biblical narratives in Genesis and beyond are filled with many sinful failures. These narratives demonstrate how sin led to death and no multiplication (the curse of death in Gen 3); how sin led to the loss of dominion over nature, animals, and other humans (Gen 3:17–19; 4:11–12); and how sin led to exile and the loss of dominion over the land (even exile from the garden in Gen 3:23–24).

But in the midst of all these negative events caused by sin, the narratives of Genesis explain that God promised to give a special blessing to one family, the seed of Abram and Jacob/Israel (Gen 12:1–3). They would be blessed with so many children in their genealogies that one could not count them (as many as the stars in the heavens or the dust of the earth in Gen 13:16; 15:5), with a promised land that God would give them (Gen 13:15–17), and with dominion over a land that others possessed at that time (Gen 15:18–21). This promise was affirmed to Abram through a covenant (Gen 15:7–21), the full implications and expectations of which being later defined in the Mosaic covenant (Exod 19–24).

Since 1 Chronicles quotes extensively from Gen 5 and 11, it is possible that some of the same thought served as a theological backdrop for the genealogies in 1 Chr 1–9. S. G. Dempster recognizes that connection and proposes a theological relationship between the blessing of God in Gen 1:28 and genealogies in 1 Chr 1–9.[17] The genealogies

---

16. C. M. Kaminski (*From Noah to Israel*) examines the fulfillment of God's blessing in later texts in Genesis and Exodus.

17. Dempster, "Geography and Genealogy," 66–82. This article suggests that the biblical genealogies testify to the fulfillment of God purpose for humanity in Gen 1:28.

in Genesis and 1 Chr 1–9 do not describe all of God's great plans, all his promises, or all the problems that were involved in the process (explained more fully in the narrative stories) of implementing his will on earth, but they do list some of the people who were involved in carrying out various parts of God's plans. Years later, when Israel failed to keep their covenant with God, the people lost the favor and blessings of God, exemplified in the loss of their land to the Assyrians (1 Chr 5:26). Nevertheless, the death of thousands and the exile of thousands more to another land under the dominion of a foreign ruler was not the end of the story; according to another narrative, God was still guiding his people in the postexilic era (2 Chr 36:22–23). God's plans for the nation of Israel were not yet complete, for it included another episode, which would be fulfilled at some future date. Thus, the narrative context of the genealogies in Genesis and Chronicles helps to fills in some information not included in the genealogy itself.

THE COMMUNITY OF ISRAEL

The community of Israel, which received God's blessing and covenant, was composed of individuals related to one of the twelve tribes described in 1 Chr 1–9. Williamson reports that the word "Israel" is used three hundred times in Chronicles: twelve times referring to the patriarch Jacob, twenty-five times appearing in the title which identified YHWH as the "God of Israel," twenty-seven times referring to the nation of Israel living in the premonarchic period, and twenty-one times referring to Israel as a people.[18] Williamson writes that, in fifty-one examples, the title "Israel" refers to the Northern ten tribes and that there are eleven cases where "Israel" refers to the Southern nation of Judah.[19] However, no examples of the latter category appear in the genealogies in 1 Chr 1–9. In the genealogies, the term "Israel" refers to: (a) the patriarch Jacob six times (1:34; 2:1; 5:1, 3; 6:38; 7:29); (b) the God of Israel twice (4:10; 5:26); (c) the Northern kingdom twice (5:17; 9:1); (d) the twelve tribes three times (2:7; 6:49, 64); and, finally, (e) "all Israel," in 1 Chr 9:2, which had the unique meaning of the "common

---

18. Williamson, *Israel in the Book of Chronicles*, 89.
19. 2 Chr 12:1, 6; 19:8; 21:2, 4; 23:2; 24:5, 16; 28:19, 23, 27.

lay Israelite" as opposed to the religious personnel like the priest and Levites.

Although the Israelites were a complex association of diverse tribal peoples who descended from the patriarch Jacob, these people included outsiders who were grafted into the community (e.g., the Canaanite woman Judah married [1 Chr 2:3]; the Egyptian servant, Jarha, who became the husband of Sheshan's daughter [1 Chr 2:35]; Bithra, the daughter of a pharaoh, who married Mered [1 Chr 4:17]; plus the mixed multitude of people who came up with the Israelites from Egypt at the time of the exodus [Exod 12:38]). Ancient Israelite literature, written long before Chronicles, records that Joseph married the Egyptian woman Asenath (Gen 41:45), Moses married the Midianite Zipporah (Exod 2:21), and Boaz married a Moabite woman, Ruth (Ruth 4). Since most of the tribes did not kill all the Canaanites living among them during Joshua's conquest of the land (Judg 1:19, 21, 27–36), it was almost inevitable that some Israelites would marry non-Israelites, that they would be influenced by the Canaanite Baal religion (Judg 2:1–3), and that these factors would contribute toward the eventual demise of both Israel and Judah. These twelve tribes suffered repeated military defeat, because they did not follow the instructions given by Moses and ignored the warnings of the prophets God sent them (2 Kgs 17:7–23; 24:10—25:21). Eventually, Israel was taken into Assyrian captivity (2 Kgs 17), and Judah was exiled to Babylon (Jer 52).

It is clear that the Chronicler's understanding of the community of Israel in 1 Chr 1–9 went beyond surface-level knowledge, for the genealogies include people who were not the descendants of Israel/Jacob. The Chronicler viewed the whole nation (including non-Israelites by birth) as the ideal "community of Israel," which inherited the blessings of God. It is important to recognize that the genealogies in 1 Chr 5 and 7 include most of the northern tribes of Israel, who went into exile in 722 BCE,[20] on the east and west side of the Jordan. Although many Hebrew people never returned to the Promised Land, a number from

---

20. Although there is no mention of the tribe of Dan, Konkel (*1 & 2 Chronicles*, 109) argues that the text of 1 Chr 7:12 "provides some textual information to indicate that Dan was once listed as a tribal name." This was based on the Greek text which had "Hushim his one son," and Hushim was a son of Dan.

the northern tribes migrated to Judah when Jeroboam led the northern nation of Israel to split off from the southern tribe of Judah (2 Chr 11:13–17). Others from the northern tribes of Manasseh and Ephraim resided in Judah (2 Chr 15:9), and people from Ephraim, Manasseh, Issachar, Asher, and Zebulun joined Hezekiah for a Passover celebration (2 Chr 30:11, 18). Thus, it seems that many families from the northern ten tribes were taken into exile with people from Judah and some of them returned to Judah.[21]

Since God made the covenant with the whole nation of Israel, it was important for the Chronicler to identify who would be included in "Israel/all Israel." In the narratives following the genealogies, there are many references to an "all Israel" who wanted David to be king (1 Chr 11:1; 12:38) and helped him capture Jerusalem (11:4). The warriors from "all Israel" came (11:10; 12:24–37) to support David while he was hiding from Saul. "All Israel" assembled with David to bring up the ark the first time (13:5, 8; 15:3), and "all Israel" fought together against their enemies (19:17). All the officials of Israel were at the important events of (1) David explaining to Solomon what his duties regarding the building of the temple would be and of (2) David installing Solomon as his successor (22:17; 23:2; 28:1; 29:6), so it was not surprising that "all Israel" obeyed/listened to Solomon (29:23). This kind of joint action with God continued into the reign of Solomon until the division of the kingdom (2 Chr 1:2; 5:3, 6; 6:6; 7:3, 8; 10:1). Although the people of Israel were divided into two nations (Israel in the north and Judah in the south) after the death of Solomon, the Chronicler did not believe that the northern tribes ceased to be important to God. The restoration of the northern tribes was always seen as a possibility, if the people would seek God and repent (2 Chr 7:14; 13:4–12).

THE IMPORTANCE OF THE COMMUNITY IN THE LIFE OF THE CHURCH

Considering the lack of theological reflection on the deeds of most people in the genealogy, it is difficult for people today, who are not part of ancient Israelite culture, to appreciate the importance of knowing

---

21. Thus, it appears that the idea of "the lost tribes of Israel" is probably a myth.

the names of distant ancestors and having an accurate record of one's genealogical history. The genealogies in 1 Chr 1–9 are important because they help the reader (1) to understand who "all Israel" refers to in the narrative sections of 1 and 2 Chronicles and (2) to glimpse a brief summary of God's relationship with his people over many past generations. The narratives in the rest of 1 and 2 Chronicles fill in many details concerning some of the people listed in 1 Chr 1–9. Although this genealogical information was originally for the benefit of the Chronicler's audience, there remains some value for people in the church today. There are four ideas to consider.

Community

The community of Israel was made up of many different tribes and thousands of people who lived in different times spanning more than a millennia, yet there remained a strong sense of connection with and appreciation for the contribution of past generations—for the unity they maintained on the basis of their common faith and common ancestor Jacob/Israel. Likewise, the church has existed in many denominations in many countries over many centuries based on a common set of beliefs that unify a diverse band of genealogically unrelated people with a common cause to honor the same God. The church should be challenged by the need for a greater sense of community among its diverse participants. Community should be cherished and strengthened, though it lacks a genealogical basis. Arguments and wrangling over small differences only hurt the reputation of the community of God (then and today) and limits its ability to carry out its mission. Minor differences should not stand in the way of creating a unified community of believers. Like Israel, the church should value the contributions of all believers and welcome strangers into the family of God.

Leadership

The genealogies of Judah (1 Chr 2–4) and Levi (1 Chr 6) record aspects of God's central plan for the political (from Judah) and spiritual (from Levi) leadership of the community of Israel. These genealogies focus on the kings in the line of Judah starting with David (1 Chr 3:10–16; 5:2), but there are no messianic hints here. In fact, the greatest emphasis was on the spiritual role of the priests and Levites, because 1 Chr 6 is the pivotal chapter in the chiastic arrangement[22] of the genealogies. Their service was integral within the community, because they were responsible for making atonement for Israel's sins (1 Chr 6:48–49). The holiness of the people and the king was far more important to the success of the nation than the abilities of any politician. Although the church lacks political power similar to a nation like Israel, the vitality of the church's influence depends deeply on godly leaders, both in the organization and oversight of its mission and strategies as well as in implementing its call for people to confess their sins, practice holiness, and honor God in worship. Without good church leadership influencing people to exhibit the characteristics of a godly servant, the political situation will risk the danger of failure, no matter the setting or circumstances.

Unity

Although the tribes of Judah and Levi were especially essential to the success of the nation, the remaining tribes of Israel were necessary in being part of "all Israel," the united community that decided what the nation should do. Although some tribes were large and others small, their destiny depended on their willingness to follow God's instructions and work together for common goals. The division of the kingdom into Israel and Judah (2 Chr 10) and the ensuing in-fighting (2 Chr 13) testify of their failure to value unity. Likewise, all members of the church, including "all churches" in each denomination, have the challenge and opportunity to play an important role in God's fulfillment of his future plan for unity. Unfortunately, many past and present leaders in the church have not valued unity as they should. While no one is required or should be encouraged to be unified with churches that do not faithfully teach God's word, there is a need to pray for and convince others to reject false teachings in order to maintain unity.

---

22. Oeming, *Das wahre Israel*, 210. Sparks (*Chronicler's Genealogies*, 29) presents a fairly complex chiastic outline. See the commentary section on 1 Chr 1–9 for the details of his outline. Andrew Hill (*1 & 2 Chronicles*, 375) has a less complicated outline of the chiasm.

COMMUNITY

Diversity and Unity

Unfortunately, some tribes depreciated the values of God's instructions and followed strange paths and ideologies that led them astray, resulting in a future overshadowed by a dark cloud of divine displeasure—a fate that every church community should strive to avoid. Although the Israelites always were a complex association of diverse tribal peoples who descended from the patriarch Jacob, they included outsiders like the Canaanite woman Judah married (1 Chr 2:3) and the mixed multitude of people who came up with the Israelites from Egypt at the time of the exodus (Exod 12:38). Some Israelites married non-Israelites who followed the Canaanite Baal religion (Judg 2:1–3), which contributed to the demise of both Israel and Judah. But these tribes suffered military defeat not because they invited strangers into their community, but because they let the strangers influence their thinking; they did not follow the instructions given by Moses, and they did not listen to the warnings of the prophets God sent them (2 Kgs 17:7–23; 24:10—25:21). The church community should always be open to strangers and new people from diverse backgrounds, but joining a community involves conforming to its rules and purposes not undermining its goals. New people should always be educated in the values of the community so that they are able contribute to its growth and vitality. Diversity should not be feared in the church, except when it deteriorates into a perverse requirement that all ideas and behaviors must be honored as equally valid. God's community of believers will include a vast multitude of diverse people from every tribe and language from vastly different cultures, but there will be no diversity when it comes to holy living in humble relationship to a loving God.

BLBLIOGRAPHY

Aufrecht, Walter E. "Genealogy and History in Ancient Israel." In *Ascribe to the Lord: Biblical and other Studies in Memory of Peter C. Craige*, edited by Lyle Eslinger, 205-35. JSOTSup 67. Sheffield: JSOT, 1988.

Berquist, Jon L. "Constructions of Identity." In *Judah and Judeans in the Persian Period*, edited by O. Lipschits and M. Oeming, 53-82. Winona Lake, IN: Eisenbrauns, 2006.

Dempster, Stephen G. "Geography and Genealogy, Dominion and Dynasty: A Theology of the Hebrew Bible." In *Biblical Theology: Retrospect*

& *Prospect*, edited by S. J. Hafemann, 66–82. Downers Grove, IL: InterVarsity, 2002.

Dyck, Jonathan E. "The Ideology of Identity in Chronicles." In *Ethnicity and the Bible*, edited by M. G. Brett, 89–116. Leiden: Brill, 1996.

Finkelstein, J. J. "The Genealogy of the Hammurapi Dynasty." *JCS* 20 (1966) 95–118.

Hartman, T. C. "Some Thoughts on the Sumerian King List and Genesis 5 and 11." *JBL* 91 (1972) 25–32.

Hill, Andrew. *1 & 2 Chronicles*. NIVAC. Grand Rapids: Zondervan, 2003.

Jacobsen, T. *The Sumerian King List*. Chicago: University of Chicago Press, 1939.

Johnson, Marshal D. *The Purpose of the Biblical Genealogies*. 2nd ed. Cambridge: Cambridge University Press, 1988.

Jonker, Louis C. *1 & 2 Chronicles*. UBCS. Grand Rapids: Baker, 2013.

Kaminski, C. M. *From Noah to Israel: Realization of the Primeval Blessing After the Flood*. JSOTSup 413. London: T. & T. Clark, 2004.

Konkel, August H. *1 & 2 Chronicles*. BCBC. Kitchener, ON: Herald Press, 2016.

Malamat, A. "King Lists of the Old Babylonian Period and Biblical Genealogies." *JAOS* 88 (1968) 163–73.

Oeming, Manfred. *Das Wahre Israel: die "genealogishe Vorhalle" 1 Chronik 1-9*. BWANT 128. Stuttgart: Kohlhamer, 1990.

Siedlecki, A. "Foreigners, Warfare and Judahite Identity in Chronicles." In *The Chronicler as Author: Studies in Text and Texture*, edited by M. P. Graham and S. L. McKenzie, 229–66. JSOTSup 26. Sheffield: Sheffield Academic, 1999.

Sparks, James T. *The Chronicler's Genealogies: Toward and Understanding of 1 Chronicles 1-9*. Atlanta: Society of Biblical Literature, 2008.

Williamson, Hugh G. M. *Israel in the Book of Chronicles*. Cambridge: Cambridge University Press, 1977.

Wilson, R. R. "The Old Testament Genealogies in Recent Research." *JBL* 94 (1975) 169–89.

5

All in the Family of David

*The Chronicler's Change from the Ammonite (2 Sam 17:25)
to the Davidic Zeruiah (1 Chr 2:16)*

PAUL S. EVANS[1]

INTRODUCTION

ROBERT GORDON WRITES: "For some reason the books of Samuel have suffered more in the process of transmission than perhaps any other part of the Old Testament."[2] While the problem passages really are only a small portion of the text, scholars frequently appeal to the Septuagint or other textual traditions (such as the Dead Sea Scrolls [DSS]) when the Masoretic Text (MT) of Samuel is problematic.[3] The short genealogy of Amasa in 2 Sam 17:25 is usually thought to be textually corrupt and is an instance where such a scholarly procedure is

---

1. I have had the privilege of working with Gus Konkel at McMaster Divinity College for the past nine years and am grateful for how his scholarship and friendship have so greatly enriched our learning community. I am glad to offer this essay in his honour. Given his research interests in both textual criticism and Chronicles, it seems a fitting tribute.

2. Gordon, *I & II Samuel*, 57.

3. Cf. Aejmelaeus, "The Septuagint of 1 Samuel," 131–49.

invariably called for. In this verse, as it stands in the MT, Amasa's mother, Abigail, is said to be the daughter of Nahash and sister of Zeruiah, who is famous as the mother of Joab, Abishai, and Asahel—often referred to as the "sons of Zeruiah" (2 Sam 2:18; 3:39; 16:10; 19:22). This information is thought by scholars to be in error, thus textual emendations abound. The main reason for these emendations, however, is not due to the evident textual problems, but due to the genealogy of Jesse in 1 Chr 2 which contradicts the information in 2 Sam 17:25. According to the Chronicler, Zeruiah, mother of Joab (and Abishai and Asahel) was David's sister (1 Chr 2:16). Therefore, "Amasa and Joab, the two army commanders, are first cousins, and both of them David's nephews."[4] While scholars[5] almost universally assume that Chronicles is correct in this regard, in this paper I will argue against this position and against reading the Chronicler's attribution of a sibling relationship between David and Zeruiah back into Samuel.

My arguments will consider both external and internal evidence. Regarding the former I will show that the best textual evidence favours the reading of Nahash as Abigail's father, and not Jesse. Regarding internal evidence, I will consider both Samuel and Chronicles at the compositional level. The book of Samuel did not present David as brother to Zeruiah or uncle to Joab and his brothers, although such familial relationships are explicitly spelled out elsewhere in regard to David's nephews. On the other hand, I will suggest that the book of Chronicles purposefully presented Zeruiah as David's sister as part of his *Tendenz* to glorify David (and by extension, Israel) by associating the sons of Zeruiah with the Davidic house, which in the Chronicler's view, had been chosen along with him. Furthermore, recognition of the Chronicler's work in this regard underscores his theology of community and his concern to build up the prestige not only of David but all Israel.

As a point of reference, the MT of 2 Sam 17:25 reads:

וַעֲמָשָׂא בֶן־אִישׁ וּשְׁמוֹ יִתְרָא הַיִּשְׂרְאֵלִי אֲשֶׁר־בָּא אֶל־אֲבִיגַל בַּת־נָחָשׁ
אֲחוֹת צְרוּיָה אֵם יוֹאָב:

---

4. Alter, *The David Story*, 302.

5. E.g., Alter, *The David Story*, 302; McCarter, *II Samuel*, 391; Levenson and Halpern, "The Political Import of David's Marriages," 512; Smith, *Samuel*, 355; Driver, *Books of Samuel*, 326; and Hertzberg, *I & II Samuel*, 357.

Community

"Amasa was the son of a man and his name was Yitra the Israelite who came unto Abigail daughter of Nahash sister of Zeruiah, mother of Joab."

I. AMASA'S FATHER

A. The Odd Construction

The first oddity in the verse is the construction in listing Amasa's father. It says Amasa is "son of a man, and his name was Yitra." The name Yitra (יתרא) in this verse differs from Chronicles where he is called Yeter (יתר). Later in 1 Kgs 2:5 Amasa's father is named Yeter with the identical spelling as Chronicles. Despite these small differences, the names Yitra and Yeter are not really textually problematic, as they basically are "longer and shorter forms—both probably 'correct'—of the same name."[6] This variation is similar to the names given for Moses' father-in-law in Exod 4:18 where he is called both Yeter (יתר) or Yitro/Jethro (יתרו) in the same verse.

What is strange about this genealogy is the construction "son of a man, and his name is." Elsewhere in the Old Testament/Hebrew Bible (OT/HB) the construction "son of a man" in a genealogical statement is always followed by a gentilic *not* by a name (e.g., Lev 24:10 lists "son of an Egyptian man" [בן־איש מצרי]; 1 Sam 9:1 has Saul described as a "son of a Benjaminite man" [בן־איש ימיני]; 1 Sam 17:12 presents David as a "son of an Ephrathite man [בן־איש אפרתי]; 2 Sam 1:13 has the messenger who reports Saul's death to David "son of a resident Amalekite man [בן־איש גר עמלקי]). The construction here instead says he is a son of a man, then lists the man's name, followed by a gentilic.

B. The Gentilic

i. Israelite

What is even stranger is that when the gentilic of Amasa's father is finally given it is "the Israelite" (הישראלי). "Israelite" as a gentilic for an individual is extremely rare in the OT/HB. It appears only one other time in the OT/HB, and that is in Lev 24:10–11 where the term is used

---

6. McCarter, *II Samuel*, 391.

to contrast a son of mixed origins (an Israelite mother and Egyptian father) and an Israelite. Given that no such contrast appears in 2 Sam 17:25, most find the reading "the Israelite" problematic here.[7] Despite the fact that LXXB (Codex Vaticanus), LXXL (Lucian Septuagint), Targums, and Vulgate all read "Israelite" along with the MT, for most scholars, in this instance internal evidence trumps external. The reading "the Israelite" does not make sense and must be rejected.

ii. Ishmaelite

Supporting this rejection of the gentilic "Israelite" is other external evidence that contain variant readings. LXXA (Alexandrinus) and 1 Chr 2:17 list Amasa's father as "the Ishmaelite." Some suggest that "a scribe would have every reason to correct *Ishmaelite* to *Israelite*."[8] For example, Hertzberg suggests that the reading "Israelite" was intended to give Amasa "a particularly suitable qualification to be leader of the host of Israel."[9] Explaining why one would change Israelite to Ishmaelite is more difficult to discern. Of course, it is quite possible that LXXA was the result of a secondary correction to bring Samuel into harmony with Chronicles. After all, as Tov notes, LXXA is "prone to harmonizing."[10]

iii. Jezreelite

Another reading is also preserved. In the Old Latin (OL) and two Greek miniscules[11] Amasa's father is said to be the "Jezreelite" (similar to Naboth's gentilic היזרעאלי in 1 Kgs 21:1). Halpern and Levenson have argued for this reading on the basis that it is unlikely that "Israelite" could have replaced "Ishmaelite." They suggest that it is unlikely that a מ was mistaken for a ר and that an ע would have just dropped out.[12] It is more probable, in their opinion, that, the sibilants ז and ש could have been switched, seeing as they sound similar before a guttural (being

---

7. Levenson and Halpern, "Political Import of David's Marriages," 512.

8. Smith, *Samuel*, 355. Driver (*Notes on the Hebrew Text*, 326) also states "*the Ishmaelite* must be read with I Ch. 2, 17 and LXX (Cod. A) here."

9. Hertzberg, *I & II Samuel*, 357.

10. Tov, "Textual Harmonization," 25.

11. See Smith, *Books of Samuel*, 356.

12. Levenson and Halpern, "Political Import of David's Marriages," 512.

weakened) and could have easily resulted in "Jezreelite" (*yizrĕʿēʾlî*). In turn then, the reading of "Jezreelite" could have plausibly led to both "Israelite" and "Ishmaelite" since each correction involves one letter only.[13] If "Jezreelite" was the original reading, it could refer to either the Issacharian city (e.g., Hos 2:2) or to the Judean town near Hebron. The latter town makes the most sense here due to Hebron's central role in Absalom's kingdom (2 Sam 19:12–15).[14] This understanding of Jezreel as a Judean town near Hebron also correlates to David's later reference to Amasa as "my own flesh and blood" (2 Sam 19:14 [Eng. 13]). If Amasa's father was an Ishmaelite, this designation would not be as meaningful. If reference is to the Judean town, Amasa is from David's homeland of Judah, so he is his own flesh and blood. Of course, David in the previous verse (2 Sam 19:13 [Eng. 12]) calls the elders of Judah his "own flesh and blood" too, so we need not read into the phrase that Amasa *was* David's nephew.

C. The Issue of the Strange Marriage Situation

Another oddity in this short genealogy of Amasa is the description of Abigail and Yeter's relationship. The text says Yeter "*had gone into/*

---

13. Levenson and Halpern, "Political Import of David's Marriages," 512. Levenson and Halpern have creatively suggested that Yeter in 2 Sam 17:25 was the real name of Nabal, Abigail's first husband in 1 Sam 25. Further, they suggest that the Abigail (אֲבִיגַיִל) from 1 Sam 25 and the Abigal (אֲבִיגַל) in 2 Sam 17:25 are one and the same woman. In this reconstruction, David took his sister Abigail away from Nabal, then proceeded to marry his sister. Amasa, then, is Nabal's son whom Abigail bore before David had married her. This understanding would mean that Amasa was David's step-son. As scholars have suggested, since Nabal was a prominent landowner in the area, David's taking Abigail as wife likely helped him gain influence in the area. If Abigail was also the sister of Zeruiah (but Zeruiah was *not* David's sister), perhaps this was instrumental in David securing the loyalty of Zeruiah's sons. After all, in the Samuel narrative, the first mention of a son of Zeruiah occurs in 1 Sam 26:6, which is only *after* David has married Abigail in 1 Sam 25:42. In the end, however, like most scholars, I still find the proposal of Levenson and Halpern unconvincing. First, if David had married his sister Abigail, and Amasa was his step-son, it seems likely this would have surfaced in the narrative (see section below on references to familial relationships in the section "C. Against the Reading Jesse." What is more, Nabal is called a Calebite (1 Sam 25:3), while Yeter is called a Jezreelite, Ishmaelite, or Israelite (2 Sam 17:25). In the end, the speculation that Yeter is Nabal is interesting but pure conjecture.

14. Levenson and Halpern, "Political Import of David's Marriages," 512.

entered unto (בא אל) Abigail." The combination of בא and אל often indicates sexual relations, but Abigail is *not* called Yeter's wife here and the strange construction has suggested to many commentators that this does not describe a marriage "in the usual sense."[15] It could indicate that Amasa was conceived of rape[16] or as the result of a "casual liaison."[17] Alternatively, the relationship could have been a so-called *sadiqa* relationship, wherein the woman and her children stay with her parents and the man/husband only periodically visits.[18] Some find this similar to Samson's marriage to the Philistine woman in Timnah in Judg 14.[19]

According to some interpreters this atypical marriage relationship could explain how Amasa could be considered a member of Jesse's house, despite his father being an Ishmaelite (or Jezreelite), because he lived with his mother's father.[20] However, since 2 Sam 17:25 never tells us that his mother's father was Jesse, this again assumes the veracity of the Chronicler's identification of Zeruiah as daughter of Jesse. If Zeruiah is daughter of Nahash, and her husband is an Ishmaelite or Jezreelite, there is actually no connection to Jesse or David whatsoever.

II. ABIGAIL'S FATHER

In the MT and LXX of 2 Sam 17:25 the father of Yeter's wife, Abigail, is given as "Nahash." Nevertheless, most scholars think that the correct name of the father of Abigail should be "Jesse." The driving force behind these emendations is their agreement with the genealogy of Jesse in 1 Chr 2:16–17 which presents Abigail and Zeruiah as sisters of David and his brothers (i.e., Jesse's daughters). There are, of course, textual witnesses for the reading "Jesse." A number of Lucianic Greek manuscripts read Ιεσσαι, instead of Ναας, ["Nahash,"].[21]

---

15. McCarter, *II Samuel*, 393.

16. Hertzberg (*I & II Samuel*, 357) questions "had the nomad come upon the young woman of Bethlehem and overpowered her?"

17. Hertzberg, *I & II Samuel*, 357.

18. Smith, *Books of Samuel*, 355; Hertzberg, *I & II Samuel*, 357; Dhorme, *Les Livres de Samuel*, 394.

19. McCarter, *II Samuel*, 393.

20. McCarter, *II Samuel*, 393.

21. Including LXXL, LXXM, and LXXN.

A. Against Reading "Nahash"

Even though McCarter considers "Nahash" in this verse "an apparent error" he also rightly concludes that "there is no reliable textual witness to contradict it."[22] He is not alone in this view as most scholars view the Greek manuscripts that read Jesse as "a result of secondary correction" or "a harmonizing alteration."[23] Despite acknowledging the lack of reliable textual evidence to support it, McCarter notes, "As Zeruiah's sister, Abigail was Jesse's daughter."[24] Of course, how does McCarter know that Zeruiah was Jesse's daughter? *Only from the claims in Chronicles.*

Some have suggested that the appearance of the name "Nahash" here in 2 Sam 17:25 could be the result of the mention of "Shobi son of Nahash" in 2 Sam 17:27.[25] However, the line in question is not in close proximity to this line but occurs two verses later, besides which, it is difficult to see how "Nahash" could replace "Jesse" if "Jesse" was the original reading.

B. In Favour of the Reading "Nahash"

First, the best manuscript evidence for 2 Sam 17:25 agrees on the reading that Abigail's father was Nahash (MT, LXX, OL, Targums). Secondly, the reading "Nahash" is the *more difficult reading* but not so difficult as to be rejected on internal grounds. Thirdly, the change to Jesse in other textual traditions is explicable due to the influence of the Chronicler's genealogy, while the change from Jesse to Nahash admits of no clear rationale.

Admittedly, the reading of 'Nahash' appears a bit odd given that it is the name of the malevolent Ammonite king who oppressed Israel back at the beginning of Saul's tenure (1 Sam 11) and wanted to gouge

---

22. McCarter, *II Samuel*, 392.

23. McCarter, *II Samuel*, 392; Driver, *Notes on the Hebrew Text*, 326; Smith, *Books of Samuel*, 355. Of course, some Jewish expositors have made "Nahash here to be another name for Jesse" which is simply a harmonizing of Chronicles with this verse. Smith, *Books of Samuel*, 354.

24. McCarter, *II Samuel*, 392.

25. Long ago Wellhausen (*Der Text Der Bücher Samuelis Untersucht*, 201) suggested, "בת־נחש ist wohl aus בן־נחש v. 27 entstanden." So Dhorme, *Les Livres de Samuel*, 394; McCarter, *II Samuel*, 392; Hertzberg, *I & II Samuel*, 357; Evans, *1 and 2 Samuel*, 213.

out an eye from every resident at Jabesh-Gilead in order to "bring disgrace on all Israel" (11:2). In the narrative, however, David clearly had ties to the Ammonite Nahash as is evident in 2 Sam 10 when David hears of the Ammonite king's passing and sends a delegation to express his sympathy to the new king, Hanun, son of Nahash. While this appears surprising given the violent history between Nahash and Israel, in one sense, Nahash was the enemy of Saul so that the adage "the enemy of my enemy is my friend" could apply here. After all, at this point in the narrative, David had been murderously pursued by Saul for years, and was even forced to go live with the enemy—the Philistines—for eighteen months. The story in 2 Sam 10 suggests that David had made a covenant with Nahash sometime in the past. The references to showing "kindness" (חסד) in 2 Sam 10:2 points to a covenant relationship.[26] It seems likely David made an agreement with Nahash when he was on the run from Saul (or perhaps when he was at war with Ish-Bosheth). The pact would likely have agreed on mutual nonaggression benefiting both sides.[27] David's indebtedness towards the Ammonite king may also be explained if some of David's most faithful men, like Abishai, Joab, and Asahel were related to Nahash. The prior positive relationship between David and Nahash may also explain why in 2 Sam 17:27 Shobi, the son of Nahash, comes in support of David, bringing him supplies when he was exiled from Jerusalem during Absalom's rebellion.

---

26. Kalluveettil, *Declaration and Covenant*, 49–50.

27. An example of such a treaty is found in the parity treaty between Hattusilis (king of Hatti) and Rameses II (Pharaoh of Egypt) wherein both kings agreed "to mutual nonaggression, mutual defense, extradition of fugitives, and even assistance in cases of contested royal accession." Long, "1 Samuel," 455. The point of the treaty is "to cause that good peace and brotherhood occur between us forever" (*ANET*, 199). Evidently, the treaty between Hattusilis and Rameses was actually a renewal of a treaty that had existed between Hatti and Egypt in the time of their fathers, and the extant treaty is reaffirming its terms. The relevant section of the treaty reads: "As to the traditional regulation [the pre-existing treaty] which had been here in the time of Suppiluliumas [Hattusili's grandfather] . . . as well as the traditional regulation which had been in the time of Muwatallis, the Great Prince of Hatti, my father, I seize hold of it . . . Behold, Ramses Meri-Amon, the great ruler of Egypt, seizes hold of [it] . . . We seize hold of it, and we act in this traditional situation" (*ANET*, 200). Similarly, upon the death of Nahash, David is likely setting out to reaffirm the terms of the treaty (showing "kindness" with the new king).

Community

The realization that the reading of Nahash is best supported has led to some unwitting attempts to harmonize the data with Chronicles. Some have suggested that Nahash was the name of "an earlier husband of Jesse's wife, to whom she bore Abigail and Zeruiah."[28] Thus, Abigail and Zeruiah were full sisters to each other, but only half-sisters to David.[29] Alternatively, some have suggested that Nahash could be a woman's name, and should be identified as a second wife of Jesse, or even the *sister* of Zeruiah.[30] Since Nahash does not appear to be a woman's name (as Wellhausen put it "ist kein Eigenname einer Frau")[31] these suggestions have not found a following.[32]

The influence of Chronicles permeates this textual issue. For example, Mauchline uncritically assumes Chronicles when he writes, "Whether we read Nahash here . . . or 'Jesse' . . . the fact remains that Amasa was a cousin of Absalom, Abishai and Joab."[33] While it is true that Amasa is presented as related to Joab regardless of the name of Abigail's father, it is *not true* that Amasa is cousin to Absalom if we read Nahash instead of Jesse. There is actually no other evidence to suggest that David or his son Absalom were close relatives of Amasa, Abishai, or Joab.

C. Against the Reading "Jesse"

While external evidence clearly did not favour reading "Jesse" in Amasa's genealogical note, internal evidence from the book of Samuel also argues against it. Chief among these internal objections to reading

28. McCarter, *II Samuel*, 394; Hertzberg, *I & II Samuel*, 357; Driver, *Notes on the Hebrew Text*, 326.

29. Hertzberg, *I & II Samuel*, 357; Evans, *1 and 2 Samuel*, 213.

30. Smith speculates that Nahash could be the sister of Zeruiah (*Books of Samuel*, 355), while Driver (*Notes on the Hebrew Text*, 326) considers the possibility Nahash was "(if we were sure that Nahash was a woman's name) a second wife of Jesse."

31. Wellhausen, *Der Text Der Bücher Samuelis*, 201. So Evans, *1 and 2 Samuel*, 213. Though Smith (*Books of Samuel*, 355) counters this assertion saying "of this we cannot be certain."

32. Along these lines, some Greek texts (LXXa and LXXb) have Nahash listed as Zeruiah's brother. McCarter (*II Samuel*, 392) rejects those readings on the grounds that Nahash is not listed as one of David's brothers in 1 Chr 2:13–15. Again, this uncritically assumes the veracity of the Chronicler's genealogy.

33. Mauchline, *1 and 2 Samuel*, 282–83.

"Jesse" is that Abigail or Zeruiah is *not* called a sister of David. This has been acknowledged by even those who would favour reading "Jesse." For example, assuming that David *is* Zeruiah's sister, Hertzberg finds it strange that "she is not called a sister of David" in 2 Sam 17:25.[34] Indeed, it would seem strange not to mention her relationship to David if it were the case.[35] After all, when David's other nephews are given some narrative space their relationship to David *is* spelled out clearly. For example, when David's nephew Jonadab helps Amnon devise a plan to get access to his incestuous love interest the text explicitly states: "Amnon had a friend whose name was Jonadab, the son of David's brother Shimeah" (2 Sam 13:3). Likewise, Jonadab's relationship to David is mentioned again when he appears later in the narrative in support of David "But Jonadab, the son of David's brother Shimeah . . . " (2 Sam 13:32). Similarly, in 2 Sam 21 when the exploits of David's mighty men against the giant Philistines are chronicled, Jonathan, who killed a six-fingered man is explicitly called "Jonathan son of David's brother Shimeah" (v. 21), yet *in the same pericope* Abishai kills a Philistine giant but is simply called the "son of Zeruiah" (21:17). Why would the text not say "Abishai, son of David's sister, Zeruiah"?[36]

Another case in point would be 1 Sam 14:50 which states "the name of the commander of [Saul's] army was Abner son of Ner, *Saul's uncle*" (1 Sam 14:50). Joab, son of Zeruiah, held the equivalent position in David's army, yet his relationship to David is *never* referenced. If Joab were David's nephew you would think it relevant to mention him in a similar way, something like "the commander of David's army was Joab, son of Zeruiah, David's sister." But no such text exists.

Similarly, when Abner is being chased by Asahel, son of Zeruiah, and is attempting to get the fleet-footed young man to stop his pursuit, Abner is very much conscious that if he is forced to kill him he would be killing Joab's brother saying, "Stop pursuing me! Why should I strike you down to the ground? How could I show my face to your brother

---

34. Hertzberg, *I & II Samuel*, 357.

35. Hertzberg (*I & II Samuel*, 357), on this account, argues that Abigail and Zeruiah were only David's half-sisters, who were born to a different mother than David—perhaps Jesse's first wife or a second wife.

36. Similarly when 2 Sam 23:18 records Abishai's heroic exploits, he is called "son of Zeruiah, the brother of Joab" with no reference to his relationship to David.

Joab?" (2 Sam 2:22). Yet, if Asahel were King David's nephew, would not Abner have some reservation to killing him for that reason? After all, in the next chapter he freely shows his face to David—coming to make a peace treaty with the king. The easiest explanation for this evidence is that the author of Samuel did *not* consider Zeruiah David's sister.

Furthermore, if one reads the Samuel narratives without the emendation "daughter of Jesse" another potential problem is satisfactorily solved—the young age of the sons of Zeruiah. If these men were David's nephews and David was only a young man of thirty when he became king in Hebron (2 Sam 2:4), the sons of Zeruiah would presumably be quite young. This is most problematic in the case of Asahel, the youngest son of Zeruiah, who was killed by Abner shortly after David's coronation in Hebron (2 Sam 2:23). Yet, despite his young age, and the way his career was cut short, Asahel was still included in the list of David's mighty men (2 Sam 23:24). If, however, Asahel was not David's nephew, Asahel's age is not an issue.

IV. THE CHRONICLER'S TENDENTIOUS GENEALOGY

A. David the Seventh Son

Against this widespread scholarly effort at harmonizing the data of 2 Sam 17:25 with Chronicles is the obvious tendentious character of the Chronicler's genealogies. For example, while in both 1 Sam 16:10 and 1 Sam 17:12-14 Jesse is said to have had eight sons and David is listed as the eighth, in 1 Chr 2:15—the very genealogy in question here—Jesse is given only seven sons and David is presented as the seventh son of Jesse, likely due to the special significance of the number seven.[37] Roddy Braun suggests, "By making David the seventh son, the writer may have wished to portray him as a uniquely favored offspring."[38] Klein

---

37. Another example can be seen in the genealogy of Esau in Chronicles is reworked from the genealogy in Gen 36 that shows the progression of Edomites to a presentation that implies that after David, Edom lost its sovereignty. Japhet writes concerning the Chronicler, "Political circumstances of Edom were thus determined: kings reigning before the accession of David, and chiefs thereafter" (*1 and 2 Chronicles*, 64). This despite the fact that there were in fact kings in Edom up until the time when the Babylonian king Nabonidus devastated the region and set up a governor there. Cf. Bartlett, *Edom and the Edomites*, 161.

38. Braun, *1 Chronicles*, 34.

points out: "Seven sons are also attributed to Elioenai, the last parent in the Davidic line (1 Chr 3:24)" and that in Chronicles "David is also in the seventh generation after Ram."[39]

B. Samuel the Levite

A well-known example of the Chronicler's purposefully changing a genealogy from the book of Samuel is found in 1 Chr 6:10–13 (Eng. 25–28) where the genealogy of the prophet Samuel is integrated with the line of Levi, though "no such correlation is made in Samuel."[40] First Samuel 1:1 lists Samuel's father, Elkanah, as a Zuphite from the hill country of Ephraim. Elkanah's lineage is traced back through Jero-ham, Elihu, Tohu, and Zuph, who is given the gentilic "Ephraimite" (אפרתי).[41] Despite his non-Levitical descent, in the early narratives of 1 Samuel, Samuel clearly acted in priestly roles. For example, he is noted as "ministering before Yahweh, a boy wearing a linen ephod" (1 Sam 2:18) and "ministering to Yahweh under Eli" (1 Sam 3:1), a task which, as Japhet comments, "was by definition considered levitical."[42] In the Chronicler's time, it was likely seen as problematic that Samuel ministered in a priestly role at Shiloh, but was not a Levite.[43] Therefore, most scholars view the Chronicler's integration of Samuel into a Kohathite genealogy as the "nonhistorical" tendentious work of the Chronicler.[44] The Chronicler managed to connect Samuel to the Levitical line through Samuel's father's name, Elkanah, which appears in the list of the sons of Korah in Exod 6:24.[45] The Chronicler's motivation could have been to

39. Klein, *1 Chronicles*, 96.

40. Knoppers, *1 Chronicles 1–9*, 421.

41. Translators usually emend "Ephrathite" to "Ephraimite" in 1 Sam 1:1, because Samuel is from Ephraim and the term is clearly used to refer to Ephraimites elsewhere (e.g., Judg 12:5). However, in Ruth 1:2 the same term (אפרתי) is used of Naomi and her husband, who are explicitly said to be from Bethlehem of Judah. Similarly, David is said to be a "son of an Ephrathite man" (אפרתי בן־איש) in 1 Sam 17:12. Thus, the term can be used either as a gentilic for someone from Ephraim or as "a sub-phratry within the tribe of Judah . . . [who] lived in Bethlehem and environs (cf. 1 Chron. 4:4)." Gordon, *1 & 2 Samuel*, 155.

42. Japhet, *I & II Chronicles*, 154.

43. Klein, *1 Chronicles*, 201.

44. Klein, *1 Samuel*, 6.

45. Braun, *1 Chronicles*, 88; Klein, *1 Chronicles*, 201.

exonerate Samuel "from the possibility of inappropriate cultic activity."[46] On the other hand, it may not have been so much about Samuel as it was about Heman, the founder-singer, who is presented as the grandson of Samuel. Japhet has suggested that this attribution of Levitical ancestry to Samuel was due to the Chronicler's concern about Heman's legitimacy.[47] Along these lines, Samuel's prophetic status may have thus been used to bolster the "prophetic function of the Levitical clans" in Chronicles (cf.1 Chr 25:1–8; 2 Chr 20:14; 29:25; 34:30; 35:15) since Heman was "their key leader."[48]

As is well known, one of the purposes of genealogies in the ancient world was to associate members with political power.[49] Genealogical presentations often sought to legitimate individuals in their office "or provide an individual of rank with connections to a worthy family or individual of the past."[50] In light of this function of ancient genealogies, it would seem this is what has happened with Samuel's Levitical genealogy. Analogously, I suggest that this is exactly what we have with the Chronicler's genealogy which associates the sons of Zeruiah with the house of David. In regard to Zeruiah, this is part of the overall *Tendenz* of the Chronicler to glorify David.

A key verse for understanding the Chronicler's rationale in including Zeruiah in the Davidic house is 1 Chr 28:4: "The LORD God of Israel . . . chose Judah to be ruler, and of the family of Judah, my father's house . . . ." This verse underscores the significance in Chronicles not only of God's choosing David, but of God's choosing the house of Jesse as well.[51] As Japhet writes, "The course of events in Samuel, including the story in 1 Samuel 16, makes it clear that it was David, and David

---

46. Klein, *1 Chronicles*, 201. The names of Samuel's ancestors also vary with Elihu changed to "Eliel" (1 Chr 6:12) or "Eliab" (1 Chr 6:19), Zuph as "Zophai" (6:11) and Jehoram as Ιδεαρ "Idear" (LXXB) Ιεροβοαμ "Jeroboam" (LXXA) or Ιερεμεελ "Jeremeel" (LXXL). Cf. Braun, *1 Chronicles*, 87.

47. Japhet, *I & II Chronicles*, 156.

48. Boda, *1–2 Chronicles*, 75.

49. Wilson, *Genealogy and History in the Biblical World*. Cf. Johnson, *The Purpose of the Biblical Genealogies*, 77–82.

50. Braun, *1 Chronicles*, 4.

51. Japhet, *I & II Chronicles*, 447.

alone, who was chosen by God . . . In Chronicles, choosing Judah and the house of Jesse has meaning in and of itself."[52]

In other words, it is not just David who is specially chosen, it is Jesse's house. Thus, by making Zeruiah out to be David's sister, her three sons are thereby included in the house of Jesse, which in Chronicles was chosen along with David.[53]

The sons of Zeruiah are clearly heroes in the stories from Samuel. The two youngest brothers are listed in the 'hall of fame' so to speak of David's mightiest soldiers (2 Sam 23:18; 23:24). This list of mighty men is repeated in Chronicles (1 Chr 11:20, 26) as is Abishai's prominent role in the war with Ammon (1 Chr 19:11, 15). Furthermore, as commentators have pointed out, the Chronicler credits Abishai with killing 18,000 Edomites in the Valley of Salt (1 Chr 18:12), something which Samuel had credited to David (2 Sam 8:13).[54] What is more, Asahel, despite his early death at the hands of Abner, is presented as an army commander (1 Chr 27:7) after David has become king (1 Chr 27:1). As Klein points out, the Chronicler was likely aware of this problem and so presents Asahel's son as succeeding him in this role.[55] Thus, the house of Asahel, as part of Jesse's house shows its continued worth. As Ristau has observed, "Although the Chr contains no sustained narrative about Asahel and Abishai, he has made redactional changes or additions to add to their accomplishments."[56]

While he is surprisingly omitted from the list of David's mighty men (2 Sam 23:8–39),[57] the eldest son of Zeruiah, Joab, is clearly the

---

52. Japhet, *The Ideology of the Book of Chronicles and Its Place in Biblical Thought*, 348, 350. As Japhet (*I & II Chronicles*, 488) notes, Isa 11:1 also underscores the significance of the "house of Jesse," though it does not use the language of "choose."

53. Klein (*1 Chronicles*, 96) speculates, "The Chronicler may also have made these women sisters of David because David calls Amasa, the son of Abigail, 'my bone and flesh' in 2 Sam 19:14 (13)."

54. McCarter (*II Samuel*, 246) has suggested this phrase crediting Abishai with the Edomite defeat was originally in Samuel as well.

55. Klein, *1 Chronicles*, 508.

56. Ristau, "In the House of Judah," 146n36.

57. In fact, Joab's armor bearer even makes the list of mighty men in 2 Sam 23:37. As I have suggested elsewhere, "It seems likely that Joab is excluded from the list due to his perennial conflicts with the king and perhaps the way in which he was ultimately found traitorous and killed by Benaiah and his elite soldiers for supporting

most prominent of the three in the stories of Samuel and he functioned as the dominant leader of Judah's army for the majority of the time. In the books of Samuel, Joab was presented as a complex character with numerous heroic qualities, but also as a shrewd, rebellious general who often disregards David's orders and undermines the king's authority (e.g., 2 Sam 3; 11; 18; 20). What is more, in 2 Sam 3:39 David describes himself as "soft/weak" (רך) in his dealings with his cunning general, and ascribes his failure to rein-in Joab as due to the wildness of the "sons of Zeruiah" (2 Sam 3:39). This picture of David being impotent in the face of Joab would not fit with the Chronicler's Davidic portrayal. However, if Joab was understood to be part of David's family, the king's 'softness' (רך) with Joab is somewhat rationalized. Of course, the Chronicler omits most of the stories of Joab in Chronicles, but his association of Joab with Jesse's house could be partly intended to affect the reading of his *Vorlage*.

An article by Ristau has underscored how the Chronicler has reworked the portrait of Joab in Chronicles, concluding that "he is presented favorably and without flaws" and that "Joab is the conqueror (11:6), builder (11:8), defender (19:13), and protector (21:6, 15)" of Jerusalem.[58] By making Joab David's nephew, the Chronicler makes the wily general part of Jesse's blessed house. Therefore, Joab's many significant contributions to David's kingdom (e.g., taking Jerusalem) bring glory to the house of David.[59]

CONCLUSION

The problem of the relation of the Deuteronomistic History to Chronicles has usually hindered the interpretation of the latter, as scholars have interpreted the differences in Chronicles within the framework of the Deuteronomistic History rather than within Chronicles itself.[60]

---

the insurrection of Adonijah (1 Kgs 2:28–34)," (*1–2 Samuel*, 501).

58. Ristau, "'In the House of Judah," 145.

59. We are never told the name of Zeruiah's husband. According to the burial notice of Asahel, the youngest of the sons of Zeruiah was buried in his father's tomb in Bethlehem (2 Sam 2:32), clearly positing Zeruiah's husband as being from "a prominent family of Bethlehem," Braun, *1 Chronicles*, 35.

60. Wright, "Innocence of David," 87–105.

However, Amasa's genealogy in 2 Sam 17:25 is an instance where the reverse is true, and the interpretation of the Deuteronomistic History has been unduly influenced by that of Chronicles. As we have seen, the best manuscript evidence does not support reading "Jesse" as the father of Abigail and Zeruiah in 2 Sam 17:25. Furthermore, the internal evidence in Samuel does not support the supposition that Zeruiah was David's sister. Finally, the Chronicler's inclusion of Zeruiah into the genealogy of Jesse fits with the Chronicler's programme of glorifying the house of David and the special choosing of Jesse's house in Chronicles. It is time for scholars to stop reading Zeruiah's Davidic pedigree into Samuel—even if that is what the Chronicler wanted.

In fact, recognizing that the association of the sons of Zeruiah with the Davidic house was a deliberate move by the Chronicler can further help interpreters discern the Chronicler's inclusive view of the postexilic community of Yehud. The Chronicler's inclusive view of Israelite community differs from that of Ezra–Nehemiah, which holds to a more segregated community, excluding northerners and only including Judah as true Israel.[61] As Konkel asserts, "The Chronicler, on the other hand, portrays a spirit of invitation to those outside the boundaries, insisting that they also belong to the community of faith."[62] As many studies have shown, against his *Vorlage* (e.g., 2 Kgs 17), the Chronicler emphasized the non-Israelite status of northerners, depicting them as (at least potentially) true Israelites who can participate in the chosen community (2 Chr 30:1, 8–9).[63] Further, by emphasizing the cultic contributions of the Davidic dynasty, the Chronicler included the entire community in the Davidic covenant, despite the lack of a ruling Davidide, through their participation in the cult.[64]

61. Tino, *King and Temple in Chronicles*, 160–61.

62. Konkel, *1 &2 Chronicles*, 399.

63. As Jonker ("Who Constitutes Society?" 717) writes, "Although a distinction between the south and the north could be made on political grounds, their unity remains a religio-cultic unity." While this call for cultic unity between the north and south in the Chronicler's Hezekiah narrative is significant, I do not hold to Williamson's thesis of a reunited Israel under Hezekiah. See my critique in "Prophecy Influencing History," 146–148.

64. As William Riley (*King and Cultus in Chronicles*, 201) suggests, "The Chronicler placed the dynastic promise into the larger context of the Temple as the major effect of the Davidic covenant, and thus demonstrated through his narrative that the

The Chronicler shows a concern with building up not only the prestige of the house of David but that of the entire Israelite community.[65] As Ristau points out, "The Chr is not only concerned to recast individuals but to recast the entire nation of Israel."[66] While his *Vorlage* excluded Joab from the list of David's mighty men (2 Sam 23:8–39), the Chronicler presented not only David as chosen by Yahweh but the whole household of Jesse (1 Chr 28:4)—and by extension Joab and the sons of Zeruiah—and thereby sought to reshape Yehud's cultural memory of Israelite community, broadening those who are considered part of 'the family of God.'[67]

BIBLIOGRAPHY

Aejmelaeus, Anneli. "The Septuagint of 1 Samuel." In *On the Trail of the Septuagint Translators: Collected Essays*, 131–49. CBET 50. Kampen: Kok Pharos, 1993.

Alter, Robert. *The David Story: A Translation with Commentary of 1 and 2 Samuel*. New York: Norton, 1999.

Bartlett, John R. *Edom and the Edomites*. JSOTSup 77. Sheffield: Sheffield Academic, 1989.

Braun, Roddy. *1 Chronicles*. WBC 14. Waco, TX: Word, 1986.

Dhorme, E. *Les Livres De Samuel*. Ebib. Paris: Lecoffre, 1910.

Driver, S. R. *Notes on the Hebrew Text and the Topography of the Books of Samuel with an Introduction on Hebrew Palaeography and the Ancient Versions and Facsimiles of Inscriptions and Maps*. 2nd ed. Oxford: Clarendon, 1913.

Evans, Mary J. *1 and 2 Samuel*. Nibcot 6. Peabody, MA: Hendrickson, 2000.

Evans, Paul S. *1–2 Samuel*. SOG. Grand Rapids: Zonderan, 2018.

———. "Prophecy Influencing History: Dialogism in the Chronicler's Ahaz Narrative." In *Prophets and Prophecy in Ancient Israelite Historiography*, edited by Mark J. Boda and Lissa Wray Beal, 143–65. Winona Lake, IN: Eisenbrauns, 2013.

---

days of the dynasty had ended while the covenant with David remained."

65. As Knoppers (*1 Chronicles 10–29*, 740) puts it, "If David is idealized in Chronicles, so are the people he leads."

66. Ristau, "In the House of Judah," 147.

67. An earlier version of this paper was originally presented in the Chronicles-Ezra-Nehemiah section at the 2016 Annual Meeting of the Society of Biblical Literature in San Antonio, Texas and I am grateful for the feedback I received from those present that day (including August Konkel).

Gordon, R. P. *I & II Samuel: A Commentary.* Library of Biblical Interpretation. Grand Rapids: Regency Reference Library, 1986.

Hertzberg, Hans Wilhelm. *I & II Samuel: A Commentary.* OTL. Philadelphia: Westminster, 1965.

Japhet, Sara. *I & II Chronicles.* Old Testament Library. Louisville: Westminster John Knox, 1993.

———. *The Ideology of the Book of Chronicles and Its Place in Biblical Thought.* Winona Lake, IN: Eisenbrauns, 2009.

Johnson, Marshall D. *The Purpose of the Biblical Genealogies: With Special Reference to the Setting of the Genealogies of Jesus.* SNTSMS 8. London: Cambridge University Press, 1969.

Jonker, Louis C. "Who Constitutes Society? Yehud's Self-Understanding in the Late Persian Era as Reflected in the Books of Chronicles." *JBL* 127 (2008) 703–24.

Kalluveettil, Paul. *Declaration and Covenant: A Comprehensive Review of Covenant Formulae from the Old Testament and the Ancient Near East.* AnBib 88. Rome: Pontifical Biblical Institute, 1982.

Klein, Ralph W. *1 Chronicles: A Commentary.* Hermeneia. Minneapolis: Fortress, 2006.

Konkel, August H. *1 &2 Chronicles.* BCBC. Harrisonburg, VA: Herald, 2016.

Knoppers, Gary N. *I Chronicles 1–9.* AB 12A. New York: Doubleday, 2004.

———. *I Chronicles 10–29.* AB 12B. New York: Doubleday, 2004.

Levenson, Jon D., and Baruch Halpern. "The Political Import of David's Marriages." *JBL* 99 (1980) 507–18.

Long, V. Philips. "1 Samuel." In *Zondervan Illustrated Bible Backgrounds Commentary: Old Testament: Volume 2, Joshua, Judges, Ruth, 1 and 2 Samuel,* edited by John H. Walton. Zondervan Illustrated Bible Backgrounds Commentary. Grand Rapids: Zondervan, 2009.

Mauchline, John. *1 and 2 Samuel.* NCB. London: Oliphants, 1971.

McCarter, P. Kyle. *II Samuel.* AB 9. Garden City, NY: Doubleday, 1984.

Riley, William. *King and Cultus in Chronicles: Worship and the Reinterpretation of History.* JSOTSup 160. Sheffield: JSOT Press, 1993.

Ristau, Kenneth A. "'In the House of Judah, My Father's House': The Character of Joab in the Book of Chronicles." In *History, Memory, Hebrew Scriptures: A Festschrift for Ehud Ben Zvi,* edited by Ian Douglas Wilson and Diana V. Edelman, 133–51. Winona Lake, IN: Eisenbrauns, 2015.

Smith, Henry Preserved. *A Critical and Exegetical Commentary on the Books of Samuel.* New York: Scribner's Sons, 1904.

Tino, Jozef. *King and Temple in Chronicles.* FRLANT. Göttingen: Vandenhoeck & Ruprecht, 2010.

Tov, Emanuel. "Textual Harmonization in the Stories of the Patriarchs." In *Rewriting and Interpreting the Hebrew Bible: The Biblical Patriarchs in the Light of the Dead Sea Scrolls*, edited by Devorah Dimant and Reinhard G. Kratz, 19–50. Berlin: de Gruyter, 2013.

Wellhausen, Julius. *Der Text Der Bücher Samuelis Untersucht*. Göttingen: Vandenhoeck, 1871.

Wilson, Robert R. *Genealogy and History in the Biblical World*. YNER 7. New Haven: Yale University Press, 1977.

Wright, John W. "The Innocence of David in 1 Chronicles 21." *JSOT* 60 (1993) 87–105.

6

Job Breaks Bad

When God Weighs In

Randall Holm

Do our names define us or do we live into our names? August Konkel is one of those person's that leaves one wondering. As an adjective, "august" according to the *OED* means "inspiring mingled reverence and admiration."[1] And Gus, as August Konkel is affectionately known, certainly reflects this description. When he enters a room, it is akin to someone stepping out of a whirlwind. His booming personality and often raucous laughter invariably fills the room, yet ironically put him in a pulpit and he may set on the listener with nothing but a still small voice barely above a whisper—such is the enigma of August Konkel.

When asked to contribute to a Festschrift in his honor, I knew immediately where to turn my attention. August Konkel is an Old Testament biblical scholar with a speciality in Wisdom Literature. Among his many accomplishments in this field, he is the author of a commentary on Job[2] and the translator of record for the book of Job in the New

---

1. Simpson and Weiner, eds., "August," *OED* 1:785.
2. Konkel and Longman, *Job, Ecclesiastes, Song of Songs*.

Community

Living Bible. And it is to this book of the Bible I dedicate an ode to "Gus."

Rich in prose, Job as a literary work is perhaps unparalleled in its ability to both repel and comfort the reader at the same time. On the one hand, reader beware, Job as a book throws classical theodicy, with its formulaic world of right and wrong, to the wind. On the other hand, reading Job can be liberating if only because it frees one from the cold reductionist world of conventional wisdom where light and darkness are visibly displayed in sharp contrast but generally to the exclusion of any possible shadows. Among other things, Job as a book accompanies readers through their shadowed pain and as such is never outdated. It is perhaps the most ongoing contemporary book in the biblical canon, if by contemporary we mean it deals with the stuff of pain and loss. In the first few pages, fate seems to deal the character[3] Job a series of blows that are incalculable in their weight. In short, Job loses his livelihood, his family, and his health. It is followed by a combative narrative between Job and a set of his so-called "friends" as they attempt to make sense of these tragic events. Are they random? Are they some kind of cosmic punitive action? Are they simply a natural consequence of "reaping what you sow"? Or is it an Olympic like training regimen designed to prepare one for some future task? Of course as readers, we already know that it is none of the above. From the onset, the curtain was pulled back and the reader overhears a conversation that involves a wager between God and the Satan—someone who is clearly not depicted as an outcast but as the Accuser.[4] The subject of the wager is Job himself.

On the surface, the story of Job is deceptively simple in its format. Yahweh is proud of Job for whom he describes as blameless and

---

3. Much has been written about the personhood of Job. Is he modeled after the real life of someone, or is he a character of fiction working much in the same way as a parable? For the purposes of this chapter, it does not really make any difference. Whether understood as a caricature of a real or fictional person, Job is readily identifiable.

4. Much could and has been said about the "wager" between God and "the Satan." At first blush the narrative resembles more Greek mythology than biblical narrative with gods duking it out to the detriment of unwitting humans below. In any event, the why of this question is a separate matter from the purposes of this chapter.

upright. Job seems to be a poster child for living and enjoying the good life. Not so fast, however, says the Accuser, Job's faith is not disinterested. He serves at Yahweh's good pleasure only because Yahweh blesses him—a hallmark of conventional wisdom. We should not, therefore, be surprised at Job's wealth, attests the Accuser. Yahweh blesses good people. But wait, ponders the Satan. "Yahweh are you now not caught in a problem of Your own making? Would Job remain upright if he didn't get anything in return? Put Job to the test, remove his wealth, his health, his livelihood and then see if he will maintain his integrity before you, O Yahweh."

Of course, neither Job nor his so-called friends who show up later to offer counsel have this reader's birds-eye view of this cosmic drama unfolding. They are all left on their own with limited resources to make sense of Job's sudden change of circumstances. In this case, their resources consisted of a long established tradition of adhering to the conventional theodic script of their time: "Good things happen to good people and bad things happen to bad people." God is never mocked. In time the wicked will be paid in misery for their misdeeds. God's ways are wider, higher, and deeper than we can possibly imagine. Everything happens for a reason. God does not wish evil on anyone unless someone truly deserves it. And by implication if bad things happen to someone, it is likely that that said person did something to merit those dire consequences. The only room for an exception clause would be if the hardship was a tool to teach and train for a future task.

From the view of those living the good life all this sounds good and reasonable. "It works because it is true, it is true because it works."[5] If and when, however, the algorithm of this accepted logic unravels, as it always does at some point in time, there was little recourse for its victims. In the case of Job, he may have claimed innocence of any wrongdoing or at least any wrongdoing that merited what he suffered, but what could he offer to the contrary? The fact was, his livelihood, family, and health were in ruin. God had abandoned him, and God never abandons the just. But Job knows what he knows. He is innocent and in no way deserves his fate. Neither will Job languish in the ashes of his life; he is determined to find a way through this valley of the

---

5. James, *Pragmatism*, 29.

shadow of death even if he has to "break bad" from his friends, from the theological conventions he has built his life upon, or even from God himself.

"Breaking Bad" is the title of a highly acclaimed five-year television series, which chronicles the life of a fictional character named Walter White. White, a middle American chemistry high-school teacher whose life spirals downhill when he discovers he has IIIA lung cancer, is almost Jobesque in his sudden demise. In addition to his cancer and that he does not have the resources to pay for treatment, his wife is pregnant and he has a son with cerebral palsy. Presumably up to this point, White played by conventional rules. When income was scarce, he picked up a second job working in a car wash. He worked hard but it was never sufficient to keep up with mounting bills. So White "breaks bad." In his case, breaking bad meant abandoning legal conventions and using his skills as a chemist to begin a double life as a meth dealer and supplier.[6]

Like Job, White is clearly a conflicted character and many would object making any comparison between White and the biblical character Job. Nowhere is White described like Job as a man who was "blameless and upright, who feared God and turned away from evil" (Job 1:1). Even so we might wonder why Walter is given the family name "White" as opposed to perhaps, "Black" or some other name. While the audience knows nothing about Walter White before episode one, we have no reason to believe his moral slate is not clean. And like Job, the circumstances behind his decision to "break bad" were not entirely of his making. White's fate may not have been the result of a cosmic wager, but it was very much the result of a broken social net combined with some simple bad luck.

From the viewer's perspective, the only thing left was to wonder how far White would go to save himself and his family from ruin. And after five seasons, sixty-two episodes, it became apparent he was willing to go as far as it took, even if it involved murder. In the end, White is shot and left dying on a concrete floor straddling a line embedded on the surface. It is as if we the viewers are left to decide on which side

6. Ironically, in the fifth season the viewer is left to conclude White has died of a gunshot wound not cancer. Of course, in Hollywood anything is possible.

of the line he belongs. Was White really a good person who went bad because of his ill-fated circumstances or was he always a bad person who when pushed by circumstances was outed for the evil person he really was? Or to put it in Job-like terms, was the pre-breaking bad White a law-abiding hardworking father, husband, and teacher in a local high school because the "work of his hands were blessed"? And if so, would he remain committed to this genteel path if circumstances were to change? For White, white faded into black as he set out to forge his own justice on earth in contrast to Job, whose struggle was to find justice in heaven.

Nonetheless, a sober reflection on the paths taken by both Job and White would certainly seem to favor Job over White. People also die in the book of Job but not at the hand of Job; we can blame God and the Satan for that. No, Job's crime is theological in nature. He calls into question the integrity and justice of God, who put him in this circumstance. In one of his many soliloquies, Job lashes out:

> Know then that God has put me in the wrong,
>   And closed his net around me,
> Even when I cry out, 'Violence!" I am not answered;
>   I call aloud, but there is not justice
> He has walled up my way so that I cannot pass,
>   And he has set darkness upon my paths
> He has stripped my glory from me,
>   And taken the crown from my head
> He breaks me down on every side, and I am gone
>   He has uprooted my hope like a tree
> He has kindled his wrath against me,
>   And counts me as his adversary.
> His troops come on together;
>   They have thrown up siegeworks against me,
> and encamp around my tent. (19:6–12 NRSV)

In a secular age, these words may simply reflect the anguished rant of an afflicted person with little moral value. To the secularist, the answer to the proverbial question "why me?" is the oft repeated response, "Why not?" Stuff happens. Anything else is dismissed as the talk of superstition. In biblical times, to speak against the wisdom of God was

Community

a pernicious act of the first order. The "fear of God is the beginning of wisdom" (Prov 1:7) was the common adage of the day. To question this was testament of someone without sense. Pay attention, Wisdom said, in the day of Job: "Think now, who that was innocent ever perished? Or where were the upright ever cut off. As I have seen, those who plow iniquity and sow trouble reap the same?" (Job 4:7–8). In this world of conventional wisdom, there is no need for statistics to demonstrate plausibility; experience and common sense are enough to rule out any objections.

Undergirding this spirit of conventional wisdom was the moral code that "everything happens for a reason."[7] Accordingly, in this world, the DNA of the cosmos is built on timeless laws of causal expectations. They may or may not be understood or appreciated but many uphold they are absolute in their integrity without which the cosmos itself would return to the chaos of Gen 1:2. And here Job and White part company. They may both begin their plight in an aura of innocence but White's lawless rebellion follows the conventional line and his story ends in his death—the ultimate price for disregarding convention. And here there is an inescapable irony, while White "breaks bad," the show itself never really "breaks bad" from the conventional wisdom script with its tools of rewards, punishments, hierarchies, and boundaries.

In the grand economy of conventional wisdom, God always remains just and good even in the face of individual suffering or death. Nothing is arbitrary; if ruin befalls a good person, the question who moved is acknowledged without asking: the answer is always the person. God is good all the time, all the time God is good. Here there is little or no room for nuance. In other words, there is no real sense in which we can measure God according to some standard of justice.[8]

---

7. For a sobering review of such logic, read Bowler, *Everything Happens for a Reason and Other Lies I've Loved*. Bowler is a young mother and Church History Professor at Duke University. She is also a survivor who has an incurable form of cancer. Her own Jobesque story is one of wisdom, heartache, and courage.

8. In a public presentation I made on the subject of abortion, I pointed out that the Bible itself does not speak to the issue of abortion nor does it directly speak to the question when a fetus becomes "human." To the objection of those who would look to passages such as Jer 1:5 ("before I formed you in the womb I knew you . . . "), I pointed out that we are dealing with poetry and need to be careful how literally we work such passages. For example, in this case if we push personhood before even

Certainly there is much to be gained by conventional wisdom. It plays a central role in the biblical tradition of Proverbs and much of Psalms[9] for good reason. Because, who does not want to cheer for conventional wisdom? We are essentially in control of our own destiny. Put in the hard work. Love God with all your heart and mind (Deut 6:5). Love your neighbor as yourself (Lev 19:18), and the good life awaits.[10] And for the curious who want answers, Lady Wisdom might even say, "Forget the reasons, they are above your earthly pay grade. Even if the curtain is pulled back and you got a glimpse behind the heavens and witness the cryptic exchange between the Satan and God you will be no closer to understanding what is happening."

Then there is Job, certainly a counter-testimony to Proverbs.[11] While Job as a book and person stops short of completely deconstructing conventional wisdom, this witness concludes such wisdom is never the last word. To wit there is not always a reason or solution for everything.

Job breaks bad with conventional wisdom and its temporal retribution. He rages against the establishment. He pleads his innocence. To the affirmation everything happens for a reason, Job complains and asks why should God even care what happens to anyone (7:20). Life is miserable and brief. Suffering is part of life. It befalls the wicked and the innocent. Can anyone tell me, asks Job, "What I have done then I will be quiet" (6:24). But of course, in the silence of God, Job will not stay quiet. Job may have resigned himself to God's absolute power to the contrary, that God does not need to justify God's actions. Job claims

---

conception this raises all kinds of problems with natural miscarriages. At least one person objected with my reasoning and retorted with no trace of ambiguity, "If God wants to abort babies via miscarriages, then that is God's business; in no way does that make God unjust."

9. Since the publication of Brueggemann's *The Message of the Psalms: A Theological Commentary* in 1984, his literary analysis of the Psalms as orientation, disorientation, and new orientation has become a standard for study.

10. See also Matt 22:37–40.

11. Teaching biblical wisdom literature in the classroom, I thematically review the traditional Wisdom collection of Job, Proverbs, Ecclesiastes, and Song of Songs under the theme of theodicy, where Job is theodic protest, Proverbs is theodic convention, Ecclesiastes is theodic skepticism, and the Song of Songs represents theodic romance.

that is precisely why if God is the God of redemption; God can act from a place of compassion instead of judgment.

In the book of Job, it is sometimes difficult to know who is on trial in this drama. Is it Job, the victim whose loyalties to the infinite are being constantly tested? Is it his hapless friends who must decide if they will stand by their companion at the cost of letting go of their carefully structured theologies? Is it conventional wisdom itself with its promise of the good life for those who play by the rules? Is it God who seems to turn aside from Job so easily to satisfy some sort of celestial bet at the behest of the Adversary? Or is it some combination of all of the above?

The one constant is that the allegiances of the reader never sway from Job. As readers, we are hooked on Job. He is the victim from the beginning to the end of the narrative. Even in his desperate outbursts directed at his friends and God, readers cannot help but cheer him on. Job, ever the underdog, never betrays the readers' sympathies. Readers may cringe at some of Job's more egregious pronouncements directed at God but their solidarity with him seldom wanes. Job's questions and judgments are the stuff of every person who through circumstances has ceased to believe in the adage "everything happens for a reason."

Much ado has been made of the fact that through the narration Job shows glimpses of creative faith. He claims there is a redeemer who can vindicate his faithfulness. He demands a trial where he can plead his case in all honesty, because he holds onto the truth that he has a witness that will plead his innocence. Unlike our hapless contemporary counterpart White, we are given ample room to cheer on Job even in the midst of his flailing questions and fits of anger and despair. But ultimately his telos is vindication not new beginnings. And vindication he receives as God praises Job for the truth he has spoken (Job 42:7, 8).

I confess, at the best of times, commentaries can be annoying. They resemble too closely the annoying friend who invites you to a baseball game only to spend the rest of the evening explaining why the players are running around the bases. In his commentary on Job, August Konkel resists this pedantic temptation, by remaining true to his own personality and at times stepping out of the whirlwind with prose meant more to inspire and provoke than instruct. And maybe that is the best one can hope for from a book like Job.

And so it is fitting at the end of this chapter to cede to Konkel's voice as he put his own stamp on this majestic tome by reflecting on God's final response to Job from out of the whirlwind:

> The final speech of God is the culmination of the argument that the universe was not created for human wishes to govern the way in which it operates. People must rethink the outrage they feel at the things they perceive to be out of order. The world is an immense arena of power and beauty amidst awesome, warring forces. The world is permeated with the order of divine providence, but it presents to humans a "welter of contradictions, dizzying variety, energies, and entities that man cannot take in."[12] This realization makes the fact that God spoke to Job and confronted him even more remarkable. God asked Job who would dare to stand before him (41:10). According to the prologue, the members of the heavenly court do so, but according to the divine speech, it is also the one whom God favors, such as Job. The pulsating life of the cosmos was his heritage, even though he was unable to comprehend it any more than he could follow the foaming wake of Leviathan as it churched the water into a boiling cauldron. The grandeur of creation is the place where mortals meet God. The home of humans displays the face of a foreign and fascinating divinity. They cannot understand his creation, much less his divine nature. Rather than challenge what they do not know about themselves in their world, they are invited to live in its mystery and to know they stand before its Creator.[13]

BIBLIOGRAPHY

Alter, Robert. "The Voice from the Whirlwind." *Commentary* 77 (1984) 33–41.

Bowler, Kate, *Everything Happens for a Reason and Other Lies I've Loved*. New York: Random House, 2018.

Brueggemann, Walter. *The Message of the Psalms: A Theological Commentary*. Minneapolis: Augsburg Fortress, 1984.

---

12. Alter, "The Voice from the Whirlwind," 41.
13. Konkel and Longman, *Job, Ecclesiastes, Song of Songs*, 237.

James, William. *Pragmatism: A New Name for Some Old Ways of Thinking.* Cambridge: Harvard University Press, 1978.

Konkel, August H., and Tremper Longman III. *Job, Ecclesiastes, Song of Songs.* TOTC. Carol Stream, IL: Tyndale House, 2006.

7

Babylon in the Book of Isaiah

H. G. M. Williamson

Most of the great ancient Near Eastern (ANE) empires featur[e] in the book of Isaiah and recent studies at both the historical and the post-colonial levels have given this matter careful attention.[1] In two recent articles I have already given consideration to two of these—Assyria and Egypt.[2] It therefore seems appropriate now to explore whether a third, Babylon, fits into a pattern I have detected in the first two instances. There seems in each case to be a movement through the long history of the composition of the book from a purely historical application of the name of the empire to a more typological or paradigmatic use in later passages, which were probably written long after the time of Isaiah of Jerusalem himself. This is helpful for hermeneutics, of course, and it leads directly into application in the modern world. I trust it will therefore be of interest to Gus Konkel, who has set us such a good example of the combination of solid historical-critical analysis

---

1. Suffice to mention as very recent examples the collection of articles in Abernethy et al., *Isaiah and Imperial Context*, and Aster, *Reflections of Empire in Isaiah 1–39*.

2. See Williamson, "The Evil Empire"; Williamson, "Egypt in the Book of Isaiah."

COMMUNITY

of the biblical text with a concern to apply it appropriately in today's church.[3]

The name Babylon occurs a total of thirteen times in the book, considerably less, therefore, than the forty-four references to Assyria and forty-nine references to Egypt. This may be partly explained as being a reflection of the fact that, unlike in the case of Assyria and Egypt, Babylon did not have much in the way of direct dealings with Judah during Isaiah's lifetime. Indeed, it is noteworthy that there are no less than four occurrences in the short chapter (only eight verses) which includes the only record of such direct contact, namely Isa 39. Despite this, the significance of the role of Babylon in the book as a whole can scarcely be exaggerated.

In a number of passages Babylon stands in parallel with "the Chaldeans," a gentilic referring to the inhabitants of the southern Mesopotamian region.[4] I shall therefore not comment separately on the latter's occurrence in those passages (13:19; 43:14; 47:1; 48:14, 20; although it occurs on its own at 47:5, that follows directly from its use where it is again parallel with Babylon in 47:1). Thus the only place where it occurs in the book of Isaiah without a direct parallel with Babylon is at 23:13, an extremely interesting verse in its own right, not least because it looks like an added comment at the end of the oracles against the nations just as the reference to Babylon opens them, but one which I regret I do not have the space to deal with in the present study.

As has already been noted by Begg in his brief but workmanlike study of our theme,[5] the thirteen references to Babylon are clustered

---

3. I recall with great pleasure how Gus worked with me long ago on an aspect of Isaiah research during a year of study leave in Cambridge; see his article on "The Sources of the Story of Hezekiah," 462-82, for the result. I am delighted to have this opportunity of renewing our collaborative friendship by way of a further article on Isaiah.

4. See Frame, *Babylonia 689-627 B.C.*, 36-43. Only later (e.g., in Daniel) did it develop the narrower sense of Babylonian sages.

5. Begg, "Babylon in the Book of Isaiah," 121-25. It may be appropriate to mention here also two other treatments of our theme: Franke focuses mainly on Isa 14 and 47 in "Reversals of Fortune in the Ancient Near East," 104-23. A much more extended treatment of some aspects of the topic than can be offered here, and that within the context of a study of this theme within the Bible as a whole, may be found in Sals, *"Hure Babylon"*; she analyzes some of the relevant passages in Isaiah on pp.

in three distinct sections of the book, namely (i) the oracles against the nations in chs. 13–23 (twice in ch. 13, twice in ch. 14, and once in ch. 21); (ii) in ch. 39, as already noted (four times); and (iii) in chs. 40–48 (four times). In looking at each group an obvious difference immediately becomes evident between uses of the name embedded within the original text itself and uses which are self-evidently editorial in some manner—in a literary heading, for instance. These latter are concentrated in chs. 13–14, and since these come first in the book Begg understandably begins his analysis there. My more diachronically determined purpose, however, suggests that we should start elsewhere, namely in chs. 40–48.

The Hebrew text of the first occurrence in 43:14 is undoubtedly difficult and almost certainly corrupt. Without entering into the detail of a text-critical discussion here I believe that the NRSV provides a good approximation:

> Thus says the LORD,
> Your Redeemer, the Holy One of Israel:
> For your sake I will send to Babylon
> and break down all the bars,
> and the shouting of the Chaldeans will be turned to lamentation.[6]

This verse comes as part of an extremely short and, therefore, perhaps accidentally truncated oracle of salvation (43:14–15). All we can conclude from it is that the addressees, the devotees of the Holy One of Israel, their creator and king (v. 15), will be redeemed by his action

---

213–330.

6. The second line of the triplet was clearly a source of difficulty even in antiquity, as the variety of renderings in the versions shows; see Goldingay and Payne, *A Critical and Exegetical Commentary on Isaiah 40–55*, 1, 295. The NRSV's rendering is possible, though it glosses over a grammatical awkwardness by collocating "all of them" with a preceding anarthrous form and it also fails to explain the present unexpected word order. Elliger attempts to defend all this, but the only one of the analogies he cites to offer any substantial support is Ps 67:4; see Elliger, *Deuterojesaja* 1, 337; personally, I prefer the conjectural emendation to "the bars of your prison," though this is admittedly far from certain. For the last line, NRSV is certainly right to follow the very widely adopted slight revocalization against MT "and Chaldeans, in the boats their ringing cry"; see already Hitzig, *Der Prophet Jesaja*, 503, and Ewald, *Die Propheten des Alten Bundes*, 424.

against Babylon and its inhabitants, the Chaldeans. It may be deduced, therefore, that Babylon is depicted as an oppressive power whose hegemony is nevertheless time-limited. The object of the verb "send" is not expressed, so that for the moment we remain ignorant of the human agent of God's purposes, as is also formally the case in 41:2-3 and 25. The closely related opening verses of ch. 45, of course, will clarify that it is Cyrus who is in view. There may thus be seen to be something of a developing picture building towards a climax in these chapters.

The second reference to Babylon in this part of Isaiah (47:1), comes beyond that particular climax and introduces a mocking taunt. Though characterized by a tight poetic syntax, the verse is more or less free of any serious textual problems.[7] The NRSV renders:

> Come down and sit in the dust,
>   virgin daughter Babylon!
> Sit on the ground without a throne,
>   daughter Chaldea!
> For you shall no more be called
>   tender and delicate.

This verse introduces a lengthy passage which differs in some respects from its wider setting in Isa 40–48, principally that it devotes extended attention to a foreign power.[8] In this respect it has sometimes been compared more with chs. 13, 14, and 21 (to which we shall return, of course) as well as with Jer 50–51.[9] For our present purpose, its significance is less in the use of the qualifier "virgin daughter," which is often used for a capital city experiencing disaster,[10] as an introduction

---

7. In addition to the commentaries, see especially Franke, *Isaiah 46, 47, and 48*, 104–12, and Franke, "The Function of the Satiric Lament," 408–18; Vanderhooft, *The Neo-Babylonian Empire*, 181–88.

8. For a strong argument that despite this distinction it is nevertheless to be read as an integral element in the triptych of chs. 46, 47, and 48, see Berges, *Jesaja 40–48*, 442–43, 478. These two observations are not, of course, mutually exclusive; cf. Sals, "Hure Babylon," 292–97.

9. See, for instance, Martin-Achard, "Esaïe 47 et la tradition prophétique sur Babylone," 83–105; Goldingay, *The Message of Isaiah 40–55*, 315–19.

10. For a full recent survey of previous work on this expression (as well as of "daughter X" such as we find in the following line), see Kartveit, *Rejoice, Dear Zion!*. I presented my own analysis of "daughter X" in *A Critical and Exegetical Commentary*

of the theme of reversal of fortune which continues through much of the subsequent poem. This is most immediately obvious in the contrast between sitting enthroned as the "mistress of kingdoms" (v. 5) and sitting in the dust on the ground. It continues, furthermore, in the last line of the verse, evoking the genteel and socially elite lifestyle of Babylon with the experience she is doomed to anticipate as a working girl, stripped of her fine clothing in order to sweat at grinding corn by the manipulation of a heavy millstone (vv. 2–3).

It has often been said that the complete destruction of Babylon and its inhabitants envisaged in this chapter so exceeds the reality of the way Cyrus eventually entered Babylon that it must pre-date the events it predicts.[11] This stark presentation is undoubtedly exaggerated, since in fact the chapter envisages the continuing existence of Babylon, albeit in a much reduced state; we should therefore be careful not to overemphasize the historical discrepancy.[12] Nevertheless the style of presentation seems to join it closely with 43:14 and its link with the opening verses of ch. 45, noted above. The tension between prediction and reality was not lost on readers in antiquity and has been held to explain the conflict within 45:1–2 over the nature of the fall of Babylon, the last line of 45:1 being perhaps a later addition to soften the implication of the surrounding lines of a violent and destructive entry.[13] Regardless of the precise date of the passage, however, it is not difficult to see how Isa 47 may be read in narrative sequence from 43:14: Israel's oppressor is herself to become the object of humiliation.

Isaiah 48:14 is another verse with some textual difficulties.[14] As they do not really affect the points of relevance for our immediate purpose, I shall not discuss them further here, however. Omitting the first line, the NRSV reads as follows:

---

on Isaiah 1–27, 1:67–70, with an update in 2:612–14.

11. See, for instance, Whybray, *Isaiah 40–66*, 118–19.

12. So correctly Sals, *"Hure Babylon,"* 299.

13. See my previous discussion in "The Setting of Deutero-Isaiah: Some Linguistic Considerations," 253–67 (259), with reference back to Kratz, *Kyros im Deuterojesaja-Buch*, 26.

14. See Hermisson, *Deuterojesaja*, 255–56 and 275–76, and Goldingay and Payne, *Isaiah 40–55*, 2:139–41.

> the LORD loves him;
> he shall perform his purpose on Babylon,
> and his arm shall be against the Chaldeans.

There is no antecedent in the text to identify the "him" whom the LORD loves, but there can be little doubt that it is again Cyrus who is in mind. Verse 15 immediately following gives this supposition very strong support; see, for instance, how it echoes 46:11 and less fully 41:25 and 45:4. It is noteworthy that, as in chs. 41 and 43 already noted, the poet is hesitant about naming him. Explanations that it might have been dangerous to do so in the prevailing political situation are not entirely convincing as otherwise it becomes difficult to account for the clear references in 44:28 and 45:1. While the immediate historical reason for this reticence is uncertain, there may well be reasons furnished by the wider literary context of the book of Isaiah as a whole which could help us in a more canonically orientated interpretation; our later discussion may help offer some explanation for this, therefore. For the moment it is enough to note the emphasis that whatever "he" does is only at God's behest; the wider context of these verses focuses emphatically on God as the one who takes the initiative and whose purposes are served by his human agent; v. 15 is again important as drawing out that implication from v. 14.

From this summarizing indication that Babylon will indeed be subject to God's purpose as outlined, among other passages, in the verses already considered, we reach finally the conclusion of this whole portion of Isaiah (Isa 40–48) with the climactic imperative in 48:20:

> Go out from Babylon, flee from Chaldea,
>   declare this with a shout of joy, proclaim it,
> send it forth to the end of the earth;
>   say, 'The LORD has redeemed his servant Jacob.'

We note at once that this emphasis on redemption makes a link back to the first of our verses, 43:14. Second, there is another link in that the shouts of joy by the Babylonians which will be turned to lamentation will here be transformed into Jacob's shout of joy (the same noun is used in each verse). The chief new element here, of course, is that for the first time in relation to a reference to Babylon the community of God's people is directly addressed and with a command to leave Babylon at that. To the extent that we have noticed a narrative thread through these verses it is clear that this is the conclusion: the Babylon whose downfall has been anticipated, whose humiliation has been envisaged, and whose final end has been assured is now no longer the place where God's people should remain.[15] Their departure has universal ramifications in that God's deliverance will be proclaimed worldwide. It brings a major section of the book to a close just as 52:11–12 does with a comparable imperative ("depart, depart, go out from there!") before the coda introduced at 52:13.[16]

In sum, the four references to Babylon in Isa 40–48 clearly reflect the historical circumstances of the Neo-Babylonian or exilic age. Babylon's fall is anticipated and the exiles are urged at the end to leave the city, so suggesting that in most if not all cases Cyrus has not yet entered Babylon. There is a reluctance here to refer to Cyrus by name, but apart from that the passages seem to be well earthed even if their hopes turned out eventually to be rather higher than the realities which followed in the Persian period. Babylon is a dominant, if not oppressive, power, but that will shortly come to an end.

Moving back through the book, we come next to consider the four references to Babylon in Isa 39. This brief chapter concludes the four that have a close parallel in 2 Kgs 18–20 and the text of our chapter is very close to that in 2 Kgs 20:12–19.[17] The composition of this section of the book of Isaiah and its relation to the parallel in Kings has been much discussed, and I have summarized that debate and sought to lay out reasons for my own position elsewhere.[18] Fortunately we can sit

---

15. Note the allusive nature of part of the description here as discussed in Halvorson-Taylor, *Enduring Exile*, 110–19.

16. That Isa 40–48 should certainly be treated as in some significant way different from 49–55 is now widely recognized. Of course there are important connections between the two sections, but that should not blind us into overlooking the distinctions, one of the more significant recent developments in the study of this portion of the book of Isaiah as a whole. For a brief outline of this case, see Berges, *Das Buch Jesaja*, 325–33 (ET, *The Book of Isaiah*, 303–11); Blenkinsopp, *Isaiah 40–55*, 59–61.

17. For synoptic presentations, with the differences highlighted, see Bendavid, *Parallels in the Bible*, 150–51; Wildberger, *Jesaja*, 3: *Jesaja 28–39*, 1494–95 (ET, *Isaiah 28–39*, 492–93).

18. *The Book Called Isaiah*, 189–211.

somewhat loose to many of the questions raised provided we are willing to accept, as I argued in line with the vast majority of scholars, that these chapters were not originally written for their present position in the book of Isaiah but have been incorporated here from somewhere else, whether that be the Books of Kings themselves or some form of sources on which both Kings and Isaiah depend.

Because it looks as though the order of events in 2 Kgs 18–20 may have been manipulated for purposes other than those of strict historical sequencing and because the result is for the collection of narratives to conclude with a reference to Babylon and, indeed, to the anticipation of exile there, it has occasionally been suggested that Isa 39 was first composed for, or at least moved to, its present position in Isaiah precisely so as to serve as a transition passage from the eighth-century setting presupposed in the first part of the book to the Babylonian setting in the chapters which follow.[19]

Several related points need to be made here, however. First, the link is worth observing but hardly so ideal as to support the view that the chapter was written explicitly to serve this purpose. As follows appropriately from the first part of the narrative, the prediction of exile relates only to Hezekiah's royal wealth and his own sons. Neither subject interests the author of the following chapters. Had Isa 39 been written explicitly to forge a connection with what follows, it would surely have focused rather on the people, whether as Jacob/Israel or as Zion, who are the subject of attention there.[20] Second, several studies have made the converse case that the strange order of the material in these chapters relates more to the concerns of the Deuteronomic Historian than to the author(s) of Isaiah so that there is no need to posit a different composition scenario in regard to this chapter than to the remainder

---

19. See, for instance, Groves, *Actualization and Interpretation in the Old Testament*, 191–201; Smelik, "Distortion of Old Testament Prophecy," 70–93. The stimulus of earlier work by Ackroyd on this material should be acknowledged even though his insights have been developed beyond anything he himself intended; see especially "An Interpretation of the Babylonian Exile," 329–52, and "Isaiah 36–39: Structure and Function," 3–21.

20. See Davies, "The Destiny of the Nations in the Book of Isaiah," 93–120 (esp. 102).

of chs. 36–39.[21] And finally—and most crucially for our present concern—the theory itself presupposes that part, at least, of chs. 1–35 and of chs. 40–66 already existed in their present setting so as to require that a connection was considered desirable. Given that, a position with which I very readily agree, there is no reason why we should not arrive at the easier conclusion that an editor used material that could usefully serve as a join (even if not perfect) than that he wrote this material specially for its present setting. In other words the suitability of references to Babylon at this point need not in any way be denied but that does not mean that we should extend this observation to introduce any further implausible hypothesis to explain what we have.

The upshot of these remarks is that the concentration of references to Babylon in Isa 39 needs to be explained at two levels. On the one hand, the original author of the material, whoever he was, used it in a simple historical sense to refer to the Babylon of the late eighth century. It was not the dominant power in the region at that time even though it often vied with the major imperial power of Assyria. A much later redactor of Isaiah, however, incorporated this chapter along with those which precede it for a variety of reasons, only one of which was to point the way forward to the Babylon of chs. 40–48.[22] At this stage of our inquiry, therefore, we may put it rather in the same line as those passages already studied in the second part of the book. The minor eighth-century power of Babylon in ch. 39 becomes the major oppressive power of the sixth-century Neo-Babylonian empire in the later chapters. But both are firmly located in the historical arena.

If we move back now to the cluster of four references to Babylon in Isa 13–14 we find ourselves in a very different situation. Only one of them is properly embedded in the main text, the other three all being in headings or a conclusion as framing elements. This is quite obvious in the case of 13:1, "An oracle concerning Babylon which Isaiah the son of Amoz saw." This form of heading is verbally close to what

---

21. See, for instance, Clements, *Isaiah and the Deliverance of Jerusalem*, 66–71; Clements, *Jerusalem and the Nations*, 120–27; Seitz, *Zion's Final Destiny*, 182–91.

22. I need not repeat the arguments advanced in *The Book Called Isaiah*, 209–11, for the suggestion that chs. 36–39 were added as late as the final redactional shaping of 40–66. See more recently with a similar conclusion Berges, *Das Buch Jesaja*, 314–21 (ET, *The Book of Isaiah*, 292–99); Stromberg, *Isaiah After Exile*, 205–22.

we find in 1:1 and 2:1 except that Babylon now stands in the place of "Judah and Jerusalem," appropriate to the shift of attention to the first of the oracles against the nations which follow. Similarly the poem in 14:4b–21, which makes no reference to Babylon or indeed any other country as the focus of its rhetoric, is introduced by a heading that concludes the prose section of vv. 1–4a with the words "you will take up this taunt against the king of Babylon." Similarly, at the end there are two verses which are clearly not part of the main poem (note especially the formula, "oracle of the Lord [of hosts]" which occurs twice in v. 22 and once in v. 23) and which mark a shift from a poem directed against an individual hubristic oppressor to an application to the collective population of Babylon: "I will rise against them . . . and will cut off from Babylon name and remnant, offspring and posterity." Self-evidently, therefore, the main part of ch. 14 is now introduced and concluded by an application to Babylon, something of which the poem itself gives us no clue.

All this means that it is only in 13:19 that we find a reference to Babylon that is properly embedded in either of the two poems that comprise the bulk of chs. 13 and 14:

> And Babylon, the most renowned of the kingdoms,
>   the glorious pride of the Chaldeans,
> will be like God's overthrow
>   of Sodom and Gomorrah.

Furthermore, this predicted overthrow is said in vv. 17–18 to be expected as a result of an invasion by the Medes:

> Now look, I am on the point of stirring up the Medes against them
> —they give no consideration to silver,
>   nor do they take any particular pleasure in gold.
> . . . . . .
> They will have no mercy on the fruit of the womb,
>   nor will their eye look with any pity on the children.[23]

---

23. The translation of these three verses is my own. While mostly free of difficulties, the first line of v. 18 is very obscure ("and bows will dash young men in pieces") and has aroused a great deal of discussion. After considering all the options, I have reached the conclusion that the words are probably misplaced here. I suspect it is too

The poet clearly anticipated, therefore, that Babylon would be overthrown by the Medes.[24] How should this be explained historically? In the first place, we should note that the Medes are not often mentioned in the Hebrew Bible (they appear most frequently in Esther; of potentially greater relevance to the occurrence here, see Isa 21:2; 2 Kgs 17:6; 18:11; Jer 25:25; 51:11, 28). Their territory was located to the southwest of the Caspian Sea on the eastern side of the Zagros Mountains. Their principal city was Ecbatana (modern Hamadan). The history of Media is not always known as well as we might wish, as it has to be put together from sources that refer to the country or region rather than from any native texts. Furthermore, archaeological research is not as advanced as in some other parts of the near East.[25] In the first part of the first millennium BCE there was not so much a single Median state as several tribal groups among a number of others of different origins. In the eighth century, the Assyrian Tiglath-pileser III and then several of his successors came to dominate the region by force, their direct impact varying somewhat according to the specifics of region and tribal affiliation. It is thus not surprising to find that on the one hand this tended to draw the Median groups closer together with each other and on the other that they came to be one of the standard eastern opponents of Assyria. Thus by the end of the period of the Neo-Assyrian

---

much of a coincidence that the rare verb "dash in pieces" occurs twice in the same passage, once (v. 16) in a regular manner and once (the present verse) in a manner which has no parallel. Furthermore, we have a reference to falling by the sword at the very end of v. 15, which might make for some sort of a link with the bows of the present verse. Finally, the "young men" here could as well belong with the list of types of people in vv. 15–16 as with the continuation of the present verse. Line lengths in v. 16 are also slightly irregular. I am therefore tempted to think that our half line may be a garbled and misplaced part of/marginal correction of/comment on that earlier passage, but its precise original form is far beyond our recall. Certainly, the flow from v. 17b to 18b is much smoother without it (note especially the unchanging subject of the plural verbs).

24. It may be added here that a similar scenario lies behind the prediction in 21:9 that "fallen, fallen is Babylon," with the one difference that there Elam is included with Media as the destroying agent (21:2; Elam is mentioned elsewhere in Isaiah only at 11:11 and 22:6). Space precludes a thorough study of this puzzling chapter here, but so far as the single reference to Babylon is concerned it seems to belong quite closely with, though probably a bit earlier than, the primary layer in ch. 13.

25. For surveys with further references, see Diakonoff, "Media," 36–148; Kuhrt, *Ancient Near East*, 652–61.

empire they were in some form of alliance with the Babylonians and they participated actively in Assyria's eventual downfall. It is during the following decades that Median power was at its height, as attested by Herodotus, the details of whose account are fiercely contested, however. The last of the main kings, Astyages, was related through his daughter to Cyrus, the rising king of neighboring Persia. In 550 BCE, Cyrus overthrew Astyages, who had initially attacked him, and Media became part of the rapidly rising Persian or Achaemenid Empire the following year with the fall of Ecbatana. And as we have already seen earlier it was Cyrus the Persian, of course, who took Babylon in 539 as a further major step in his imperial progress.

It follows from this brief account that Isa 13:17–19 cannot refer to events in the eighth-century lifetime of Isaiah himself, for the Medes and Babylonians were both subject to Assyria at the time and came to have close relations in their resistance to it.[26] Equally, however, it is difficult to see how this prophecy could be a *vaticinium ex eventu*, since it was to the Persians, not the Medes, that Babylon eventually fell.[27] These considerations suggest a time of composition when Media was at the height of its power, namely shortly before (or a little after if the news took time to travel) 549 BCE, the year in which Media fell to Cyrus.

This conclusion receives further support from the fact that, contrary to the prediction in v. 19, Babylon was not completely overthrown and destroyed, as comparison with the "overthrow of Sodom and Gomorrah" implies (according to the similar reference in 1:9 the suggestion is that there will not even be so much as a remnant left).

---

26. Contrast, for instance, with varying attempts to circumvent the obvious difficulties: Kissane, *The Book of Isaiah*, 155–56 (who thought that Babylon had been substituted for an original Assyria); Erlandsson, *The Burden of Babylon* (for specific criticism of whom see Hom, *The Characterization of the Assyrians in Isaiah*, 55–60); Oswalt, *The Book of Isaiah Chapters 1–39*, 300–301, 307–9; Krause, "Historical Selectivity," 175–212; Heater, "Do the Prophets Teach," 23–43; Smith, *Isaiah 1–39*, 293–94, 304–5. The suggestion that the reference here is to some Medes who had been "incorporated into the Assyrian military" (as mercenaries?), as suggested by Hayes and Irvine, *Isaiah, the Eighth-Century Prophet*, 222–23, is completely contradictory to the obvious sense of the first line of v. 17.

27. I cannot take seriously as influencing the present verse such considerations as that in Esther the Medes and Persians are often mentioned together or the fact that in Dan 11:1 there is a reference to Darius the Mede.

Historically Babylon was not finally destroyed in this way during the biblical period.[28] Although there is some possible evidence that there was an element of conflict close to the date of Cyrus's entry in 539 BCE,[29] and although of course there was a major battle earlier at Opis,[30] the reality and recollection of the entry into Babylon itself is of a largely peaceable affair. This was not expected, and indeed, as noted already above in the discussion of 47:1, the text of 45:1–2, which also recalls this event, gives signs of having been revised to take account of the unexpected course of events over against the violence which was previously anticipated. This looks like unequivocal evidence, to be joined with that in v. 17, that this part of the chapter, at any rate, must have been written before, not after, the fall of Babylon to Cyrus.[31]

If this anchoring of the last part of the poem in a clear historical setting thus seems assured, even if the details of the prediction did not work out precisely as expected, how does that relate to the rest of the poem which precedes it? The general shape of the poem is clear: a vivid anticipatory description of the Day of the Lord reaches its goal and climax in the final stanza (vv. 17–22) where, as we have seen, the Medes are identified as God's specific agents and Babylon is named as their target. It will be completely overthrown and never again inhabited. On this general basis, some commentators have defended the view that the whole of the poem in 13:2–22 was composed as it stands for its present context;[32] Wildberger, for instance, defends this conclusion on

28. This applies as much to Xerxes' attack on Babylon in 482 BCE as to any earlier conquest, so that I cannot see any advantage in trying to find a reference to that event behind the present passage, contra Berges, *Das Buch Jesaja*, 152 (ET, *The Book of Isaiah*, 135–36). Dandamayev ("Babylonia in the Persian Age," 326–42 [esp. 329]), whom Berges cites in support, is quite clear that, though the Babylonian kingdom was "liquidated," life continued there and, indeed, later prospered again, quite contrary to what our passage states.

29. See Tolini, "Quelques éléments," *ARTA* 2005.003: http://www.achemenet.com/ressources/enligne/arta/pdf/2005.003-Tolini.pdf.

30. See Kuhrt, *Ancient Near East*, 602.

31. Loader, *A Tale of Two Cities*, 60–61, follows the first edition of Watts's commentary in what he considers a "convincing" argument to date this verse to the reign of Ahaz. In his revised edition, however, Watts correctly alters this to the Neo-Babylonian period; see Watts, *Isaiah 1-33*, 188, 200; rev. ed., 2005, 239, 250.

32. This, of course, was the standard older critical view; see for instance, Duhm, *Das Buch Jesaia*, and Marti, *Das Buch Jesaja*, 1900. Gray (*A Critical and Exegetical*

the ground that the implied question raised by vv. 2–5 is answered by v. 17 just as that raised by 7–16 is answered by v. 19.[33] If allowance is made for the fact that we should not look for mathematically logical or conceptual unity in a poem that uses such evocative and emotionally-charged phraseology, that position is certainly not to be dismissed out of hand.

Despite this, there is one striking feature of the poem which seems to suggest that there may, in fact, more probably be two (or more) stages of composition. The bulk of the poem (vv. 2–16) describes the imminent arrival of the Day of the Lord in terms which are universal. Without listing all the details, it is sufficient here to note that, for instance, the army which God is mustering comprises kingdoms and nations from earth's remotest ends (vv. 4–5) and that the object of their onslaught seems equally to be directed against the whole world (vv. 5, 9, 11). Only with v. 17, which has its own standard introductory form ("Now look, I am on the point of stirring up . . . "), is this historicized by reference to the Medes in their assault on Babylon. This disjuncture between the universal tone of the first part of the poem and its separate application to an historically specific context which makes the poem fit the introduction in v. 1 has generally been thought to be strongly suggestive of an earlier poem being reused for its new present context.[34] This conclusion does not in any way discredit the legitimacy of a synchronic reading of the passage as a whole; after all, that is what our editor has deliberately bequeathed to us. It does, however, also open the door to consideration of the longer history that may lie behind the text we have received.

There are two basic approaches to this question. The first is that there was a pre-existing poem with universal scope (vv. 2–16), which was

---

Commentary on the Book of Isaiah I-XXVII), found some suspicious unevenness in composition but refrained from a detailed composition history; in his view the problems arose by later additions rather than by the incorporation of earlier material. In addition to some more recent commentaries (e.g., most recently Roberts, *First Isaiah*), see also Vermeylen, *Du prophète Isaïe à l'apocalyptique*, 286–87; Høgenhaven, *Gott und Volk bei Jesaja*, 140–41; Eidevall, *Prophecy and Propaganda*, 107–13.

33. Wildberger, *Jesaja*, 2, 507–8 (ET, *Isaiah 13–27*, 13–14).

34. For a clear exposition of this relatively common opinion, see Jeppesen, "The *Maśśa' Babel* in Isaiah 13–14," 63–80.

then applied by the main redactor of the passage specifically to Babylon in vv. 17–22. The alternative approach sees things completely the other way round. While it had sometimes been adumbrated previously,[35] it has become more popular following its fullest exposition by Zapff.[36] On this view an original anti-Babylon oracle in vv. 17–22 was later given a universal application by the addition of vv. 2–16. Given that elsewhere too there are examples of a day of the Lord passage being developed in a universalizing direction (e.g., the use of the day of the Lord in Joel 1–2 followed by 3–4, and similarly in the change introduced at Obad 15[37]), there seems to be an inherent attraction about this alternative approach. I should like to offer some further refinements to Zapff's work in support of it.

First, there is a problem with Zapff's proposal as it stands, though he does not refer to it, so far as I can see. In v. 17, which opens the oracle as he understands it, the expression "against them" has no antecedent.[38] It would be easier if there were at least something before 13:17 to which this could refer.

Second, there seem to me to be grounds for challenging the original unity of vv. 2–16. The most obvious duplication is that the Day of the Lord is introduced twice, in vv. 6 and 9. Beyond that, vv. 2–3 and 4–5 seem to sit uneasily alongside one another. In the former, God addresses a plural audience and speaks in the first person singular (v. 3). In vv. 4–5, by contrast, God is referred to in the third person and the standpoint shifts to those whom the army is approaching. It is therefore possible that we have two introductions to the oracle about the mustering of the army. Finally, Bosshard-Nepustil[39] has noted that there is a

---

35. See very briefly Marti, *Jesaja*, 128; Eissfeldt, *Einleitung in das Alte Testament*, 429–30 (ET, *The Old Testament: An Introduction*, 319–20); Barton, *Isaiah 1–39*, 85.

36. Zapff, *Schriftgelehrte Prophetie—Jes 13 und die Komposition des Jesajabuches*, followed, for instance, by Bosshard-Nepustil, *Rezeptionen von Jesaia 1–39 im Zwölfprophetenbuch*, 68–72; Berges, *Das Buch Jesaja*, 155–56 (ET, *The Book of Isaiah*, 139–40); Schmid, *Jesaja*, i: *Jesaja 1–23*, 129.

37. On both see Barton, *Joel and Obadiah*, 12–14, 92–93, 151–54.

38. This has been noted by Bosshard-Nepustil, *Rezeptionen von Jesaia 1–39*, 72, and Jeremias, "Der 'Tag Jahwes' in Jes 13 und Joel 2," 129–38 (133), albeit with varying consequences.

39. It should be noted that Bosshard-Nepustil's own final analysis effects something of a median position between the two that I have summarized above: he thinks

sharp difference between 9–13 and 14–16 in terms of the effects of the day of the Lord: the former is cosmic, the latter terrestrial; the former is selective in that it regards the day as punishment for the wicked and the proud (who v. 12 admittedly implies are the vast majority) whereas the latter is all-embracing in terms of application and furthermore speaks only of their flight in terror, without any reference to judgment or punishment;[40] the former is marked off by a strong *inclusio*: 9a and 13b both describe the day of the Lord as characterized by "fury and burning anger" (joined in construct in 9a, distributed over the two halves of the line in 13b), while the latter follows on very smoothly from v. 8: note especially the use of the idiom "at each other" in v. 8 which is the same as the repeated words "each person to" in 14b.

I therefore propose that we entertain as a working hypothesis that we have two broadly parallel passages in vv. 2–16, namely 2–3 + 6–8 +14–16 and 4–5 + 9–13. It then emerges as further support of this hypothesis that the universalizing features are in fact all restricted entirely to the second group of verses. So far as that feature of the passage is concerned, I can see nothing in 2–3, 6–8, and 14–16 that has ever been claimed to be part of this universalizing tendency.

The basic layer of the chapter in vv. 17–22 as identified by Zapff may therefore be amplified by adding vv. 2–3, 6–8, and 14–16 to it. Those who suffer at the approach of the day of the Lord in vv. 6–8 + 14–16 then make a good antecedent for the expression "against them" in v. 17. Furthermore the whole of the now extended form of the original layer of the chapter fits very well with the form of the book as shaped (in my opinion) in the late exilic period, just like (parts at least of) chs. 40–55.

The question then arises as to why this poem should later have been expanded by the verses which in a more concentrated form bring a universal—even a cosmic—dimension to the whole day of the Lord scenario. The answer lies, I believe, in observing the close link with the

---

the earliest layer in the chapter comprised vv. 2–8 + 14–16, that vv. 1 and 17–22 were then added to it, and finally that vv. 9–13 were added subsequently.

40. This tension was noted already by Gosse, *Isaïe 13,1–14,23*, 153, and by Höffken, *Das Buch Jesaja*, 130–31, albeit without any literary-critical consequences being drawn.

outlook of chs. 24–27 (and 24 in particular).[41] If true, this means that this material will have been added so as to introduce the collection of oracles against the nations in a way that closely parallels the larger universal application of them in the so-called Isaiah Apocalypse. At this stage it may suffice to draw attention on the one hand to the shared use of such major themes as the wholesale destruction of the earth for its wickedness by divine agents and the decimation of its population (13:12; 24:6). On the other hand we should also note such specific points of contact as the use of Hebrew *tebel*, "world," as a way of describing "the earth" in 13:11 and 24:4, 26:9, 18, and 27:6; the "shaking" of the world by violent earthquake in 13:13 and 24:18; the genuinely cosmic scope of the description, with reference to the sun and moon, in 13:10, 13 and 24:21–23;[42] the application to the whole of humanity of the vocabulary for wickedness, sin and guilt in 13:9, 11 and 24:5–6 and 26:10; the use of the same vocabulary for the description of divine action as "punishment" in 13:11 and 24:21; the use of "tyrants/ruthless" (same Hebrew word) in 13:11 and three times in 25:3–5;[43] and the use of "desolation" to describe the eventual outcome (13:9; 24:12). While of course one or other of these elements may be put down to coincidence, their accumulation is impressive. We may agree with Scholl's conclusion that "Stil, Wortgebrauch und theologisches Denken stimmen zwischen Jes 13*/(14*) und Jes 24–27 in erstaunlichem Maße überein."[44]

---

41. This has been noted by some others as a possibility, but with only little or no substantiation from textual evidence; see, for instance, Seitz, *Isaiah 1–39*, 118, 123; Schmid, *Jesaja*, 129; Sals, *"Hure Babylon,"* 218; Heskett, *Reading the Book of Isaiah*, 53. For somewhat fuller studies, see Vermeylen, *Du prophète Isaïe à l'apocalyptique*, 354–55; Berges, *Das Buch Jesaja*, 143–44, 152–53 (ET, *The Book of Isaiah*, 127–28, 136–37); and Scholl, *Die Elenden in Gottes Thronrat*, 199–203. Others tend to focus on one or two points of connection only, without trying to put together a comprehensive collection; see, for instance, Polaski, *Authorizing an End*, 104–5; Hibbard, *Intertextuality in Isaiah 24–27*, 100–101; Cunha, "'Kingship' and 'Kingdom,'" 61–75 (esp. 65–66).

42. The force of this particular feature will be strengthened by the observation of Collins that descriptions of cosmic destruction are extremely rare elsewhere (though he does not apply this in our particular case because of his different, and I believe mistaken, narrowing of the application in 13:10–13); see "The Beginning of the End of the World in the Hebrew Bible," 137–55.

43. Cf. Vanderhooft, *Neo-Babylonian Empire*, 125

44. Scholl, *Die Elenden in Gottes Thronrat*, 207.

Applying this conclusion to our composition-historical analysis, it needs to be pointed out that so far as Isa 13 is concerned the closest parallels in both thought and diction occur exclusively in what I have argued is the smaller amount of later amplification of the chapter (i.e., vv. 4–5 + 9–13) than previous studies have recognized. The material which I have now ascribed to the original layer does not feature at all in the preceding comparison. This distinction, coupled with the closer points of comparison of the earlier layer with Isa 40–55, helps confirm this fresh analysis while at the same time answering the main problems which Zapff's pioneering analysis has raised. It also helps explain how the later redactor who included chs. 24–27 (or somebody else who was working along the same lines) gave shape to his extended section of Isa 13–27 by way of a comparable universalizing of the oracles against specific nations that he was thus enclosing with fresh introduction and conclusion.

I conclude, therefore, that the history of composition of Isa 13 helps us to understand how a description of the overthrow of the historical Babylon came over time to be interpreted as paradigmatic of God's wider, universal purposes for the world, and to introduce the way in which the enigmatic "city" of chs. 24–27 can equally be regarded as a paradigmatic Vanity Fair rather than the subject of any more specific restricted historical identification. In this late form of the book, Babylon is no longer just the historical city but stands as a representative of arrogant human institutions which set themselves as equal to, if not superior to, God himself. They may have their day in the sun, but their long-term fate is sealed.

In moving towards a conclusion, we should note the hermeneutical significance of this redacted text now coming as the first point at which we encounter Babylon in the book and indeed as the first of the oracles against the nations. The original layer of the chapter, which was surely placed in its present location at more or less the same time as the bulk of chs. 40–55, took its stance as a prophecy of the fall of Babylon from which, as we have seen in 40–48, the exiles might be delivered and freed. As time went on, however, it became clear that this prophecy was indeed fulfilled in general terms but not in the specific way that was first envisaged. Working very much in the spirit of the author of chs. 24–27, who opened the way to a universal application of the preceding oracles against the nations, a redactor gave a similar twist to our chapter by his additions which were of modest extent but of radical reapplication. Once put in place, this redaction had a forward effect on the way that references to Babylon later in the book might also be read. As so often, a diachronic analysis leads to a fuller appreciation of the final form of the text. The satire against Babylon and her idols, the prospect of deliverance, and the urgent command to flee may now be treated paradigmatically by any who find themselves oppressed by the circumstances of their present condition in "exile" from God and his concern.[45] The promise is not just to a single generation but may be reapplied with appropriate recontextualization "to children's children" "from everlasting to everlasting" (Ps 103:17).

BIBLIOGRAPHY

Abernethy, A. T., et al. *Isaiah and Imperial Context: The Book of Isaiah in the Times of Empire.* Eugene, OR: Pickwick, 2013.

Ackroyd, P. R. "An Interpretation of the Babylonian Exile: A Study of II Kings 20, Isaiah 38–39." *SJT* 27 (1974) 329–52.

———. "Isaiah 36–39: Structure and Function." in *Von Kanaan bis Kerala: Festschrift für Prof. Mag. Dr. Dr. J. P. M. van der Ploeg O.P. zur Vollendung des siebzigsten Lebensjahres am 4. Juli 1979*, edited by W. C. Delsman et al., 3–21. AOAT 211. Neukirchen-Vluyn: Neukirchener Verlag, 1982.

———. Joel and Obadiah: A Commentary. OTL. Louisville: Westminster John Knox, 2001.

Barton, J. *Isaiah 1–39*. OTG. Sheffield: Sheffield Academic, 1995.

Begg, C. T. "Babylon in the Book of Isaiah." In *The Book of Isaiah*, edited by J. Vermeylen, 121–25. BETL 81. Leuven: Peeters, 1989.

Bendavid, A. *Parallels in the Bible*. Jerusalem: Carta, 1972.

Berges, U. *The Book of Isaiah: Its Composition and Final Form.* HBM 46. Translated by M. C. Lind. Sheffield: Sheffield Phoenix, 2012.

———. *Das Buch Jesaja: Komposition und Endgestalt.* Herders biblische Studien 16. Freiburg: Herder, 1998.

———. *Jesaja 40–48.* HTKAT. Freiburg: Herder, 2008.

Blenkinsopp, J. *Isaiah 40–55: A New Translation with Introduction and Commentary.* AB 19A. New York: Doubleday, 2002.

---

45. This may go some way towards explaining the reticence we noted previously about specifying the historical circumstances too precisely.

Bosshard-Nepustil, E. *Rezeptionen von Jesaia 1-39 im Zwölfprophetenbuch: Untersuchungen zur literarischen Verbindung von Prophetenbüchern in babylonischer und persischer Zeit.* OBO 154. Göttingen: Vandenhoeck & Ruprecht, 1997.

Clements, R. E. *Isaiah and the Deliverance of Jerusalem: A Study of the Interpretation of Prophecy in the Old Testament.* JSOTSup 13. Sheffield: JSOT, 1980.

———. *Jerusalem and the Nations: Studies in the Book of Isaiah.* HBM 16. Sheffield: Sheffield Phoenix, 2011.

Collins, J. J. "The Beginning of the End of the World in the Hebrew Bible." In *Thus Says the Lord: Essays on the Former and Latter Prophets in Honor of Robert R. Wilson*, edited by J. J. Ahn and S. L. Cook, 137–55. LHBOTS 512. New York: T & T Clark, 2009.

Cunha, W. de A. "'Kingship' and 'Kingdom': A Discussion of Isaiah 24:21–23; 27:12–13." In *Formation and Intertextuality in Isaiah 24-27*, edited by J. T. Hibbard and H. C. P. Kim, 61–75. Ancient Israel and Its Literature 17. Atlanta: Society of Biblical Literature, 2013.

Dandamayev, M. "Babylonia in the Persian Age." In *The Cambridge History of Judaism. I. Introduction; The Persian Period*, edited by W. D. Davies and L. Finkelstein, 326–42. Cambridge: Cambridge University Press, 1984.

Davies, G. I. "The Destiny of the Nations in the Book of Isaiah." In *The Book of Isaiah*, edited by J. Vermeylen, 93-120. BETL 81. Leuven: Peeters, 1989.

Diakonoff, I. M. "Media." In *The Cambridge History of Iran, 2: The Median and Achaemenian Periods*, edited by I. Gershevitch, 36–148. Cambridge: Cambridge University Press, 1985.

Duhm, B. *Das Buch Jesaia.* HKAT 3/1. 4th ed. Göttingen: Vandenhoeck & Ruprecht, 1922.

Eidevall, G. *Prophecy and Propaganda: Images of Enemies in the Book of Isaiah.* ConBOT 56. Winona Lake, IN: Eisenbrauns, 2009.

Eissfeldt, O. *Einleitung in das Alte Testament.* Neue theologische Grundrisse. 3rd ed. Tübingen: Mohr, 1964.

———. *The Old Testament: An Introduction.* Translated by P. R. Ackroyd. Oxford: Blackwell, 1965.

Elliger, K. *Deuterojesaja 1: Jesaja 40,1–45,7.* BKAT 11.1. Neukirchen-Vluyn: Neukirchener Verlag, 1978.

Erlandsson, S. *The Burden of Babylon: A Study of Isaiah 13:2–14:23.* ConBOT 4. Lund: Gleerup, 1970.

Ewald, H. *Die Propheten des Alten Bundes.* Vol. 2. Stuttgart: Krabbe, 1841.

Frame, G. *Babylonia 689-627 B.C. A Political History.* PIHANS 69. Istanbul: Nederlands Historisch-Archaeologisch Instituut te Iİstanbul, 2007.

Franke, C. "The Function of the Satiric Lament over Babylon in Second Isaiah (xlvii)." *VT* 41 (1991) 408–18.

———. *Isaiah 46, 47, and 48: A New Literary-Critical Reading*. BJSUCSD 3. Winona Lake, IN: Eisenbrauns, 1994.

———. "Reversals of Fortune in the Ancient Near East: A Study of the Babylon Oracles in the Book of Isaiah." In *New Visions of Isaiah*, edited by R. F. Melugin and M. A. Sweeney, 104–23. JSOTSup 214. Sheffield: Sheffield Academic, 1996.

Goldingay, J. *The Message of Isaiah 40–55: A Literary-Theological Commentary*. London: T. & T. Clark International, 2005.

Goldingay, J. and D. Payne, *A Critical and Exegetical Commentary on Isaiah 40–55*. ICC. 2 vols. London: T. & T. Clark, 2006.

Gosse, B. *Isaïe 13,1–14,23 dans la tradition littéraire du livre d'Isaïe et dans la tradition des oracles contre les nations*. OBO 78. Göttingen: Vandenhoeck & Ruprecht, 1988.

Gray, G. B. *A Critical and Exegetical Commentary on the Book of Isaiah I–XXVII*. ICC. Edinburgh: T. & T. Clark, 1912.

Groves, J. W. *Actualization and Interpretation in the Old Testament*. SBLDS 86. Atlanta: Scholars, 1987.

Halvorson-Taylor, M. A. *Enduring Exile: The Metaphorization of Exile in the Hebrew Bible*. VTSup 141. Leiden: Brill, 2011.

Hayes, J. H., and S. A. Irvine. *Isaiah, the Eighth-Century Prophet: His Times and his Preaching*. Nashville: Abingdon, 1987.

Heater, H. "Do the Prophets Teach that Babylonia Will Be Rebuilt in the Eschaton?" *JETS* 41 (1998) 23–43.

Hermisson, H.-J. *Deuterojesaja: Jesaja 45,8–49, 23*. BKAT 11.2. Neukirchen-Vluyn: Neukirchener Verlag, 2003.

Heskett, R. *Reading the Book of Isaiah: Destruction and Lament in the Holy Cities*. New York: Palgrave Macmillan, 2011.

Hitzig, F. *Der Prophet Jesaja*. Heidelberg: Winter, 1833.

Höffken, P. *Das Buch Jesaja: Kapitel 1–39*. NSKAT 18/1. Stuttgart: Verlag Katholisches Bibelwerk, 1993.

Høgenhaven, J. *Gott und Volk bei Jesaja: Eine Untersuchung zur biblischen Theologie*. ATDan 24. Leiden: Brill, 1988.

Hom, M. K. Y. H. *The Characterization of the Assyrians in Isaiah: Synchronic and Diachronic Perspectives*. LHBOTS 559. London: T. & T. Clark, 2012.

Jeppesen, K. "The *Maśśa' Babel* in Isaiah 13–14." *PIBA* 9 (1985) 63–80.

Jeremias, J. "Der 'Tag Jahwes' in Jes 13 und Joel 2." In *Schriftauslegung in der Schrift: Festschrift für Odil Hannes Steck zu seinem 65. Geburtstag*, edited by R. G. Kratz et al., 129–38. BZAW 300. Berlin: de Gruyter, 2000.

Kartveit, M. *Rejoice, Dear Zion! Hebrew Construct Phrases with "Daughter" and "Virgin" as Nomen Regens*. BZAW 447. Berlin: de Gruyter, 2013.

Kissane, E. J. *The Book of Isaiah, Translated from a Critically Revised Hebrew Text with Commentary*, 1:i–xxxix. Dublin: Browne and Nolan, 1941.

Konkel, A. H. "The Sources of the Story of Hezekiah in the Book of Isaiah." *VT* 43 (1993) 462–82.

Kratz, R. G. *Kyros im Deuterojesaja-Buch: Redaktionsgeschichtliche Untersuchungen zu Entstehung und Theologie von Jes 40–55*. FAT 1. Tübingen: Mohr, 1991.

Krause, A. F. "Historical Selectivity: Prophetic Prerogative or Typological Imperative?" In *Israel's Apostasy and Restoration: Essays in Honor of Roland K. Harrison*, edited by A. Gileadi, 175–212. Grand Rapids: Baker, 1988.

Kuhrt, A. *The Ancient Near East c. 3000–330 BC*. London: Routledge, 1995.

Loader, J. A. *A Tale of Two Cities: Sodom and Gomorrah in the Old Testament, Early Jewish and Early Christian Traditions*. CBET 1. Kampen: Kok, 1990.

Marti, K. *Das Buch Jesaja*. KHC 10. Tübingen: Mohr, 1900.

Martin-Achard, R. "Esaïe 47 et la tradition prophétique sur Babylone." In *Prophecy: Essays Presented to Georg Fohrer on his Sixty-Fifth Birthday 6 September 1980*, edited by J. A. Emerton, 83–105. BZAW 150. Berlin: de Gruyter, 1980.

Oswalt, J. N. *The Book of Isaiah Chapters 1-39*. NICOT. Grand Rapids: Eerdmans, 1986.

Polaski, D. C. *Authorizing an End: The Isaiah Apocalypse and Intertextuality*. BibInt 50. Leiden: Brill, 2001.

Sals, U. *Die Biographie der "Hure Babylon": Studien zur Intertextualität der Babylon-Texte in der Bibel*. FAT 2/6. Tübingen: Mohr Siebeck, 2004.

Schmid, K. *Jesaja: Jesaja 1–23*. Zürcher Bibelkommentare 19.1. Zurich: Theologischer Verlag, 2011.

Scholl, R. *Die Elenden in Gottes Thronrat: stilistisch-kompositorische Untersuchungen zu Jesaja 24–27*. BZAW 274. Berlin: de Gruyter, 2000.

Seitz, C. R. *Isaiah 1–39*. IBC. Louisville: John Knox, 1993.

———. *Zion's Final Destiny: The Development of the Book of Isaiah: A Reassessment of Isaiah 36–39*. Minneapolis: Fortress, 1991.

Smelik, K. A. D. "Distortion of Old Testament Prophecy: The Purpose of Isaiah xxxvi and xxxvii." *OtSt* 24 (1986) 70–93.

Smith, G. V. *Isaiah 1–39*. NAC 15A. Nashville: B&H, 2007.

Stromberg, J. *Isaiah After Exile: The Author of Third Isaiah as Reader and Redactor of the Book*. Oxford Theological Monographs. Oxford: Oxford University Press, 2011.

Tolini, G. "Quelques éléments concernant la prise de Babylone par Cyrus (octobre 539 av. J.-C.)." *ARTA* 2005.003.

Vanderhooft, D. S. *The Neo-Babylonian Empire and Babylon in the Latter Prophets*. HSM 59. Atlanta: Scholars, 1999.

Vermeylen, J. *Du prophète Isaïe à l'apocalyptique: Isaïe, I–XXXV, miroir d'un demi-millénaire d'expérience religieuse en Israël*. EB. 2 vols. Paris: Gabalda, 1977–1978.

Watts, J. D. W. *Isaiah 1–33*. WBC 24. Waco: Word, 1985; rev. edn. 2005.

Whybray, R. N. *Isaiah 40–66*. NCB. London: Oliphants, 1975.

Wildberger, H. Jesaja: Jesaja 13–27. BKAT 10.2. Neukirchen-Vluyn: Neukirchener Verlag, 1978.

———. *Isaiah 13–27*. CC. Translated by T. H. Trapp. Minneapolis: Fortress, 1997.

———. *Isaiah 28–39*. CC. Translated by T. H. Trapp. Minneapolis: Fortress, 2002.

———. *Jesaja: Jesaja 28–39: Das Buch, der Prophet und seine Botschaft*. BKAT 10.3. Neukirchen-Vluyn: Neukirchener Verlag, 1982.

Williamson, H. G. M. *The Book Called Isaiah: Deutero-Isaiah's Role in Composition and Redaction*. Oxford: Clarendon, 1994.

———. *A Critical and Exegetical Commentary on Isaiah 1–5*. ICC. London: T. & T. Clark, 2006.

———. *A Critical and Exegetical Commentary on Isaiah 6–12*. ICC. London: T. & T. Clark, 2018.

———. "Egypt in the Book of Isaiah." In *Israel in Egypt*, edited by A. Salvesen et al., 27-55. Ancient Judaism and Early Christianity 110. Leiden: Brill, 2020.

———. "The Evil Empire: Assyria in Reality and as a Cipher in Isaiah." In *Imperial Visions: The Prophet and the Book of Isaiah in an Age of Empires*, edited by R. G. Kratz and J. Schaper, 15–40. FRLANT. Göttingen: Vandenhoeck & Ruprecht, 2020.

———. "The Setting of Deutero-Isaiah: Some Linguistic Considerations." In *Exile and Return: The Babylonian Context*, edited by J. Stökl and C. Waerzeggers, 253–67. BZAW 478. Berlin: de Gruyter, 2015.

Zapff, B. M. *Schriftgelehrte Prophetie—Jes 13 und die Komposition des Jesajabuches: Ein Beitrag zur Erforschung der Redaktionsgeschichte des Jesajabuches*. Forschungen zur Bibel 74. Würzburg: Echter, 1995.

8

Where is the Study of the Septuagint Going, and Should It?

STANLEY E. PORTER

INTRODUCTION

IT IS NOT UNCOMMON to witness August Konkel walking around McMaster Divinity College with either a Hebrew Bible or Greek New Testament, or possibly both, in his hands.[1] In fact, his facility with the biblical languages and his ability to provide spontaneous translations for whatever occasion are legendary. Gus takes his biblical text with him to class, to chapel, and even to faculty meetings on occasion—where he will turn directly to the Hebrew or Greek text and provide his own translation and even commentary or sermonic points as needed. Gus preaches directly from the biblical text, often with no

---

1. I offer this short article in honour of my colleague Dr. Gus Konkel, who is now Professor of Old Testament at McMaster Divinity College, after having served Providence University College and Theological Seminary (in its various manifestations and under a variety of names) for a number of years. As I write this essay, Gus has also joined Dr. Mark Boda and me in teaching our new graduate-level Septuagint Studies Seminar as part of the MA/PhD programs of MDC. Gus has been a unique and tremendously important addition to our faculty and the general ethos of MDC. I congratulate him on receiving this volume in his honor.

notes but the biblical passage in front of him, with elegance and power in his delivered word supported by direct reference to the text. Gus will often elegantly extemporize as he preaches, bringing the ancient wording into play with his spontaneous translation (although admittedly the translations do often sound a bit like a mix of the King James and a somewhat newer translation—one of the many he has used through the years or perhaps one that he had a part in translating). In his handling of the inspired text in this way—without apology and without faultering—Gus provides a model especially for his students but also, if we are honest with ourselves, for his fellow faculty members. In many if not most ways, Gus embodies and exemplifies the characteristics that we all long to see developed in our seminary students, as well as in ourselves—those who are completely under the authority of God's Word, without hesitation or excuse.

This characteristic of Gus is not one of recent development. Gus's facility with the Bible began years ago, presumably as a young child, and continued to be nurtured through years of informal and formal education and continuing practice. As a result, it is not surprising to discover that Gus wrote an important article that in many ways embodies both the traits that he constantly exemplifies in his handling of the Bible in his daily activities as a faculty member and most of the major issues at play in contemporary Septuagint studies, which in varying ways combine both Hebrew and Greek study. In 1993, Gus published an article in the respected journal, *Vetus Testamentum*, that was modestly entitled "The Sources of the Story of Hezekiah in the Book of Isaiah."[2] In many ways, this article evidences Gus's apparently equal facility in both Hebrew and Greek. More than that, however, the article evidences exposure to and consideration of many, if not most, of the major issues in contemporary study of the Septuagint.[3] These include questions of

---

2. Konkel, "Sources."

3. The astute reader—and perhaps some not-so-astute readers—will notice that I unashamedly use the term "Septuagint" to refer to the composite, mostly but not entirely translated, version of the Jewish Scriptures of the Second Temple period. There is no entirely satisfactory and completely unproblematic term to use for this document, with Old Greek, Greek Bible, and other terms having their own limitations. The fact that the creation of this document seems to have originated with an event or series of events involving a number of bilingual Jewish translators in Egypt

the pre-Masoretic text, Greek translation of the Jewish Scriptures, later Greek versions (especially the *kaige* recension), translation technique of earlier and later versions, evidence of exegetical and interpretive influence in the Greek, levels of language and exegesis involving syntax, semantics, and context, textual corruption and criticism, textual retroversion, theological interpretation, and even literary shaping of the account. This is a broad range of topics, especially to find in a single article; as a result, for some of them he can only hint at the topic concerned. In fact, one of the few major issues that Gus does not seem to address is the nature of producing a commentary on the Septuagint. This may be because neither of the recent two major English-language commentary series on the Septuagint had been formally announced in 1993.[4]

WHERE CONTEMPORARY SEPTUAGINT STUDIES ARE HEADING

From the outset, there have been two major views of how to conceptualize the Septuagint. The way that the Septuagint is conceptualized has resulted in two major ways in which it is examined and treated within both common use and scholarship. This bifurcation goes back at least as early as the disagreement between Augustine and Jerome over what constitutes the basis of our older Testament. To some extent this situation was predicated upon the language, Greek, being widely used throughout the church, but also dictated by the fact that the Greek New Testament appears to draw upon the Greek Old Testament for most of its citations.[5] Jerome, however, disputed the account of the translation

(see the Letter of Aristeas; Philo, *Moses* 2:26–44; Josephus, *Ant.* 12.11–118; *Ag. Ap.* 2.45–47) is sufficient to lend the nomenclature to the entire document. Those who use the document will know of the critical issues attending to both the document and its name.

4. The commentary series connected with the NETS translation (completed in 2007), to be published by the Society of Biblical Literature, was first announced in the mid 1990s, and the Brill Septuagint Commentary Series was first announced soon after that. The NETS group has yet to publish a single commentary, while the SEPT series has published thirteen volumes, with several more in various stages of editing and production.

5. See Harl, Dorival, and Munnich, *La Bible grecque*, 274–80; and Swete, *Introduction*, 381–405.

of the entire Old Testament by the seventy and also noticed a number of difficulties and discrepancies between the Hebrew and Greek. Augustine attempted to find a compromise by claiming that God had inspired and superintended the Septuagint, even if there were differences from the Hebrew that had been corrected by later authors.[6] The result was that for the western church the Jewish Bible became the basis of the Old Testament and for the eastern church the Greek Bible became the Old Testament.[7] For those who have regarded the Septuagint as Scripture, including the Orthodox church (including especially the Greek Orthodox, but all of those Orthodox traditions that use the Septuagint as either their Scripture or the basis of their translated Scripture), there has been an appreciation of the Greek Bible (Old and New Testaments) as holy text. In other words, the issue in reading the Septuagint (in Greek or translation) is to appreciate it as a living scriptural document for the worshiping community and profitable for spiritual instruction.

Despite this, in conjunction with developments in critical study of the Bible, this was not the approach that came to capture the attention of western biblical scholars. With the rise of historical criticism came the need to subject the Septuagint to similar study, even if such study occurred somewhat belatedly after attention was first given to the Old and New Testaments in Hebrew and Greek. This Septuagint criticism involved, among other critical perspectives, (1) textual criticism in relation to its textual base, (2) Greek language study, and (3) what must be called a type of source criticism. I wish to concentrate upon these three areas in establishing the direction of contemporary Septuagint studies.

(1) To begin with textual criticism, one need only trace the development of critical editions of the Septuagint.[8] Septuagint textual criticism early on adopted a single manuscript tradition as its textual base. Even though the Complutensian Polyglot (1514–1517) and the Aldine Greek Bible were eclectic texts (but based upon a relatively few number of late manuscripts), the Sixtine edition of 1587 (promoted

---

6. See Hengel, *Septuagint*, 47–54.

7. Hengel, *Septuagint*, 63–64, 125.

8. I draw upon Jobes and Silva, *Invitation*, 64–70, for this history of editions, supplemented by some of the personal information on scholars provided on pp. 265–88.

by Pope Sixtus V) adopted Codex Vaticanus as its base—despite there being some missing portions. This adoption is understandable, because Codex Sinaiticus had not yet been discovered (Codex Alexandrinus was known, and was used for some other editions, but was clearly not as early). In the late eighteenth and early nineteenth centuries, Robert Holmes and then James Parsons produced a five-volume edition of the Greek Old Testament based upon the Sixtine text. The Sixtine text was also used as the basis of the several editions of the Septuagint prepared in the middle of the nineteenth century by Constantine Tischendorf, to which he compared several other early codexes (such as LXXA, LXXC, and LXXS = Sinaiticus, once he had discovered it).[9] Near the end of the nineteenth century, a number of Cambridge scholars began to produce a new edition of the Septuagint of Vaticanus, compared with many other available manuscripts. Henry Barclay Swete published a three-volume hand-edition of this Septuagint in 1887–1894 (third edition 1901–1907),[10] while work continued on the Larger Cambridge edition under the editorship of Alan E. Brooke and Norman McLean,[11] joined later by Henry St. John Thackeray.[12] This large edition was never completed, although it produced nine fascicles (from 1906 to 1940). At the same time that the Cambridge edition was being produced, there was a turn in textual criticism with the rise of eclectic texts. It is at this point that Septuagint textual criticism began to become much more like textual criticism of the Greek New Testament. Instigated but never accomplished by Paul de Lagarde (who died in 1891, the subject of controversy),[13] the development of a critical text was taken up by Alfred Rahlfs,[14] along with the founding of a Septuagint studies institution in Göttingen (1908), still in existence. Rahlfs himself produced

---

9. Jobes and Silva, *Invitation*, 265–66. Cf. Porter, *Constantine Tischendorf*, 65–67, for a more positive view of Tischendorf's accomplishments—including his having discovered one of the two most important Old Testament Greek texts, Codex Sinaiticus, an accomplishment that puts him in a class by himself; and Swete, *Introduction*, 187.

10. Jobes and Silva, *Invitation*, 273–75.

11. Jobes and Silva, *Invitation*, 275–76.

12. Jobes and Silva, *Invitation*, 276–78.

13. Jobes and Silva, *Invitation*, 268–71.

14. Jobes and Silva, *Invitation*, 272–73.

a hand-edition of the Septuagint based upon three major codexes—Vaticanus, Sinaiticus, and Alexandrinus—as a stopgap measure while full critical (by this is meant eclectic) editions of the individual books were produced (this hand-edition revised by Robert Hanhart in 2006). Rahlfs himself produced the individual volume on Psalms in 1931, and many other volumes have been published in the Göttingen Septuagint series, under a succession of editors such as Werner Kappler, Joseph Ziegler,[15] Hanhart, John Wevers,[16] and Udo Quast, among others,[17] to the point where this series is often claimed to provide preferable eclectic texts than single manuscript texts.[18] But eclectic texts they are, nonetheless. In other words, they are not texts of any particular Septuagint manuscript but texts gleaned from all of the possible manuscripts. Thus, even though textual criticism of the Greek Old Testament generally began with single manuscripts, especially Codex Vaticanus, still often recognized as the single most reliable Greek Old Testament text, the eclectic text, as it did in New Testament studies, soon came to prominence and has continued to dominate Septuagint studies, to the point in some people's minds of there being only one legitimate text-critical approach, use of the Göttingen eclectic text—a text that never existed in the ancient world but was only created in the universities of Germany.

(2) The second area is study of the Greek language of the Septuagint. In a recent survey of changing opinions regarding the Greek language of the Septuagint, I trace the history of discussion over four major periods.[19] Although there has been debate over the nature of the Greek of the New Testament since the sixteenth century, discussion of the Greek of the Septuagint is much more recent, with major

---

15. Jobes and Silva, *Invitation*, 282–83.

16. Jobes and Silva, *Invitation*, 286–87.

17. See Jobes and Silva, *Invitation*, 70n17, for a list of the volumes published to the date of their publication.

18. As Jobes and Silva (*Invitation*, 276) say regarding the Brooke–McLean text in relation to the Göttingen edition, it was abandoned in light of "what many textual critics considered to be a better approach."

19. Porter, "History of Scholarship." The third and fourth viewpoints are clearly represented by various authors within the volume in which my essay appears. Some of the authors mentioned below are contributors to this volume.

works first appearing in the nineteenth century. (a) The first period is the Semitic Greek Hypothesis period. Scholars during this period often posited something called Biblical Greek, in reaction to those earlier scholars who had denigrated the Greek of the Bible for its comparative classical inferiority. The result was comparative study that defined the characteristics of Biblical Greek with reference to its Hebraic features. Heinrich G. J. Thiersch, followed by Zechariah Frankel and Eduard Reuss, made such proposals,[20] which reached a highpoint in the monograph on Biblical Greek by Edwin Hatch, in which he saw the Greek of the Septuagint as having its own integrity in relation to other forms of Greek and reflecting a Semitic mindset.[21] This perspective was enshrined in the still-referenced Septuagint grammar of F. C. Conybeare and St. George Stock, until recently one of only two grammars of the Septuagint in English.[22] The Semitic position held that, though written in Greek, the Septuagint evidenced a distinctive Jewish Greek identifiable by particular linguistic constructions foreign to Greek but dependent upon Hebrew, a view that has persisted in various forms to the present.[23] (b) The Hellenistic/Koine Greek Hypothesis emerged after 1895 in light of discoveries of numerous Greek documentary papyri that resembled the Greek of the Septuagint in both vocabulary and syntax. These discoveries confirmed the speculations of some previous scholars who thought that the Greek of the Septuagint was part of the common language of the time. The two major figures in this reevaluation of Septuagint Greek were Adolf Deissmann and James Hope Moulton. First in his *Bible Studies* and then in his *Light from the Ancient East*, Deissmann made widely known the importance of these Greek documentary papyri, along with inscriptions, by showing that, though a translated document and hence with some Semitic elements, the

---

20. Adolf Deissmann made the observation that such theories were, apart from a few exceptions, made not by linguists but by theologians. See Deissmann, "Hellenistic Greek," 39.

21. Hatch, *Essays*, 1–35.

22. Conybeare and Stock, *Selections*, 1–24.

23. For example, this view was claimed in the first edition (1896) of Friedrich Blass's grammar of New Testament Greek (*Grammatik*, 4–5) and is maintained in the latest German edition of 1990 (*Grammatik*, 4–6).

Septuagint vocabulary was thoroughly Hellenistic.[24] Moulton argued similarly for its syntax, especially in his *Prolegomena*.[25] The influence of this hypothesis was large, affecting general works on Koine Greek, such as the important research of Albert Thumb; monographs and related work on the Septuagint, such as the introduction by Swete; and a number of grammars that addressed the Septuagint in significant ways, such as by Thackeray.[26] This perspective is also reflected in a number of histories of Greek written in the mid to late twentieth century and into the twenty-first century, such as by Geoffrey Horrocks.[27] This position holds that Hellenistic Greek was the natural result of linguistic development and was essentially a single variety used throughout the Mediterranean world of the Second Temple period and the language used in the translation of the Septuagint, even if there were examples of Semitic enhancement.[28] (c) The third period encompasses the Hebraic/Jewish Greek Hypothesis, which re-emerged especially after World War II. In 1951, Henry Gehman explicitly argued for the "Hebraic Character of Septuagint Greek," in which he emphasizes what he sees as difficulties in the translation. He was followed by Nigel Turner, who went further and emphasized what he identified as the "unique character of Biblical Greek." This position—even though it proposed little new that had not already been addressed previously—was promoted more widely by Matthew Black in terms of this Greek being "a peculiar language, the language of a peculiar people." Since the 1960s, this position has been argued at length by the Finnish School of Septuagint studies, for whom Hebraisms loom large, arguably too large, as they are often not

---

24. Deissmann, *Bible Studies* (a one volume translation of originally two German volumes, published respectively in 1895 and 1897); Deissmann, *Light from the Ancient East* (originally published in 1908); among other works.

25. Moulton, *Prolegomena*, 1–41; among many other works.

26. Thumb, *Griechische Sprache*; Swete, *Introduction*, 19–20; and Thackeray, *Grammar*.

27. Horrocks, *Greek*, 56–59, following Thackeray. Other Greek historians are P. S. Costas, L. R. Palmer, and F. R. Adrados, as well as contributors such as Nicholas de Lange in the composite history of A.-F. Christidis. All of these are listed in Porter, "History of Scholarship," 25–26.

28. The notion of distinguishing Semitic enhancement from intervention and direct translation is sometimes overlooked by those attempting to marshal evidence of Semitisms. The distinction is found in Moulton and Howard, *Accidence*, 16.

considered in light of comparative phenomena or whether they reflect Semitic enhancement or intervention.[29] This hypothesis believes that a blending of Greek and Hebrew is a linguistically recognizable phenomenon that occurred in Egypt beginning in the third century BCE and that clear instances of such a combination can be detected in the Septuagint and the phenomena can only be explained on the basis of knowledge of such a relationship between Hebrew and Greek. The interlinear approach to studying the Septuagint, which will be discussed further below, grows directly out of this conceptualization of the Greek of the Septuagint. (d) The fourth and final viewpoint is one that concurrently revives the Koine Greek Hypothesis along with the continuation of the Hebraic/Jewish Greek Hypothesis. In around 1980, there was a resurgence of the Greek hypothesis in biblical Greek study, with publication of an essay by Moisés Silva. In an article on bilingualism, Silva addressed the opposition between Semitic and Greek theorists, arguing that it revealed a failure to distinguish between *langue* and *parole*, with the result that the viewpoint of Deissmann and others was not fairly represented.[30] Silva has been followed in his position by Greg Horsley, who disputes the notion of there being a Jewish Greek.[31] John Lee, beginning with his work on Septuagint lexicography published in 1980 and in many articles since, has argued that the vocabulary of the Septuagint fits within the Koine paradigm, and he has more recently been followed by James Aitken, drawing upon inscriptions.[32] This approach has been taken in the introduction to the Septuagint by Marguerite Harl, Gilles Dorival, and Olivier Munnich[33] and a number of recent

---

29. The Finnish school was inaugurated by Ilmari Soisalon-Soininen and is directly seen in the work of Raija Sollamo, Anneli Aejmelaeus (who was the director of the Göttingen Septuagint institute from 1993 to 2000), and Anssi Voitila, among others (see Porter, "History of Scholarship," 29–31). Their studies often focus upon a singular linguistic phenomenon, such as the infinitive, Hebrew semiprepositions, possessive pronouns, and parataxis, among others. For representative works, see Aemelaeus, *On the Trail*; and Voitila, *Présent et imparfait*. The work of Georg Walser also falls into a similar position, although he attempts to straddle the categories by positing a synagogue style of Greek. See Walser, *Greek of the Ancient Synagogue*.

30. Silva, "Bilingualism."
31. Horsley, "Fiction of 'Jewish Greek.'"
32. Lee, *Lexical Study*; Aitken, *No Stone Unturned*.
33. Harl, Dorival, and Munnich, *La Bible grecque*, esp. 223–66.

grammatical works, including the exploration of the verbal syntax of the Greek Pentateuch by Trevor Evans and especially the recent and finally fulfilled syntax of Septuagint Greek by Takamitsu Muraoka.[34] As a result, there are currently two competing approaches to the Greek of the Septuagint, the Semitic and the Koine perspectives. As will be seen further below when discussing the interlinear approach to the Septuagint, especially in relation to the Finnish school, along with how some issues are presented in Septuagint studies, the Semitic hypothesis seems to have the ascendency at this time.

(3) The third area concerns what I am calling source criticism. Source criticism in biblical studies has been a major focus since at least the eighteenth century. Theories regarding the Pentateuch, from Astruch to Wellhausen and beyond,[35] and those regarding the Synoptic Gospels, from Holtzmann and Streeter to the present, are all types of source theories with which most biblical scholars are familiar.[36] Source criticism in Septuagint studies takes on a different cast, depending upon whether one wishes to focus upon the Hebrew or the Greek text as the source of authoritative study. As a result, Septuagint studies reflects two alternative approaches to source criticism. Muraoka calls these two different theories translator-centered or reader-centered approaches.[37] He equates the translator-centered approach with the Finnish School of Septuagint studies already mentioned above, as starting "from the source text," that is, the Hebrew text.[38] This is similar to the approach taken in the "interlinear paradigm" associated with the NETS/SBL translation and commentary project.[39] Those who are responsible for

---

34. Evans, *Verbal Syntax*; Muraoka, *Syntax*, esp. xxxvii–xlvii.

35. I find it interesting to note (on the basis of Jobes and Silva, *Invitation*, 69n14) that one of the founders of the Göttingen Septuagint Institute was Julius Wellhausen, a major Hebrew Bible source critic.

36. See Porter, "History of Biblical Interpretation," 15–18, for a brief overview of major contributors.

37. Muraoka, *Syntax*, xl.

38. Muraoka, *Syntax*, xl.

39. This paradigm was defined by Albert Pietersma, first in his *Translation Manual* and then more fully in his "New Paradigm," to serve as the basis of the NETS/SBL commentaries (none has been published to date). For other attempts at defining and utilizing this approach, see Boyd-Taylor, "Place in the Sun" and *Reading between the Lines*; and Wagner, *Reading the Sealed Book*, among some others.

this project make a distinction between the text as produced (the NETS Bible and anticipated commentary series) and the text as received (see below for further comments, including on the Brill Septuagint Commentary Series). They wish to emphasize the text as produced. In the introduction to the NETS, the editors characterize this approach as assuming the "translationese" of the Septuagint, even to the point of claiming that the Septuagint is often not even Greek but Hebrew essentially in Greek characters. They therefore utilize the Hebrew text as a means to interpret the Greek text, and as a result defend the Greek being as bad as it is because it was rendered for a particular educational purpose, that of providing "interlinear" interpretation of the source text.[40] At least one scholar connected with this approach has gone so far as to frame the relationship between the Hebrew and Greek text to place priority upon the Hebrew text as source: the Septuagint means "the LXX *qua translation*, that is to say, the LXX as an entity standing in an immediate relationship to its source text, in distinction from the LXX, cut loose from its historical moorings, and thus the LXX as a free standing entity, in short, the LXX *qua translation* in distinction from the LXX *qua text*."[41] At least within English-language scholarship of the last fifty or so years, this approach to the Septuagint in relationship to the Hebrew can be seen as the predominant source theory. The emphasis is upon the Hebrew, with the Greek providing a means to access this originating source.

The second approach, what Muraoka calls a reader-centered approach, despite some of the comments above, also merits notice, not least because it has emerged in more recent times as a competing model of source analysis. From the comments above by Pietersma and others, one would think that there is in fact only one approach to the Septuagint, but this is hardly the case. Although Muraoka recognizes that the two approaches that he outlines "do not have to be mutually contradictory but [complement] each other,"[42] the translator-centered approach or "intertextual paradigm" often does not appear to accept their complementarity. Muraoka notes, however, that there are features

40. Pietersma and Wright, "To the Reader," xiv–xv.
41. Pietersma, "Context Is King," 165.
42. Muraoka, *Syntax*, xl.

of the Greek in the Septuagint, even if one wishes to emphasize the Hebrew, that simply do not correspond. As a result, "not only original compositions, but also translated books of the Septuagint could be read and analysed as a running Greek text."[43] After all, Muraoka states, "That is how it was read by the majority of readers for whom Hebrew was, say, Basque, not Greek (!), of course."[44] In other words, there is a legitimate position for those who wish to examine the Septuagint *qua text*, rather than simply *qua translation*. This is the position that is taken in the Brill Septuagint Commentary Series. This is a literary commentary on the Greek text of the Septuagint, with the Greek text of the individual biblical books treated in their own right and with their own integrity, structure, and compositional shape, that is, as each was "received" in Greek by its early users (at least as evidenced by the codex manuscript tradition).[45] Nevertheless, despite the fact that sixteen of such commentaries have been produced, there is still a widespread belief, at least in some circles, that to be a Septuagint commentary is to examine the Hebrew text as the primary source. That simply is not the case.

As a result of such misguided conceptions, it comes as no surprise to find, for example, Jobes and Silva's introduction to the Septuagint in its 2015 edition, despite its co-authorship by Silva (see comments on his view of language, above), oriented to this approach. In discussing the history of manuscripts of the Septuagint, after describing the several major single manuscript editions, they state that, since "every manuscript contains scribal errors" and "no one existing manuscript preserves in its entirety the Greek text as it originally came from the translator or reviser," a "different approach can be taken, namely, the production of a critical text," such as the Göttingen eclectic text.[46] This

---

43. Muraoka, *Syntax*, xl.

44. Muraoka, *Syntax*, xl; cf. xliv. Muraoka is attempting to make his own play on the "it's all Greek to me," for those who had Greek but not Hebrew.

45. See Hengel, *Septuagint*, 57–74. This is also the approach taken in the La Bible d'Alexandrie commentary series. See Harl, "La Bible d'Alexandrie," 181–97, esp. 184: "A text written in any language should be read and analysed only in the context of this language" (cited in Jobes and Silva, *Invitation*, 229). See also Muraoka, *Syntax*, xliv: "The LXX as a whole, when translated or composed, was most likely designed for public consumption, either for cultic use or personal study . . . ."

46. Jobes and Silva, *Invitation*, 68.

is clearly seen by Jobes and Silva as superior to any single manuscript edition, despite, as even though they admit "the resulting printed text is not identical to any manuscript in its entirety" and "the text that appears on the printed page of such an edition is not found in any one surviving manuscript."[47] Further, when it comes to speaking about how to examine the Septuagint, the examples that they provide are geared toward using the Greek text as a window to the Hebrew text. In a chapter entitled "Interpreting the Septuagint," Jobes and Silva give brief recognition to both reader- and translator-centered approaches, but they clearly privilege the latter or "interlinear paradigm" by providing extended examples using this approach.[48] They provide two parallel columns of Hebrew and Greek text, with translations of each, and then offer word and phrase commentary on the Greek text and its Hebrew equivalent in relation to the underlying Hebrew source text. They often make comments about how literal or free the Greek is in relation to the Hebrew. Even their treatment of the two Greek texts of Esther is in relation to the Hebrew source text. Also published in 2015, James Aitken's edited companion to the Septuagint—despite some examples to the contrary—also seems overall to reflect a translator-centered approach in the structure of its comments on each book, with many of them making explicit comparisons between the Hebrew and Greek texts as the basis of their discussion.[49]

In other words, even though there have been recognized competing views of how to approach the Septuagint, there remains a consistent orientation that conforms to a particular approach to the text, despite acknowledged diversity.

---

47. Jobes and Silva, *Invitation*, 68–69.

48. Jobes and Silva, *Invitation*, 228–62.

49. Aitken, ed., *Companion*. This is perhaps not surprising considering how few Brill Septuagint Commentary Series authors are participants in this volume (two maximum)—although a couple are participants in the La Bible d'Alexandrie commentary series. Many of the contributors are identified with the SBL/NETS group. More surprising—and a major shortcoming of a book that purports to represent scholarship on the Septuagint—is the failure of the *Companion* to list the Greek editions or translations of the Brill Septuagint Commentary Series in the introductory information on editions for each biblical book (apart from mentioning the Greek text of 3 Maccabees, the only one cited so far as I can tell), even if they are included in the bibliographies.

SHOULD CONTEMPORARY SEPTUAGINT STUDIES BE HEADED IN THIS DIRECTION?

On the basis of critical summary of these three areas of textual criticism, Greek language, and source criticism, we can see that contemporary Septuagint studies are generally oriented in a particular direction. To summarize, this orientation is to rely upon an eclectic text, emphasize the Semitic character of the Septuagint Greek language, and be translator-centered in nature as reflected in the interlinear paradigm. As I have attempted to point out along the way, there is no compelling reason why Septuagint studies should continue to be headed in this direction. There are in fact good reasons to be noted in each of the areas that I have discussed above why it should not, if for no other reason than to provide a balanced and complementary approach.

Concerning the text of the Septuagint, I observed above that there has been a mixed history of use of single manuscript and eclectic texts. Despite the fact that some think that an eclectic text has a better chance of representing the original or at least the earliest recoverable text, there are good reasons to question this assertion. The fact remains that any eclectic text is a (much) later scholarly creation. The only authority it has is the contemporary scholarship that created it.[50] While I recognize that there are still text-critical issues with using a single-manuscript text for study of the Septuagint (as is done in the Brill Septuagint Commentary Series), at least with the use of such manuscripts we return to and re-enter the world of manuscripts that were actually created and used within the ancient world. This alone would seem to provide a compelling reason to continue to develop single-manuscript textual commentary and scholarship.

Concerning the language of the Septuagint, we have seen the alternation between perspectives, with the Semitic hypothesis tending to have residual predominance. In some ways, this is understandable, as the language of the Jewish Bible was originally Hebrew. However, we must also recognize that the Septuagint, from early in its creation, assumed the status of sacred text that has continued through the New Testament period and even into the present. To make a statement about

---

50. For a similar proposal for New Testament studies, see Porter, *How We Got the New Testament*, 72–75.

the Septuagint's sacred status is not only to make a theological statement but also (and arguably more importantly for the scholarly issues involved) to make a statement about how this text was interpreted, transmitted, and used in antiquity, on the basis of the language in which it was written, the Greek language. On this basis, the Greek Old Testament merits interpretation on the basis of the language in which it is written and it functioned in the ancient world.

Concerning the source-critical issues relating to the Septuagint, we have noted that whether by default or intention the translator-centered approach to the Septuagint has had a strong continuing emphasis upon examination of the Septuagint. This has occurred to the point of orienting entire schools of thought (e.g., the Finnish) and in the form of the "interlinear paradigm" coming to be a dominant (or at least widely asserted) interpretive framework for recent translation and possibly commentary writing (though none has been published to date). However, as we have seen, not only is a translator-centered approach not the only approach but it is not necessarily the best approach to coming to terms with the Septuagint itself. The use of a single Greek manuscript and emphasis upon studying the language of the Septuagint in relation to the Greek found within it, as it was read by its original users and as it is analyzed today, are both ways of refashioning the perspective from the translator and concentration upon the Hebrew source to the reader and user of the Septuagint, both in the original context and in contemporary scholarship.

The Brill Septuagint Commentary Series is just one possible way to take a literary or reader-oriented approach. It is not the only way that this can be done, but I believe that it corrects some of the major misperceptions and even limitations of other, previous Septuagint scholarship. Attention to Greek manuscripts, understanding the Greek of the Septuagint as Koine Greek, and approaching it from the perspective of its readers redresses some of the faulty perspectives so as to correct the basis of interpretation of a text that has not just served religious communities in various ways over the centuries but has sufficient textual, linguistic, and source-critical integrity to merit such examination.

BIBLIOGRAPHY

Aemelaeus, Anelli. *On the Trail of the Septuagint Translators: Collected Essays.* CBET 50. Rev. ed. Leuven: Peeters, 2007.

Aitken, James K. *No Stone Unturned: Greek Inscriptions and Septuagint Vocabulary.* Winona Lake, IN: Eisenbrauns, 2014.

Aitken, James K., ed. *T&T Clark Companion to the Septuagint.* London: Bloomsbury, 2015.

Blass, Friedrich. *Grammatik des Neutestamentlichen Griechisch.* Göttingen: Vandenhoeck & Ruprecht, 1896. 17th ed., revised by Albert Debrunner and Friedrich Rehkopf, 1990.

Boyd-Taylor, Cameron. "A Place in the Sun: The Interpretive Significance of LXX–Psalm 18:5c." *BIOSCS* 31 (1998) 71–105.

———. *Reading between the Lines: The Interlinear Paradigm for Septuagint Studies.* Leuven: Peeters, 2011.

Conybeare, F. C., and St. G. Stock. *Selections from the Septuagint According to the Text of Swete.* Boston: Ginn, 1905.

Deissmann, Adolf. *Bible Studies: Contributions Chiefly from Papyri and Inscriptions to the History of the Language, the Literature, and the Religion of Hellenistic Judaism and Primitive Christianity.* Translated by Alexander Grieve. Edinburgh: T. & T. Clark, 1901.

———. "Hellenistic Greek with Special Consideration of the Greek Bible." In *The Language of the New Testament: Classic Essays,* edited by Stanley E. Porter, 39–59. Sheffield: Sheffield Academic, 1991.

———. *Light from the Ancient East: The New Testament Illustrated by Recently Discovered Texts of the Graeco-Roman World.* Translated by Lionel R. M. Strachan. London: Hodder & Stoughton, 1910.

Evans, T. V. *Verbal Syntax in the Greek Pentateuch: Natural Greek Usage and Hebrew Interference.* Oxford: Clarendon, 2001.

Harl, Marguerite. "La Bible d'Alexandrie: I. The Translation Principles." In *X Congress of the International Organization for Septuagint and Cognate Studies, Oslo, 1998,* edited by Bernard A. Taylor, 181–97. SBLSCS 51. Atlanta: Society of Biblical Literature, 2001.

Harl, Marguerite, Gilles Dorival, and Olivier Munnich. *La Bible grecque des Septante: Du judaïsme hellénistique au christianisme ancien.* Paris: Cerf/CNRS, 1988.

Hatch, Edwin. *Essays in Biblical Greek.* Oxford: Clarendon, 1889.

Hengel, Martin. *The Septuagint as Christian Scripture: Its Prehistory and the Problem of Its Canon.* Translated by Mark E. Biddle. Edinburgh: T. & T. Clark, 2002.

Horrocks, Geoffrey. *Greek: A History of the Language and its Speakers.* London: Longman, 1999.

Horsley, G. H. R. "The Fiction of 'Jewish Greek.'" In *New Documents Illustrating Early Christianity*. V. *Linguistic Essays*, 5–40. Sydney: Macquarie University, 1989.

Jobes, Karen H., and Moisés Silva. *Invitation to the Septuagint*. 2nd ed. Grand Rapids: Baker, 2015.

Konkel, August H. "The Sources of the Story of Hezekiah in the Book of Isaiah." *VT* 43 (1993) 462–82.

Lee, John A. L. *A Lexical Study of the Septuagint Version of the Pentateuch*. SBLSCS 14. Chico, CA: Scholars, 1983.

Moulton, James Hope. *Prolegomena*, vol. 1 of *A Grammar of New Testament Greek*. Edinburgh: T. & T. Clark, 1906.

Moulton, James Hope, and W. F. Howard. *Accidence and Word-Formation*, vol. 2 of *A Grammar of New Testament Greek*. Edinburgh: T. & T. Clark, 1929.

Muraoka, Takamitsu. *A Syntax of Septuagint Greek*. Leuven: Peeters, 2016.

Pietersma, Albert. "Context Is King in Septuagint Lexicography—or Is It?" In *Biblical Greek in Context: Essays in Honour of John A. L. Lee*, edited by James K. Aitken and Trevor V. Evans, 165–76. Biblical and Theological Studies 22. Leuven: Peeters, 2015.

———. "A New Paradigm for Addressing Old Questions: The Relevance of the Interlinear Model for the Study of the Septuagint." In *Bible and Computer: The Stellenbosch AIBI-6 Conference. Proceedings of the Association Internationale Bible et Informatique "From Alpha to Byte," University of Stellenbosch 17–21 July, 2000*, edited by Johann Cook, 337–64. Leiden: Brill, 2002.

———. *Translation Manual for "A New English Translation of the Septuagint" (NETS)*. Ada, MI: Uncial, 1996.

Pietersma, Albert, and Benjamin Wright. "To the Reader of NETS." In *A New English Translation of the Septuagint*, edited by Albert Pietersma and Benjamin Wright, xiii–xx. Oxford: Oxford University Press, 2007.

Porter, Stanley E. *Constantine Tischendorf: The Life and Work of a 19th Century Bible Hunter*. London: Bloomsbury, 2015.

———. "The History of Biblical Interpretation: An Integrated Conspectus." In *Pillars in the History of Biblical Interpretation*, edited by Stanley E. Porter and Sean A. Adams, 1–70. 2 vols. McMaster Biblical Studies Series 2. Eugene, OR: Pickwick, 2016.

———. "History of Scholarship on the Language of the Septuagint." In *Die Spracher der Septuaginta/The Language of the Septuagint*, edited by Eberhard Bons and Jan Joosten, 15–38. Handbuch zur Septuaginta/Handbook of the Septuagint LXX.H 3. Gütersloh: Gütersloher Verlagshaus, 2016.

———. *How We Got the New Testament: Text, Transmission, Translation.* Grand Rapids: Baker, 2013.

Silva, Moisés. "Bilingualism and the Character of Palestinian Greek." *Bib* 61 (1980) 198–219.

Swete, Henry Barclay. *An Introduction to the Old Testament in Greek.* Cambridge: Cambridge University Press, 1902.

Thackeray, Henry St. John. *Introduction, Orthography and Accidence*, vol. 1 of *A Grammar of the Old Testament in Greek according to the Septuagint.* Cambridge: Cambridge University Press, 1909.

Thumb, Albert. *Die griechische Sprache im Zeitalter des Hellenismus: Beiträge zur Geschichte und Beurteiling der Κοινή.* Strassburg: Trübner, 1901.

Voitila, Anssi. *Présent et imparfait de l'indicatif dans le pentateuque grec: Une étude sur la syntaxe de traduction.* Helsinki: Société d'exégèse de Finlande à Helsinki; Göttingen: Vandenhoeck & Ruprecht, 2001.

Wagner, J. Ross. *Reading the Sealed Book: Old Greek Isaiah and the Problem of Septuagint Hermeneutics.* Tübingen: Mohr Siebeck, 2013.

Walser, Georg. *The Greek of the Ancient Synagogue: An Investigation on the Greek of the Septuagint, Pseudepigrapha and the New Testament.* Stockholm: Almqvist and Wiksell International, 2001.

9

Lexicographical Notes on the Septuagint of Zechariah

AL WOLTERS[1]

INTRODUCTION

IN THE COURSE OF my work on the book of Zechariah, I have often been struck by the degree to which scholars differ on how they understand the Greek text of the Septuagint version of this book.[2] In saying this what I have in mind is not just the vexed question of how the Greek text of the LXX relates to its Hebrew *Vorlage*, which is often quite different from the MT, but rather the question of what the Greek text, considered in its own right and without regard to its parent text, would have meant to its intended readership. Closer examination reveals that there is often very little unanimity on how specific Greek words and phrases are to be understood on the level of lexical semantics. A

---

1. I am pleased to offer the following notes to Gus Konkel as a token of my admiration and respect for him as a scholar, teacher, administrator, and all-round Christian gentleman.

2. See Wolters, *Zechariah*. See p. 8 for a general discussion of the text-critical value of the LXX of Zechariah, and scattered comments throughout the commentary on individual philological points involving the LXX.

comparison of existing translations of the LXX, as well as the available standard lexica and commentaries, reveals that these sources often differ dramatically among themselves on how the text of LXX Zechariah should be understood and translated. The present essay is an attempt to shed some new light on some of these points of disagreement.

To accomplish this goal I have taken as my point of departure the Septuagint text of Zechariah as established by Ziegler in the Göttingen edition.[3]

(1) ΨΑΡΌΣ, "GRAY."

Zechariah 1:8: ἵπποι πυρροὶ καὶ ψαροὶ καὶ ποικίλοι καὶ λευκοί ("red, gray, dappled and white horses").

Zechariah 6:3: καὶ ἐν τῷ ἅρματι τῷ τετάρτῳ ἵπποι ποικίλοι ψαροί ("and in the fourth chariot dappled gray horses").

Zechariah 6:7: καὶ οἱ ψαροὶ ἐξεπορεύοντο ("and the gray ones were going out").

In these three verses the adjective ψαροί evidently refers to a horse color, but it is disputed what specific color is meant. The underlying Hebrew is of no help, because the meaning of the Hebrew (which is different in ch. 1 from what it is in ch. 6) is itself disputed. In 1:8 ψαροί corresponds to שְׂרֻקִּים in the MT, variously translated as "speckled" (KJV), "having ruddy tinge over white" (BDB), "sorrel" (NRSV), and "chestnut sabino/mealy chestnut" (Abernethy).[4] In 6:3 and 6:7 ψαροί corresponds to אֲמֻצִּים, variously translated as "bay" (KJV), "piebald" (*HAL*), "powerful" (NIV), "and "steeds" (NRSV).[5]

With respect to the Greek of Zech 1:8, it needs to be pointed out that the two adjectives ψαροὶ καὶ ποικίλοι together correspond to the single word שרקים in the Hebrew, suggesting that these Greek words were originally alternative translations of that obscure Hebrew word. This possibility is supported by the fact that Jerome, in his translation of the LXX text in his commentary on Zechariah, has only *varii*

---

3. Ziegler, *Duodecim prophetae*.

4. See Abernethy, "Translation of Horse Colors," 596. Abernethy lists other proposed translations as well.

5. Other proposed translations are listed in Wolters, *Zechariah*, 173–74.

at this point, reflecting ποικίλοι, while neglecting to translate ψαροί altogether.⁶

Where existing translations do reflect ψαροί, the proposed renderings are also confusingly diverse. In 6:3 and 6:7 Jerome uses *sturnini*, "starling-like," a rare Latin adjective based on *sturnus*, "starling," no doubt based on the assumption that the Greek adjective is based on ψάρ, "starling." The CP has *multicolores* in 6:7. Thomson has "ash coloured" in 1:8 but "bay" in 6:3 and 6:7. Brenton has "grey" in 1:8, but "ash-coloured" in 6:3 and 6:7. NETS has "gray" in 1:8 but "dapple-gray" in 6:3 and 6:7. Giguet has "gris-pommelé" ["dapple-gray"], and BG has "grises" ["gray"] in all three places.

The Greek lexicographer Hesychius (fifth–sixth century CE) has the following two entries on our adjective: ψαροί· ποικίλοι. εἶδος χρώματος. ψαρόν· ποικίλον. σποδοειδές ("ψαροί [means] 'dappled,' 'a kind of color;' ψαρόν [means] 'dappled,' 'ash-like'").⁷ He thus seems to vacillate between the meanings "dappled," some indeterminate color, and "ash-like." Modern lexica of ancient Greek generally follow the lead of LSJ, which has the following entry s.v. ψαρός (A): "*like a starling*, i.e. speckled, dappled, ψ. ἵππος a *dapple-grey* horse, Ar. Nu.1225, Lxx Za.1.8." Thus LEH and GELS have "dapple-grey" in the relevant entries, and GE has "having the color of a starling, piebald with gray." Septuaginta-Vokabular mistakenly glosses the word as a noun: "Star" (that is, "starling"). On the other hand, *HAL* s.v. שָׂרֹק takes an entirely different tack: "G ψαροί 'starenfarbig' [καὶ ποικίλοι], gemeint ist damit wohl der in Syrien u. Kleinasien beheimatete sog. Rosenstar, eine Starenart mit rosarotem Schnabel u. einem Rosaschimmer am Rücken."

The trouble with defining ψαρός in terms of the bird "starling" is that the starling's plumage varies widely in color, depending on species, gender, and season of the year (see the entry "Sturnus" in Wikipedia). According to LSJ s.v. ψάρ, the Greek word refers specifically to the *Sturnus vulgaris*, or common starling.⁸ If this is correct, then it is

---

6. See Jerome as found in Adriaen, ed., *Hieronymi presbyteri opera*, 754.201. Note that the Latin translation in CP echoes Jerome's on this point.

7. Hesychius Alexandrinus, "ψαροί," 4:242; Hesychius Alexandrinus, "ψαρόν," 4:242.

8. See also Thompson, *A Glossary of Greek Birds*, 198.

significant that this species has "glossy black plumage with a metallic sheen, which is speckled with white at some times of year" (Wikipedia entry on "Common starling"). However, since other species of starling are also found in the lands where Greek was spoken, some of which have quite a different coloring (like the "Rosenstar" or "rosy starling" mentioned in *HAL*), to say that a horse is "starling-like" tells us nothing about its color. This leads us to suspect that the adjective ψαρός actually has nothing to do with starlings at all. Note that Greek has another word, ψαρός (B) in LSJ, which refers to some kind of powder of unknown color. A review of the examples of ψαρός listed in the *TLG* reveals that some ancient Greek philologists linked ψαρός not with the noun ψάρ but with the verb ψαίρω, "to skim," and thus gave ψαρός the meaning "swift."[9]

If neither the Hebrew of the *Vorlage* nor the presumed connection with the starling help us to define ψαρός, where can we turn to find out its meaning? I would submit that the most plausible answer is found in the testimony of Modern Greek. We find the following in G. P. Shipp's *Modern Greek Evidence for the Ancient Greek Vocabulary*: "Ψαρός is now 'grey' of hair, replacing πολιός, also of a horse, as already in Ar[istophanes], with noun ψαρής ['gray horse' AW]. Du Cange has ψαροὶ ἵπποι."[10] The reference to Du Cange is to his *Glossarium ad scriptores mediae et infimae graecitatis*, which defines ψαρός as "*canus, albus*, Πολιός, Ψαράδα," that is, "gray."[11] It would seem that ψαρός has nothing to do with starlings and means neither "multi-colored" nor "dappled" nor "dapple-gray" nor "bay"—let alone "pink" as per *HAL*— but simply "gray."[12]

(2) ἈΝΑΤΟΛΉ, "RISING."

Zechariah 3:8: διότι ἰδοὺ ἐγὼ ἄγω τὸν δοῦλόν μου Ἀνατολήν ("therefore behold, I am bringing my servant Rising").

---

9. See for example Koster, *Scholia in Aristophanem, Pars I*, 425 (under 1225a,b).

10. Shipp, *Modern Greek Evidence for the Ancient Greek Vocabulary*, 579.

11. Du Cange, *Glossarium ad scriptores*, 1779. The citation of ψαροὶ ἵπποι is from Zech 1.

12. See also Reiter, *Die griechischen Bezeichnungen der Farben Weiss, Grau und Braun*, 92–93.

Zechariah 6:12: Ἰδοὺ ἀνήρ, Ἀνατολὴ ὄνομα αὐτῷ ("Behold a man, whose name is Rising").

Translators usually take one of three approaches to rendering ἀνατολή in these two verses, where it clearly has a messianic reference. One is to look to the corresponding Hebrew, namely צֶמַח, and to translate "The Branch" (so Brenton), "(plant) sucker" (so BA: *Surgeon*), or "shoot of plants" (so GELS; similarly LEH). Another is to emphasize the general idea of "rising" (so Jerome: *oriens*; similarly CP, Giguet, Doutreleau, BG). A third is to focus on the specific meaning "sunrise" as the beginning of the day (so Thomson: "Anatole [Day-spring]" and SD: *[Sonnen-] Aufgang*). Curiously, BG first has *Oriente* (which normally means "east" in Spanish) in 3:8 but then *Naciente* (which means "nascent," "rising" or "east") in 6:15.

In a recent carefully argued essay, Lanier has demonstrated that the semantic range of ἀνατολή/ἀνατέλλω overlaps substantially with the semantic range of the Hebrew root צמח. They both share five common "categories of use," namely "plant growth (literal)," "bodily growth (literal)," "arise/emerge (plant metaphor)," "arise/emerge (non-plant metaphor)," and "messianic (metaphor)."[13] It thus turns out that the translation of צֶמַח by ἀνατολή is altogether justified, despite considerable scholarly opinion to the contrary.[14] What all these shared categories have in common is the notion of "(a)rising." Consequently, Lanier in his conclusion proposes that ἀνατολή in the three messianic passages of Jer 23:5, Zech 3:8, and Zech 6:12 be translated as "(a/the) Arising One."[15] I would endorse Lanier's overall argumentation but suggest a slight revision of his conclusion. Since ἀνατολή is an abstract noun, I would prefer to render it in these verses as "Rising."

(3) ΛΑΜΠΆΔΙΟΝ, "LAMP-SUPPORT."

Zechariah 4:2: ἑώρακα καὶ ἰδοὺ λυχνία χρυσῆ ὅλη, καὶ τὸ λαμπάδιον ἐπάνω αὐτῆς, καὶ ἑπτὰ λύχνοι ἐπάνω αὐτῆς, καὶ ἑπτὰ ἐπαρυστρίδες τοῖς λύχνοις τοῖς ἐπάνω αὐτῆς· 4:3 καὶ δύο ἐλαῖαι ἐπάνω αὐτῆς, μία

---

13. See Lanier, "The Curious Case," 505–27 (esp. 517 and 523).

14. See for example Cimos, "Observations on the Greek Translation of the Book of Zechariah," 91–108 (99).

15. Lanier, "The Curious Case," 527.

ἐκ δεξιῶν τοῦ λαμπαδίου καὶ μία ἐξ εὐωνύμων ("I saw, and behold, a menorah all of gold, and the *lampadion* on it, and there are seven lamps on it, and seven refilling vessels for the lamps on it. 4:3 And over it are two olive trees, one on the right of the *lampadion*, and one on the left").

In a vision, Zechariah sees a lampstand or menorah (λυχνία) with seven lamps (λύχνοι). The menorah is also supplied with pouring vessels (ἐπαρυστρίδες, for refilling the lamps with oil), together with another feature called a λαμπάδιον (sometimes written λαμπαδεῖον), which is of disputed meaning. Proposed translations of this disputed word range from "lamp" (so Jerome and CP: *lampas*; similarly BG), "lamp dish" (so Thomson), "bowl" (Brenton, SD), and "torch" (NETS). Giguet and BA both use the French word *lampion*, which normally means a Chinese lantern, but BA explains: "Le *lampádion* (ou *lampadeîon*) est en grec une 'petite torche', un lampion."[16] Doutreleau, curiously, has *lampadaire*, "standard lamp" or "street lamp." The lexica have a similar diversity of renderings, including "small lamp" (Schleusner: *parva lampas*), "bowl" (LSJ), "small torch" (SV: *kleine Fackel*), "bowl (of a lamp), small lamp" (LEH), "*bowl* of a lamp" (GELS), and "bowl, cup" (GE).

The translation "bowl" can be explained by reference to the corresponding Hebrew (גֻּלָּה), which is itself of disputed meaning, but which is usually taken to mean "bowl."[17] However, there is nothing to indicate that the Greek has that hypothetical meaning of the Hebrew word. Instead, λαμπάδιον in ordinary Greek usage is the diminutive of λαμπάς, "torch," which accounts for another one of the proposed renderings, namely "(little) torch." However, this meaning seems incongruous in the context, since it evokes the odd image of a menorah that is furnished with both lamps and torches. The translation "lamp" is also strange, since the menorah (λυχνία) is already supplied with seven lamps (λύχνοι). How can we make sense of this strange use of the Greek word in the LXX?

A plausible point of departure is to take a closer look at the two other places in the LXX where the word λαμπάδιον occurs, especially since it turns out that these two places also describe the menorah in

---

16. 249.

17. See the discussion in Wolters, *Zechariah*, 115-16.

Israel's central place of worship (whether tabernacle or temple), and uses much of the same Greek vocabulary that we find in Zech 4. These places are the following:

Exodus 38:16: καὶ τὰ λαμπαδεῖα αὐτῶν, ἅ ἐστιν ἐπὶ τῶν ἄκρων, καρυωτὰ ἐξ αὐτῶν· καὶ τὰ ἐνθέμια ἐξ αὐτῶν, ἵνα ὦσιν ἐπ' αὐτῶν οἱ λύχνοι, καὶ τὸ ἐνθέμιον τὸ ἕβδομον ἀπ' [variant reading: ἐπ'] ἄκρου τοῦ λαμπαδείου ἐπὶ τῆς κορυφῆς ἄνωθεν, στερεὸν ὅλον (text according to Rahlfs). "And [he made] their *lampadeia*, which are on the ends, almond-like out of them, and the sockets out of them in order that the lamps might be on them, and the seventh socket on [reading ἐπ'] the end of the *lampadeion* on the top above, entirely solid" (after the NETS translation).

3 Kingdoms 7:35 (49): καὶ τὰς λυχνίας, πέντε ἐκ δεξιῶν καὶ πέντε ἐξ ἀριστερῶν κατὰ πρόσωπον τοῦ δαβιρ, χρυσᾶς συγκλειομένας, καὶ τὰ λαμπαδεῖα καὶ τοὺς λύχνους καὶ τὰς ἐπαρυστρίδας χρυσᾶς (Rahlfs). "and [Salomon gave] the lampstands, five on the right and five on the left, in front of the dabir—overlaid gold, and the *lampadeia* and the lamps and the golden pouring vessels" (after the NETS translation).

It should be pointed out first of all that the existing translations of these two passages exhibit the same confusion as before with respect to the meaning of λαμπάδιον. For example, in Exod 38:16 Brenton translates it first as "lamp" and then as "lampstand" and in 3 Kgdms 7:35 (49) as "candlestick." NETS has "lampholder" in Exod 38:16 (both times) and "lampstand" in 3 Kgdms 7:35 (49). Secondly, it should be noted that the Hebrew *Vorlage* is again of no help. In Exod 38:16 (= MT 37:20) it is unclear whether the corresponding Hebrew (at least for λαμπάδια at the beginning) is מְנֹרָה, "menorah" (so tentatively the concordance of Hatch and Redpath under λαμπάδιον) or פֶּרַח, "bud, flower" (here referring to a bud-like feature on the branches of the menorah). In 3 Kgdms 7:35 (=MT 7:49), it is definitely פֶּרַח.

Although it seems clear that the LXX text of Exod 38:16 underlies the vocabulary of both 3 Kgdms 7:35 (49) and Zech 4:2–3, there seems to be no consistency in the way the three passages use the word λαμπάδιον. This confirms what Gooding writes in his study of the LXX description of the tabernacle in Exodus: "The only conclusion that one can come to is that in the Septuagint the terms relating to lampstands are inextricably confused."[18] Thus, according to the Exodus text, the word seems to designate two quite different things: (1) Six objects situated atop each of the six branches of the menorah, with the lamps of the menorah "on them" (ἐπ' αὐτῶν), that is, on those objects and thus also on the upper ends (ἄκρα) of the branches. The translation "lamp dish" or "lamp-holder" would fit this use of the term. (2) A single object of which it is said that the seventh socket is on its upper end (ἄκρον), "on the top above." This appears to refer to the central shaft of the menorah, which in some reconstructions of the menorah rises higher than the six curving branches.[19] If we look at 3 Kgdms 7:35 (49) in the light of these two meanings of λαμπάδιον, it is clear that the former one fits its usage here (multiple objects belonging to a single menorah).

However, when we turn to Zech 4:2–3, we find that the word is being used in a different sense again. The menorah described in the vision has only one λαμπάδιον, of which it is said that it is "on" (ἐπάνω) the menorah (v. 2), and that the two olive trees are "over" (ἐπάνω) it, presumably meaning that they overhang it (v. 3). Although its second occurrence here could be understood of the central shaft, that meaning does not work for its first occurrence. The central shaft of the menorah cannot be said to be "on" or "over" (ἐπάνω) the menorah. In what sense then is λαμπάδιον being used in Zechariah?

I would suggest that the term here is an accurate rendering of the Hebrew גֻּלָּה but that the latter does not refer to a "bowl" situated above the menorah (the traditional interpretation); rather, it designates the curved upper part of the menorah, consisting of the branches on either side of the central shaft. It can be said to be "on" the menorah because מְנוֹרָה in Hebrew, strictly speaking, refers to what in Exod 25:34 and 37:20 is called "the menorah itself," consisting of the central shaft and base, without the branches. For lack of a better word, this complex of the menorah's branches could be called its "branchwork."[20]

18. Gooding, *Account of the Tabernacle*, 57.

19. See also the extensive discussion of the term in the note on Exod 38:16 in *L' Exode*, 365–66, where it is also concluded that λαμπάδιον is used in two different senses.

20. See the detailed defense of this interpretation in Wolters, *Zechariah*, 115–16.

It seems, therefore, that the term λαμπάδιον in the LXX has a variety of specific meanings, all related in some way to the menorah of the central sanctuary. Perhaps we can say that it refers in general to a lighting apparatus which can take on different concrete forms, and must in each case be interpreted in the light of its specific context. One feature which the various senses do have in common is that they all support a lamp or lamps, whether that be the multiple "lamp dishes" of the first meaning, the single central shaft of the second, or the collective "branchwork" of the third.[21] As a common generic designation we might therefore choose the translation "lamp-support."

A related question is the issue of the proper spelling of the term we have been discussing. So far we have treated λαμπάδιον and λαμπαδεῖον as though they were variant spellings of the same word. That is also how they are generally treated in printed editions and lexica. Thus, Rahlfs's edition prints the form λαμπαδεῖον throughout, although that form is not listed in LEH or GE. It is only in LSJ and GELS that we find an entry spelled λαμπαδεῖον. The assumed interchangeability is understandable, since due to itacism ει and ι were not distinguished in pronunciation in post-classical Greek, and manuscripts generally used them indiscriminately.

However, Peter Walters has made the suggestion that λαμπαδεῖον and λαμπάδιον are not just variant spellings of the same word, but are actually distinct lexemes, each with its own meaning, which later came to be spelled the same way. He points out that there are many other examples of distinct lexemes ending in -εῖον and -ιον, which in Attic Greek were still kept orthographically distinct, but later became indistinguishable in writing.[22] In his view λαμπάδιον properly means "small torch," and that it is another word, λαμπαδεῖον, which occurs in the LXX. Of the latter he writes:

> λαμπαδεῖον. This must be claimed as the correct spelling in the LXX, in which the word nowhere means *small torch*. In Exod 38:16 (37:19) it renders גְּבִיעַ, cup or *calyx of a flower*, here used metaphorically of the bowl for the lamps on the

---

21. There was a lamp also atop the central shaft, making a total of seven lamps. See Zech 4:2.

22. See Walters, *Text of the Septuagint*, 46–47, 50–51, 285, 286.

candelabra. The same thing is called גֻּלָּה in Zech. 4:2 f., where it is translated λαμπαδεῖον (κρατήρ in Exod 25:30 (31) ff.). This bowl was filled with water as a protection against pieces of wicks from the lamps, which, when falling down, were extinguished in the water (Horst, explaining Zech. 4:2 f.).[23]

Of this quotation I would note that it is doubtful that λαμπαδεῖον in Exod 38:16 (MT 37:19) renders the Hebrew word גָּבִיעַ (see above), or that the latter means "*cup* or *calyx of a flower*," or that λαμπαδεῖον in Zechariah 4 corresponds to κρατήρ in Exod 25. I would also dispute the validity of Horst's idiosyncratic interpretation of גֻּלָּה in Zech 4:2.[24] Leaving all that aside, however, what is important for our purposes is that Walters, on the basis of what he takes to be the meaning of the underlying Hebrew, understands λαμπαδεῖον in the LXX to mean "the bowl for the lamps" on the menorah. As I see it, this interpretation makes sense of the first meaning we discerned in Exod 38:16, but it does not fit with the second.[25]

Although Walters's proposal to identify λαμπαδεῖον as a distinct lexeme was adopted by his student Gooding, and is also reflected in the entry λαμπαδεῖον in GELS, I do not believe it can be sustained.[26] It is very telling that a search of the *TLG* does not turn up a single example of λαμπαδεῖον. It is true that Walters cites an example of this spelling in an Attic inscription of the fourth century BCE, but this appears to be the only recorded example, since the same example is listed in LSJ s.v. λαμπαδεῖον. This could easily be a one-off misspelling and, in any case, is of uncertain meaning. LSJ gives it the meaning "torch-holder,"

---

23. Walters, *Text of the Septuagint*, 50.

24. See Horst, *Die zwölf kleinen Propheten*, 223. I am not aware of any other commentator who has adopted Horst's view on this point.

25. It is perhaps a misunderstanding of Walters's words here which led to the gloss "bowl (of a lamp)" in LEH and GELS.

26. See Gooding, *Account of the Tabernacle*, 56. It is also of interest to note that Muraoka has vacillated on the spelling of our word. In his *A Greek-English Lexicon of the Septuagint* he has the spelling λαμπαδεῖον, but in his subsequent *A Greek-English Lexicon of the Septuagint* he has the spelling λαμπάδιον. In GELS (2009) he reverted to λαμπαδεῖον.

but Meisterhans the meaning *Kandelabra*.²⁷ Neither of these meanings fit the uses of λαμπάδιον in the LXX.

(4) ΜΥΞΩΤΗΡΕΣ, "OIL-PRESSERS."

Zechariah 4:12: Τί οἱ δύο κλάδοι τῶν ἐλαιῶν οἱ ἐν ταῖς χερσὶ τῶν δύο μυξωτήρων τῶν χρυσῶν τῶν ἐπιχεόντων καὶ ἐπαναγόντων τὰς ἐπαρυστρίδας τὰς χρυσᾶς; ("What are these two branches, which are in the hands of the two golden oil-pressers which pour (oil) into the golden refilling vessels and top them up?")

There is considerable diversity of opinion as to the meaning of the μυξωτῆρες which are here mentioned. Some translators have opted for literal "nostrils" (so Jerome, CP, SV, NETS), but this evokes a rather bizarre picture of nasal mucus pouring into refilling vessels. Other proposals are "funnels" (Thomson), "spigots" (so Schleusner: *epistomia*), "pipes" (so Brenton, BG), "lamp spouts" (so Giguet: *becs de lampe*), and simply "spouts" (so Doutreleau: *becs*, BA, SD).²⁸ LSJ1996 glosses the word as *"vessel for pouring* oil into a lamp," and this has been adopted in LEH, GELS, and GE.

The current consensus of the standard lexica is therefore that μυξωτῆρες in Zech 4:12 means "vessels for pouring (oil into lamps)." This interpretation is based, not on the meaning of this Greek word elsewhere, but on the immediate context in the present verse, which states that these μυξωτῆρες "pour (oil) into the golden refilling vessels and top them up." However, not only is this meaning unattested for the word elsewhere, but it also makes it a synonym of the ἐπαρυστρίδες which it is here said to supply with oil. The word ἐπαρυστρίδες, which also occurs in Zech 4:2, is familiar from the description of the tabernacle menorah in Exod 38:17 (= MT 37:23) and the temple menorah in 3 Kgdms 7:35 (49), where it refers to the oil vessels used to replenish the lamps of the menorah with oil.²⁹ It cannot be right that Zech 4:12 is

---

27. See Meisterhans, *Grammatik der attischen Inschriften*, 51. Walters, *Text of the Septuagint*, 285n30, and 286n39, glosses it as both "chandelier" and "torch-holder."

28. I myself previously defended the translation "lamp spouts." See Wolters, "The meaning of Ṣantĕrôt (Zech 4:12)," 1–15 (13).

29. See the relevant entries in LSJ, LEH, GE. Compare the synonymous ἐπαρυστήρ in Exod 25:38. I see no reason to differentiate between ἐπαρυστήρ, *"vessel for pouring* oil into a lamp," and ἐπαρυστρίς, *"channel for pouring oil into a lamp"*

saying that what fills one kind of refilling vessel (the ἐπαρυστρίδες) is another kind of refilling vessel (the μυξωτῆρες).

A search of the *TLG* brings up eighty occurrences of the word μυξωτήρ in ancient and medieval Greek, almost always in the plural. A survey of these occurrences reveals that it is recorded only once in extant Greek literature before its appearance in Zechariah, namely in Herodotus (*Hist.* 2.86), where it means "nostrils." Almost all other occurrences of the word, with the exception of places where Zech 4:12 is cited or alluded to in patristic writings, are found in medical writers like Galen, where it consistently refers to human or animal nostrils. In three places there is also reference to the nostrils of a brazen bull. But Zech 4:12 appears to be the only place where the Greek word is ever used in any of the unusual senses ascribed to it here by LXX translators and lexicographers. The word appears to be used here in a unique sense.

Unfortunately, the eleven patristic places where the μυξωτῆρες of our text are mentioned are also quite unhelpful, although occasionally there is the suggestion that it designated a part of λύχνοι, "lamps."[30] This association was probably suggested by the analogy with μυκτήρ, the much more common Greek word for "nostril," which can also refer to the wick of a lamp. It is the assumed parallel with μυκτήρ which underlies the note on μυξωτῆρες (understood to be *becs* or "spouts") in BA: "il est le doublet de *mukter*, plus fréquent. Outre leur emploi chez les médecins, ces mots désignent le bec d'une lampe (depuis Aristophane, *Ass.* 5)."[31] Unfortunately, this note is mistaken on two counts. The first mistake is that μυκτήρ when used of lamps does not mean "spout," but "wick," as is clear from the place in Aristophanes which the note cites (*Women of the Assembly* or *Ecclesiazusae* 5). See LSJ s.v. The second mistake is that there is no attested example of μυξωτήρ meaning any part of a lamp. In any case, in the present context it makes no sense

---

(so GELS).

30. The *Patristic Greek Lexicon* s.v. μυξωτήρ 1 claims that the word is used by Oecumenius in the sense "*hole* in lamp to hold wick." However, an examination of the passage in question (*Commentarius in Apocalypsin* 129, 7) reveals that Oecumenius is there giving the two lampstands of Rev 11:4 the same allegorical significance as the two μυξωτῆρες of Zech 4:12, without specifying the lexical meaning of the latter.

31. 258.

to understand the word as designating the part of a lamp, since the μυξωτήρ functions as the means of providing lamps with oil.

I would propose an entirely different interpretation of the Greek term, namely that it here refers to a person, specifically a person who presses out oil. It is well established that nouns ending in -τήρ are commonly agent nouns, as in σωτήρ, "savior."[32] Furthermore, it is significant that μυξωτήρ is part of a family of Greek words that implicitly compare the oil of lamps with nasal mucus. Consider μύξα, meaning both "nasal mucus" and "wick (of an oil lamp)," δίμυξος and πολύμυξος, used respectively to describe an oil lamp with two wicks or many, μυκτήρ meaning both "nostril" and "wick," προμύσσω, meaning both "to wipe one's nose" and "to snuff a lamp wick," and προμύσσω, "to snuff a lamp wick."[33] In the light of this, it is a reasonable hypothesis that μυξωτήρ originally meant "μύξα-producer."[34] On the one hand, this would account for its well-attested meaning "nostril" in later Greek. On the other hand, given the frequent association of nasal mucus with lamp oil, the same word could well have acquired the meaning "oil-producer," or more specifically "oil-presser," since oil was produced by pressing it from olives. When the translator of Zechariah used the word, it was apparently still a relatively new coinage, and therefore its etymological root meaning was still relatively fresh.

What makes this proposal especially attractive is that the meaning of the Greek now matches what I take to be the meaning of צַנְתְּרוֹת, the corresponding Hebrew in the MT. Although this enigmatic Hebrew word has received many different interpretations, a plausible case can be made for the meaning "oil-pressers."[35] Another advantage of understanding μυξωτῆρες of persons is that it gives a plausible meaning to the phrase ἐν ταῖς χερσί, which then refers straightforwardly to the hands with which the oil-pressers press out the oil from the olives on

---

32. See Goodwin and Gulick, *Greek Grammar*, 184 (§818).

33. See LSJ in the relevant entries.

34. We could speculate that there was an unattested verb *μυξόω, "produce μύξα," which would explain the *omega* in μυξωτήρ.

35. See Wolters, "The Meaning of Ṣanterôt," 1–15, and Wolters, *Zechariah*, 144–47. I should point out that I have only recently come to realize that the LXX translation μυξωτήρων can be taken as support for my proposal regarding צנתרות. That proposal was adopted in Boda, *The Book of Zechariah*, 305, 311–12.

the branches. It is no longer necessary to wonder what the "hands" of these metaphorical "nostrils" might be, or to resort to such awkward translations of the phrase as "in the handles [of]" (so Thomson), "by the side [of]" (so Brenton, Giguet), or simply "in" (Doutreleau: *dans*). A third advantage of this interpretation is that it makes sense of there being two μυξωτῆρες, one on either side of the menorah, whereas metaphorical "nostrils" would belong together as parts of the same metaphorical nose.

The objection may be raised that the adjective "golden" implies that the μυξωτῆρες are made of metal, like the lampstand itself, and therefore cannot refer to persons. However, this objection can be readily countered by the observation that χρυσοῦς in Greek is often used metaphorically, and is not infrequently applied to divine persons (see LSJ s.v. III,a). In the present context it no doubt suggests that the μυξωτῆρες were heavenly figures.

The overall picture which emerges, therefore, is that of two "golden" oil-pressers, each of whom takes an olive-laden branch in his hand to press out the oil, and subsequently pours the oil thus acquired into the refilling vessels.

(5) ἘΠΑΝΆΓΩ, "TOP UP."

Zechariah 4:12: Τί οἱ δύο κλάδοι τῶν ἐλαιῶν οἱ ἐν ταῖς χερσὶ τῶν δύο μυξωτήρων τῶν χρυσῶν τῶν ἐπιχεόντων καὶ ἐπαναγόντων τὰς ἐπαρυστρίδας τὰς χρυσᾶς; ("What are these two branches, which are in the hands of the two golden oil-pressers which pour (oil) into the golden refilling vessels and top them up?")

A separate discussion is warranted for the participle ἐπαναγόντων in this verse. It appears to reflect the Hebrew מַעֲלִים (the *hiphil* of עָלָה, "bring up") rather than the מֵעֲלֵיהֶם, "from on them" of the MT.[36] The Greek verb has been translated in a bewildering variety of ways. Renderings range from "draw back" (so Jerome and CP: *retrahunt*), "supply" (Thomson), "communicate with" (Brenton), "feed" (BA: *alimentent*), "flow to" (NETS), "lead up" (SD: *hinaufleiten*), "bring" (BG: *traen*),

---

36. See among others Lowe, *The Student's Commentary on Zechariah, Hebrew and LXX*, 18; Rudolph, *Haggai, Sacharja 1–8, Sacharja 9–14, Maleachi*, 104–5; Hanhart, *Sacharja*, 253.

"bring up" (LEH s.v.), and "cause to move up" (GELS s.v.). Giguet omits altogether to translate the verb, and Doutreleau introduces oil as the subject, which is said to "spread" (*où . . . se répand l'huile*).

I suspect that the bafflement of the translators is rooted in the fact that it is difficult to imagine how the oil-pressers (μυξωτῆρες) could be said to actually "bring up" the refilling vessels. I believe the solution of the puzzle lies in the parallelism with the participle ἐπιχεόντων, here meaning not "pour over" but "pour in" (see LSJ s.v. A,II). As the "oil-pressers" of the olive trees pour oil into the refilling vessels they "bring them back up," that is, return them to their previous level of fullness. Or, as we say in idiomatic English, they "top them up." In this understanding of the verb the meaning of both of its pre-verbs comes into play, with ἀνα- suggesting both "back" and "up" (see LSJ s.v. F,1 and F,4) and ἐπι- indicating the point of fullness "up to" which the vessels are brought (see LSJ s.v. ἐπί G,2,d).

(6) ΛΗΜΜΑ, "MESSAGE."

Zechariah 9:1: Λῆμμα λόγου κυρίου· ἐν γῇ Σεδραχ καὶ Δαμασκοῦ θυσία αὐτοῦ ("Message of the word of the Lord: his sacrifice is in the land of Sedrach and Damascus.")

Zechariah 12:1: Λῆμμα λόγου κυρίου ἐπὶ τὸν Ισραηλ· λέγει κύριος . . . ("Message of the word of the Lord: the Lord says . . . ")

The word λῆμμα here functions, as it often does in the LXX, as a translation of the Hebrew word מַשָּׂא, "oracle." It should be noted that the Hebrew noun is related to the verb נָשָׂא, "to lift" or "carry." Although its original sense was therefore something carried, a burden or load, it is also used in many places as a general term for "prophetic revelation" or "oracle." This was first clearly articulated by the Dutch biblical scholars Joannes Coccejus and Campegius Vitringa in the seventeenth century. The term therefore essentially refers to any message which the prophet "carries" or "conveys" from God to his addressees.[37]

In the light of this background information about the Hebrew term, we can understand why the Greek λῆμμα in Zechariah is

---

37. See Wolters, *Zechariah*, 261–62. For the seventeenth-century recognition of the meaning "oracle," see Pressel, *Commentar zu den Schriften der Propheten Haggai, Sacharja und Maleachi*, 262.

sometimes translated "burden" (so Thomson and Brenton), or "load" (BG: *carga*), and sometimes "oracle" (so BA). If it means "oracle" we can also understand why Giguet translates λῆμμα λόγου κυρίου in both places as simply "parole du Seigneur," leaving the first Greek word untranslated, since "oracle" and "word of the Lord" are virtually synonymous. This background also explains the separate meaning category in LSJ s.v. λῆμμα IV: ""in Lxx, *burden* laid on one, *commission received*, esp. of *prophecy*."

However, λῆμμα is not to be simply equated with the Hebrew word מַשָּׂא. The Greek word is related to the verb λαμβάνω and means essentially "something received" and then by extension "profit" or "assumption" (that is, something taken for granted." See LSJ s.v. (The latter meaning explains Jerome's translation of λῆμμα here as *assumptio*). The underlying image of the Greek word is not something that is carried or conveyed by the prophet, but rather something that is *received* by him, namely a message from God. The best translation of the prophetic λῆμμα is therefore "message," with the implication "message received." So SD, which translates *Botschaft*.

I have not been able to account for one of the published translations of λῆμμα. It is the rendering found in NETS, namely "an issue (of the Lord's word)." It is unclear to me what "issue" here means, or how it was arrived at.

(7) ΦΑΝΤΑΣΙΑ, "VISION"

Zechariah 10:1: Αἰτεῖσθε παρὰ κυρίου ὑετὸν καθ' ὥραν πρόϊμον καὶ ὄψιμον· κύριος ἐποίησεν φαντασίας, καὶ ὑετὸν χειμερινὸν δώσει αὐτοῖς ("Ask rain from the Lord, early or late according to the season. The Lord brought about visions, and he will give them winter rain").

When he came to the word φαντασίας in this verse Jerome frankly declared himself baffled. "I do not know with what intent the Seventy gave the translation φαντασίας, unless they perhaps wished to describe the greatness of [God's] grace and the marvel of his gifts with the noun φαντασία."[38] To judge from this tentative comment he seems to have

---

38. Adriaen, *Hieronymi presbyteri opera*, 838: "Et nescio quid uolentes LXX phantasias interpretati sunt, nisi forte magnitudinem gratiae admirationemque donorum, nomine phantasiae uoluere describere."

taken the word to refer to things that are "fantastic" in the sense of "wonderful." However, in his Latin translation he did not even attempt to find an equivalent for the Greek word, contenting himself with the transliteration *phantasias* (so too CP). Subsequent translators, however, although they have not avoided the challenge of translating φαντασίας, have come up with widely divergent results. Thomson has "appearances," Brenton "bright signs," Giguet "manifest signs" (similarly SD), BA "flashes of lightning" (*fulgurances*), NETS "representations," and BG "displays" (*ostentaciones*). There is no agreement among LXX lexica either: LEH has "*sign* (from God)," and GELS s.v. has "*what visibly manifests itself,* 'image.'"

It is possible to make a pretty good guess as to what the translator *intended* to convey by φαντασίας here, but it is less clear what the word in fact actually conveyed to a Greek speaker. The corresponding word in the MT is חֲזִיזִים (itself a multivalent word of disputed interpretation; I have translated it "thunder showers"[39]), but it has long been recognized that what the LXX translator read in his *Vorlage* was either חֲזְיֹנִים or חֲזוֹנִים, both meaning "(prophetic) visions."[40] On φαντασία meaning "vision," see Schleusner s.v., LEH s.v., and GE s.v. A. Note also that in Job 20:8 the word חִזָּיוֹן is translated by the related word φάσμα (variant reading φάντασμα). It follows that what the LXX translator of our verse intended to convey with the word φαντασίας was "visions."

However, for a reader of the Greek text who has no knowledge of the probable Hebrew *Vorlage* of this verse, it is at best a remote possibility that φαντασίας would actually have conveyed the meaning "visions," especially since the immediate context speaks of rain. The most straightforward way of understanding φαντασίας in this context would probably be to assume that it refers to natural "phenomena" in general, or more specifically to "displays" of God's power, as in lightning, or to "signs" of a coming rainstorm. This suspicion is confirmed by the history of interpretation, beginning with the commentaries written by the Greek church fathers, specifically those by Didymus the Blind, Cyril of Alexandria, Theodore of Mopsuestia, and Theodoret of Cyrrhus, who

---

39. See Wolters, *Zechariah*, 309.

40 See for example Schleusner s.v.; J. Z. Schuurmans Stekhoven, *De Alexandrjnse vertaling van het Dokekapropheton*, 101; Rudolph, *Haggai–Sacharja*, 190.

uniformly understood the φαντασίας here of bolts of lightning (see the references given in BA *ad locum*). Unwittingly, they thus got close to the meaning of the MT reading חֲזִיזִים. There is no indication that any Greek Church father understood the word here to refer to visions.[41]

This raises the philosophical point whether a translation of the LXX should seek to reflect the intention of the translator or to give the most plausible reading of the text in its literary context. I tend to the former view and would therefore argue that the best translation here is "visions."

An additional grammatical point to observe in this verse is that the adjectives πρόϊμον and ὄψιμον modify ὑετόν, not ὥραν. This is clear from Deut 11:14, to which our verse is clearly alluding. NETS gets it wrong, translating "in the early and later season" (so too BG). The correct construal is indicated in GELS s.v. πρόϊμος.

(8) ΒΑΡΥΝΩ, "HARDEN."

Zechariah 11:8: καὶ βαρυνθήσεται ἡ ψυχή μου ἐπ' αὐτούς ("and my soul will be hardened against them").

The verb βαρύνω means "make heavy," "weigh down," so that a literal rendering of this sentence would be "and my soul will be *made heavy* or *weighed down* against them." However, it is clear that this cannot here be understood literally but must have a metaphorical or idiomatic meaning. Translators and commentators have made many stabs at capturing this idiomatic meaning. The fifth-century church father Cyril of Alexandria paraphrased the sentence as βαρείαν αὐτοῖς ἐποίσω τὴν δίκην, ("I shall impose a heavy penalty on them").[42] Some have given a fairly literal rendering, for example "my soul will be heavy against them" (so NETS; similarly Jerome, CP, Thomson, BG). Others say that the soul "will be very irritated" (so Schleusner: *exacerbatus valde erit*), "be distressed (or provoked)" (so Wright[43]), "grieve" (so

---

41 According to the notes on this verse in BA (313), Basil the Great, when he quoted this verse in his *Letter* 210.6 (not 210.16 as indicated in those notes), may have understood φαντασία to mean "vision." This is based on a misreading of the passage in question. When the authors quote Basil as saying that "toute vision n'est pas une prophétie" the Greek word translated "vision" is actually ἐνύπνιον, "dream."

42. See his commentary on Zechariah at *PG* 72.192B.

43. Wright, *Zechariah and his Prophecies*, 580.

Brenton) or "be sore displeased" (so Brenton in a marginal note), or "closed off" (so SD: *verschlossen*). Schrenk has glossed the idiom here as meaning *zürnen, streng sein*, "be angry, be severe."[44] French translators have chosen the rendering *s'appesantira* (literally "weigh down;" so Giguet, Doutreleau, BA).[45] Muraoka in 1990 glossed the line as "I shall be gravely distressed over them,"[46] but in 2009 as "my attitude towards them will become unfriendly" (so GELS s.v.). How are we to find our way in this welter of conflicting opinions?

As I have argued elsewhere, the answer to this question lies in the fact that the verb βαρύνω in the LXX often takes on one of the senses of the Hebrew כבד hiphil, namely "to harden" (the heart) or "dull" (the senses).[47] I would argue, therefore, that the sentence we are considering should be translated "and my soul *will be hardened* against them."

This conclusion is reinforced if we recognize that the verb in the parallel line which follows is an example of inner-Greek corruption. That line reads as follows: καὶ αἱ ψυχαὶ αὐτῶν ἐπωρύοντο ἐπ' ἐμέ ("and their souls were roaring against me"). This does not seem to make much sense in the context. However, a good case can be made for the view that the verb ἐπωρύοντο here originally read ἐπωροῦντο, from the verb πωρόω, "to harden" (literally "to turn to stone [πῶρος]").[48] The change would be the result of the metathesis of two letters, a common cause of textual corruption. Standing in parallelism with βαρυνθήσεται, this verb thus means essentially the same thing.

(9) ῎ΙΣΤΗΜΙ, "WEIGH OUT," "PAY."

Zechariah 11:12: καὶ ἐρῶ πρὸς αὐτούς Εἰ καλὸν ἐνώπιον ὑμῶν ἐστι, δότε [στήσαντες] τὸν μισθόν μου ἢ ἀπείπατε· καὶ ἔστησαν τὸν μισθόν μου τριάκοντα ἀργυροῦς ("and I will say to them, 'If it is good in your

---

44. See G. Schrenk in *TDNT* 1.559 (= *TWNT* 1.557).

45. The French *s'appesantir* commonly has the meaning "to dwell at length (on a subject)," but this meaning does not fit the present context.

46. Muraoka, "Septuagintal Lexicography," 42.

47. See Wolters, "Semantic Borrowing," 686. Note that this use of βαρύνω is found also at Zech 7:11.

48. See Wolters, "Semantic Borrowing," 688–90.

eyes pay my wages [after weighing them out], or else refuse.' And they weighed out my wages, thirty silver coins").

It should be noted that the word στήσαντες after δότε, though without a counterpart in the MT and absent from the editions of Rahlfs and Ziegler, has considerable manuscript support.[49] It is also found in the text used for the patristic commentaries on Zechariah by Didymus the Blind and Jerome.[50]

It is clear that ἔστησαν here means "weigh (out)," and thus "pay." The image is that of a certain amount of silver being put (literally "made to stand") on one tray of a pair of scales to make sure it is the correct amount, and then paid out to a worker as wages. This is a well-established meaning of ἵστημι (see LSJ s.v. A,IV,2; BDAG s.v. 6,b; GE 1,D), and is confirmed here by the underlying Hebrew וַיִּשְׁקְלוּ), "and they weighed out"). It is correctly translated by Thomson, Brenton, Giguet, and BG. See also GELS s.v. II,4.

It is therefore surprising that so many contemporary translations get it wrong. See for example BA ("ils fixèrent mon salaire"), NETS ("they fixed my salary"), and SD ("sie bestimmten meinen Lohn"). It is even more surprising that Jerome, who had an excellent command of Greek and who correctly translated the Hebrew as *appenderunt*, rendered ἔστησαν here as *statuerunt*.[51] This anomaly can probably be explained by the fact that his commentary on Zechariah was heavily dependent on that of Didymus the Blind, who although his native tongue was Greek, also misinterpreted the Greek verb here, writing στήσαντες, τοῦτ' ἔστιν ὁρίσαντες, τὸν μισθόν μου, thus equating ἵστημι here with ὁρίζω, "to determine."[52] No doubt the mistake has to do with the fact that, after the introduction of coinage in the Greek world around 400 BC, the actual weighing of silver to determine the exact value of a sum of money was no longer common practice, since coins had a standardized weight.

---

49. See the apparatus *ad locum* in Ziegler.

50. See Doutreleau, *Sur Zacharie*, 858, and Adriaen, *Hieronymi presbyteri opera*, 856.

51. Adriaen, *Hieronymi presbyteri opera*, 856.

52. For Jerome's dependence on Didymus, see Doutreleau, *Sur Zacharie*, 129-35. The quote is found on p. 860 of Doutreleau's edition.

We find a similar confusion in translations of Matt 26:15, where we read of the chief priests who had been approached by Judas Iscariot that they ἔστησαν αὐτῷ τριάκοντα ἀργύρια, a clear allusion to our verse. The verb is here correctly translated as "weigh out" or "pay" in most contemporary versions, but Jerome (in the Vulgate) has *constituerunt*, and the KJV has "they covenanted with him for thirty pieces of silver." Compare also the curious entry in BDAG s.v. ἵστημι A,6,b, which acknowledges that the verb in Zech 11:12 meant "weigh out," but claims that in the allusion to that verse in Matt 26:15 it means "determine a monetary amount."

A number of subordinate points in this verse also require a brief comment. One is the meaning of ἀπείπασθε. GELS s.v. ἀπεῖπον 1 assigns the following meaning to its use here: "*rescind* an agreement." I can find no lexicographical evidence for this meaning, and suspect a confusion with the verb διασκεδάζω (or rather its Hebrew counterpart פרר *hiphil*), which occurs three times in the immediate context (vv. 10, 11, and 14). The Greek verb ἀπεῖπον here simply has its common meaning "refuse" (see LSJ s.v. II and IV,2). Another point is the translation of μισθός, which BG renders with the Spanish word *jornal*, "day's wages." This is a mistake, however, since the wage in question was in all likelihood a month's wages.[53] Finally, it should be noted that ἀργυροῦς is the accusative plural of the contracted form of the adjective ἀργύρεος, here used as a substantive, meaning "silver coins" (see LSJ s.v. II, which mentions this place). This rendering therefore (unlike the Hebrew original[54]) does presuppose the introduction of coinage. As noted above, it is replaced by its equivalent ἀργύρια in Matt 26:15.

(10) ἈΣΤΡΆΓΑΛΟΙ, "ANKLEBONES."

Zechariah 11:16: καὶ τὰ κρέα τῶν ἐκλεκτῶν καταφάγεται καὶ τοὺς ἀστραγάλους αὐτῶν ἐκστρέψει ("and he shall eat the meat of the choice ones and twist off their anklebones").

There is again great diversity in the rendering of ἀστραγάλους in this verse. Published translations include the following: "heels" (so Jerome and CP: *talos*, Doutreleau: *talons*), "joints" (Thomson, Giguet:

53. See Wolters, *Zechariah*, 381–82.
54. See Wolters, *Zechariah*, 379.

jointures, BA: *articulations*), "joints *of their necks*" (Brenton), "hooves" (Brouwer: *hoeven*),[55] "vertebrae" (NETS), "necks" (Brenton in marginal note, BG), and "ankle" (Rudolph: *Knöchel*).[56] The LXX lexica also disagree among themselves. SV s.v. has "vertebrae" (*Wirbelknochen*), LEH s.v. has "the joints of the anckle [*sic*]," and GELS s.v. has "one of the vertebrae of the neck: of sheep."

Although it is true that ἀστράγαλος can refer to vertebrae, especially in the neck, as well as bones elsewhere in the body (see LSJ s.v.), we do not need to settle for this wide array of possible meanings in the present context. When applied to animals, as here, ἀστράγαλος regularly refers to the bones of the ankle (see LSJ s.v. II,1). One of the most common uses of the word in Greek is in reference to the game of *astragalismos*, in which the anklebones of sheep and goats were used like dice (see LSJ s.v. III). Note also that the word "astragalus" has entered the English language as a technical term for a bone in the ankle.[57] Consequently, the bones here mentioned are most likely those found in the ankles.

As it happens, this meaning is also a good match for the corresponding Hebrew in the MT, namely פַּרְסֵיהֶן. This is usually translated as "their hoofs," but since it appears to refer to something edible, it should probably be understood to mean "their trotters," where "trotters" refers to "the feet of a quadruped, esp. those of sheep and pigs as used for food."[58] They are often eaten as a delicacy.

(11) ΔΈΡΡΙΣ ΤΡΙΧΊΝΗ, "MANTLE OF HAIRCLOTH."

Zechariah 13:4: καὶ ἐνδύσονται δέρριν τριχίνην ("and they will put on a mantle of haircloth").

This sentence is usually interpreted to mean that the prophets will wear "a hairy skin" (so Thomson, BA, NETS, BG), which evokes the strange image of prophets wearing a shaggy animal's hide. Somewhat less strange is the rendering "hairy leather garment" (so GELS s.v.; similarly SD: *einen haarigen Ledermantel*). LSJ (s.v. I) also gives the

---

55. See Brouwer, *Wachter en herder*, 196.
56. See Rudolph, *Haggai, Sacharja*, 203.
57. See the *Oxford English Dictionary* s.v. 1.
58. Wolters, *Zechariah*, 396.

meaning "skin" for the δέρρις here, but this is corrected in LSJ1996 s.v. with the note: "II. *cloak* or sim.; perh. fr. similarity to Hebr. *aderet* [*sic*; read *adderet*]." In other words, the garment in question is not necessarily made of skin or leather. This is confirmed by the use of δέρρις in the Pentateuch, where it refers to the curtains of the tabernacle, which are explicitly said to be made of goat's hair (Exod 26:7, 26:12, and Num 4:25). This in turn sheds light on the meaning of the adjective τρίχινος here, which does not mean "hairy" in the sense "covered with hair," but rather "made of hair" (so GELS s.v.; BDAG s.v.). In other words, the garment in question was woven of hair, probably goat's hair. This is confirmed by the Hebrew *Vorlage*, which has שְׂעַר אַדֶּרֶת, "a mantle of haircloth," where the word שֵׂעָר is related to שָׂעִיר, "he-goat." It should also be borne in mind that a mantle of goat's hair was worn by Elijah and may have become a kind of symbol of the prophetic office.[59]

The phrase was correctly understood by Brenton, who has "a garment of hair," and Giguet, who has "*cilices de crin.*" We find a curiously hybrid translation in Jerome, who has "*pelle Cilicina,*" literally "Cilician skin," where the adjective *Cilicinus* is a variant of *Cilicius*, "Cilician," which when applied to fabrics means "made of goat's hair" (*Oxford Latin Dictionary* s.v. "Cilicius" c). Obviously this cannot apply to "skin." (Incidentally, the Latin adjective is based on the Greek Κιλίκιον, which means "*coarse cloth*, strictly of Cilician goat's hair" [LSJ s.v.], and itself gave rise via *cilicium*, "hairshirt," to French *cilice*, "hairshirt"). We find a similar disconnect between noun and adjective in the entry for τρίχινος in GELS, where we read: "*made of hair*: δέρρις τ. 'hairy leather garment' Exod 26.7, Zech 13.4." It is unclear how a leather garment can be "made of hair!"

The suggestion in LSJ1996 that the translation δέρρις was here chosen because it sounded like Hebrew *'adderet* (see above) seems dubious to me. It is more probable, given the propensity of later LXX translators to draw on the vocabulary of the Pentateuch, that the translator of Zechariah is here echoing the expression δέρρεις τριχίνας in Exod 26:7, where it refers to the goat's hair curtains of the tabernacle.

---

59. See Wolters, *Zechariah*, 428–29.

BIBLIOGRAPHY

Abernethy, Diana. "Translation of Horse Colors in Zechariah 1:8; 6:2–3, 6." *JBL* 136 (2017) 593–607.

Adriaen, M., ed. *Hieronymi presbyteri opera. Pars I: Opera exegetica 6: Commentarii in prophetas minores*. CCSL 76A. Turnholt: Brepols, 1970.

Brouwer, Cornelis. *Wachter en herder: Een exegetische studie over de herderfiguur in het Oude Testament, inzonderheid in de pericopen Zacharia 11 en 13:7-9*. Wageningen: Veenman & Zonen, 1949.

Brown, Francis, S. R. Driver, and Charles A. Briggs. *Hebrew and English Lexicon of the Old Testament, with an Appendix Containing the Biblical Aramaic*. Oxford: Clarendon, 1906.

Casevitz, Michel, Cécile Dogniez, and Marguerite Harl. *Les Douze Prophètes: Aggée Zacharie*. BA 23.10–11. Paris: Cerf, 2007.

Cimos, Mario. "Observations on the Greek Translation of the Book of Zechariah." In *IX Congress of the International Organization for Septuagint and Cognate Studies. Cambridge, 1995*, edited by Bernard A. Taylor, 91–108. SBLSCS 45. Atlanta: Scholars Press, 1997.

Doutreleau, Louis. *Didyme l'Aveugle, Sur Zacharie*. SC 83–85. Paris: Cerf, 1962.

Du Cange. *Glossarium ad scriptores mediae et infimae graecitatis*. 2 vols. Lyon: Rigaud, 1688.

Glare, P. G. W., ed. *Greek-English Lexicon. Revised Supplement*. Oxford: Clarendon, 1996.

Gooding, D. W. *The Account of the Tabernacle. Translation and Textual Problems of the Greek Exodus*. Cambridge: Cambridge University Press, 1959.

Goodwin, W. W., and C. B. Gulick. *Greek Grammar*. Boston: Ginn, 1930.

Hanhart, Robert. *Sacharja*. BKAT 14.7. Neukirchen-Vluyn: Neukirchener Verlag, 1990–1998.

Hesychius Alexandrinus. *Hesychiui Alexandrini Lexicon*. Edited by Peter Allan Hansen and Ian C. Cunningham. 4 vols. SGLG 11. Berlin: de Gruyter, 2009–2020.

Horst, Friedrich. *Die zwölf kleinen Propheten: Nahum bis Maleachi*. HAT 1.4. Tübingen: Mohr Siebeck, 1938.

Koehler, L., W. Baumgartner, and J. J. Stamm. *Hebräisches und aramäisches Lexikon zum Alten Testament*. Leiden: Brill, 1967–1995.

Koster, W. J. W. *Scholia in Aristophanem, Pars I: Prolegomena de comoedia, scholia in Acharnenses, Equites, Nubes. Fasc. III2 continens scholia recentiora in Nubes*. Groningen: Bouma's Boekhuis, 1974.

Lanier, Gregory R. "The Curious Case of צמח and ἀνατολή: An Inquiry into Septuagint Translation Patterns." *JBL* 134 (2015) 505–27.

Le Boulluec, Alain, and Pierre Sandevoir. *L'Exode*. BA 12. Paris, Cerf, 1986.
Liddell, Henry George, and Robert Scott. *A Greek-English Lexicon*. 9th ed. Oxford: Clarendon, 1940.
Liddell, Henry George, et al. *A Greek-English Lexicon*. 9th ed. with revised supplement. Edited by P. G. W. Glare with A. Thompson. Oxford: Clarendon, 1996.
Lowe, W. H. *The Student's Commentary on Zechariah, Hebrew and LXX*. London: MacMillan, 1882.
Lust, Johan, et al., eds. *Greek-English Lexicon of the Septuagint*. Rev. ed. Stuttgart: Deutsche Bibelgesellschaft, 2003.
Meisterhans, K. *Grammatik der attischen Inschriften*. Dritte vermehrte und verbesserte Auflage, besorgt von Eduard Schwyzer. Berlin: Weidmann, 1900.
Montanari, Franco. *The Brill Dictionary of Ancient Greek*. Leiden: Brill, 2015.
Muraoka, T. *A Greek-English Lexicon of the Septuagint*. Louvain: Peeters, 2009.
———. "Septuagintal Lexicography: Some General Issues." In *Melbourne Symposium on Septuagint Lexicography*, edited by T. Muraoka, 17–48. SBLSCS 28. Atlanta: Scholars, 1990.
Rehkopf, Friedrich. *Septuaginta-Vokabular*. Göttingen: Vandenhoeck & Ruprecht, 1989.
Reiter, Gerhard. *Die griechischen Bezeichnungen der Farben Weiss, Grau und Braun. Eine Bedeutungsuntersuchung*. Commentationes Aenipontanae XVI. Innsbruck: Universitätsverlag, 1962.
Rudolph, Wilhelm. *Haggai, Sacharja 1–8, Sacharja 9–14, Maleachi*. KAT. Gütersloh: Gerd Mohn, 1976.
Schleusner, J. F. *Novus thesaurus philologico-criticus; sive lexicon in LXX. et reliquos interpretes graecos, ac scriptores apocryphos Veteris Testamenti*. 3 vols. Leipzig: Weidmann, 1822.
Shipp, G. P. *Modern Greek Evidence for the Ancient Greek Vocabulary*. Sydney: Sydney University Press, 1979.
Thomson, Charles. *The Old Covenant Commonly Called the Old Testament: Translated from the Septuagint*. Edited by S. F. Peels. 2 vols. London: Skeffington & Son, 1904.
Thompson, D'Arcy Wentworth. *A Glossary of Greek Birds*. Oxford: Clarendon, 1895.
Walters, Peter. *The Text of the Septuagint: Its Corruptions and their Emendation*. Edited by D. W. Gooding. Cambridge: Cambridge University Press, 1973.
Wolters, Al. "The Meaning of Ṣantĕrôt (Zech 4:12)." *JHebS* 12 (2012) 1–15.
———. "Semantic Borrowing and Inner-Greek Corruption in LXX Zechariah 11:8." *JBL* 118 (1999) 685–90.

———. *Zechariah*. HCOT. Leuven: Peeters, 2014.
Wright, C. H. H. *Zechariah and his Prophecies, Considered in Relation to Modern Criticism*. London: Hodder & Stoughton, 1879. Reprint, Minneapolis: Klock & Klock, 1980.
Ziegler, Joseph, ed. *Duodecim prophetae*. Septuaginta. Vetus Testamentum graecum auctoritate Societatis Litterarum Gottingensis XIII. Göttingen: Vandenhoeck & Ruprecht, 1943.

10

The Congregation of the Poor
Poverty as a Self-Designation in the Dead Sea Scrolls

Daniel K. Falk

INTRODUCTION

SINCE THE EARLY DAYS of research on the Dead Sea Scrolls, the usage of poverty language with regard to the covenantal community invited comparison with the New Testament.[1] The purpose of this short study is to survey some of the more recent investigations of poverty language in the Dead Sea Scrolls and to assess their significance for the study of the New Testament and early Christianity. Such a reassessment is in order due to several factors. First, New Testament scholarship is still deeply influenced by studies prior to the full publication of the Dead Sea Scrolls (the official series Discoveries in the Judaean Desert was completed in 2010). Much relevant new material from Qumran has been published in the last twenty years, especially a large body of previously unknown wisdom texts and critical editions of all of the

---

1. I gratefully dedicate this article to Gus Konkel, whose love of the biblical text is infectious.

Hodayot manuscripts.[2] Second, with full publication of multiple copies, it has become increasingly clear that intertextual relationships and redaction among key texts are complicated and non-linear. Third, in the last couple decades in particular, scholars have increasingly applied new methods to the study of the Dead Sea Scrolls, especially drawing on social-scientific models and cognitive science of religion.[3] This is reflected in a shift in focus from historical reconstruction to social affect.

At the risk of over-simplification, I would distinguish two broad trends in the study of poverty language in the Dead Sea Scrolls. On the one hand are those with predominantly philological and historical-critical interests, using historical and textual models to pursue such questions as the meaning of the terms in their grammatical and literary context, the historical and social context of the writings, and what this language says about the referents. On the other hand are those that primarily use models from the social sciences to pursue questions about how groups use labels to differentiate themselves, and the effects of such language on subjectivity and group identity. After a summary of some of the main observations of the former studies, this paper will discuss the contributions of studies in the latter vein.

HISTORICAL AND PHILOLOGICAL APPROACHES

Most investigations of poverty in the Dead Sea Scrolls have sought, through close philological and literary study, to explain the meaning of the terms in their contexts, to identify their referents, and to clarify the implications for the social location of the movement and its history. The main terminology is similar to the Hebrew Bible (אביון, עני, ענו, מחסור, דל, רש) with a similar spectrum of usage from socio-economic to metaphorical poverty, including material deprivation, persecution, lowly standing before God, and a spiritual quality of humility.[4]

---

2. DJD 20; DJD 34; DJD 29; DJD 40.

3. See Jokiranta, "Sociological Approaches," for an overview.

4. For the distribution and usage of these terms, see Fabry, "דַּל dal; דלל dalal," 681–85; Wold, "אֶבְיוֹן ʾæbjôn"; Zanella, "חָסֵר ḥāser"; Gregory, "רוש rwš," 645–48; Markl, "עָנָה II ʿānāh"; and Fabry, "Die Armenfrömmigkeit."

COMMUNITY

Poverty as Self-Designation

The greatest amount of attention has been devoted to the usage of poverty terminology as a self-designation, especially as a potential parallel to the use of "the Poor Ones" as a title for the early Christian community in Jerusalem (e.g., Gal 2:10).[5] For example, David Flusser argued in 1960 that a psalm in the Hodayot that praises God for raising up a herald "to proclaim good news to the poor (ענוים) . . . [the contr]ite in spirit (נכאי רוח) . . . and those who mourn" (1QH[a] 23:13–16) shares with Matt 5:3–5 a common midrash on Isa 61:1 and 66:2, and they must have some sort of literary connection.[6] Moreover, a practice of shared wealth is attested of the early Christians in Acts, of the Essenes in reports by Philo and Josephus, and of the sectarian community in the Community Rule found at Qumran (1QS 1:11–12; 5:1–4).[7] Thus, some have suggested that the use of poverty language as a self-designation in both movements is related to a similar chosen lifestyle of shared property, and even that early Christianity perhaps had a historical connection to the Essene movement.[8]

Leander Keck showed that the evidence does not support such connections.[9] He noted, "It is essential to distinguish between the practice of sharing wealth and calling one's community 'the Poor,' for they are not at all the same."[10] He also noted that in neither the New Testament nor the Dead Sea Scrolls is poverty language used as a designation in contexts describing shared wealth. With regard to the Qumran texts, "the passages which speak of the economic arrangements of the community contain no references whatsoever to 'the Poor' and those passages which speak of 'the Poor' (or the poor) do not discuss the

---

5. See Keck, "The Poor Among the Saints in the New Testament," 100–101.

6. Flusser, "Blessed Are the Poor." All references to 1QH[a] are according to the reconstruction of Stegemann and Schuller, DJD 40. Throughout, translations of the Dead Sea Scrolls are from Parry and Tov, *The Dead Sea Scrolls Reader* (with occasional adaptations).

7. Philo, *Hypoth.* 10:11–13; *Prob.* 84–88; Josephus, *War* 2:122.

8. E.g., Flusser, *Judaism of the Second Temple Period*, 1:34.

9. Keck, "The Poor Among the Saints in the New Testament"; Keck, "The Poor Among the Saints in Jewish Christianity and Qumran."

10. Keck, "The Poor Among the Saints in Jewish Christianity and Qumran," 68.

shared life at all."[11] This observation continues to be true even after the publication of the full corpus of scrolls found at Qumran.

In fact, the evidence for the use of "the Poor" as a technical title in either the New Testament or the Dead Sea Scrolls is weaker than is often assumed. Poverty language as a community designation is relatively rare in both corpora, and in neither case does it seem to have been a prominent title. The distribution of poverty language is revealing. For now, it is important to note merely that in the Dead Sea Scrolls, the only certain cases of "the poor" as a title for the sectarian community are found in a commentary (pesher) on Psalms: the "meek" and the "righteous" of Ps 37:11, 21–22 who will inherit the earth interpreted as "the congregation of the Poor Ones" (עדת האביונים) who faithfully endure a time of affliction and are vindicated in God's eschatological judgment (4QpPsa 1–10 ii 9–12; 1–10 iii 8–11). A similar phrase in a hymn about transformation (4Q491 11 i 11) is probably also a titular use: "the company of the Poor Ones (ועצת אביונים) shall become an eternal congregation" (לעֲדֹת עולמים)." This is probably a Hodayot hymn, as a different recension occurs in three Hodayot manuscripts.[12] There are a few other references where the eschatological community of the faithful is described as "the poor" or "the humble": in a pesher on Isaiah (4QpIsaª [4Q161] 8–10 3) and in the War Scroll (1QM 11:9, 13; 13:14; 14:7). Other instances of poverty language for the faithful community are mostly from direct citation of Scripture in pesher texts (e.g., 4QpIsaᶜ [4Q163] 21 7 [Zech 11:11]; 8–10 13 [Isa 14:30]; 18–19 2 [Isa 29:19]; 4QTanh [4Q176] 1–2 ii 2 [Isa 49:14]; cf. CD 6:16 [Isa 10:2]; 19:9 [Zech 11:7]). In a number of the Hodayot hymns, the speaking voice self-identifies as a "poor one." In short, the use of poverty language as a self-designation in the Dead Sea Scrolls is limited to a narrow group of texts: the pesher texts, the Hodayot, and the War Scroll. That is, it occurs in a few exegetical, poetic, and eschatological texts that take up language of the pious poor from post-exilic Psalms and prophetic texts. On the other hand, such usage is conspicuously lacking in the rule books (Rule of the Community, Damascus Document) which describe

---

11. Keck, "The Poor Among the Saints in Jewish Christianity and Qumran," 68.

12. On the difficulties of this remarkable hymn, see Wise, "מי כמוני באלים"; Collins, "Self-Glorification Hymn."

the aims and way of life of communities in this movement, including the practice of shared wealth (e.g., CD 13:11-12; 1QS 1:11-13).[13] As Keck noted, this makes it highly doubtful that the use of "the Poor" as a self-designation is due to the practice of voluntary shared property.

Social Location

Numerous studies also examine the use of poverty language for potential clues to social location, in particular whether it reflects actual socio-economic poverty and/or experience of persecution.[14] Such investigations focused initially on the pesher texts and Hodayot. Whereas some of the Hodayot—the so-called "Community Hymns"—use poverty language metaphorically in expressions of humility and nothingness before God (*niedrigkeitsdoxologie*), others—the so-called Teacher Hymns—seem to describe persecution and betrayal experienced by a leader.[15] The latter hymns have frequently been interpreted in light of passages in the pesher texts that speak of the Teacher of Righteousness persecuted by the Wicked Priest and betrayed by members of his own community.[16] Some have argued that these hymns reflect the actual experience of an individual, whereas others argue that they were for communal use—whether liturgical or didactic—and express the community's experience of persecution.[17] It is generally agreed now that neither the pesher texts nor the Hodayot offer reliable data for historical reconstruction, and a sharp distinction between two types of Hodayot as Community versus Teacher or Leader Hymns is increasingly questioned.

---

13. There are two passages in the Damascus Document where the eschatological faithful community is described as "the poor" in quotations from the prophets: CD 6:16 (Isa 10:2); 19:9 (Zech 11:7). On the treatment of wealth in the Rule of the Community and the Damascus Document, see Murphy, *Wealth in the Dead Sea Scrolls*, 25-162.

14. E.g., Flusser, *Judaism of the Second Temple Period*, 1:35; Murphy, *Wealth in the Dead Sea Scrolls*; Fabry, "Die Armenfrömmigkeit"; Wright, "Categories of Rich and Poor."

15. E.g., Douglas, "Teacher Hymn Hypothesis"; Schuller, "Recent Scholarship," 120, 139-46.

16. E.g., 1QpHab 11:4-8; 4QpPsa (4Q171) 1-10 iii 15-16 cf. 1-10 ii 9-25 (esp. 18-20).

17. E.g., Holm-Nielsen, *Hodayot*, 48n4; 49n11.

With the full publication of the Dead Sea Scrolls, it has become clear that some of the key works are composite, incorporating diverse materials, and survive in different recensions, most notably, the Damascus Document, the Rule of the Community, the Hodayot and the War Scroll.[18] Scholars have attempted to plot works and redactions in a developmental progression from pre-sectarian to early sectarian and full sectarian.[19] Especially important with regard to poverty language are the numerous sapiential works found at Qumran—especially 4QInstruction—which scholars generally judge to be "pre-sectarian" but very influential on the language and ideology of the sectarian movement.[20] The portrayal of community life and relationships with outsiders differs significantly among different texts and recensions, including the language and attitudes related to poverty and wealth.

Catherine Murphy's massive study, *Wealth in the Dead Sea Scrolls and in the Qumran Community*, exemplifies this developmental approach.[21] In lengthy chapters on the Damascus Document, Rule of the Community, 4QInstruction and other literature, she exhaustively examines the material related to wealth and poverty in light of relative dating and redactions, and relates these data to the archaeological evidence from Qumran and the secondary testimony about the Essenes from Philo, Josephus, and Pliny the Elder. She describes her approach as "socio-redactional": "This method begins with the assumption that traditions are shaped according to the socio-political pressures experienced by the communities behind the texts... Religious expressions... are part of a symbol system that encompasses other institutions (family, ecnomy, politics), and thus we can expect that economic categories will shed light on religious expressions and *vice versa*."[22] It is impossible to

---

18. E.g., Hempel, *Damascus Texts*, 44–53; Hempel, *Qumran Rule Texts*, 65–119; Metso, *Serekh Texts*, 15–20; Schofield, *From Qumran to the Yaḥad*, 69–130; Schuller, "Recent Scholarship," 133–146; Kim Harkins, "Observations"; Kim Harkins, "A New Proposal"; Duhaime, *War Texts*, 12–44; Schultz, "Compositional Layers in the War Scroll."

19. Dimant, *History, Ideology, and Bible Interpretation in the Dead Sea Scrolls*, 171–83.

20. Goff, *4QInstruction*, 27–29.

21. Murphy, *Wealth in the Dead Sea Scrolls*.

22. Murphy, *Wealth in the Dead Sea Scrolls*, 23.

do justice to the details of this study here, but distinctive of her study is the priority she gives to the rule books, as she is primarily concerned with the legal and social practices related to wealth and poverty. The Hodayot and pesher texts, on the other hand, are treated briefly in a chapter on "Other Literature." Her main thesis is that "real economic deprivation and rival theodicies that justified economic oppression and religious persecution lie behind the sectarian economic critique and practice."[23] Murphy finds throughout the sectarian texts concern for economic inequality, and blames the arrogance of the wicked. She finds little evidence for an idealization of poverty, but rather the development of an alternative economy to meet needs in the present, while looking forward to the eschatological reversal of fortunes. The evidence from the archeology of Qumran and external descriptions of Essenes she regards as consistent with this picture. Murphy suggests that the pre-sectarian 4QInstruction resonated in the sect because it addresses those who experience poverty and are in danger of falling into real need, and advises them to seek wisdom while awaiting eschatological reversal.

Notably, Murphy focuses on poverty language as directly related to socio-economic conditions and not as metaphorical or as an ideal. Not all scholars are optimistic about the ability to reconstruct social location of the community from the language in these texts. With regard to 4QInstruction, for example, scholars differ quite markedly over how to understand the repeated address to the sage as "you are poor."[24] Few have accepted Eibert Tigchelaar's suggestion that this should be read as a conditional, "If you are poor."[25] Similar to Murphy, Benjamin Wright, and Matthew Goff both believe that the instruction addresses those of low social and economic status, but not destitute.[26] Wright, however, also finds possible hints of metaphorical and idealized poverty, especially the line "Do not esteem yourself highly for your poverty

---

23. Murphy, *Wealth in the Dead Sea Scrolls*, 232; see overall summary, 447–55.

24. E.g., "Remember that you are poor (ראש)"; "You are poor (אביון)" (4Q416 2 iii 2, 8, 12).

25. Tigchelaar, *The Addressees of 4QInstruction*, 69–71.

26. Wright, "Categories of Rich and Poor"; Goff, *Worldly and Heavenly Wisdom*, 127–67; Goff, *4QInstruction*, 23–27.

when you are (anyway?) a pauper, lest you bring into contempt your (own way) of life" (4Q416 2 ii 20–21; Hebrew omitted). Goff acknowledges that the text assumes the addressee is poor, but asks "what is meant by such assertions."[27] In addition to "concern for the addressee as a poor person," 4QInstruction also refers to metaphorical poverty as an "ethical ideal"; Goff argues that this is the only way to understand the repeated reminders "you are poor": it "means not simply that he is materially poor but also that he should live in a way which is humble, simple and reverent."[28] Benjamin Wold also notes that the statement "you are poor" would not make sense as reminding the poor of their impoverished state. Rather, he argues that such poverty language is metaphorical, but as a negative rather than idealized condition, referring to the human condition of lacking knowledge in relation to heavenly beings.

In stark contrast to Murphy, a more recent study by Unsok Ro focuses on the Hodayot and the pesher texts, and argues that the use of poverty language as self-description is not related to economic impoverishment but rather a self-assessment in relation to God and enemies.[29] Indeed, he agrees with Hartmut Stegemann that the Essenes were relatively wealthy due to their practice of shared property, which had to do with concerns of ritual purity.[30] Similar to Norbert Lohfink, he finds a piety of the poor that has its roots in religious conflict of the Persian-Hellenistic period.[31] The self-designations with poverty language describe on the one hand the distress of the pious in relation to their enemies, and their humble acknowledgment of nothingness in relation to the redeeming God on the other hand. Unsok Ro argues that the crisis is eschatological and religious rather temporal and material, that the priority is on "being poor before God" rather than "poor before the adversaries," and thus that it is poverty as a spiritual attitude not a condition that is primarily in view.[32]

27. Goff, *4QInstruction*, 25.
28. Goff, *4QInstruction*, 26.
29. Unsok Ro, "Piety of the Poor"; cf. Unsok Ro, *Die sogenannte 'Armenfrömmigkeit'.*
30. Unsok Ro, "Piety of the Poor," 68–69; 65n55.
31. Lohfink, *Lobgesänge der Armen*.
32. Unsok Ro, "Piety of the Poor," 62–64.

Theological Themes

Another set of questions concerns the theological and anthropological views related to poverty and the poor evinced in the Dead Sea Scrolls. Lohfink, for example, argues that poverty language in the sectarian scrolls is not primarily about material poverty or voluntary sharing of property, but about suffering violence.[33] In the Hodayot it is above all a theological motif in the context of judgment, justification, and grace. The language expresses the sense of human lowliness before God, in need of divine justification.[34] He finds some similarities to New Testament conceptions, although he thinks poverty language in the Qumran texts is more distant from social reality.

Fabry similarly believes that poverty language in the sectarian scrolls primarily has a theological orientation, although he thinks it must also be grounded in experience of poverty and persecution.[35] He gives special weight to the passages about the "poor of spirit" (רוח ענוה; ענוי רוח) in the context of salvation and justification (e.g., 1QM 14:7; 1QS 3:8; 4:3; 1QHª 6:14–16).

SOCIAL SCIENTIFIC MODELS

More recently, a variety of studies informed by social-scientific approaches offer new insights. Drawing on models of sect and group formation, speech-acts, social identity and categorization theory, social and cultural memory, sociolinguistics, and labelling theory, such studies work by analogy to explore the function and social affect of the practiced use of such rhetoric. In particular, how does the cultivated use of such language train individuals to think of oneself in relation to God, their group, and others?

Rhetoric and Identity Formation

Carol Newsom's 2004 monograph, *The Self as Symbolic Space: Constructing Identity and Community at Qumran*, has had a profound influence on methods of studying the Dead Sea Scrolls. Particularly

---

33. Lohfink, *Lobgesänge der Armen*, 32–37.
34. Lohfink, *Lobgesänge der Armen*, 99–100.
35. Fabry, *Die Armenfrömmigkeit*, 150–51.

of interest for the present study, she moves the focus away from the text as witness to history, behavior and beliefs of communities to the rhetorical world of the text as discourse. Rather than looking to the text as a reflection of the self and community, she analyzes it as formative discourse in the construction of the self. Her study focuses on the Community Rule and the Hodayot, and the way these texts configure a symbolic world for constructing a sectarian identity, drawing on a wide range of theorists of language and culture.[36] From Mikhael Bakhtin and others she takes the idea that groups develop distinctive social dialects both by their language repertoire and by using traditional language with different "accentuation," and she examines how the sectarian texts "reaccentuate" language and images to develop a counter discourse.[37] As she notes, "Making a sectarian is, above all, a matter of remaking the language he speaks."[38] She uses Michel Foucault's ideas of discourse as power and "technologies of the self" in examining how the individual is configured in texts as both an object and subject of knowledge.[39] Drawing on Kenneth Burke, she emphasizes that language is symbolic action that does things, and in analyzing the Hodayot, she asks what these hymns do in shaping one's subjectivity as they are repetitively prayed by a community.[40] She also uses Dorothy Holland's concept of "figured worlds," the "social and symbolic construction of selves and communities."[41] Newsom argues:

> [Figured worlds are] the 'as if' structures that persons take as meaningful reality. They are 'as if' in the sense that they are culturally constructed, furnished with model narratives, typical character roles, objects and activities that are part of the social performances conducted within these worlds, sets of appropriate and inappropriate emotions and responses to recurrent situations, posited beliefs about the nature of reality,

---

36. Newsom, *Self as Symbolic Space*, see esp. 6–19, 77–79, 92–101, 191–93 on method.
37. Newsom, *Self as Symbolic Space*, 6–12.
38. Newsom, *Self as Symbolic Space*, 92.
39. Newsom, *Self as Symbolic Space*, 19–20, 95–101.
40. Newsom, *Self as Symbolic Space*, 16, 77–78, 191–286.
41. Newsom, *Self as Symbolic Space*, 92 (92–95).

and so forth. In this regard figured worlds bear considerable resemblance to game-playing and fantasy . . . .

Newsom notes that "persons enter into figured worlds as novices and become both more proficient and more shaped by the worlds as they continue to engage in their discourses and practices."[42] This concept of practice and proficiency is especially important for Newsom's analysis of these texts and their role in a process of internalizing a subjectivity and a world. She repeatedly interrogates how these texts train a sectarian to speak and think about oneself in order to be this type of person.

Although she does not address the use of poverty language except in passing, her analysis as a whole examines the rhetorical function of such language. Two samples are illustrative. The first is her treatment of the psalm in 1QH[a] 11:20–37, which addresses the "problem of anxiety about the essential similarity between 'the saved and the damned.'"[43] Newsom notes that it responds thematically to the previous psalm, which ended with describing the lot of the speaker's enemies, who go down to the pit. In this psalm, the speaker begins by distinguishing himself from his enemies, thanking God for delivering him from the pit and purifying him so that he might join the heavenly community. But then the speaker experiences a crisis of knowledge within himself, acknowledging that he is but a creature of clay and his lot is with the wicked. In this context, the speaker describes himself as "the soul of the poor one (נפש אביון)" who is surrounded by disaster. He describes in detail the fury of Belial and his helpless terror in the face of it. The psalm switches to scenes of eschatological judgment, and the speaker finds resolution in the confession of God's predetermined purposes and his self-knowledge. Newsom adopts Lohfink's film-making metaphor to describe the abrupt shifts in point of view, from heavenly to earthly, from "worm's eye view" to "bird's eye view." The dramatic swing in mood reflects what Newsom calls the "masochistic sublime": relishing the nothingness of one's being in contrast to God as absolute.[44] She

---

42. Newsom, *Self as Symbolic Space*, 93–94.

43. Newsom, *Self as Symbolic Space*, 253 (253–61). In her book, Newsom gives the reference as 11:19–36.

44. Newsom, *Self as Symbolic Space*, 220.

writes, "In reciting the wonderful acts of God, the speaker must tell of himself and in so doing encounter his own bifurcated identity as one who belongs to an 'eternal lot with the spirits of knowledge' and also the 'lot of the vile.'"[45] Poverty language in the Hodayot belongs to this sort of cultivated speech of oneself in relation to God.

In the second example, 1QH^a 13:22—15:8, the speaking voice is a leader who is betrayed by disaffected associates.[46] The introductory strophe blesses God for not abandoning the speaker, who refers to himself as the "orphan" and the "poor one" and identifies with the community of the faithful poor.

> Blessed are You, O Lord, for you have not abandoned the orphan, and you have not despised the poor one (רש), for your strength is witho[ut en]d and your glory without measure. And wonderful warriors are your servants, but a humble people (עם ענוים) (has a place) in the mud of yo[ur] feet [together] with those who are eager for 24 righteousness (נמהרי צדק) so that all the faithful poor (אביוני חסד)) may be lifted up from the mire together. (1QH^a 13:22–24)[47]

The rest of the psalm alternates between accounts of distress from this betrayal, and statements of God's aid, ending on a note of distress. It uses language and imagery from psalms of complaint, and Newsom notes that in the opening lines, "there is no doubt that the speaker is claiming for himself a traditional identity within a well-known moral language. He himself is to be seen as the 'orphan' and the 'poor one.' By the second century BCE these were terms that not only drew on the ancient paternalistic ethos of the Near East but also on a specifically religious reinterpretation of those terms as labels of rectitude and piety."[48]

The sectarian nature of the conflict is revealed in the charge that the defectors divulged esoteric knowledge to outsiders: "With the

---

45. Newsom, *Self as Symbolic Space*, 261.

46. Newsom, *Self as Symbolic Space*, 331–45. In her book, Newsom gives the reference as 13:20—15:5.

47. Adapted from Newsom's translation in Parry and Tov, *The Dead Sea Scrolls Reader*, with added Hebrew; this translation differs from her translation in Newsom, *Self as Symbolic Space*, 332–37.

48. Newsom, *Self as Symbolic Space*, 342.

secret you have hidden in me they go about with slander to the children of destruction" (1QH^a 13:27). Traditional psalm language is—in Bakhtin's sense—reaccented, "to colonize the new moral territory of sectarian ethics."[49] By means of the leadership myth, casting disaffection as betrayal, and discipline and repentance as the context of divine provision, the psalm serves to encourage loyalty to the community and its leadership. Those who recite the psalms learn to think and speak of themselves in these terms. The psalms serve as a template: "Both by hearing others describe themselves in these poetic prayers and by the practice of articulating one's own experience in terms of the shaped story of the self in the Hoyadot, the sectarian is drawn into a radical reinterpretation of his identity."[50] The leader is offered as a model, and poverty as a model identity.

Sectarian Theory

Eyal Regev uses models drawn from cross-cultural studies of modern sectarian movements in analyzing the social functions of beliefs and practices in the sectarian communities reflected in the Dead Sea Scrolls.[51] He notes that the attitudes and behaviors related to wealth in the scrolls reflect an ideology characteristic of introversionist sectarian groups.[52] He identifies the following aspects.[53] (1) Wealth of the outside world is viewed as corrupt and defiling (e.g., CD 6:14–16). Therefore, strict boundaries between insiders and outsiders are drawn in relation to wealth, and the "attempt to avoid contact with the wealth of the outside society was a means to withdraw socially from evil."[54] (2) Accumulation of wealth is seen as incompatible to the service of God, and even immoral (e.g., CD 4:15–18; 1QH^a 6:31). (3) The community is obligated to care for the poor and needy (e.g., CD 14:12–17), but not merely out of humanitarian concern. It is also related to the ideology

---

49. Newsom, *Self as Symbolic Space*, 342.
50. Newsom, *Self as Symbolic Space*, 348.
51. Regev, *Sectarianism in Qumran*.
52. Regev, *Sectarianism in Qumran*, 336.
53. Regev, "Wealth and Sectarianism," 213–20; cf. Regev, *Sectarianism in Qumran*, 335–50.
54. Regev, "Wealth and Sectarianism," 214–15.

of corrupt wealth: the poor, uncontaminated by wealth, are associated with those loyal to God. For example, in CD 19:9, "those who give heed to God are the 'poor of the flock'" of Zech 11:7. "The poor" in 1QpHab 12:2–10 are associated with "the simple-hearted of Judah who obey the Law." In 1QH ͣ 13:22–24, a "humble people (עם ענוים)" and "those who are eager for righteousness (נמהרי צדק)" make up "all the faithful poor (אביוני חסד)." The self-designation of the community as the poor has to do with these ideological associations (e.g., "the congregation of the Poor Ones" in 4QpPsa 1–10 ii 10; 1–10 iii 10; "the poor" identified with the "Yahad" in 1QpHab 12:2–10), and is not related to the actual economic situation.[55] (4) The community closely regulates economic activity in order to avoid economic ties with outsiders and accumulation of wealth within the community. (5) The practice of communal shared property thus served as both a boundary against the outside world and its corrupt wealth, and to ensure equality within the community.

Regev notes surface similarities between the sectarian scrolls and the New Testament in social approaches toward wealth. "Both condemned the accumulation of wealth which led to impiety, criticised the wealthy, helped the poor, perhaps even regarded themselves (probably metaphorically) as 'the poor,' and under certain circumstances, enacted communal property ownership." But he believes they differ in that the sectarian movement reflected in the scrolls required "strict separation from the wealth of outsiders" whereas the early Christian movement "expressed social criticism but was not sectarian."[56]

Alex Jassen also uses sectarian theory, but whereas Regev focuses on the social function of economic ideology, Jassen analyzes the rhetoric of violent language in the Dead Sea Scrolls, drawing on scarce resources theory.[57] As originally developed by economists, scarce resources theory posits that violence erupts when critical resources—particularly ecological (e.g., food, water, energy) and spatial (e.g., land, shelter)—are in short supply."[58] In the context of religious conflict, however, there are other—and potentially more important—resources

55. Regev, *Sectarianism in Qumran*, 347.
56. Regev, "Wealth and Sectarianism," 227–29.
57. Jassen, "Dead Sea Scrolls and Violence."
58. Jassen, "Dead Sea Scrolls and Violence," 17.

than material resources. Jassen applies this theory to the sectarian movement represented by the scrolls in four areas of religious conflict: Scripture, sacred space, group privileging, and salvation.[59] Especially in a sectarian context, these areas represent limited goods: a claim to be the guardians of correct interpretation is a claim that others are false; a claim to be the unique people of God is a claim that others are not. Jassen discusses each area, in terms of sectarian formation and eschatological imagination. In the scrolls, he finds a unique combination of two uses of violent language: the infusion of violent language in debate over interpretive authority and identity as God's people, and defusion of violence in the present by relegating it to an eschatological setting. He notes that, "In the present time, the sect's 'weapons' are twofold: (1) social separation and meticulous observance of law, thereby ensuring the imminent unfolding of its 'revolutionist' ideology and its own salvation in the eschatological carnage; (2) A discourse of imagined violence that serves to 'empower' the 'weak' community in the face of outside Roman and Jewish power." Thus Jassen concludes, "The violent eschatological vision serves in the present primarily as a rhetorical tool to empower the disempowered community."[60] We can recognize the same tension between present conflict and future resolution that is addressed in relation to poverty language in very different ways by Murphy and Unsok Ro. Jassen's analysis highlights the rhetorical use of poverty language beyond economic, as metaphor for conflict over scarcity of religious resources.

Social Identity Approach

Jutta Jokiranta also applies sociological models of sectarianism in her study of the Dead Sea Scrolls, focusing especially on social psychological approaches.[61] In addressing the use of poverty language in the scrolls, she draws on the social identity approach. As defined by Henri Tajfel, social identity is "that part of an individual's self-concept which

---

59. He draws these four categories from Hector Avalos, who applied scarce resources theory to religion; Jassen, "Dead Sea Scrolls and Violence," 18–19.

60. Jassen, "Dead Sea Scrolls and Violence," 16.

61. E.g., Jokiranta, "Sociological Approaches"; Jokiranta, *Social Identity and Sectarianism*.

derives from his knowledge of his membership of a social group (or groups) together with the value and emotional significance attached to that membership."[62] The social identity approach explores both how and why people define themselves as members of a group.[63] It recognizes that when people categorize themselves as members of a social group, they tend to "exaggerate the perceived similarities within groups and the perceived differences between groups."[64] Furthermore, group membership is not static: one's sense of identification with the group may wax and wane. Jokiranta notes,

> When members of a group are not satisfied with its present status but cannot leave the group, they have to create a positive reevaluation of the in-group. This is done by means of several strategies: groups may find new dimensions with which to compare themselves; they may redefine the value of an existing comparison so that what was regarded as weakness is seen as a strength; or groups may also select new out-groups for intergroup comparisons. These strategies, if successful, will bring the group a positive social identity, even if its status has not changed.[65]

Jokiranta regards the use of poverty language in the Dead Sea Scrolls as such a group-identification strategy.

The most important text for Jokiranta is the reinterpretation of Ps 37 in the Psalms pesher (4QpPsa = 4Q171). Psalm 37 is a wisdom psalm addressing the problem of the suffering of the righteous and

---

62. Jokiranta, "Social Identity in the Qumran Movement," 284, citing H. Tajfel.

63. Trebilco, *Self-Designations*, 10, cites a helpful description of social identification theory by Hinkle and Brown: In this theory, it is argued that our sense of who we are stems in large part from our membership of and affiliation to various social groups, which are said to form our social identity. This identity is thought to be maintained through evaluative comparison between in-groups and relevant out-groups. When these comparisons are favourable, that is, when some positive distinctiveness has been achieved, our social identity is said to be positive and, by implication, our more general self-concept. Since it is assumed that there is a general preference for a positive rather than a negative self-concept, this introduces a motivational element into our comparative activity; we will be more disposed to look for and recognize intergroup differences which favour our in-groups over out-groups.

64. Jokiranta, "Social Identity Approach," 86, citing J. C. Turner.

65. Jokiranta, "Pesharim," 32.

how to respond to the wicked. The righteous as helpless victims of the wicked are referred to as the "afflicted" (עָנָוִים; Ps 37:11) and the "poor and needy" (עָנִי וְאֶבְיוֹן; Ps 37:14). They are urged not to give in to anger but to wait on God to reverse their fortunes. In the pesher, the psalm is reinterpreted in light of the sectarian community. The opposition concerns interpretation of Torah and, in the present, they are to return to the law and submit to the community. The "poor" becomes collectivized as "the congregation of the poor" (עֲדַת הָאֶבְיוֹנִים).

> And the afflicted (וַעֲנָוִים) will take possession of (the) land and will delight in abundant peace (Ps 37:11). Its interpretations concerns the congregation of the Poor Ones, (עֲדַת הָאֶבְיוֹנִים) who will accept the appointed time of affliction, and they will be delivered from all the traps of Belial. But afterwards they will delight [in] all [. . .] of the land and will grow fat in all [. . .] flesh. (4Q171 1–10 ii 2 9–12; cf. 1–10 iii 10).

That is, "poor" becomes a collective designation for the in-group. They do not merely suffer abuse, but accept their distress as an appointed time of affliction.[66] Jokiranta writes, "Instead of openly challenging the out-group's position and practices, the Pesher Psalms promotes strategies of social change that would establish the positive social identity but leave the reversal of circumstances in the future."[67] She concludes,

> In summary, the ideology of the in-group as the congregation of the poor in the period of humiliation is able to strengthen the group identity by adding to its positive dimensions (the poor are in the right ethical and spiritual relationship with God) and by promoting a positive view of its low-status attributes (period of humiliation is self-chosen and belongs to the divine plan; it will be reversed in the future).[68]

Jokiranta notes that "poor" is not a common collective designation in the scrolls, and the connotations vary in different texts. But she helps to clarify that the identification with the biblical poor is strategic in helping to promote a positive social identity.

---

66. Jokiranta, *Social Identity and Sectarianism*, 142–48.
67. Jokiranta, *Social Identity and Sectarianism*, 141.
68. Jokiranta, *Social Identity and Sectarianism*, 148.

Sociolinguistics and Labeling Theory

Paul Trebilco's two monographs on insider and outsider designations in the New Testament draw on further methodological insights that could fruitfully be applied to poverty designations in the Dead Sea Scrolls.[69] In addition to social identity theory, Trebilco incorporates insights from sociolinguistics, labeling theory, and social deviance theory. From sociolinguistics Trebilco takes the idea that "communities of practice"—that is, communities engaged in a common enterprise such as a religious group—develop their own distinctive repertoire of shared language. Trebilco argues, "This social dialect includes technical terms not found elsewhere in the wider culture, abbreviations and specialised use of otherwise common language, including self-designations" and "terms for outsiders."[70] Moreover, their language and identity are constructed in relation to each other: language not only expresses identity but also shapes identity.[71] The labeling of both insider and outsider groups plays an important role in social identity as a key element of categorizing and stereotyping, since "we are what we are because *they* are not what we are."[72] What a group names itself not only expresses its self-perception but has an influence on shaping both how it sees itself and also its behavior.[73] Correspondingly, the labels it applies to outsiders not only reflect but also influence its group identity and group behavior, and its construction of boundaries.[74]

Matthew Collins interacts briefly with labeling theory and social deviance theory in a monograph on sobriquets in the Dead Sea Scrolls, although his study is primarily concerned with historical development in the use of labels.[75] He emphasizes that labels are evaluative, and impute either moral superiority or inferiority.[76] By means of "reverse labelling," the community may seek "to define itself over and against

---

69. Trebilco, *Self-Designations*; Trebilco, *Outsider Designations*.
70. Trebilco, *Self-Designations*, 7; Trebilco, *Outsider Designations*, 15.
71. Trebilco, *Self-Designations*, 8.
72. Trebilco, *Outsider Designations*, 9, citing Tajfel and Forgas; italics original.
73. Trebilco, *Self-Designations*, 5–6.
74. Trebilco, *Outsider Designations*, 12–13.
75. Collins, *Use of Sobriquets*, 196–207.
76. Collins, *Use of Sobriquets*, 201–2.

the rest of society by deviantizing all those who are not members of the community."[77]

Neither Trebilco nor Collins investigate the use of poverty language as self-designation, but there is much scope for analyzing the poverty designations through the perspectives they engage. There can be no question that there is a distinctive social dialect reflected in the sectarian scrolls.[78] What part does poverty language play in that social dialect? As various scholars have noticed, poverty language is not a common self-designation in the scrolls, but it plays a role in certain contexts more than others. How is this traditional language imbued with new signification? How is a traditional negative designation (poor) turned into a positive social identification? And how is wealth used as a deviantizing label? As some scholars have noted, poverty and wealth are often not presented as polar terms; the Hodayot, for example "pits the wealth of the outsiders against the knowledge of community members."[79] Considering labels as formative of social identity, there is potentially more to be gained by inquiring what sort of identity and behavior is encouraged by the adoption of poverty designations than in trying to recover social realities behind the language (i.e., whether economic poverty or persecution).

CONCLUSION

In this paper, I distinguish two broad categories of approaches to studying the use of poverty language in the Dead Sea Scrolls. The first category includes those studies that seek to identify what that language tells about the community: that is, what does it reveal about the history, social location, or theological ideas of the community. Is this language related to voluntary adoption of poverty and the practice of communal property, to the experience of persecution and disadvantage by the pious due to their uncompromising commitment to God's law, or simply to the actual socio-economic status of the community? Can lines of historical and social contact, influence, or development be drawn between communities that used poverty language similarly? There can be

---

77. Pietersen, "False Teaching," 173, cited in Collins, *Use of Sobriquets*, 202.
78. See e.g., Schniedewind, "Qumran Hebrew."
79. Murphy, *Wealth in the Dead Sea Scrolls*, 243, referring to 1QH^a 18.

little doubt that there is some relationship between the use of language and historical and social realities, and many sophisticated studies have explored these relationships. Nevertheless, the disagreement among scholars on such questions sends a strong signal of caution. We only have texts to examine, not communities. Moreover, the fact that the pattern of usage of poverty language differs markedly between different genres and contexts also reinforces that there is no direct connection between the worlds of text and living community.

The second category includes a variety of approaches that instead focus on the function of language in the formation of community identity and behavior, drawing on models from sociology, psychology, linguistics, and rhetoric. That is, they are concerned with what the language does rather than what the language reflects. These have the advantage that they are based on studies of living people and groups but, to apply the insights to the ancient world, of course, one is still dependent primarily on textual data, and working from analogy. The application of such approaches specifically to poverty language in the Dead Sea Scrolls and the New Testament is still limited, and I suggest that there is much yet to be gained. Recognizing poverty language as part of a social dialect, for example, highlights that vocabulary similarities between the Dead Sea Scrolls and the New Testament are less significant than how that language is reaccented in the different communities. The use of poverty language in relation to the motif of knowledge is especially striking in the Dead Sea Scrolls, and it seems that there are two distinct usages: poor with regard to knowledge in contrast to God and angels and poor but with knowledge in contrast to outsiders. This invites further investigation from the perspective of knowledge as a scarce resource. It is important to consider both how a group practices poverty language as self-description as well as the group identity and boundaries such language cultivates. These additional questions and models offer new perspectives on the use of poverty language, for example, as counter discourse in differentiating from outsiders and as a strategy of cultivating a positive social identification. Since the same language may be used for very different rhetorical purposes by different groups, attention to these questions may contribute a more nuanced basis for comparison between the Dead Sea Scrolls and the New Testament.

BIBLIOGRAPHY

Collins, John J. "The Self-Glorification Hymn from Qumran." In *Crossing Boundaries in Early Judaism and Christianity: Ambiguities, Complexities, and Half-Forgotten Adversaries*, edited by Kimberly B. Stratton and Andrea Lieber, 25–40. Supplements to the Journal for the Study of Judaism 177. Leiden: Brill, 2016.

Collins, Matthew A. *The Use of Sobriquets in the Qumran Dead Sea Scrolls*. LSTS. London: T. & T. Clark, 2009.

Dimant, Devorah. *History, Ideology and Bible Interpretation in the Dead Sea Scrolls: Collected Studies*. FAT 90. Tübingen: Mohr Siebeck, 2014.

Douglas, Michael C. "The Teacher Hymn Hypothesis Revisited: New Data for an Old Crux." DSD 6 (1999) 239–66.

Duhaime, Jean. *The War Texts: 1QM and Related Manuscripts*. Companion to the Qumran Scrolls 6. London: T. & T. Clark, 2004.

Elgvin, Torleif, et al., eds. *Qumran Cave 4: XV: Sapiential Texts, Part 1*. Discoveries in the Judaean Desert 20. Oxford: Claredon Press, 1997.

Fabry, Heinz Josef. "דַּל Dal; דלל Dalal." *ThWAT* 1:681–85.

Fabry, Heinz-Josef. "Die Armenfrömmigkeit in den qumranischen Weisheitstexten." In *Weisheit in Israel: Beiträge des Symposiums "Das Alte Testament und die Kultur der Moderne" anlässlich des 100. Geburtstags Gerhard von Rads (1901–1971) Heidelberg, 18.–21. Oktober 2001*, edited by David J. A. Clines, Hermann Lichtenberger, and Hans-Peter Müller, 145–65. Münster: LIT, 2003.

Flusser, David. "Blessed Are the Poor in Spirit . . . " *IEJ* 10, 1 (1960) 1–13.

———. *Judaism of the Second Temple Period: Sages and Literature*. Translated by Azzan Yadin. 2 vols. Grand Rapids: Eerdmans, 2009.

Goff, Matthew J. *4QInstruction*. WLAW 2. Atlanta: SBL, 2013.

———. *The Worldly and Heavenly Wisdom of 4QInstruction*. STDJ 50. Leiden: Brill, 2003.

Gregory, Bradley. "Rwš רוש." In *ThWAT* 3:645–48.

Hempel, Charlotte. *The Damascus Texts*. Companion to the Qumran Scrolls 1. Sheffield: Sheffield Academic Press, 2000.

———. *The Qumran Rule Texts in Context*. Texts and Studies in Ancient Judaism 154. Tübingen: Mohr Siebeck, 2012.

Holm-Nielsen, Svend. *Hodayot: Psalms From Qumran*. ATDan 2. Aarhus: Universitetsforlaget, 1960.

Jassen, Alex P. "The Dead Sea Scrolls and Violence: Sectarian Formation and Eschatological Imagination." *BibInt* 17 (2009) 12–44.

Jokiranta, Jutta. "Pesharim: A Mirror of Self-Understanding." In *Reading the Present in the Qumran Library: The Perception of the Contemporary by Means of Scriptural Interpretations*, edited by Kristin De Troyer and Armin Lange, 23–34. SymS 30. Atlanta: Society of Biblical Literature, 2005.

———. *Social Identity and Sectarianism in the Qumran Movement*. STDJ 105. Leiden: Brill, 2013.

———. "Social Identity Approach: Identity-Constructing Elements in the Psalms Pesher." In *Defining Identities: We, You, and the Other in the Dead Sea Scrolls. Proceedings of the Fifth Meeting of the IOQS in Gröningen*, edited by Florentino García Martínez and Mladen Popović, 85–110. STDJ 70. Leiden: Brill, 2008.

———. "Social Identity in the Qumran Movement: The Case of the Penal Code." In *Explaining Christian Origins and Early Judaism: Contributions from Cognitive and Social Science*, edited by Petri Luomanen, Ilkka Pyysiäinen, and Risto Uro, 277–98. BibInt 89. Leiden: Brill, 2007.

———. "Sociological Approaches to Qumran Sectarianism." In *The Oxford Handbook of the Dead Sea Scrolls*, edited by Timothy H. Lim and John J. Collins, 200–31. Oxford: Oxford University Press, 2010.

Keck, Leander E. "The Poor Among the Saints in Jewish Christianity and Qumran." *BZNW* 57 (1966): 54–78.

———. "The Poor Among the Saints in the New Testament." *BZNW* 56 (1965) 100–29.

Kim Harkins, Angela. "A New Proposal for Thinking About 1QH^a Sixty Years After Its Discoverty." In *Qumran Cave 1 Revisited: Texts From Cave 1 Sixty Years After Their Discovery. Proceedings of the Sixth Meeting of the IOQS in Ljubljana*, edited by Daniel K. Falk et al., 101–34. STDJ 91. Leiden: Brill, 2010.

———. "Observations on the Editorial Shaping of the So-called Community Hymns from 1QH^a and 4QH^a (4Q427)." *DSD* 12 (2005) 233–56.

Lohfink, Norbert. *Lobgesänge der Armen: Studien zum Magnifikat, den Hodajot von Qumran und einigen späten Psalmen*. Stuttgart: Verlag Katholisches Bibelwerk, 1990.

Markl, Dominik. "עָנָה II ʿānāh." In *ThWAT* 3:166–72.

Metso, Sarianna. *The Serekh Texts*. LSTS 62. London: T. & T. Clark, 2007.

Murphy, Catherine. *Wealth in the Dead Sea Scrolls and in the Qumran Community*. STDJ 40. Leiden: Brill, 2002.

Newsom, Carol A. *The Self as Symbolic Space: Constructing Identity and Community at Qumran*. STDJ 52. Leiden: Brill, 2004.

Parry, Donald W., and Emanuel Tov, eds. *The Dead Sea Scrolls Reader*. 6 vols. Leiden: Brill, 2014.

Pietersen, Lloyd Keith. "'False Teaching, Lying Tongues and Deceitful Lips' (4Q169 Frgs 3-4 2.8): The Pesharim and the Sociology of Deviance." In *New Directions in Qumran Studies: Proceedings of the Bristol Colloquium on the Dead Sea Scrolls, 8-10 September 2003*, edited by Jonathan G. Campbell, William John Lyons, and Lloyd Keith Pietersen, 166-81. LSTS 52. London: T. & T. Clark, 2005.

Regev, Eyal. *Sectarianism in Qumran: A Cross-Cultural Perspective*. RelSoc 45. Berlin: de Gruyter, 2007.

———. "Wealth and Sectarianism: Comparing Qumranic and Early Christian Social Approaches." In *Echoes from the Caves: Qumran and the New Testament*, edited by Florentino García Martínez, 211-29. STDJ 85. Leiden: Brill, 2009.

Schniedewind, William M. "Qumran Hebrew as an Antilanguage." *JBL* 118 (1999) 235-52.

Schofield, Alison. *From Qumran to the Yaḥad: A New Paradigm of Textual Development for the Community Rule*. STDJ 77. Leiden: Brill, 2009.

Schuller, Eileen M. "Hodayot." In *Qumran Cave 4.XX. Poetical and Liturgical Texts, Part 2*, edited by Esther Chazon, et al, 69-254. DSD 29. Oxford: Clarendon, 1999.

———. "Recent Scholarship on the Hodayot 1993-2010." *CurBR* 10 (2011) 119-62.

Schuller, Eileen M., and Carol A. Newsom. *The Hodayot (Thanksgiving Psalms): A Study Edition of 1QH^a*. EJL 36 Atlanta: Society of Biblical Literature, 2012.

Schultz, Brian. "Compositional Layers in the War Scroll (1QM)." In *Qumran Cave 1 Revisited; Texts from Cave 1 Sixty Years After Their Discovery. Proceedings of the Sixth Meeting of the IOQS in Ljublana*, edited by Daniel K. Falk et al., 153-64. STDJ 91. Leiden: Brill, 2010.

Stegemann, Hartmut, and Eileen Schuller. *1QHodayota: With Incorporation of 1QHodayotb and 4QHodayota-f*. DSD 40. Oxford: Clarendon, 2009.

Strugnell, John, et al., eds. *Qumran Cave 4. XXIV. Sapiential Texts, Part 2; 4QInstruction (Mûsār lĕ Mēvîn): 4Q415 ff. With a Re-edition of 1Q26 and an Edition of 4Q423*. DSD 34. Oxford: Clarendon, 1999.

Tigchelaar, Eibert. "The Addressees of 4QInstruction." In *Sapiential, Liturgical and Poetical Texts from Qumran: Proceedings of the Third Meeting of the International Organization for Qumran Studies, Oslo 1998. Published in Memory of Maurice Baillet*, edited by Daniel K. Falk et al., 62-75. STDJ 35. Leiden: Brill, 2000.

Trebilco, Paul R. *Self-Designations and Group Identity in the New Testament*. Cambridge: Cambridge University Press, 2011.

Unsok Ro, Johannes. *Die sogenannte "Armenfrömmigkeit" im nachexilischen Israel*. BZAW 322. Berlin: de Gruyter, 2002.

———. "Piety of the Poor in the Community of Qumran and Its Historical Origins." In *From Judah to Judaea: Socio-Economic Structures and Processes in the Persian Period*, edited by Johannes Unsok Ro, 54–85. Sheffield: Phoenix, 2012.

Wise, Michael O. "מי כמוני באלים? A Study of 4Q491c, 4Q471b, 4Q427 7 and 1QH ͣ 25:35—26:10." DSD 7 (2000) 173–219.

Wold, Benjamin G. "אֶבְיוֹן 'æbjôn." In *ThWAT* 1:13–17.

Wright, Benjamin G. III. "The Categories of Rich and Poor in the Qumran Sapiential Literature." In *Sapiential Perspectives: Wisdom Literature in Light of the Dead Sea Scrolls. Proceedings of the Sixth International Symposium of the Orion Center for the Study of the Dead Sea Scrolls and Associated Literature, 20-22 May, 2001*, edited by John J. Collins et al., 101–23. STDJ 51. Leiden: Brill, 2004.

Zanella, Francesco. "חָסֵר Ḥāser." In *ThWAT* 1:1036–41.

11

Reading Luke-Acts as a Mennocostal

Pentecostals, Mennonites, and the Prophethood of All Believers[1]

MARTIN W. MITTELSTADT

INTRODUCTION

I AM A CRADLE Pentecostal. As a young boy, I loved to read, hear, and experience biblical stories. Like many Pentecostal children, I would picture myself standing in a crowd to listen to the parables of Jesus, climbing a tree like Zacchaeus, or singing hymns in prison with Paul and Silas. I learned early that these stories were somehow my stories, a continuation of the gospel. In this essay, I reflect upon my spiritual and academic formation from my years as a young college student, to a wannabe theologian, and to a mature scholar (at least in my own eyes). After decades of passion and energy given to biblical studies, I remain a Pentecostal (not begrudgingly), but I also embrace the designation "Mennocostal."[2] For this emerging identity, I must thank (or blame) Pastor Luke, possibly the most important voice in my formation. In

---

1. An earlier version of this paper was published in *Mennocastals*, 14–28.
2. See Mittelstadt, "My Life as a Mennocostal."

the following narrative, I recount the impact of many years of reading, writing, and reflecting on Luke-Acts, particularly through the lens of various Pentecostal and Mennonite scholars, who, unbeknownst to them, contributed to my ever-evolving Mennocostal worldview.

Though much has changed from the day I enrolled in a small Canadian Pentecostal college in 1982, I begin with a summary of the primary scholarly voices to shape my early years. My initial exposure to methodologies for biblical interpretation would both jumpstart and stunt my reading of Scripture. Second, I choose to reject, if only for a moment, the advice I regularly give to my students; I succumb to an oversimplified use of Luke-Acts by applying oft-held stereotypes, namely the correlation of Pentecostals to Spirit and Mennonites to peace. I reflect upon two scholars, Roger Stronstad and John Howard Yoder, both of whom produced monumental contributions to their respective traditions (and beyond). Third, I turn to Luke Timothy Johnson, whose scholarship has helped me piece together the Mennocostal puzzle. In his *Prophetic Jesus and Prophetic Church*, Johnson, a Catholic, captures well both the Stronstadian Jesus of the Spirit and the Yoderian Jesus of peace and justice. Fourth, I reflect upon my continuing formation by way of Mennonite and Pentecostal contributions to Lukan scholarship. Along the way, I draw not only on Pentecostal and Mennonite scholars but on others who enlarged my Mennocostal worldview. Finally, I conclude with an open invitation for ongoing Pentecostal and Mennonite convergence.

TWENTIETH-CENTURY FISTICUFFS: MORE OR LESS HISTORY?

My introduction to biblical studies came at the height of historical criticism. As I entered college in the early 1980s, a full century of scholarship on the historical (un)reliability of the Gospels and Acts had surely fulfilled John's declaration "that the whole world does not have room for the books that would be written on the life of *historical* Jesus" (John 21:25, slightly modified).[3] Dissertations, monographs, and textbooks filled libraries on topics such as source criticism (who used what?),

---

3. Unless otherwise noted, all Scripture quotations are from the NRSV.

form criticism (what is the raw form of any story?), synoptic studies (what might Mark and Q have to do with Luke and Matthew?), and redaction criticism (how did editors cut and paste their stories?). On the one hand, certain scholars called for increasing suspicion regarding the historical plausibility of the New Testament. Many of these same scholars worked tirelessly to undermine the credibility of scholars who chose to "err" on the side of historical reliability. On the other hand, twentieth-century "Evangelical" scholars engaged in a spirited defense of early Christian historicity. It is here where I encountered my first predicament.

Initially, this debate proved overwhelming. My Pentecostal pastors and Sunday School teachers never mentioned hermeneutical questions concerning historical reliability. Espousing the old adage akin to "the Bible said it, I believe it, and that settles it for me," my pastors and teachers had either resolved the issue for themselves and felt no need to enlighten me or they were not even familiar with the academic fisticuffs. Fortunately, at least as I understood things at that time, my professors steeped in Evangelical hermeneutics walked me through this tumultuous period. Thus, the primary goal of my Synoptic Gospels course was to slither through A. T. Robertson's *Harmony of the Gospels* to properly reconstruct the life of Jesus. In an Acts course, I tackled F. F. Bruce's *Acts*, the go-to commentary of Evangelicals and Pentecostals (sigh) primarily for his defense of Luke the historian.[4]

Though my Pentecostal professors (trained by Evangelicals) saved me from the "evil liberals," I stumbled to the next quandary. This time I found myself standing before an insider, a Pentecostal. Gordon Fee, a theological father to many academicians in the Pentecostal tradition and a premier Pauline theologian, turned my world upside down. In his *How to Read the Bible for All its Worth*, co-authored with Douglas Stuart, Fee "conceded" Pentecostal methodology to the growing Evangelical perspective. Though Fee continued to defend historical reliability, he expressed strong concerns over "normativity," that is, the idea that writers of biblical narrative would expect normative theologies and practices to be gleaned by readers. Fee wrestled with the

---

4. Robertson, *A Harmony of the Gospels*; Bruce, *Commentary on the Book of the Acts*.

"Question of Historical Precedent" and produced a controversial conclusion. At best, he would only acknowledge that "biblical precedents may sometimes be regarded as repeatable patterns—even if they are not understood to be normative."[5] Needless to say, this chapter received not a little bit of attention among Pentecostals.[6]

Before moving on, I must comment briefly on the contributions of two further "Evangelicals" (they are Anglican but cherished by Evangelicals), who published their inaugural monographs in 1970. James Dunn, in his *Baptism in the Spirit*, sounded like an earlier version of Fee. Dunn's resistance to the didactic value of biblical narrative pushed Pentecostals to the brink; since Luke comes off as a fanatic (Dunn's preferred term is "enthusiastic" and reminiscent of Pentecostals), readers must turn to Paul the teacher for guidance on life of the Spirit. Luke's use of Spirit must agree or succumb to Paul's use of similar language. I. Howard Marshall, on the other hand, declared that Luke should be read as historian *and* theologian. Marshall maintained, that "Luke has a theological interest [and] his narratives, though they are historical, are always more than . . . the record of brute facts."[7] Though Dunn and Fee run a different course than Marshall, these three men would impact the journey of many Pentecostals and Mennonites.

By the mid-1980s, I had concluded (with the help of my professors) that the biblical narratives as recorded in the Scriptures proved to be historically accurate. I survived (sigh) and came to appreciate the historical accuracy, if not yet the literary artistry, of NT writers. As I look back, the efforts of my teachers and the extensive reading on defense of historicity may have dulled my ability to read, hear, and experience the stories of Jesus and the early church. (I say these things not to slight them, for they were simply products of their methodological era.)

---

5. Fee and Stuart, *How to Read the Bible for all Its Worth*, 111.

6. Fee and Stuart, *How to Read the Bible for all Its Worth*, 111. Fee and Stronstad engaged in what seemed to be a lifelong battle on this matter. See my *Reading Luke-Acts in the Pentecostal Tradition*.

7. Stronstad, *The Charismatic Theology of St. Luke*, 8.

TURNING THE CORNER: THANK GOD FOR ROGER STRONSTAD AND JOHN HOWARD YODER

I graduated college in 1985, the year Roger Stronstad published what became the go-to rebuttal against Dunn and Fee. I entered part-time pastoral ministry and discovered Stronstad's *Charismatic Theology of St. Luke* at a critical juncture in my journey. For many Pentecostal students and pastors, Stronstad provided the methodological tools necessary not only to survive but thrive in our tradition. If adoption of the evangelicalized readings of biblical narratives (Dunn and Fee) would prevail, my Pentecostal impulses on the Spirit-filled life, upheld by way of Luke and Acts, would be severely threatened. Stronstad took up this challenge and guided many Pentecostals through this difficulty.[8] He provided me with timely answers. First, though Paul and Luke both employ language of "baptized" and "filled" with the Spirit, Luke's decidedly greater use of the terms (3-to-1 and 9-to-1, respectively) must not be relegated to a Pauline meaning. Second, Luke employs Spirit in the life of Jesus and his followers in continuity with charismatic (think "prophetic") enablement of OT agents who fulfill God's purposes (e.g., Moses, David, Elijah). The same Spirit transferred from the likes of Moses to Joshua and Elijah to Elisha is transferred by Jesus to his disciples and beyond. And the same Spirit previously limited to OT leadership (e.g., prophets and kings) now becomes universally available for all believers. Finally, Luke's Jesus also functions as the consummate man of the Spirit, the model for future followers who will continue "all that Jesus began to do and teach" (Acts 1:1). In so doing, Stronstad amplified Luther's axiomatic "priesthood of all believers" to "prophethood of all believers," a new Pentecostal/Charismatic axiom.[9]

Shortly after discovering Stronstad, I began studies at Providence Seminary, a non-denominational institution with a predominance of Mennonite faculty, students, and constituents. At Providence, I first encountered the theologies of Mennonites. I owe my initial exposure to Mennonite scholarship to Edmund Neufeld (note the name), who introduced me to John Howard Yoder's *Politics of Jesus*. Deemed by

---

8. See my *Reading Luke-Acts in the Pentecostal Tradition*.
9. Stronstad, *Prophethood of All Believers*.

many to be one of the most influential theological works of the twentieth century, I first detested Yoder's thesis, only to realize many years later that I had adopted his vision of the Lukan Jesus' radical worldview. If Stronstad's Jesus is the exemplary man of the Spirit, Yoder's Jesus is "a model of radical political action."[10] Yoder rejects any attempt to bypass the life of Jesus only to receive a heavenly-minded salvation. His Jesus is the preeminent model for radical discipleship and nonviolent resistance.[11]

It is no exaggeration for me to state that these scholars changed my life! First, Stronstad and Yoder refused to settle for the debate over historicity. Instead, they endeavored to give Luke voice not simply as historian but as theologian and pastor. They reminded me that the biblical stories I embodied as a child remained critical to discipleship. Second, Stronstad and Yoder rescued me from a view of Jesus that made his life distant, unattainable, and irrelevant for everyday life. Instead, they strove to give Luke's Jesus precedent in our lives. Finally, their scholarship gave rise to a dawning convergence. The prophetic Jesus, filled with the Spirit and the model of nonviolent resistance to the powers, should produce a prophetic church. Enter Luke Timothy Johnson.

LUKE TIMOTHY JOHNSON: A CATHOLIC GUIDE TO MENNOCOSTAL LIFE

If I had to choose the one biblical scholar who has most influenced my academic and spiritual formation, I would say, without hesitation, Luke Timothy Johnson. His emergence as the premier Lukan scholar of narrative criticism provided the technical language for biblical methods I had felt as a Pentecostal. In his recent *Prophetic Jesus, Prophetic Church*, Johnson addresses *The Challenge of Luke–Acts to Contemporary Christians*:

---

10. Yoder, *The Politics of Jesus*, 2. I would be remiss not to note the recent news concerning the predatory life led by Yoder. Sadly, a man committed to non-violence preyed upon vulnerable women. I agree with the stance of Herald Press, the leading Mennonite press. Yoder remains an important voice, but I condemn his behaviour (see https://heraldpress.com/yoder/).

11. See "My Life as a Mennocostal."

COMMUNITY

> The pertinent question for believing readers is not 'Is Luke's rendering of Jesus historically accurate?' but rather, 'How does Luke's imaginative construal challenge the values of the world?' The pertinent question is not 'Was the early church as Luke describes it?' but rather, 'How does Luke's portrayal of the early church challenge the church in every age?'[12]

I read Johnson's dissertation during my seminary years and could not have imagined the role his lifework would have on my dissertation, future scholarship, and formation.[13] His use of narrative methodology set the bar for a generation of Lukan scholars, and his theological conclusions provided a new surge of meaning for the ecclesial import of Luke's story. For Johnson, if Luke's Jesus is the consummate prophet and the people of God continue Jesus' work, the church then and now embodies the prophetic life of Jesus. The Spirit of the living Jesus calls people to repent, demands their unmitigated allegiance, and challenges all powers that usurp God's rule. The prophetic Jesus and all subsequent prophets commit to radical poverty signaled by shared possessions, prayerful dependence upon God, and dramatic itinerancy (see section 4). Though classical Pentecostals taught me about Acts as an open-ended narrative, how ironic that a Catholic scholar would hone my reading of Luke–Acts and further my development as a Mennocostal.

READING LUKE-ACTS AS A MENNOCOSTAL

With roughly two decades of Luke-Acts research behind me, I am occasionally asked why I do not just move on from Luke-Acts, only to respond that every time I am ready to say, "Enough," Pastor Luke refuses to let me go. I say unequivocally that obsession with Luke-Acts does not primarily serve to advance my academic pursuits; instead it results from the pervasive impact of Luke's story upon my life. In stating this, I owe much to the methodological advances made by Pentecostal

---

12. Johnson, *Prophetic Jesus, Prophetic Church*, 6. I would describe this particular work as a pastoral commentary on Luke-Acts. Johnson has spent a lifetime in Lukan studies, and produced numerous volumes on Luke-Acts. In this work, as I see it, he writes as a seasoned pastor-scholar and gives his reading of Luke based upon a life of meticulous study. See my review: "Prophetic Jesus, Prophetic Church," 120–22.

13. Johnson, *The Literary Function of Possessions in Luke-Acts*.

theologian Amos Yong, who calls upon Pentecostals (and all Christians) to expand our collective "pneumatological imagination." For Yong, the many tongues of Pentecost serve metaphorically to enliven our contemporary Christian experience and praxis. If Pentecost launches the Spirit-filled life and if Pentecost is the domain not only of Pentecostals but of all Christians, including Mennonites, then Pentecost provides the impetus for continuous prophetic speech. Pentecost offers an early glimpse into Luke's many-tongued vision for the people of God.[14] For the final part of this essay, I describe my sojourn with Luke, a journey highlighted by seasons of pneumatological imagination.[15]

Spirit and Peace

In the fall of 2008, I was invited to deliver the Schrag Lecture Series at Messiah College (Mechanicsburg, PA), and I chose to share with my Anabaptist friends our common pacifistic impulses. Since many Pentecostals remain unfamiliar with this heritage and those of us who maintain this impulse find the path difficult to tread, I sought fresh insight into Spirit-filled peacemaking from my newfound friends. For the first lecture, I mined scenes in Luke-Acts that brought together "Spirit and Peace."[16] I would not have launched into this paper without what I believe to be Mennonite NT scholar Willard Swartley's *magnum opus*. In his *Covenant of Peace*, Swartley cleverly seeks to discover *The Missing Peace in New Testament Theology and Ethics*. He surveys some twenty-five major studies of NT theology and laments that not a single study on Luke and Acts paid attention to the peace motif. To counter this gaping hole, Swartley marches through Luke–Acts and opens my eyes yet again to a broken world inclined toward power, self-interest, and conflict. For Swartley, Luke's Jesus enters this world to announce the path/way of peace and to embody the gospel's radical hospitality; if Jesus' vision for radically inclusive communities is to come to fruition,

---

14. Yong, *The Spirit Poured Out on All Flesh*.

15. The following categories do not reflect a linear journey but lengthy and complex developments. The order seems fitting given the primacy of peace and justice for Mennonite theology and praxis.

16. Mittelstadt, "Spirit and Peace in Luke-Acts," 17–41. An earlier version was presented at Messiah College, Schrag Lectureship Series on April 9, 2008.

his disciples must follow his path. Not surprisingly, Luke first labels Jesus' followers as people of "The Way" (see section C!).[17]

As I examined Luke's use of the peace motif, I found that Luke revealed his agenda via Spirit-filled agents. The Lukan birth narrative includes three prophetic and programmatic announcements: Zechariah longs for "the way of peace" (Luke 1:79); an angelic army (note the irony) sings to shepherds concerning "peace on those whom [God] favors" (Luke 2:14; compare Luke 19:38); and Simeon, an old priest, receives fulfillment of a promise that he would see God's messiah before death—"now dismiss your servant in peace" (Luke 2:29). The adult Jesus filled with Spirit (Luke 3:22; 4:1, 14, 18) proclaims *shalom* for specific individuals (Luke 7:50; 8:48) and commissions his disciples to announce, "Peace to this house" (Luke 9:51—10:24) in a world ill prepared for "the things that make for peace" (Luke 18:35—19:44). At the Gentile Pentecost in Acts 10, a passage revered by Pentecostals for Luke's emphasis on Spirit reception, Peter's declaration of the "good news of peace by Jesus Christ who is Lord of all" fulfills Luke's programmatic hopes announced at the beginning of the Third Gospel (Acts 10:36). Contrary to rule marked by heavy-handed propaganda that promotes an idyllic but corrupt *pax Romana* (not unlike *pax Americana*), the church counters with *pax Christi*. The ever-maturing Peter slowly but surely comes to understand that God is not impartial (see Acts 2:39). Peter pronounces Jesus as Lord and invites searching individuals and communities to experience the loving embrace of Jesus and his followers. The gospel provides a way for anyone looking to replace hatred and hostility with love and inclusion under the Lordship of Jesus Christ. I had a firm grip on Luke's pneumatology (detect sarcasm), yet I had failed to see the message of Spirit and peace without the help of my Mennonite friends.

Evangelism or Social Justice

On May 22, 2011, an F5 tornado ripped through Joplin, MO, only seventy miles from my home in Springfield. A twenty-two-mile tornadic track resulted in the death of 158 people, some one thousand injuries,

---

17. Luke 1:79; 2:14; 2:29; 7:50; 8:48; 10:5; 10:6 (2); 11:21; 12:51; 14:32; 19:38; 19:42; 24:36; Acts 7:26; 9:31; 10:36; 12:20; 15:33; 16:36; 24:2.

and the destruction of more than seven thousand homes and businesses. My family and I made several trips to Joplin to support with cleanup. We learned that the Mennonite Disaster Service (MDS) was the first volunteer-based relief service on the ground and later discovered they were the last to go.[18] On a trip to Joplin in the summer of 2012, I visited the MDS station, and my mind rushed to childhood memories of Mennonite Central Committee and MDS in Winnipeg. I found myself reflecting upon the compartmentalization I had learned as a Pentecostal, where relief and development via food, clothing, and shelter set up the gospel. On this day, I was reminded that Mennonites view such work *as* the gospel of the kingdom.

Until recently, the Assemblies of God (AG), my current denominational affiliation, cited three reasons for existence, namely, to evangelize the lost, worship God, and disciple believers. At the 2009 General Council of the AG, a resolution to add a fourth reason produced a hard-fought debate. The resolution was defeated but revisited due to the earnest plea of General Superintendent George O. Wood. The second vote passed narrowly, and the AG added compassion—not social justice—as a fourth purpose and emphasis. Not surprisingly, some cringed at the possibility that the AG that would mix evangelism and social justice and thereby slide down the slippery slope of Social Gospelers. Still others decided not to vote for the addition of compassion, since evangelism and compassion function as hand and glove. Whereas the AG resolution sought to heighten awareness and intentionality concerning compassion, some delegates wondered why the AG should distinguish between what is part and parcel of the gospel. Fortunately, some were swayed, and the AG announced a fourfold purpose with compassion alongside evangelism, worship, and discipleship.[19] Given the confusion over inclusion of compassion, I am reminded that a Mennonite reading

---

18. See http://www.mennoworld.org/archived/2011/6/6/mds-provides-leadership-joplin/ and
http://www.mennoworld.org/archived/2013/4/29/mds-concludes-joplin-project/.

19. In fairness, the success of Pentecostals has been marked not only by verbal proclamation but by transformational ministries. See Miller and Yammamori, *Global Pentecostalism*.

of Luke might help us better understand social justice (yes, I said it) as prophetic work.

Swartley states, "I would venture that Luke 4:18–19 has been used more often in pulpits and conference programs within Mennonite circles than any other Scripture."[20] Like Pentecostals, Mennonites place significant paradigmatic stock in Jesus' words both fulfilled and launched in his hometown. Similarly, I cannot count the number of sermons and references to Pentecostal appropriation of Jesus' exclamation, "The Spirit of the Lord is on me, because he has anointed me to proclaim good news" (v. 18). But what does this good news sound like? What does good news produce? Luke's Jesus provides such a bridge. For Mennonite and Pentecostal convergence, I cannot imagine a more passionate conversation concerning the nature of Spirit-anointed preaching to the poor, restored vision and health, release of captives, and the announcement of Jubilee. More than buzz words, Pentecostals and Mennonites preach and practice the gospel. Both traditions employ the word *euangelion* used in v. 18 with respective emphases, whether "good news" (think proclamation) or social justice (think action). Concerning their order of importance, I would answer only "yes." Surely, and through the Spirit, we have much to teach each other.

Nachfolge, (Im)migration, and Refugees

Given the evangelistic (think missionary) impulse of Pentecostals, movement proves crucial to our identity. Pentecostalism has been described as "a religion made to travel."[21] I picture preachers making use of John 3:16 and Acts 1:8 to implore Spirit-filled believers to leave their local Jerusalem and take the message of God's love throughout the world. Though a cursory reading of Luke-Acts delivers fulfillment of Jesus' words as the story moves from "Jerusalem, Judea, Samaria, and to the end of the earth" (Acts 1:8). Luke embeds the often-unplanned circumstances for movement. In Jesus' inaugural post-resurrection announcement, Jesus calls upon "witnesses" to fulfill this task (Luke 24:48). Unfortunately, the English translation fails to capture the Greek root for "martyr." Such an oversight often causes readers to miss Luke's

20. Swartley, "Smelting for Gold," 297.
21. Dempster et al., *The Globalization of Pentecostalism*.

twist on the movement of Jesus' witnesses. God's people often embark on "The Way" not because of a strategic "Missions Conference." Instead, Philip flees Jerusalem upon the death of his martyred friend Stephen, only to take the gospel to the Samaritans, and Paul consistently bolts from city to city on account of persecution and finally travels to Jerusalem and Rome not as a missionary but as a prisoner for the gospel. Once again, these stories find their beginning in Jesus' teaching, and I found that the Mennonite story offered sobering clarity.

In the mid-1990s, I pastored in Morden-Winkler, the heart of the Manitoba Mennonite belt (it is noteworthy that many in my congregation identified as ex-Mennonites). In 1994, Winkler Bible Institute hosted a summer long exhibition of Thieleman Van Bragt's *Martyrs Mirror*, based upon a seventeenth-century commemoration of martyrological accounts from early Christianity to the Anabaptists of his day.[22] The exhibit displayed thirty of 104 recently discovered copper plates etched by the gifted Mennonite artist, Jan Luyken, for his 1685 edition.[23] In a new publication on the social history of *Martyrs Mirror*, David Weaver-Zercher, American religious historian at Messiah College, claims that no other book (and drawings) apart from the Bible has produced a greater impact on Mennonite identity. For me, I have been drawn to, and haunted by, the specific account and illustration of Dirk Willems. As Willems runs to safety across a frozen river, his pursuer falls through the ice, and Willems must make a split-second decision to continue his flight or save a life. In dramatic fashion, Luyken "captures" the moment Willems rescues his pursuer. Willems is subsequently returned to town and burned at the stake. Not unlike a Pentecostal testimony, Willems' story calls upon Mennonites to consider Jesus' hard teachings such as his exhortation to "love your enemies [and] do good to those who hate you" (Luke 6:27); his prediction "they will seize you and persecute you" and "hand you over to synagogues and put you in prison, and you will be brought before kings and governors, and all on

22. Originally published in Dutch. Translated by Joseph E. Thom in 1837 as *The Bloody Theatre, or Martyrs' Mirror, of the Defenceless Christians Who Baptized only upon Confession, and Who Suffered and Died for the Testimony of Jesus, Their Savior, from the Time of Christ until the Year A. D. 1660*.

23. https://kauffman.bethelks.edu/martyrs/index.html (accessed March 30, 2017).

account of my name" (Luke 21:12); and his promise that "those who want to save their life will lose it, and those who lose their life for my sake, and for the sake of the gospel, will save it" (Luke 9:24).[24]

Mennonites make much use of the German word *Nachfolge*, their "way" to embody discipleship. Jesus' call to be a disciple cannot be reduced to individual belief (i.e., theological assent); the call demands that communities of believers literally "follow after" him.[25] In short, the Mennonite story tells of a people whose collective witness reads like a continuous migration narrative. If discipleship demands a daily walk in accordance with Jesus' radical teachings, the call to witness will include the kind of enemy love and possible martyrdom exhibited by Willems. And amid such difficulties, Mennonite history is replete with countless migration stories that resemble Acts; the Mennonites are a people ever-scattered because of witness and for witness. *Nachfolge* befits a life fraught with suffering, danger, and struggle. When they are pushed from "home," Mennonites must depend on the hospitality of others to reestablish their communities. Whether they flee persecution or go willingly to the ends of the earth, they are living examples of a people given second and third chances. As these movements remain etched upon their contemporary memory, Mennonites preserve their identity and inspire contemporary witness.

As I look back upon my early Pentecostal experience of Acts, I recall stories of Spirit-driven triumph. The classic invitation to participate in Acts-like reenactment typically began with Spirit-baptism, followed by a call to the world and the triumph of the gospel, something akin to "look out world, here comes Mittelstadt." Needless to say, my exploits failed to resemble anything like the sermonic rhetoric. In fact, my struggle with theological triumphalism nearly led to my departure from my Pentecostal roots. Had it not been for about a three-year personal investigation of Luke-Acts during my pastorate in Morden, I might have gone another direction. As I lived among Mennonites and learned their stories, I completed my dissertation entitled *Spirit*

---

24. Weaver-Zercher, *Martyrs Mirror*.

25. Sadly, the English title of Dietrich Bonhoeffer's monumental *Cost of Discipleship* does not reflect the German title *Nachfolge*, and thus fails to capture a deliberate link to Anabaptist thought and praxis.

and Suffering in Luke-Acts. The dissertation proved autobiographical. I wrote to see if I could remain Pentecostal. As I wrestled with the rhetoric of triumphalism versus my experience, I discovered that to be filled with the Spirit means living in the tension between acceptance and rejection, between the triumph and the tragedy of the gospel. God's agents from Jesus through the Twelve, Stephen, James, and Paul witnessed regularly under duress. Luke's Jesus not only modeled suffering for his followers, but he predicted opposition and persecution against future witnesses (Luke 12:1–12; 21:12–15). Far from a story of glory to glory, Luke strategizes a narrative of expansion driven by followers on the run.

Many Christians around the world live daily in such a climate. Life at home requires boldness and enemy love. Other Christians choose to leave their Jerusalem, enter volatile regions as agents of the gospel, and prepare, as much as they are able, for the difficulties ahead of them. But I must press further. My delineation of *Nachfolge* thus far employs terms such as "the Way," journey motif, and migration, but what about a turn toward current language caught by the much-debated battle over immigration and refugees? *Nachfolge* compels me to perceive in Luke-Acts and among Mennonites, an immigration narrative, a story of refugees. Like Jesus' first followers and Mennonites of days gone by, still other Christians leave home because of allegiance to the gospel. Severely persecuted and exhausted from ever-visible death, they finally flee for their lives. Like the Mennonites of old, many contemporary Christians receive gracious hospitality in new lands. I am deeply saddened when I listen to fellow Pentecostals (and Christians in general) unwilling to follow Luke's barrier-breaking Pentecost, an event that launches welcome by and to all humans. For me, the Mennonite story, coupled with their radical obedience to the Gospels and Acts, makes Pentecost more plausible. Pentecostals with our emphasis on Spirit-led witness would do well to integrate the Spirit's call to provide a "way of peace," thoughtful compassion toward the migrant embodied by our Mennonite friends.

Community

DISCLAIMER AND INVITATION

First, I assume that readers will recognize limitations of this account. This is my story; a partial account of a life lived entirely in the church. This story is a testimony based upon reading and rereading the Gospels and Acts among fellow academicians and believers. As I and others explore stories of Pentecostal and Mennonite convergence, we assume that all Christians, with even a little history in the greater Christian community and the smallest amount of intentionality, find points of convergence with those of other traditions. I also want to make it clear that impulses described as emblematic of one tradition do not imply the other should be declared wanting. For example, if my discovery that "any gospel which is not social is not gospel" first found meaning among Mennonites, I do not suggest that Pentecostals fail to teach and practice compassion.[26] Similarly, I am committed to non-violence. I came to this position through Mennonites long before I discovered that my Pentecostal (hi)story included a rich peace tradition. Having said this, I maintain that encounter with other traditions opens our eyes to new understanding and practices not necessarily well articulated in every tradition. For me, early interaction with Mennonites not only gave birth to my formation of a social gospel and a life dedicated to non-violence but encouraged me to reimagine and integrate these values with a Pentecostal vision for life in the Spirit.

Finally, I propose that the most substantive dialogue partner for Pentecostals should be Mennonites. Sadly, on more than one occasion, I have been told both by church officials and ecumenists that Pentecostal/Mennonite dialogue amounts to "small potatoes"; ecumenical investment with Mennonites, a tradition small-in-number and influence, seems futile compared to the large and powerful Catholic and Anglican traditions. To the contrary, I would suggest that such a dialogue might further enliven the vision of two traditions committed to radical apostolic Christianity. Both traditions work best as counter-cultural movements, yet struggle daily with temptation to accommodate the gospel; on this matter, I fear a gospel message that ranges from one extreme that settles primarily for an introspective faith to a gospel defined by

---

26. Kraybill, *The Upside-Down Kingdom*, 35.

cultural domination, Christians bent on power. Both traditions derive their *raison d'être* from the Gospels and Acts and would do well to share their ongoing experience of these texts. Our shared approach to Scriptures that tell and envision the stories of God's people then and now should inspire common exposition, particularly among pastors and theologians. Both traditions would serve our larger Christian family well by modelling life together. Given our collective commitment to prophethood, I am hard pressed to imagine two traditions more in need of one another and more able to work together. It is my hope that Mennocostals scattered within our respective traditions will foster relationships that inspire Spirit-inspired life and witness.

WHAT HAS GUS KONKEL TO DO WITH MENNOCOSTALS?

Gus Konkel serves not only as the consummate Old Testament professor, but he possesses remarkable facility to read Scripture through the lens of Jesus. Konkel may not have used Stronstad's axiom "prophethood of all believers," but he surely captures and conveys the visionary continuity between the prophets of old, the prophetic Jesus, and the prophetic church. Konkel remains committed to his Mennonite roots, specifically, the Mennonite struggle not only to receive but advocate for compassionate justice, not least to the foreigner-immigrant, and the outsider-refugee. Konkel may not be a Pentecostal, but he shares with conviction the longing of Moses—and people of Pentecost—"that all the Lord's people were prophets and that the Lord would put His Spirit upon them!" (Num 11:29). In so doing, I am grateful for an exemplary individual who "*follows after*" the Prophet like Moses, and has assisted many students, colleagues, and friends to embrace the Mennocostal life. Gus, it is not too late to join the Mennocostal family!

BIBLIOGRAPHY

Bruce, F. F. *Commentary on the Book of the Acts: The English Text with Introduction, Exposition, and Notes*. Grand Rapids: Eerdmans, 1977.

Dempster, Murray, et al., eds., *The Globalization of Pentecostalism: A Religion Made to Travel*. Oxford: Regnum, 1999.

Fee, Gordon, and Douglas Stuart. *How to Read the Bible for all Its Worth*. Grand Rapids: Zondervan, 1981.

Good, Sheldon. "MDS Provides Leadership in Ravaged Joplin." *Mennonite World Review*, June 6, 2011. http://www.mennoworld.org/archived/2011/6/6/mds-provides-leadership-joplin/.

Johnson, Luke Timothy. *The Literary Function of Possessions in Luke-Acts.* Missoula, MT: Scholars Press, 1977.

———. *Prophetic Jesus, Prophetic Church: The Challenge of Luke-Acts to Contemporary Christians.* Grand Rapids: Eerdmans, 2011.

Kraybill, Donald. *The Upside-Down Kingdom.* Updated Edition. Harrisonburg, VA; Herald, 2011.

"MDS Concludes Joplin Project." *Mennonite World Review*, April 29, 2013. http://www.mennoworld.org/archived/2013/4/29/mds-concludes-joplin-project/.

Miller, Donald, and Tetsunao Yammamori. *Global Pentecostalism: The New Face of Christian Social Engagement.* Berkeley: University of California Press, 2007.

"The Mirror of the Martyrs." https://kauffman.bethelks.edu/martyrs/index.html.

Mittelstadt, Martin W. "My Life as a Mennocostal: A Personal and Theological Narrative." In *Pentecostals and Nonviolence: Reclaiming a Heritage*, edited by Paul Alexander, 333–51. Eugene, OR: Pickwick, 2012.

———. *Reading Luke-Acts in the Pentecostal Tradition.* Cleveland, TN: Center for Pentecostal Theology Press, 2010.

———. Review of *Prophetic Jesus, Prophetic Church: The Challenge of Luke-Acts to Contemporary Christians*, by Luke Timothy Johnson and *The Spirit and the 'Other': Social Identity, Ethnicity, and Intergroup Reconciliation in Luke-Acts*, by Aaron J. Kuecker. *Pneuma* 35 (2013) 120–22.

———. "Spirit and Peace in Luke-Acts: Possibilities for Pentecostal/Anabaptist Dialogue." In *Didaskalia* 20 (2009) 17–41.

Robertson, A. T. *A Harmony of the Gospels for Students of the Life of Christ.* San Francisco: Harper & Row, 1922.

Stronstad, Roger. *The Charismatic Theology of St. Luke.* Grand Rapids: Baker, 2012.

———. *Prophethood of All Believers.* Sheffield: Sheffield Academic, 1999.

Swartley, Willard M. "Smelting for Gold: Jesus and Jubilee in John H. Yoder's Politics of Jesus." In *A Mind Patient and Untamed: Assessing John Howard Yoder's Contributions to Theology, Ethics, and Peacemaking*, edited by Ben C. Ollenburger and Gayle Gerber Koontz, 288–302. Telford, PA: Cascadia, 2004.

Weaver-Zercher, David. *Martyrs Mirror: A Social History.* Baltimore: Johns Hopkins University Press, 2016.

Yoder, John Howard. *The Politics of Jesus.* Grand Rapids: Eerdmans, 1994.

Yong, Amos. *The Spirit Poured Out on All Flesh: Pentecostalism and the Possibility of Global Theology*. Grand Rapids: Baker Academic, 2005.

12

The Word of God and Christian Community

David Johnson

INTRODUCTION

The Reverend Doctor August Konkel was my faculty colleague at Providence Theological Seminary for twenty-two years, from August 1990 to July 2012. During that time we also served on the President's Cabinet together, with him as President of Providence University College and Seminary and me first as Dean of the Seminary then as Executive Vice President and Provost. During this long association, I learned that Gus was a man of the Word. His ability to sight-read Hebrew and Greek texts was legendary in southern Manitoba, from among students in class to governors at board meetings. I remember one day when he forgot he was supposed to speak in Seminary chapel. A student went to retrieve him from his office. As he walked down the hall, while speaking with the student he also prepared a fine message from his Hebrew Bible. Of course, being able to prepare a message from the Hebrew Bible on the fly does not come naturally. It comes from years of in-depth study of Hebrew, the text of Scripture, and biblical theology. But Gus also has a natural ability (some might call it a gift) in preaching. Even though Gus has this "gift," he does not use it to pontificate. He uses his gift of preaching to bring forth the Word of God from the Bible.

Gus is also a community person. I remember once as we talked in his office early in my years at Providence, he said to me, "People are the most important thing in this world." He is a natural storyteller. He has long poems memorized, like "The Ballad of the Ice-Worm Cocktail" by Robert Service and ones written by his father. He could recite these poems on command. Students loved it when he came as president to the residence hall to tell stories and spend time with them.

Gus is a man of the Word and he is a community person. So it is with great delight that I offer to him this short study of the Word of God and the Christian community. The major part of the paper is a biblical theology of the Word of God. The last section briefly discusses the implications of this theology for the life of the Christian community.

A BIBLICAL THEOLOGY OF THE WORD OF GOD

It has been said (and I have said it myself) that the early verses of Genesis are assertions, not about *how* God created the world but *that* God created the world. But, in fact, the early verses of Genesis state precisely *how* God created the world. Genesis 1:2 paints a picture of a dark, empty, and chaotic land (*'areṣ*). Then v. 3 says, "And God said (*wayyō'mer 'Elohim*), 'Let there be light, and there was light.' God overcame the darkness by speaking light into existence. On days two and three God overcomes the chaos of the land by speaking (*wayyō'mer 'Elohim*) separations into existence between waters above and below and between waters and land. On days four through six God speaks (*wayyō'mer 'Elohim*) into existence all living creatures in the heavens, in the seas, and on the land. God also does other things with words in these early verses like naming things and creatures. The Mishnah points out that it is important to note that there are ten occurrences of the phrase *wayyō'mer 'Elohim* in the opening creation narrative (*m. 'Abot* 5.1; cf. vv. 3, 6, 9, 11, 14, 20, 24, 26, 28, 29). God could have created everything with one speech act, but he did it with ten.[1] How did

---

1. On the artistry of the ten sayings, cf. Cassuto, *A Commentary on the Book of Genesis*, 14.

God create the heavens and the land? He did it by speech, by the word. From the very beginning, God's word is powerfully creative.

In the Torah, God speaks Ten Words again in Exod 20 and Deut 5. The actual phrase "ten words" occurs in Exod 34:28.[2] The Ten Words were given as Israel began her wilderness wanderings and then again near the end. If there is a connection, the point is that as God overcomes the chaos, emptiness, and darkness of creation by speaking, so God overcomes the chaos, emptiness, and darkness of human life by speaking ten instructions for living. Throughout the stories of the wilderness wanderings Moses often represents the speech of God (e.g., Num 11:24-25). That is why Moses is refused entrance into the Promised Land in Num 20. God tells Moses to speak to the rock to bring water out of it, but instead Moses strikes the rock with the staff and is thereby accused of not trusting God (i.e., not trusting God's word). It is also why a prophet like Moses is promised to the people (Deut 18:15-22).

God's speech, whether direct or usually mediated through Moses, is a key theological theme in the Torah. That is why, near the end of the Torah, Moses gathers the people and after finishing his poem about Israel's future, he says to them, "Take to heart these words . . . for it is not an empty word for you, for it is your life" (Deut 32:46-47).[3] The passage certainly refers to the poem of ch. 32 but probably also to the blessings and curses in earlier chapters of Deuteronomy and perhaps to the whole of the Torah. Moses is not saying this word is about your life. One can almost picture Moses holding up a scroll and saying that this is the word that constitutes your life. This word (this book) defines you as a people, it makes you who you are. It is a powerful, creative word.

It is not surprising that, as the Torah ends with this emphasis on God's word, the Former Prophets begin with the same emphasis: "Only be strong and very courageous, being careful to do according to all the law that Moses my servant commanded you. Do not turn from it to the right or to the left, that you may have success wherever you go. This book of the Law shall not depart from your mouth, but you shall

---

2. In Exod 34:28, Moses or the LORD (it is unclear which) wrote the ten words on stone tablets, but these ten words in the context (vv. 10-26) are different than the ten in Exod 20.

3. All biblical translations are my own.

meditate on it day and night, so that you may be careful to do according to all that is written in it, then you will prosper and succeed" (Josh 1:7–8). The implicit "written" word of Deut 32:47 is now explicitly a written word. It is a word that will bring success, which is what it does for Joshua. The Former Prophets are filled with stories of the powerful word of God. They include the stories of young Samuel (1 Sam 3:1–18); the rejection of Saul (1 Sam 15:22–23); various prophecies and their fulfillment (e.g., the prophecy about Jericho [Josh 6:26 and 1 Kgs 16:34] or 2 Kgs 4:43–44); David's oracle (2 Sam 23:1–7); the stories of Elijah and Elisha, especially Elijah's encounter with the still small voice of the Lord (1 Kgs 19:9–18); Josiah's discovery of the book of the Law of the Lord (2 Kgs 22–23), and others.

The Latter Prophets are also filled with references to the powerful word of God. "The word of the LORD came to . . ." or "And God said (or says) . . ." occurs in every prophetic book often many times over. Isaiah is a prime example emphasizing the word of God. The grand vision of Isa 2 is that the nations will stream to Mount Zion because it is from there that the word of the LORD shall spread. This word will judge disputes between peoples, and they shall build a lasting peace among themselves (vv. 3–4). After his vision in the temple Isaiah is commissioned to preach from cleansed lips (6:6–7). The word of God that comes from his lips will dull the people's ears and blind their eyes. The word will bring a lack of understanding (6:9–10).[4] It is a powerful word which accomplishes God's will of judgment. In 34:16, Isaiah calls on the nations to read from the book of the LORD. After judgment God promises to gather his people into an Edenic place of refuge (34:16—35:10). In ch. 40, the word of promise is explicit that the people will return from their captivity. This promising word is sure: "Grass withers, flowers fade, but the word of our God endures forever" (40:8). This word is the "good news" of salvation of the LORD's coming (40:9–10; cf. 52:7). Chapter 41 contrasts the idols which do not speak with God who calls the future into existence through the Servant (42:9). God gave the Servant of the LORD a mouth which is sharp like a sword (Isa 49:2). God taught him the word which will sustain the weary, he wakens to hear the word of

---

4. Alec Motyer (*The Prophecy of Isaiah*, 78) calls this "the oddest commission ever given to a prophet."

the Lord (50:4). The promise of return from captivity is like water for the thirsty and food for the hungry (Isa 55:1–2). This word of promise accomplishes God's work. As the rain and snow come from heaven and water the earth causing it to bear fruit, so is God's word that goes forth from God's mouth. It does not return without succeeding in its purpose (55:10–11). As with creation, God's word accomplishes God's purpose. It is a powerful word. It is the ultimate speech act.

Isaiah's theology of the powerful word of God is also found in the other Latter Prophets. Both Jeremiah and Ezekiel are called by God's word and commissioned to speak it (Jer 1:2, 4, 9–12; Ezek 2–3). Jeremiah pronounces judgment on the false prophets who have not stood in the council of the Lord (23:18, 22). God says, "Is not my word like fire and like a hammer that shatters rock" (23:29)? Hosea alludes to the Ten Commandments (4:2), then explicitly pronounces judgment because the people have ignored God's law (4:6). Amos says there is a famine for the word of the Lord (8:11–12). Micah echoes Isaiah's prophecy about the word of the Lord proceeding from Zion (4:1–4); Habakkuk is told to write the revelation God gives him (2:2). Later he deplores the one who makes an idol that cannot speak (2:18). Zechariah refers to the words of earlier prophets as the word of God (7:7, 12). At the end of the Latter Prophets there is a call to remember the law of Moses given at Horeb (Mal 4:4). It is to be noted that, as in the Former Prophets, as the history of redemption moves forward the concept of the powerful, active, and creative word of God is considered to be inscripturated in the text of the Torah.

The Writings also contain an emphasis on the word of the Lord. The first verses of their first book recall the opening of the Former Prophets. The only two passages in the OT that use the phrase "meditate on them day and night" are Josh 1:8 and Ps 1:2. The idea of meditating on the Law of God works like a thread that ties together all three sections of the Hebrew Bible. The first psalm, without a prescript, functions to introduce one of the major themes of the Psalter, that is, the law, the word of God.[5] God's word/law is prominent in Pss 19 and 119.

---

5. Likewise, the second psalm, without prescript, also functions to introduce a major theme of the Psalter, namely the anointed king, the son of God. Cf. Sheppard, *The Future of the Bible*, 66–74. The lack of prescript is unusual in the first book of

It is speech that acts upon its hearers. Psalm 18:30 says the Lord's word is flawless. In Ps 29 the voice of the Lord is powerful and shakes the earth.[6] The creative word of God also occurs in Ps 33:6, "By the word of the Lord the heavens were made, and by the breath of his mouth all their host." This word is called right and true (v. 4). God spoke and the earth came to be; he commanded and it stood firm (v. 9). In Ps 105:8–19 God's word proved true as God kept the covenant with Abraham. In vv. 31 and 34 the plagues on Egypt are attributed to God speaking. God finally speaks at the end of Job. The words of mother and father in Proverbs are the words of God. Near the end of the Writings, Ezra and Nehemiah speak of the Law and its effect on people (Ezra 3:2, 4; 7:6, 10). It takes a central role in Neh 8–9. It is read out and interpreted by the Levites under the care of Ezra. Nehemiah 9:5–37 is the interpretation of the story of Israel as it is told in the Scriptures.

If we picture the OT as a rope of many strands, one of the thematic strands in that rope is the powerful word of God. It is sometimes visible on the surface of the rope and sometimes is buried among the other threads. But it is certainly always there. It is one of the threads that ties the OT together. The NT picks up this theme at many places and brings it into messianic perspective.

The Gospel of Matthew begins the story of Jesus by rehearsing events that "fulfill" the prophecies of the OT (cf. Matt 1–2). As the story develops, there are many times where "fulfillment" is mentioned until we come to 26:56, where the text asserts, "But all this has taken place that the Scriptures of the prophets may be fulfilled." In addition to texts which assert fulfillment in the life of Jesus, we find Jesus citing Scripture three times in the temptation narrative in Matt 4 (// Luke 4:1–13). In Matt 5:17–20, he asserts that nothing will pass from the Law until everything is accomplished. The word of God is found in the words of Jesus in 7:24–27, where building one's life on Jesus words is like building one's house on solid rock. As God overcame the chaotic sea in Gen 1 (mentioned also in the divine speeches in Job), so Jesus calms the sea

---

the Psalter, giving a hint that these two psalms were placed here as an introduction.

6. The voice of the Lord in Ps 29 occurs seven times. It may be a reference to thunder and lightning.

by his word (8:26). Jesus heals by speaking (9:1–8).[7] He is the sower who sows the word (13:18–23), and he brings about judgment by his word symbolized in the cursing of the fig tree (21:19).

Although the Gospel of Mark does not contain as much of Jesus' teaching as the other gospels, it does emphasize Jesus the teacher. For example, in 2:2 Jesus preached the word to the crowd but the content of that word is not stated here. It is not until ch. 4 that the contents of Jesus' word is given, and then it is given in parables. As in Matthew, the word is the seed that the sower sows (4:14). "With many other parables he spoke the word to them" (4:33). The Olivet Discourse in Mark 13 is the second main speech of Jesus in the Gospel. It is more than prediction, it is cause. In the midst of the sufferings of the end times, the disciples are to speak whatever the Holy Spirit gives them to say (13:11).

The Gospel of Luke contains a number of references to the word of God. In almost a Johannine way, the prologue speaks of those who were eyewitnesses and servants of the word (1:2).[8] The angel Gabriel tells Mary that no word of God will ever fail (1:37). The crowds recognize the authority and power of the words of Jesus (4:32, 36). In 5:1 the word of God is heard in the teaching of Jesus. The power of Jesus' word is seen in the healing of the centurion's child (7:7). Luke's record of the parable of the sower is similar to Matthew and Mark. At the end of the parable Jesus identifies his family as those who hear and keep the word of God (8:21; cf. 11:28).[9] Mary sits at Jesus' feet listening to his word (10:39). At the end of the Gospel, the resurrected Jesus opens the minds of the disciples to understand the Scriptures and shows them how the Scriptures find their fulfillment in him.

The word of God in the Gospel of John is prominent from the very first verse: "In the beginning was the word." Reference to the word in John is not limited to the prologue.[10] Robert Gundry highlights the

---

7. In fact, many of Jesus' miracles are narrated in such a way as to put emphasis on the power of the word. For example, see the stories of Peter's denial. Does Jesus merely foretell, or does his word actually bring about the events?

8. Perhaps a reference to both Jesus and the gospel.

9. In the parallel passages in Matthew and Mark, it is those who do the will of God who are Jesus' kin.

10. In the Fourth Gospel, Jesus from the outset is the incarnate Word of God. As the Gospel moves past the prologue, the incarnate Word speaks words. For further

prominence of the word in the Fourth Gospel, so only a brief rehearsal is given here.[11] Jesus speaks in the Gospel of John more than in any other Gospel. Jesus asserts that the one whom God sends speaks the words of God (3:34; cf. 7:16–18; 12:47–50). Many Samaritans believed because of his word (4:41). Jesus claims that his words are spirit and life (6:63) so Peter says, "Lord to whom shall we go? You have the words of eternal life" (6:68). In his speeches Jesus says the word (Scripture) cannot be broken (10:35) and that God's word is truth (17:17).

The Book of Acts, with regard to the word of God, brings to full flower that which began to bud in the Gospel of Luke. To describe the first volume, *logos* is used, instead of a word like *biblion* (1:1). The word of God occurs in three of the summary statements which divide the book (6:7; 12:24; 19:20). On the day of Pentecost, the word of God comes to the people in many languages through the apostles (2:1–13). The apostles, in Acts, are the tradents of God's word so that the early disciples devote themselves to the apostles teaching (2:43) and the church prays that the apostles would be able to speak the word with all boldness before all people (4:29). The apostles recognize the priority of the word of God and so devote themselves to its ministry (6:2, 4). As Acts develops, the word of God is the gospel of Christ. God works so that Philip brings the word to the Ethiopian leader (8:26). Later a large number of Gentiles receives the word of God (11:1). Paul preached the word of God in synagogues (13:5), and Sergius Paulus wanted to hear the word of God (13:7). When Paul is asked to deliver a speech in a synagogue he brings a word of encouragement (*paraklesis*) which is a recitation of the OT story. In 15:7 Peter calls the message "the word of the gospel." So throughout the rest of the book the word is the gospel (16:6, 32; 17:11, 13; 18:11; 19:10, 20; 20:32).

The Pauline epistles[12] also emphasize the powerful word of God. Right at the beginning of Romans, it says that the gospel is the power of God for salvation (1:16). The word of the cross is the power of God to those who are being saved (1 Cor 1:18; cf. 15:1–2). We have the

---

reflection, see Grundy, *Jesus the Word according to John the Sectarian*.

11. Gundry, *Jesus the Word according to John the Sectarian*.

12. I use Paul and Pauline Epistles for convenience, recognizing that not everyone holds that Paul is the immediate source of these letters.

message in jars of clay to show that its power is God's (2 Cor 4:7). As Paul defends his ministry of the word, he says that the weapons of our warfare are divinely powerful. This applies to his letters as well as his speech (2 Cor 10:3–12; cf. Eph 6:10–17). The gospel bears fruit and grows (Col 1:6). To the Thessalonians, the gospel came with power and they received it as the word of God (1 Thess 1:5, 13). Teaching the word brings salvation to its hearers (1 Tim 4:11–16). Although Paul was in prison, the word of God was not chained, it was free to do its work (2 Tim 2:9). Every Scripture is from the very mouth of God and is useful in equipping people for service (2 Tim 3:16–17). The word of God acts upon its hearers.

Paul notes that there is a particular pattern of teaching to which believers conform (6:17). This pattern is the message of Jesus Christ according to the revelation of the mystery now manifested through the exposition of prophetic writings (Rom 16:25–26). The word is a mystery taught by the Spirit (1 Cor 2:6–16). It is a mystery made known by revelation and enacted through the preaching of the gospel (Eph 3:1–13; Col 1:27; 2:2). It is crucial that this word is passed on faithfully and is not distorted (2 Cor 4:2; Gal 2:5, 14; 2 Tim 1:14).

According to Paul, the word is central to ministry. Preaching the gospel is Paul's first priority (1 Cor 9:15–23; Phil 1:15–18). He teaches the word everywhere in every church (1 Cor 4:17). He is not like the philosophers who sell the word (2 Cor 2:17). He tells Timothy to preach the word and not human ideas (2 Tim 4:2). This is the word of reconciliation (2 Cor 5:19).

In the past God spoke through prophets, but in these final days God has spoken definitively through his Son (Heb 1:2). This is why it is crucial that today when we hear God's voice we do not harden our hearts (Heb 3:7, 15; 4:7). God's word is living and active and penetrates to the very depths of the human heart (Heb 4:12–13).

The first chapter of James highlights the work of the word. It is by the word that we experience new birth (1:18). It is a word that is planted in us (1:21) and it acts like a mirror by which we are able to correct our living (1:22–25). Likewise, 1 Peter says we have been born again through the word after which Peter cites Isa 40:6–8: "All flesh is as grass and all its glory as the flower of grass. The grass withers and the flower falls, but the word of the Lord remains forever" (1 Pet 1:23–25). With a different image, 2 Peter says the same thing, we participate in the divine nature through the promises of God (1:4). Second Peter is a summarizing text when it comes to a biblical theology of the Word of God. It notes that Scripture comes from the moving of the Spirit of God (1:20–21). The word comes by the prophets and the apostles of the Lord and Savior (3:2). It is by this very word that the world was created, and it is by this word that the world will be recreated in the end (3:13). The final verses of 2 Peter speak of the writings of Paul as in the same class as the rest of Scripture (3:15–16).[13]

The final book of the Bible begins with what John saw, namely, the word of God to which he bore witness (Rev 1:2). The whole prophecy, even about all the evil doings of beasts and harlots, is about God's purpose, which he has put in the hearts of his enemies until his words are fulfilled (17:17). The end will come with the Rider on the white horse (19:11–16). The description of the Rider in these verses allows one to picture the Rider as a super being, but the picture is distorted by the reference to the sword that comes from his mouth (19:15; cf. 1:16; Isa 49:2). This is a metaphor for the word that proceeds from his mouth by which he controls the nations. In the end, it is the word of the Rider that will bring peace and justice to the world.

It is clear that the powerful word of God is a central theme in all of Scripture from Genesis to Revelation. Even recognizing the notion of confirmation bias when reading the text, it is apparent that this statement is true, just by the sheer number of references. God is often said to "speak," and this in contrast to foreign gods and dumb idols. It is not always clear how God speaks, at times it is loud and at times it is soft. It is clear that God often speaks the word through chosen servants (once even through a donkey). It is also clear that God speaks through the writing and rehearsing of Scripture, to the point where these writings can be called the word of God.

God's speech does things, this is how God acts. God creates the heavens and the earth by the word. God prophesies and in the prophecy, the word can be said to cause the events. This is a living and active

---

13. See Vögtle, "Die Schriftwerdung der apostolischen Paradosis nach 2. Petr 1,12–15," 297–305.

word. When God makes a promise, for example of a return from captivity, it is actually that promise that makes it happen. When God speaks a word of blessing or judgment, it is that word that brings them about. In both testaments it is God's word that brings salvation to God's people. Fulfillment is more than God foreseeing the future and announcing it. Fulfillment is due to the sovereign word of God doing God's work. Therefore, God's people can put absolute trust in God's word and they can act upon it.

THE WORD OF GOD AND THE CHRISTIAN COMMUNITY

So what can we say about the relationship between the word of God and the Christian community? I conclude with four short statements.

First, the word is formative for the church. The Word of Christ is to dwell richly in the midst of the church (Col 3:16). When the church gathers the Word is to be central because God speaks to the church in the Word. Scripture, as opposed to mere human thoughts, is God's speech. This gospel is powerful in the changing of people's lives. It is not a psychological trick, God's word actually works powerfully. Hence, the word must be studied carefully, then preached, then discussed, and then applied to the life of the church and to the lives of those who form the body of Christ, all under the guidance of the Holy Spirit. Much of what passes for preaching today is therapeutic rather than proclamatory. It is anthropological rather than theological. Certainly, people need self-awareness. They also need God-awareness. James Packer opens his classic book, *Knowing God*, by quoting a Charles Spurgeon sermon preached in 1855:

> It has been said by someone that "the proper study of mankind is man." I will not oppose the idea, but I believe it is equally true that the proper study of God's elect is God; the proper study of the Christian is the Godhead. The highest science, the loftiest speculation, the mightiest philosophy, which can ever engage the attention of a child of God is the name, the nature, the person, the work, the doings, and the existence of the great God whom he calls Father.[14]

---

14. Packer, *Knowing God*, 13.

Second, the church is the divinely appointed tradent of the word of God. This word is present primarily as the canon of Scripture. The relationship of church and canon is symbiotic. The church is the means by which the canon is recognized and preserved, and it is the canon that creates and sustains the church. The canon is both an accident of history and an inspired work of God.[15] As the Westminster Confession (1.4–5) stated in the seventeenth century:

> The authority of the Holy Scripture, for which it ought to be believed and obeyed, dependeth not upon the testimony of any man or church, but wholly upon God (who is truth itself), the author thereof; therefore it is to be received because it is the Word of God. We may be moved and induced by the testimony of the Church to an high and reverent esteem of the Holy Scripture; and the heavenliness of the matter, the efficacy of the doctrine, the majesty of the style, the consent of all the parts, the scope of the whole (which is to give glory to God), the full discovery it makes of the only way of man's salvation, the many other incomparable excellencies, and the entire perfection thereof, are arguments whereby it doth abundantly evidence itself to be the Word of God; yet notwithstanding, our full persuasion and assurance of the infallible truth, and divine authority thereof, is from the inward work of the Holy Spirit, bearing witness by and with the Word in our hearts.

Third, the Christian community is charged with faithfully preserving the word of God and passing it on to succeeding generations (i.e., interpretation). The history of the interpretation of Scripture is long and twisted. One of the major twists happened in the seventeenth and eighteenth centuries with the development of "history" and the rise of historical criticism.[16] Johann Salomo Semler and others separated the word of God and Scripture, noting that the Scripture more or less contained the word of God. Loosed from the mooring of the canon, the word of God became captive to the word of human beings. Human criticism ruled over the word of God. In keeping with the biblical

---

15. Cf. Chapman, "Reclaiming Inspiration for the Bible," 167–206.
16. Cf. Frei, *The Eclipse of Biblical Narrative*.

theology of the word of God, the church must return to *lectio divina*.[17] The canon is the word of God. The word of God is a transformative word. Humans do not stand in judgement over Scripture. Scripture is the mirror in which humans see their situation defined and which offers both correction (in Luther's terms *adversarius noster*, our adversary) and a way to know God. *Lectio divina* recognizes the transformational purpose of Scripture as the word of God living and active. It aligns itself with what the word of God declares about itself.

Finally, the church hears the polyphonic word of God through Scripture. Within the Christian community the Bible is the main avenue by which God speaks. It is also the veritable critic of all the human claims to speak the word of God. As R. W. L. Moberly points out, the Bible is a book of ancient history, and it is a cultural classic.[18] But it is more than these. It is also a word from God. It is the "privileged vehicle of divine truth in today's world."[19] How do believers hear God's word in Scripture? They are called upon to test this word, and in the testing they have found, and will continue to find, it to be true.[20] The test is believing that the word is from God and then acting upon that word. "This dimension of personal faith and engagement is a necessary corollary to the persuasive force of a Christian plausibility structure."[21] All of this is not to say that each person hears or speaks the word of God in the same way. God speaks one message in a variety of ways and words. It is a polyphonic word. The polyphony speaks to different people in

---

17. By the term *lectio divina*, I mean reading Scripture as the word of God, not in the technical sense of continuous reading following more or less strict forms. See the interaction of Francis Young with Jean Vanier's commentary on the Gospel of John in "Towards Transformational Reading of Scripture," 236–54. Young points out the importance of Vanier's reading and theorizes on how it can be integrated into a critical reading of the text. *Lectio divina* does not require the reader to put their mind on the shelf. There is a place for sophisticated and even critical reading of the text. At the same time, readers must allow the Scripture to be a critic of all their readings of the word of God.

18. Moberly, *The Bible*, 41–52.

19. Moberly, *The Bible*, 129.

20. Moberly, *The Bible*, 134–40.

21. Moberly, *The Bible*, 139. The plausibility structure of which Moberly speaks is the church throughout its history.

different languages and cultures and historical settings. Scripture draws the church together in its commitment to follow the will of God every day.

The word of God is a major theme of biblical theology. So what is the relationship between the powerful word of God and the Christian community? The word of God forms the Christian community. The community is the tradent of the word of God in the canon of Scripture. The community interprets Scripture as the word of God. And finally, and most profoundly, God speaks to the community through the word of God which is the Bible.

BIBLIOGRAPHY

Cassuto, U. *A Commentary on the Book of Genesis: Part 1, From Adam to Noah*. Translated by Israel Abrahams. Jerusalem: Magnes, 1961.

Chapman, Stephen B. "Reclaiming Inspiration for the Bible." In *Canon and Biblical Interpretation*, edited by Craig Bartholomew et al., 167–206. Scripture and Hermeneutics Series 7. Grand Rapids: Zondervan, 2006.

Frei, Hans. *The Eclipse of Biblical Narrative*. New Haven: Yale University Press, 1974.

Gundry, Robert. *Jesus the Word according to John the Sectarian: A Paleofundamentalist Manifesto for Contemporary Evangelicalism, Especially Its Elites in North America*. Grand Rapids: Eerdmans, 2001.

Moberly, R. W. L. *The Bible in a Disenchanted Age: The Enduring Possibility of Christian Faith*. Theological Explorations for the Church Catholic. Grand Rapids: Baker, 2018.

Motyer, Alec. *The Prophecy of Isaiah: An Introduction and Commentary*. Downers Grove, IL: InterVarsity Press, 1993.

Packer, J. I. *Knowing God*. Downers Grove, IL: InterVarsity Press, 1973.

Sheppard, Gerald. *The Future of the Bible: Beyond Liberalism and Literalism*. Toronto: The United Church Publishing House, 1990.

Vanier, Jean, and Francis Young. "Towards Transformational Reading of Scripture." In *Canon and Biblical Interpretation*, edited by Craig Bartholomew et al., 236–54. Scripture and Hermeneutics Series 7. Grand Rapids: Zondervan, 2006.

Vögtle, Anton. "Die Schriftwerdung der apostolischen Paradosis nach 2. Petr 1,12–15." In *Neues Testament und Geschichte*, edited by Heinrich Baltenswelter and Bo Reicke, 297–305. Tübingen: Mohr, 1972.

13

Destruction and Restoration of Genuine Human Community in Dietrich Bonhoeffer's *Creation and Fall*

Patrick S. Franklin

INTRODUCTION

PEOPLE HAVE ALWAYS BEEN attracted to Dietrich Bonhoeffer. Many respect him as a hero of the resistance movement and leader of the Confessing Church in Nazi Germany during the Second World War. Many others know him as a writer of insightful devotional classics, such as [Cost of] *Discipleship, Life Together,* and *Prayerbook of the Bible.* Some are captivated by the creative, courageous, and suggestive and innovative quality of his later theological writings, especially *Letters and Papers from Prison* and his *Ethics.* Still others have been drawn to the centrality of friendship in Bonhoeffer's life (as evidenced in and in his personal letters), especially his deep friendship with Eberhard Bethge (his closest friend, biographer, and frequent theological conversation partner), but also his receptivity and openness to friends from various cultural and ethnic backgrounds, such as Jean Lasserre (a French pacifist), Albert Fisher (an African American, with whom Bonhoeffer attended Abyssinian Baptist Church in Harlem during his time in the USA), Erwin Sutz (a Swiss theological student who was instrumental

PATRICK S. FRANKLIN—*Destruction and Restoration of Genuine Humanity*

in arranging for Bonhoeffer to meet Karl Barth), Paul Lehmann (a student at Union Seminary, who helped deepen Bonhoeffer's appreciation for the plight of the oppressed and the importance of civil rights), and George Bell (a bishop in England who became an important ally during the resistance period). Recently, Bonhoeffer's life-long devotion to ministering to and caring for young people—whether young children in Sunday school, or poor and underprivileged kids, or teens in youth groups, or university students in discussion groups—has been celebrated and explored theologically.[1]

During his own life Bonhoeffer invested himself deeply in relationships and community, and many—students, teachers, theologians, pastors, and church congregants of various ages and backgrounds—found themselves drawn to him. He had a sharp mind, a deep interest in people, and a winsome personality. Throughout his theological career, he was fascinated with ecclesiology and especially the nature and expression of church and of genuine Christian community. His reflections on Christian community in his (now classic) book *Life Together* are profound and continue to be a source of spiritual inspiration, theological reflection, ecclesial imagination, and practical instruction to pastors, theologians, church and parachurch leaders, and thoughtful Christian believers all over the world.

While most of Bonhoeffer's admirers are familiar with *Life Together*, many are less familiar with (or even unaware of) the development of its central theological themes in Bonhoeffer's earlier works, namely *Sanctorum Communio*, *Act and Being*, the *Christology Lectures*, and *Creation and Fall*. This essay will explore Bonhoeffer's theology of community in the latter book. *Creation and Fall* is a fascinating work for many reasons. It helpfully sees the Old Testament as an important source for ecclesiological reflection, whereas too often people begin their thinking about the church with the New Testament (e.g., Acts 2, 4) and thus fail to grasp important aspects of the church's *telos*, especially its connection to biblical and theological anthropology. It draws important doctrinal themes together, including creation, christology, anthropology, soteriology, ecclesiology, and eschatology. And, as a theological work, it represents an important point of transition in

1. See Root, *Bonhoeffer as Youth Worker*.

Bonhoeffer's writing, connecting his earlier academic work with his later contemplative, devotional, and ethical writings. *Creation and Fall* is not a flawless book; but it is a highly insightful, creative, suggestive, provocative, contextual, and theologically stimulating piece of writing, worthy of attention and consideration.

A final word of introduction before proceeding: It is a great honour to dedicate this chapter contribution to Dr. Gus Konkel. While we never formally worked together at Providence Theological Seminary in Manitoba, Canada (though as outgoing President, he did interview me as a candidate for the position of Assistant Professor of Theology and Ethics in November, 2011), we have had many opportunities to connect and discuss matters of life, faith, Bible, and theology. Whether during Gus's visits to teach modular classes at Providence, or at meetings of the Canadian-American Theological Association, or by personal correspondence through email, Gus has been generous in providing ongoing encouragement, advice and wisdom, feedback on presented papers and articles, and dialogue and perspective on ideas and issues over which I have wrestled. I regard him as a model Christian scholar: deeply devoted to loving God and loving others, deeply committed to excellent biblical and theological scholarship, and deeply immersed in Christian community at many levels (church, academy, broader networks, friends, and colleagues). Thank you, Gus.

A THEOLOGICAL EXPOSITION

Reading *Creation and Fall* is not like reading a typical modern commentary written by an Old Testament scholar working in the professional guild of academic biblical studies. Thus, before explicating the theology of human community in *Creation and Fall*, it is important to identify and understand Bonhoeffer's interpretive aims and methodological commitments. Most significantly, Bonhoeffer's approach to the text in this work is decidedly and intentionally theological, as his subtitle suggests (*A Theological Exposition of Genesis 1–3*).[2] Bonhoeffer

---

2. His previous two published books, *Sanctorum Communio* (pub. 1930, an updated version of Bonhoeffer's doctoral dissertation) and *Act and Being* (pub. 1931, an updated version of Bonhoeffer's *Habilitation*), were more philosophical and systematic in nature. See also: Godsey, *Theology of Dietrich Bonhoeffer*, 119–43; Bonhoeffer,

does not claim, or even aim, to be doing something like 'pure exegesis' or 'presuppositionless exegesis' when explicating Gen 1–3. Following the example of Karl Barth, Bonhoeffer takes a post-critical approach to the text,³ which breaks free of the epistemological and methodological limitations of the Enlightenment and the trends in modern biblical and theological scholarship stemming from it.⁴ Bonhoeffer does not discard the methods of grammatical-historical criticism, or the importance of serious historical scholarship,⁵ but he relativizes and subjugates them to serve his primary theological and ecclesiological commitments and aims.⁶ "That is, he in principle accepted the findings of historical and literary criticism but sought to move *beyond* them to grapple with the question, What is the word of God as it addresses itself to us today in this scripture?"⁷

Bonhoeffer was an early advocate and practitioner of what we now refer to as the theological interpretation of Scripture.⁸ Theological interpretation is defined not primarily by its methods (its practitioners employ a variety of methods), but by its commitments, concerns, posture or orientation(s), interpretive aims, and intentional habits and

---

"The Interpretation of the New Testament," in *No Rusty Swords*, 308–25; and Bonhoeffer, *Life Together*, 58–65.

3. De Gruchy, "Editor's Introduction," 7.

4. For a brief discussion of this history, see Fowl, *Theological Interpretation*, 13–53.

5. Bonhoeffer took classes with the great liberal theologian, Adolf von Harnack, and was impressed with his emphasis on history. Bonhoeffer looked to Harnack as a mentor and often walked to school with him. He contributed to a Festschrift dedicated to Harnack in 1926, and spoke at Harnack's memorial service on behalf of Harnack's students (his speech was published). See: Schlingensiepen, *Dietrich Bonhoeffer*, 27–30, 58–59; and Marsh, *Strange Glory*, 43–46, 99.

6. As Bonhoeffer (*Creation and Fall*, 22) puts it, "This is its presupposition [that the Bible is the book of the church] and this presupposition constitutes its method; its method is a continual returning from the text (as determined by all the methods of philological and historical research) to this presupposition."

7. De Gruchy, "Editor's Introduction," 7.

8. See, for example, Billings, *The Word of God for the People of God*; Fowl, *Engaging Scripture*; Treier, *Introducing Theological Interpretation of Scripture*; Vanhoozer, Bartholomew, and Treier, *Theological Interpretation of the Old Testament*; Vanhoozer, Treier, and Wright, *Theological Interpretation of the New Testament*; and Webster, *Holy Scripture* and *The Domain of the Word*.

practices. Above all, theological interpreters seek to keep theological concerns primary.⁹ This does not mean simply mining the Bible for propositional content related to particular doctrines and their construction; rather, and more broadly, it means seeking to indwell the biblical text in order to encounter and attend to the triune God that is revealed and actively speaks in and through it. "In this way, theology becomes a form of scriptural interpretation, not simply its result."¹⁰ This endeavor rests upon explicit commitments held by the interpreter about the nature and *telos* of Scripture and the God that ordained, inspired, sanctified, and now illumines it.¹¹ As Stephen Fowl writes, "Scripture needs to be understood in the light of a doctrine of revelation that itself flows from Christian convictions about God's triune life. Scripture is a gift from the triune God that both reflects and fits into God's desire to bring us into ever deeper fellowship with God and each other."¹² Thus, "theological interpretation ... will involve those habits, dispositions, and practices that Christians bring to their varied engagements with

---

9. Watson, *Text, Church and World*, vii.

10. Fowl, *Theological Interpretation*, 39. In addition, theological interpretation is first and foremost a practice of the church and is thus ecclesially oriented (23), uses Scripture "as a way of ordering and comprehending the world" rather than the other way around (23), involves reading guided by the rule of faith (29), recognizes Christ as the centre of Scripture and thus the subject of both the OT and the NT (33–37), accepts that theology – not textual and hermeneutical theories – provides the *telos* for reading scripture (39), employs the methods of grammatical-historical criticism when helpful, but also gains from the insights of pre-modern forms of exegesis such as figural reading (56), and is formed by practices laying at the centre of Christian life and leading to the cultivation of virtue, such as: truth seeking/telling; repentance, forgiveness, reconciliation; and patience (66–70).

11. For a rigorous and fascinating theological discussion of these themes, and their relation to conventional biblical scholarship, see Webster, *Holy Scripture* (chapter 1).

12. Fowl, *Theological Interpretation*, 13. Drawing on the work of John Webster, Fowl writes, "God's self-revelation to humans is both the source and content of a Christian doctrine of revelation. Revelation is directly dependent upon God's triune being and it is inseparable from God's freely willed desire for loving communion with humans. In this light, the written text of Scripture is subsidiary to and dependent upon a notion of revelation that is itself directly dependent on God's triune being." (Fowl, *Theological Interpretation*, 6).

Scripture so they can interpret, debate, and embody Scripture in ways that will enhance their journey toward their proper end in God."[13]

Reading Scripture theologically entails, in addition, an adequate self-awareness on the part of the interpreter,[14] which includes knowledge of oneself (including one's virtues and vices) and of one's present context (socio-cultural, ethnic, philosophical, ecclesial, community/school/social context of interpretation, etc.). For example, Stephen Fowl underscores the importance of the ethical formation of the reader for interpreting Scripture well and Francis Watson points to a threefold orientation situating the reader theologically (before God) to text, church, and world.[15] Taken together, their insights suggest that theological interpretation is a holistic practice, aiming to bring *the whole reader* (and their context) before *the whole of Scripture*, to be addressed and transformed through Word and Spirit by the Triune God who is *Lord over the whole of Reality*. Thus, theological interpretation seeks to move beyond the dualisms[16] posited by modernity and often reinforced methodologically within the guilds of modern biblical and theological

---

13. Fowl, *Theological Interpretation*, 14.

14. Thus, Calvin wisely begins his famous *Institutes*, a work which he intended as a guide for reading Scripture, with the words: "Our wisdom, in so far as it ought to be deemed true and solid Wisdom, consists almost entirely of two parts: the knowledge of God and of ourselves" (Calvin, *Institutes* I.I.1–3, 37).

15. For a detailed introduction to the work of these two prominent voices in theological interpretation, see my chapter "Francis Watson and Stephen E. Fowl as Theological Interpreters of Scripture." For the relevant works by the authors, see especially: Fowl, *Engaging Scripture*; *Philippians*; and Fowl and Jones, *Reading in Communion*; and Watson, *Text, Church and World*; and *Text and Truth*.

16. Examples of these dualisms include objectivity-subjectivity, reason-faith, facts-values, description-prescription, 'what a text meant' vs. 'what a text means,' past-present, text-reader, and so forth. Theological interpreters need not deny 'softer' distinctions here that are seen to operate together in dialogical relationship and inter-dependence; what they reject is a kind of modernist prioritization of detached, impersonal methods of engaging the text as a 'thing,' akin to the methodological naturalism proper to the physical sciences. The latter, while appropriate given the subject matter (physical reality, broken down into distinct parts and studied according to their proximate causal relations), is unbefitting of the subject matter of Christian interpretation (the personal Word-address of the transcendent, Triune God, self-disclosed as Father, Son, and Spirit via the biblical witness and the interpretive traditions of the church).

scholarship.[17] Theological interpreters engage intentionally as whole persons situated in their contexts before God, who read Scripture with explicitly theological commitments and aims, guided by the rule of faith, in communion with the church past and present, in order to encounter God and be formed by that encounter, as it is mediated by the text and guided by the active presence and working of the Holy Spirit.

In *Creation and Fall*, Bonhoeffer exemplifies many of the tenets of theological interpretation.[18] First, he understands his reading of the Bible to be an explicitly and inherently theological practice. This means that Bonhoeffer reads unapologetically as a Christian and as a theologian seeking after God's Word in the words of the text.[19] Repeatedly in *Creation and Fall*, Bonhoeffer speaks of the Bible as an address to God's people, and not simply one taking place in the past but an address that also speaks to readers and hearers today.[20] This is because God indwells the text, and we readers and listeners imaginatively find ourselves in the text too, drawn into its world and concerns and called to account.[21] Moreover, Bonhoeffer finds Christian doctrine to be a useful aid in interpreting the text.[22] For example, in his reading of Gen 1–3, Bon-

---

17. I refer here to the consequences for biblical scholarship following Johann Gabler's distinction of biblical scholarship (doing exegesis as a purely descriptive task) and theology (a prescriptive task involving reflection, synthesis, and application to contemporary concerns) as well as Krister Stendahl's famous differentiation of 'what a text meant' (the task of biblical scholarship) and 'what a text means' (the task of theology). On these developments, see: Gabler, "Oration;" and Hasel, "Relationship." For Watson's critique of Gabler's distinction, see *Text, Church and World*, 30–33, and *Paul and the Hermeneutics of Faith*, 531–32. Agreeing with Brevard Childs, Watson argues that genuine scriptural interpretation begins from an explicit framework of faith.

18. Which is not to say that he gets everything right. In places, more attention to the contemporary Old Testament scholarship of his day could either improve his exegesis (especially his reading of Gen 1) or augment and lend further support to this own insights and reflections.

19. De Gruchy, "Editor's Introduction," 7.

20. Bonhoeffer, *Creation and Fall*, 29, 30, 43, 82, 83, 89, 100.

21. Bonhoeffer, *Creation and Fall*, 81–82. With respect to Gen 1–3, as we will see later, 'Adam' is *we ourselves* (89, 100), such that we are meant to hear God's address to Adam as if to us.

22. This is another common feature of theological interpretation (though how one construes and "uses" doctrine varies amongst practitioners). As Reno ("Series Preface," 12) writes in his series preface to the Brazos theological commentary, "This

hoeffer draws on christology, the sacraments, ecclesiology, theological anthropology, the resurrection of Christ, and more.[23]

Second, Bonhoeffer reads Scripture in light of Jesus Christ. Bonhoeffer's reading of Scripture is both christocentric and christotelic,[24] with Christ as the Centre and goal of Scripture's witness to the self-revelation of God. With respect to Creation, Bonhoeffer notes that we cannot go back to "the beginning" in some pure, unproblematic way. Perhaps with affinities to Gadamer's notion of effective history (that there is no pure 'past' accessible to scholars as some object, only the past as already operative in and partially determinative of the present),[25] yet further complicated by the theological problem of sin, Bonhoeffer writes that we find ourselves in the 'middle': "Humankind no longer lives in the beginning; instead it has lost the beginning. Now it finds itself in the middle, knowing neither the end nor the beginning, and yet knowing that it is in the middle."[26] Then, perhaps with John 1:1–2 ringing in the background, Bonhoeffer writes, "No one can speak of the beginning but the one who was in the beginning."[27] Christ alone, who is God Incarnate comes to us in the midst of time to unveil to us the true beginning and end of human existence: "only from Christ . . . can we know about the original nature of humankind . . . . Only in the middle, as those who live from Christ, do we know about the beginning."[28] Thus, for example, Bonhoeffer interprets the image of

---

series of biblical commentaries was born out of the conviction that dogma clarifies rather than obscures." In particular, Reno mentions that contributors are trained in the Nicene tradition, by which he means not merely learning a set of words and creeds but "a pervasive habit of thought" and "the animating culture of the church in its intellectual aspect" (14).

23. Bonhoeffer, *Creation and Fall*, 35–36, 62, 72, 79, 89, 92, 99, 100–101.
24. Enns, *Inspiration and Incarnation*, 144–55, 158–59.
25. Ringma, *Gadamer's Dialogical Hermeneutic*, 34.
26. Bonhoeffer, *Creation and Fall*, 28.
27. Bonhoeffer, *Creation and Fall*, 29.
28. Bonhoeffer, *Creation and Fall*, 62. Elsewhere, he writes, "The church . . . views the creation from Christ; or better, in the fallen, old world it believes in the world of the new creation, the new world of the beginning and the end, because it believes in Christ and in nothing else" (22)

God in Gen. 1 in light of Jesus Christ who is the true Image, the true revelation of God and prototype of the authentically human.[29]

Third, Bonhoeffer reads the biblical text (here Gen 1–3) canonically, a method that is closely linked with his christological convictions.[30] Bonhoeffer is not attempting, naively and simplistically, to read Christ out of the Old Testament exegetically or to read Christ into the Old Testament eisegetically. Rather, Bonhoeffer reads the entire biblical text in its final form as a coherent but diverse and complex whole: "indeed one can read [Genesis] as a book that moves toward Christ *only when one knows* [i.e., from the New Testament] that Christ is the beginning, the new, the end of our whole world" (emphasis added).[31] This canonical reading leads Bonhoeffer to revive and employ pre-modern methods of reading the text, such as figural reading and typological reading.[32]

---

29. Bonhoeffer, *Creation and Fall*, 65, 113. And linking the two themes, Bonhoeffer writes: "Adam is a human being like us and Adam's history is our history, with the one decisive difference, to be sure, that for us history begins where for Adam it ends. Our history is history through Christ, whereas Adam's history is history through the serpent. But precisely as those who live and have their history through Christ alone we are enabled to know about the beginning not by means of our own imagination but only from the new center, from Christ" (92).

30. Specifically, concerning the present text, Bonhoeffer reads the Old Testament in light of the New Testament and especially in light of Jesus Christ. In Bonhoeffer's work, this commitment to canonical reading centred in Christ leads him both to interpret the OT in light of the NT, but also the NT in light of the OT. In fact, as Bonhoeffer's theology matured, he came increasingly to see how important the OT is to understanding the true nature of Christianity. For example, "Does the question about saving one's soul appear in the Old Testament at all? Aren't righteousness and the Kingdom of God on earth the focus of everything, and isn't it true that Rom 3.24ff. is not an individualistic doctrine of salvation, but the culmination of the view that God alone is righteous? It is not with the beyond that we are concerned, but with this world as created and preserved, subjected to laws, reconciled, and restored. What is above this world is, in the gospel, intended to exist *for* this world; I mean that, not in the anthropocentric sense of liberal, mystic pietistic, ethical theology, but in the biblical sense of the creation and of the incarnation, crucifixion, and resurrection of Jesus Christ," 285–286. Or, "While you're in Italy I shall write to you about the Song of Songs. I must say I should prefer to read it as an ordinary love song, and that is probably the best 'Christological' exposition," 315.

31. Bonhoeffer, *Creation and Fall*, 22. Or, regarding one of his interpretive decisions later in the book: "To be sure, this judgement . . . arises only from listening to and understanding scripture as a whole," 71.

32. For example, reminiscent of Irenaeus, Bonhoeffer draws the following connection between Eve and Mary: "Eve, the fallen, wise mother of humankind – that

Fourth, Bonhoeffer grants primacy to the church, not the academy, as the proper locus for reading and interpreting Scripture. He writes, "Theological exposition takes the Bible as the book of the church and interprets it as such." The church "is founded upon the witness of Holy Scripture"; the "church of Holy Scripture" thus "reads the whole of Holy Scripture as a book of the end, of the new, of Christ." "*In the church*, therefore, the story of creation must be read in a way that begins with Christ and only then moves on toward him as its goal" (emphasis added).[33] This is not to suggest that the church should be naively ignorant of biblical and theological scholarship; it is simply to affirm that primarily, "Our concern is the text as it presents itself to the church of Christ today."[34]

Fifth and finally, Bonhoeffer approaches biblical interpretation as an ethical task. Bible reading aims at the formation of the reader through one's encounter with God as one seeks to indwell the text; and, one's ethical formation—one's character formed in Christ and one's characteristic love for God and neighbour—inevitably shapes one's reading of Scripture (one's heart and character partially predetermines what one cares about, and thus, what one sees and attends to). Moreover, Bible reading is teleologically oriented toward practice; in other words, genuine interpretation of the text (according to the text's theological nature as God's Word-address to us) includes the embodiment of its narrative and teachings in the lives of Christian believers, both individually and corporately (e.g., Matt 7:24–27; Jas 1:22–25). As Erich Klapproth recalls from Bonhoeffer's opening words to his course on Creation and Fall on Nov. 8, 1932, "One can never hear it, if one does not at the same time live it—and this involves specially *exercitium* ['practice']."[35] The interpreter's heart and formation, context and concerns, loom large yet subtle (beneath the surface) in *Creation and Fall*. Readers of the book do well to be mindful of Bonhoeffer's historical,

---

is the one beginning. Mary, the innocent, unknowing, mother of God – that is the second beginning," *Creation and Fall*, 138.

33. Bonhoeffer, *Creation and Fall*, 22.
34. Bonhoeffer, *Creation and Fall*, 83.
35. Bonhoeffer, *Creation and Fall*, 23n11.

cultural, and political context (1932–33 Germany). As John de Gruchy helpfully reminds us:

> It was a winter of profound discontent in Germany; it was also a time of confusion, anxiety, and for many, false hope, as social and political upheavals led to the demise of the Weimar Republic and the birth of the Third Reich. In the midst of these events Bonhoeffer called his students to focus their attention on the word of God as the word of truth in a time of turmoil.[36]

These words are important to keep in mind as we turn now to unpacking Bonhoeffer's theology of personhood and community in *Creation and Fall*.

GENUINE COMMUNITY

According to Bonhoeffer, human beings were created to find meaning, fulfilment, and completion not in themselves, but in God. The human being, like all other creatures, is a contingent lifeform, one dependent upon God for everything that it is and has, as well as for its ongoing existing and becoming. Genuine human community arises within this reality. Genuine human community is not a creation of humanity. It is not, as Bonhoeffer puts it in a later work, a human ideal that we must achieve, but a divine reality that God establishes and into which God calls and draws us to participate.[37] Our original participation, as depicted in Gen 2 in the story of the first humans living together in the Garden of Eden, was not itself the fullness and completion of all that God intended human personhood and community ultimately to become. Rather, the original human community depicted in the early chapters of Genesis foreshadows what would be achieved in fullness later, through Christ and in the Spirit. It is Christ, not Adam, who is the true prototype for human beings;[38] and it is through Christ in the Spirit that Adam's *telos* is fully revealed, his nature consummated, and his destiny secured.

---

36. De Gruchy, "Editor's Introduction," 1.

37. Bonhoeffer, *Life Together*, 35–38. See also *Sanctorum Communio*, 125, 153, 157–61, 198–99, 211, 275–282.

38. Bonhoeffer, *Creation and Fall*, 65.

Bonhoeffer's reflections about human personhood and community in *Creation and Fall* flow from his interpretation of the two trees located at the centre of the Garden of Eden. The centrality of the two trees in this setting strikes Bonhoeffer as being deeply significant. Bonhoeffer sees both trees as occupying the focal point of all life, goodness, meaning, knowledge, wisdom, and social harmony. As such, the trees represent God, because they occupy the space and perform the functions that belong properly to God alone.[39] "The life that comes from God is at the center; that is to say, God, who gives life, is at the center. . . . Adam's life comes from the center which is not Adam but God; it revolves around this center constantly, without ever trying to take possession of this center of existence."[40] God alone has Life, in the sense of non-contingent, necessary, self-sustaining, eternal life.[41] Human beings do not of themselves possess this kind of life; theirs is contingent, non-necessary, temporary life, dependent outside of itself for sustenance. As creatures made of the dust of the earth, the original humans are depicted as mortal beings, dependent upon God for their very life and breath.[42] As David Kelsey says in his magisterial work on theological anthropology, human beings *live on borrowed breath*.[43] Genuine, authentic human existence recognizes this existential fact. God is the Source and Centre of human life, meaning, and fulfilment. "Human

---

39. Bonhoeffer's interpretation of the two trees in the Garden of Eden strikes me as being deeply consonant with Gus Konkel's reading of the text (through, of course, as an Old Testament scholar, Konkel would add layers of historical and exegetical detail not present in Bonhoeffer's reading). In a personal email correspondence, written to me on October 25, 2017, Gus explained: "[The] [t]ree of knowledge and tree of life are both representative of that which is exclusive to the holy (they could of course be real trees, just like bread and wine at communion are real bread and wine). That is holy in the absolute sense, that which defines God. Life on earth is continuously dependent on God, it is the gift of the holy to the common. Knowledge of that life is also exclusive to the source. This is defined by the terms 'good and evil.' This is a common Hebrew merism that can be found everywhere (e.g. Gen 31:24). All knowledge belongs to God alone."

40. Bonhoeffer, *Creation and Fall*, 84.

41. In his *Systematic Theology*, Millard Erickson points out that, properly speaking, Life is a divine attribute (297–98).

42. Walton, "Reading Genesis," 166.

43. Kelsey, *Eccentric Existence* (Part One).

beings have life from God and *before* God."⁴⁴ Authentic human existence accepts this as unproblematic. "Indeed this tree first gains its particular significance only after humankind has fallen prey to death by eating from the tree of knowledge. Before that, life is not something problematic or to be sought after or snatched at; instead it is just here, as a given life, indeed life before God."⁴⁵ Adam and Eve are not alone in their being creatures that derive their life and *telos* from God; but as *human beings* made *in God's image* they do this in unique and distinctive ways: by the Word-address of God, human beings are enabled to respond to God intelligibly and responsibly as those who converse with God, love God, and serve God through their vocation as stewards of creation. With God as their Centre, and with their lives oriented toward and given meaning and guidance in light of that Centre, they are predisposed to obeying God 'naturally' as a characteristic outflow of their being. "Adam has life in the unity of unbroken obedience to the Creator—has life just because Adam lives from the center of life, and is oriented toward the center of life, without placing Adam's own life at the center."⁴⁶ Adam lives this life of obedience in a truly authentic way, in innocence flowing from freedom to be that which his Creator calls him to be. Adam and Eve possess this life "in their obedience, in their innocence, in their ignorance; that is, they possess it in their freedom. The life that human beings have happens in an obedience that issues from freedom."⁴⁷

In this context of wholeness, freedom, and innocence (one might say, "purity of heart," i.e., Matt 5:8), Adam and Eve enjoy perfect community with God and each other. At this point in the story, there is not a hint of pride, fear, distrust, envy, distorted desire or lust, competitiveness, inequality, selfishness, or dissatisfaction within or between humans. Adam receives Eve as pure gift and loves her as such:

---

44. Bonhoeffer, *Creation and Fall*, 84.

45. Kierkegaard says that authentic Christian life is found not by grasping at it or by losing one's sense of self by falling into passivity (both of these are forms of despair), but when the self "rests transparently in the power that established it," Kierkegaard, *Sickness Unto Death*, 44.

46. Bonhoeffer, *Creation and Fall*, 84.

47. Bonhoeffer, *Creation and Fall*, 84.

> That Eve is derived from Adam is a cause not for pride, but for particular gratitude, with Adam. Adam does not infer from it any claim for himself; instead Adam knows that he is bound in a wholly new way to this Eve who is derived from him. This bond is best described in the expression: he now belongs to her, because she belongs to him. They are now no longer without each other; they are one and yet two. . . . But this becoming one never means the merging of the two or the abolition of their creatureliness as individuals. It actualizes to the highest possible degree their belonging to each other, which is based precisely on their being different from each other.[48]

Eve represents grace to Adam in a way more fundamental to his humanness than just being a relational partner (important as that is); she is a concrete, embodied manifestation of Adam's limit. "The other person is the limit that God sets for me, the limit that I love and that I will not transgress because of my love. . . . By the creation of the other person freedom and creatureliness are bound together in love."[49] One could say that the other person is a sacrament, a physical manifestation of an invisible grace (the grace of transcendence of self through communion with the other) and thus an instrument of divine grace and love, though Bonhoeffer himself does not use this language. Adam and Eve are thus truly *free*—not 'free' in the modern sense of the (almost absolute) autonomy of the individual, i.e., freedom *from* God and other people. They are truly free *for God* and free *for one another*. "For in the language of the Bible freedom is not something that people have for themselves but something they have for others."[50] For Bonhoeffer, freedom is not primarily a quality, an ability, or a possession; it is a relation

---

48. Bonhoeffer, *Creation and Fall*, 97–98.

49. Bonhoeffer, *Creation and Fall*, 99. In *Santorum Communio*, 45–55, Bonhoeffer had employed this concept to explain that human beings encounter in both God and other human beings' ethical limits on their own existence. Thus, their own subjectivity is conditioned and limited by the subjectivity of other persons who confront them from outside of themselves. Bonhoeffer's views here on personhood share some affinities with the views of Buber and Levinas. For a discussion of the differences between Bonhoeffer and Levinas, see Zimmerman, *Recovering Theological Hermeneutics*, 278–81, 285; and between Bonhoeffer and Buber, see Green, "Human Sociality and Christian Community," 116.

50. Bonhoeffer, *Creation and Fall*, 62.

between persons. "Being free means 'being-free-for-the-other', because I am bound to the other. Only by being in relation with the other am I free."[51] Such freedom is an image of God's own freedom.[52] Bonhoeffer writes, "God wills not to be free for God's self but for humankind. Because God in Christ is free for humankind, because God does not keep God's freedom to God's self, we can think of freedom only as a 'being free for. . . .'"[53] Humans were created to be *exocentric* creatures, beings that find their centre and completion outside of themselves, in God and in other human persons.[54]

This idyllic picture is complicated by the presence of the other tree, the tree of the knowledge of good and evil. To grasp what Bonhoeffer says about this tree, it is important to understand that Bonhoeffer does not regard the events recorded in Gen 2–3 as being historical; he is not troubled by this or by questions related to the historicity of the stories.[55] His interpretation is more existential—or better, *theological*—

---

51. Bonhoeffer, *Creation and Fall*, 63.

52. Green, "Human Sociality and Christian Community," 117. The classic treatment of Bonhoeffer's theology of human sociality is Green's *Bonhoeffer: A Theology of Sociality*.

53. Bonhoeffer, *Creation and Fall*, 63. Bonhoeffer famously expounds the concept of *imago Dei* in terms of humans being free-for-God and free-for-others, i.e., he interprets the imago relationally (Barth follows Bonhoeffer on this in his *Church Dogmatics* 3/1). However, Bonhoeffer's interpretation of the *imago Dei* is not restricted to this. Primarily, being in God's image means *representing God*, and one of the ways in which humans represent God is by their being-in-relation in genuine love and freedom. Another important way that humans represent God is by ruling over creation, having been commissioned and empowered by God to do so and accountable to God in this function, 65–66.

54. The term exocentric comes from Pannenberg, *Anthropology in Theological Perspective*, 43–79.

55. For example, Bonhoeffer writes, "Whether the creation occurred in rhythms of millions of years or in single days, this does no damage to biblical thinking. We have no reason to assert the latter or to doubt the former; the question as such does not concern us. That the biblical author, to the extent that the author's word is a human word, was bound by the author's own time, knowledge, and limits is as little disputed as the fact that through this word God, and God alone, tells us about God's creation." Later, when discussing God's fashioning the human out of clay, Bonhoeffer writes, "Surely no one can gain any knowledge about the origin of humankind from this! To be sure, as an account of what happened this story is at first sight of just as little consequence, and just as full of meaning, as many another myth of creation. And yet in being distinguished as the word of God it is quite simply *the*

in nature.⁵⁶ He is concerned with how the text addresses *us* (for him, those who read and heard the text in 1932–33 Germany).⁵⁷ Adam is *we ourselves*.⁵⁸ When the text describes Adam, it is describing us; when it is addressing, judging, and holding forth grace to Adam, it is doing all of this to us.⁵⁹ The picture of genuine human community depicted in Gen 2 "is the church [Kirche] in its original form" and "in its deepest sense the community of husband and wife [depicted in Gen. 2] . . . is destined to be the church (Eph 5:30–32)."⁶⁰ That Genesis speaks to us in pictures is not an indication of its limitations, but of its great depths:

> Who can speak of these things except in pictures? Pictures after all are not lies; rather they indicate things and enable the underlying meaning to shine through. To be sure, pictures do vary; the pictures of a child differ from those of an adult, and those of a person from the desert differ from those of a person from the city. One way or another, however, they remain true, to the extent that human speech and even speech about

---

source of knowledge about the origin of humankind" (Bonhoeffer, *Creation and Fall*, 49, 75–76, original emphasis).

56. Bonhoeffer is not seeking, in modernist fashion, to separate the kerygmatic kernel of universal truth from the cultural shell of its ancient, primitive form. Rather, it is precisely through its form, in the actual stories that we have, that God's theological Word of address comes to us as readers. Later, in the prison letters, Bonhoeffer distances himself from Bultmann's existential demythologization on this point: "You can't, as Bultmann supposes, separate God and miracle, but you must be able to interpret and proclaim *both* in a 'non-religious' sense. Bultmann's approach is fundamentally still a liberal one (i.e. abridging the gospel), whereas I'm trying to think theologically," Bonhoeffer, *Letters and Papers from Prison*, 285.

57. He writes, "This is God's word; this is an event at the beginning of history, before history, beyond history, and yet in history; this is a decision that affects the world; *we ourselves* are the ones who are affected, are intended, are addressed, accused, condemned, expelled; *God, yes God*, is the one who blesses and curses; it is our primeval history [Urgeschichte], truly our own, every individual person's beginning, destiny, guilt, and end – so says the church of Christ," Bonhoeffer, *Creation and Fall*, 82, original emphasis.

58. Though he might nuance this a little differently, Gus Konkel similarly places an emphasis on the text's significance for the people of God in the present: "As I always tell my students, Gen 1–11 is not to tell us about some world in the past, it is to explain to us the world of the present" (email correspondence, October 25, 2017).

59. Bonhoeffer, *Creation and Fall*, 89, 100.

60. Bonhoeffer, *Creation and Fall*, 100, 101.

abstract ideas can remain true at all—that is, to the extent that God dwells in them.[61]

While the tree of life points to the source, and thus the fullness and richness, of life with and before God, the tree of the knowledge of good and evil points to the limit or boundary of human existence. This boundary is Adam/humanity's creatureliness. Adam does not initially regard this tree as a temptation, but recognizes it as "the grace that belongs to his creatureliness and freedom."[62] Adam is not God; he was created to be *like God*, made in God's own image, but not to *be God*, or to be like God in such a way that he *takes or usurps God's proper place*.[63] He is to be like God, in dependency upon and obedience to God. Adam's contingent "I exist" is properly derivative of God's absolute "I AM." To many who read the story of the tree of the knowledge of good and evil for the first time, God's prohibition against eating of it seems arbitrary (why the silly test?), duplicitous (doesn't the New Testament, e.g., Jas 1:13–15, say that God tempts no one?), or even fearful and defensive (is God afraid of what the humans are becoming in Gen 3:22?). Taking Gen 2–3 as a literal, historical account raises these and other troubling questions.[64] But Bonhoeffer does not read it this way; what

61. Bonhoeffer, *Creation and Fall*, 81.

62. Bonhoeffer, *Creation and Fall*, 87. Moreover, "Adam knows neither what good nor what evil is and lives in the strictest sense *beyond good and evil*; that is, Adam lives out of the tree of life that comes from God," 87–88, original emphasis.

63. Wenham and several other interpreters (he cites Cassuto, Westermann, Vawter, and Clark) regard the tree as being associated with wisdom, not wisdom generally but specifically wisdom that belongs properly to God. He notes that "the wisdom literature . . . makes it plain that there is a wisdom that is God's sole preserve, which man should not aspire to attain (e.g., Job 15:7–9, 40; Prov 30:1–4), since a full understanding of God, the universe, and man's place in it is ultimately beyond human comprehension. To pursue it without reference to revelation is to assert human autonomy, and to neglect the fear of the Lord which is the beginning of knowledge (Prov 1:7)," 63. Wenham notes that this interpretation is likely confirmed by Ezek 28:6, 15–17, which he sees as the closest parallel to Gen 2–3, where the king of Tyre is expelled from Eden for excessive pride, regarding himself "wise as a god," 64.

64. Thus, I find solutions such as that proposed by Walton to be theologically unconvincing: "God's prohibition of the tree need not lead us to conclude that there was something wrong with what the tree gave (remember, everything was created 'good'). Rather than God's putting the tree there simply to test Adam and Eve, it is more in keeping with his character to understand that the tree would have use in the future. When the time was right, the first couple would be able to eat from it"

he finds important is the theological meaning of what the text depicts "in pictures": "The prohibition means nothing other than this: Adam, you are who you are because of me, your Creator; so now be what you are. You are a free creature, so now be that. You are free, so be free; you are a creature, so be a creature."[65] For Bonhoeffer, then, the early chapters of Genesis reveal that God intends human persons to be creatures that love God and one another genuinely and freely. Thus, centred and oriented outside of themselves, toward God and one another, they find meaning, purpose, significance, flourishing, and harmony.

DESTRUCTION OF HUMAN COMMUNITY

When Adam and Eve eat of the tree of the knowledge of good and evil in Gen 3, they do more than simply disobey God's command and incur guilt. They *do* act in disobedience and so incur guilt, but much more fundamentally they betray their own nature *as creatures* and as *human beings made in God's image*. The significance of their eating of the tree goes beyond the act itself. According to Bonhoeffer, the story symbolizes the fundamental problem of human existence: that human beings do not acknowledge God as the Source and Centre of their existence, but instead attempt to usurp God's place as Centre and be gods unto themselves in place of God.[66] Human beings want to be

(Walton, *NIVAC: Genesis*, 205). This interpretation seems to me to be constrained by an overly literalistic and historicist reading, i.e., that the tree was an actual tree in real historical time.

65. Bonhoeffer, *Creation and Fall*, 85.

66. Gus Konkel corroborated this interpretation for me when he wrote (email correspondence, October 25, 2017): "Of course the tempter readily deceives arrogant humans—they can be god. So they think. Partaking of the tree of knowledge describes humanity, not simply some event in the past. Modernists partook vigorously from that tree, believing there is nothing to be known outside of what their minds can think or perceive. (As Conrad Black puts it, "faith in the non-existence of anything greater than themselves.) It is the claim made since Adam and Eve. . . . An implication of claiming to have all knowledge is the claim to know what is good and what is evil. . . . Only if you have all knowledge is this possible. The whole book of Genesis is about this experiment. The narrator has very deliberately drawn the whole to a conclusion in the words of Joseph in Gen 50:19–20: 'Am I in the place of God?' Rhetorical question to the brothers. 'You intended this for evil but God intended it for good so as it is this day a great people is preserved alive.' The claim to be god, the claim to all knowledge failed, and of course it also resulted in severance from

their own source of life, their own source of meaning and purpose, and they want to decide for themselves what is good and what is evil.[67] They "renounce the life that comes from [the word of God] and grab it for themselves."[68] The result? By "eating of the tree," humankind now stands in the centre, having no limit and living from its own resources. But to do so is to destroy their very creatureliness and to introduce a rupture into their nature (of all creatures, only humans negate their own nature; their good and evil acts result from this rupture in their being). Bonhoeffer writes,

> Humankind lives in a circle; it *lives* out of its own resources; it is alone. Yet *it cannot live*, because in fact it does not live but in this life is dead, because it *must* live, that is, it *must* accomplish life out of its own resources and just that is its death (as the basis at once of its knowledge and of its existence!). Humankind whom God's commandment confronts with a demand is thrown back upon itself and now has to live in this way. Humankind now lives only out of its own resources, by its knowledge of good and evil and thus is dead.[69]

Norman Wirzba explains, "Bonhoeffer proposes that prior to the transgression Adam lives in respectful obedience to the grace of life. His obedience made possible a unified, singularly focused form of life in which the two-sidedness of good and evil ... had not yet emerged." Further, "The option is not between good and evil but between a 'life obedient to God' and 'a life of good and evil.'"[70] The latter path can only

---

the tree of life. But the punishment is mitigated. *Eve* (*khawwah* = life) is the means of preserving life in the present (Gen 3:20). But Genesis is the story of the blessing all nations may participate in (Gen 12:3), the working out of which is expressed by Joseph in the blessing of Jacob (Israel) as seen at the end of the book of Genesis."

67. Later, Bonhoeffer picks up this theme of human beings, as autonomous individuals, desiring to be their own source of the knowledge of good and evil in his *Ethics* (written 1940–1943; first German edition published posthumously in 1949; first English edition published in 1955). There he argues that Christian ethics primarily concerns our being formed in Christ, not as making use of *our* knowledge of good and evil, our "knowing good and evil in disunion with the origin," as Bonhoeffer puts it, *Ethics*, 308.

68. Bonhoeffer, *Creation and Fall*, 117.

69. Bonhoeffer, *Creation and Fall*, 91, original emphasis.

70. Wirzba, "The Art of Creaturely Life," 14n14.

lead to death, or as Wirzba describes Bonhoeffer's interpretation, to "deathly 'life.'"[71]

Not content to be the image of their Creator (*imago Dei*), human beings fall prey to the serpent's suggestion that they can be *more* like their Creator (*sicut Deus*) by transgressing their creaturely limit. The temptation is subtle, even 'pious,'[72] because it begins with the truth (i.e., that human beings *are* to be like God) and plays off of that truth by redirecting and thus distorting it. "This is disobedience in the semblance of obedience, the desire to rule in the semblance of service, the will to be creator in the semblance of being a creature, the dead in the semblance of life."[73] Bonhoeffer teases out the differences with the use of two Latin descriptors, *imago Dei* and *sicut Deus*:

> Imago dei—humankind in the image of God in being for God and the neighbour, in its original creatureliness and limitedness; sicut deus—humankind similar to God in knowing-out-of-its-own-self about good and evil, in having no limit and acting-out-of-its-own-resources, in its aseity, in its being alone. Imago dei—bound to the word of the Creator and deriving life from the Creator; sicut deus—bound to the depths of its own knowledge of God, of good and evil. Imago dei—the creature living in the unity of obedience; sicut deus—the creator-human-being who lives on the basis of the divide [Zwiespalt] between good and evil. Imago dei, sicut deus, agnus dei—the human being who is God incarnate, who was

---

71. Wirzba says that such deathly life is both dishonest and damaging: "It is dishonest because it denies that we daily depend on others and upon God for life. It is damaging because it transforms a world of grace into an arena of competitive grasping and self-glorifying manipulation," Wirzba, "The Art of Creaturely Life," 14.

72. By appealing to God's own word, but distorting it, the serpent attacks not with flagrant malice but under the garb of religious piety and profundity: "In this way the serpent purports somehow to know about the depths of the true God beyond this given word of God. . . . The serpent knows of a more exalted God, a nobler God, who has no need to make such a prohibition" (Bonhoeffer, *Creation and Fall*, 106). Bonhoeffer sees a lesson in this for Christians in his own time: "Were the question to come to us with its godlessness unveiled and laid bare, we would be able to resist it. But Christians are not open to attack in that way; one must actually approach them with God, one must show them a better, a prouder, God than they seem to have, if they are to fall," 107.

73. Bonhoeffer, *Creation and Fall*, 117.

sacrificed for humankind sicut deus, in true divinity slaying its false divinity and restoring the imago dei.[74]

The human being that has made itself to be the ultimate centre of its own existence has become alienated from God and other humans; such a person is profoundly alone. Both God and other persons become threats to one's centrality, one's personal sovereignty, one's will to power as Nietzsche puts it (because once God is 'dead' the sheer will to power takes over and human beings can live 'beyond good and evil' in a sense vastly different from Bonhoeffer's notion of pre-fallen innocence of good and evil).[75] Now the human being regards the natural limit or boundary that God had set as being arbitrary, patronizing, or even malevolent. "Now he no longer accepts the limit as God the Creator's grace; instead he hates it as God begrudging him something as Creator."[76] Adam can no longer trust God; he has become disoriented, distorted, and divided—relationally, volitionally, epistemologically,[77] psychologically, and bodily. As a corollary of this, Adam can no longer trust Eve, the 'other' that God has given him, since "in the same act of transgressing the boundary he has transgressed the limit that the other person represented to him in bodily form. Now he no longer sees the limit that the other person constitutes as grace but as God's wrath, God's hatred, God's begrudging."[78] Now, instead

74. Bonhoeffer, *Creation and Fall*, 113.
75. See footnote 62 above.
76. Bonhoeffer, *Creation and Fall*, 122.

77. Bonhoeffer writes about the epistemological consequences of this state (the mind turned in upon itself) in *Act and Being*, 45, 137, in *Ethics* (e.g., 299–304), and in his Christology lectures (on the latter, see Franklin, "Bonhoeffer's Anti-Logos"). An important passage connecting this theme in *Creation and Fall* back to Bonhoeffer's earlier *Act and Being* reads as follows: "For 'in Adam' means to be in untruth, in culpable perversion of the will, that is, of human essence. It means to be turned inward into one's self, *cor curvum in se*. Human beings have torn themselves loose from community with God and, therefore, also from that with other human beings, and now they stand alone, that is, in untruth. Because human beings are alone, the world is 'their' world, and other human beings have sunk into the world of things (cf. Heidegger's '*Mitsein*', 'being-with'). God has become a religious object, and human beings themselves have become their own creator and lord, belonging to themselves," *Act and Being*, 137.

78. Bonhoeffer, *Creation and Fall*, 122.

of existing in freedom-for-God-and-each-other, human beings exist radically for-self, as "one person sees the other in terms of their being over against each other; each sees the other as divided from himself or herself."[79] 'Freedom' has now become freedom *for*-self and freedom-*from*-God-and-other-persons.

Elsewhere, Bonhoeffer describes this state by appealing to Luther's notion of the *cor curvum in se* (the heart turned or curved in upon itself). Rejecting their God-ordained creaturely limit, which inherently oriented them toward finding their Centre and completion outside of themselves, human beings have become radically self-centred, or "wrongly centred" as Miroslav Volf puts it.[80] Ironically, in finding themselves in this way, they lose themselves. They become 'lost,' alienated from God, from others, and from themselves. They exist in a state of living death,[81] contradiction,[82] despair (Kierkegaard), and restlessness (Augustine), unable truly to know God and themselves (Calvin), unable genuinely to love God and others as they should (Wesley[83]). They are compelled to live, defining and striving after their own self-appointed *telos*,[84] but unable truly to live and flourish as God intended since gaining this life lies beyond their own power and even comprehension (e.g., Matt 15:24–26; John 12:24–26). Human beings are now 'cursed' to live in the

79. Bonhoeffer, *Creation and Fall*, 122.

80. Volf, *Exclusion and Embrace*, 69. See also Pannenberg's discussion of sin as 'centrality' in *Anthropology*, 80–153.

81. Bonhoeffer's description is profound: "For what causes despair in Adam's situation is just this, that Adam lives out of Adam's own resources, is imprisoned within Adam, and thus can want only Adam, can hanker only after Adam; for Adam has indeed become Adam's own god, the creator of Adam's own life. When Adam seeks God, when Adam seeks life, Adam seeks only Adam. On the other hand it is just this solitude, this resting in oneself, this existing in and of oneself, that plunges Adam into an infinite thirst. It is therefore a desperate, an unquenchable, and eternal thirst that Adam feels for life. It is essentially a thirst for death; the more passionately Adam seeks after life, the more completely he is ensnared in death," *Creation and Fall*, 143.

82. Bonhoeffer, *Creation and Fall*, 92.

83. See Shepherd, "'. . . That We May Perfectly Love Thee.' John Wesley and Sanctification."

84. "And those who have attained the knowledge of good and evil, who live as people who are split apart within themselves [im Zwiespalt], have lost their life," Bonhoeffer, *Creation and Fall*, 89.

world they have chosen: "The curse is the Creator's affirmation of the world that has been destroyed. That humankind must live in the fallen world, that humankind gets what it wants, that as the being who is *sicut deus* it must live in its *sicut deus* world—that is the *curse*."[85] Having rejected their true Centre and Source of genuine community, human beings struggle to live together and to love one another; they strive to achieve their own ideals and visions of community.[86] They long for love, belonging, affirmation, acceptance, harmony, and a sense of social utility (i.e., a sense that they contribute something unique and needed to their communities). However, their deepest longings and aspirations are always beyond their grasp, beset by human ego, pride, distorted and obsessive desires, envy, defensiveness, greed, corruption, laziness, lack of empathy, idolatry, ethnocentricity, ideology, and the consequences of socio-economic, racial, and gender inequality (to name just a handful of issues). Just as the true Source and Centre of human community lies transcendently beyond human beings (in God, the Creator), so too the redemption, reconciliation, restoration, and realignment of human community must come from beyond the confines of human will, achievement, authority, and power.

RESTORATION OF COMMUNITY

Since *Creation and Fall* focuses on giving a theological exposition of Gen 1–3, it can only hint at and foreshadow what the restoration of human community requires and involves. First, the restored human community is centred in God, more precisely—*in Christ*. Christ is our *new* Centre, the one who restores and completes our genuine creatureliness and frees us from our own 'knowledge of good and evil.' It is in Christ that our lives are preserved and in whom we find our *telos* or end. It is

---

85. Bonhoeffer, *Creation and Fall*, 132, original emphasis.

86. For an analysis and critique of non-theological attempts to ground personhood and community, see Franklin, *Being Human, Being Church*, chapters 1–2, where I explicate and evaluate six types: a) a social contract between consenting individuals (Locke, Hobbes); b) a moral association of cause and duty (Kant); c) erotic communities of desire and self-assertion (Nietzsche); d) phileic communities of common interest and expression (Sartre; existentialism); e) community as an instrumental good for its members (sociobiology/evolutionary psychology); and f) community as concentric circles of care (Noddings).

through Christ that we learn about our true beginning and true nature, through whom also we are reoriented toward the new creation, and in whom we find ourselves addressed from the centre of our existence (as, indeed, Christ is the Centre of all human life and history).[87] It is in Christ that we learn what it means to be creatures made in God's image.[88] Even our bodies find their completion and transformation in and through Christ: "The body and blood of the Lord's Supper are the new realities of creation promised to fallen Adam. Because Adam is created as body, Adam is also redeemed as body [and God comes to Adam as body], in Jesus Christ and in the sacrament."[89] Christ stands at the centre of restored human community as Mediator and Priest. As Bonhoeffer writes in *Life Together*, "Christian community is not an ideal we have to realize, but rather a reality created by God in Christ in which we may participate."[90] For, "Only in Jesus Christ are we one; only through him are we bound together. He remains the one and only mediator throughout eternity."[91]

Second, the restoration and completion of genuine human community in Christ requires redemption from our own captivity to self, a reversal of the *cor curvum in se*. Through Christ and in the Spirit, God comes to set us free to be truly *for God*, truly *for others* and *for the world*.[92] It is in Christ and in the Spirit that we are enabled to love God, love neighbour, and even love ourselves (our true selves, not our

---

87. Bonhoeffer, *Creation and Fall*, 29, 34–35, 62, 65, 92–93, 140. For Bonhoeffer's explication of Christ as the Centre of human history, see his "Lectures on Christology," 324–27.

88. Bonhoeffer, *Creation and Fall*, 65, 113.

89. Bonhoeffer, *Creation and Fall*, 79.

90. Bonhoeffer, *Life Together*, 38. Bonhoeffer had written much earlier in his doctoral dissertation: "It is extremely dangerous to confuse community romanticism [Gemeindschaftsromantik] with the community of saints [Gemeinschaft der Heiligen]. For the latter must always be acknowledged as something that is already established by God. The community of saints is, of course, something we ourselves must will. But it can be willed by us only once God wills it through us" *Sanctorum Communio*, 278.

91. Bonhoeffer, *Life Together*, 33.

92. Volf writes that our new centre in Christ is a de-centred centre. He helpfully highlights the Spirit's role in achieving this: "The Spirit enters the citadel of the self, decenters the self by fashioning it in the image of the self-giving Christ, and frees its will . . . ," Volf, *Exclusion and Embrace*, 92.

imagined or ideal selves). For example, "God does not want me to mold others into the image that seems good to me, that is, into my own image. Instead, in their freedom from me God made other people in God's own image.... God creates every person in the image of God's Son, the Crucified...."[93] Thus, it is in and through Christ and by the Spirit that we can fulfill our calling and function as persons made in the divine image and patterned after Christ the prototype, the "man for others" who shows us that genuine Christian life entails "existence for others."[94] This being-for-others informs both the content and shape of Christian witness; it is central to what the church *is* in Christ and what the church is called to embody and proclaim in the world as it bears witness.[95] For Bonhoeffer, the church is only the church when it exists for-others, since Christ is Saviour in virtue of his being fully God and fully human, and thus his being fully *for*-God and *for*-human-beings.

Third, it is important to point out that the church as the "new humanity" bears witness to the eschatological, new creation community in a real yet proleptic way, as a sign and foretaste of the coming kingdom of God. Bonhoeffer writes, "the church of Jesus Christ is the place—that is, the space—in the world where the reign of Jesus Christ over the whole world is to be demonstrated and proclaimed."[96] Its witness points to something real, but as a sign sharing in the reality to which it points, not as the ultimate fulfillment of that reality itself (the church is a *penultimate* participation in this *ultimate* eschatological reality).[97] Thus, a fellow Christian is "a physical sign of the gracious presence of the triune God."[98] In this sense, the church itself and especially the Christian community is sacramental in nature, pointing beyond itself to the true source and destiny of the relational nature of human beings, namely the Father-Son-Spirit Life of the triune God. This highlights the inherently social nature of Christian soteriology: being saved includes (as part of its intrinsic *telos*) being in community,

---

93. Bonhoeffer, *Life Together*, 95.
94. Bonhoeffer, *Letters and Papers from Prison*, 381–82.
95. See Franklin, "Bonhoeffer's Missional Ecclesiology," 115–17.
96. Bonhoeffer, *Ethics*, 63.
97. For Bonhoeffer's discussion of ultimate and penultimate, see *Ethics*, 146–70.
98. Bonhoeffer, *Life Together*, 29.

which means being in the church. As Bonhoeffer writes, "Whoever seeks to become a new human being individually cannot succeed. To become a new human being means to come into the church, to become a member of Christ's body."[99]

CONCLUDING REMARKS

Bonhoeffer's theology of personhood and community focuses on being reconciled, restored, renewed, and re-oriented—in short, *centred*—in Christ. This is insightful and important, but also incomplete. More needs to be said to articulate a fully trinitarian and participatory ecclesiology that biblical faith and classical theology demand. I propose that such an ecclesiology would include a theological explication of God's sending forth of the Holy Spirit to indwell (be *in*) those whom Christ has redeemed, thereby placing them *in* Christ who *is* in the Father.[100] Moreover, it would draw this biblical pattern into a robust theology of participation, in dialogue with patristic and medieval sources.[101] Bonhoeffer hints in this direction when he writes: "The church of Christ is Christ present through the Holy Spirit. . . . The life of believers in the church-community is truly the life of Jesus Christ in them (Gal 2:20; Rom 8:10; 2 Cor 13:5; 1 John 4:15."[102] However, Bonhoeffer never had the opportunity to develop this insight theologically into a fuller trinitarian model.[103]

BIBLIOGRAPHY

Billings, Todd J. *The Word of God for the People of God: An Entryway to the Theological Interpretation of Scripture*. Grand Rapids: Eerdmans, 2010.

Bonhoeffer, Dietrich. *Act and Being: Transcendental Philosophy and Ontology in Systematic Theology*. Vol. 2 of *Dietrich Bonhoeffer Works*, edited

---

99. Bonhoeffer, *Discipleship*, 219.

100. Köstenberger and Swain, *Father, Son and Spirit*, 176; Gorman, *Becoming the Gospel*.

101. See, for example, Dennis Ngien's *Gifted Response*. See also my article, "The God Who Sends is The God Who Loves."

102. Bonhoeffer, *Discipleship*, 221.

103. I began to sketch out a trinitarian, participatory account of human personhood and community in my *Being Human, Being Church*, chapters 3 and 6.

by Wayne Whitson Floyd, Jr. Translated by H. Martin Rumscheidt. Minneapolis: Fortress, 1996.

———. *Creation and Fall: A Theological Exposition of Genesis 1–3*. Vol. 3 of *Dietrich Bonhoeffer Works*, edited by John W. de Gruchy. Translated by Douglas Stephen Bax. Minneapolis: Fortress, 1997.

———. *Ethics*. Vol. 6 of *Dietrich Bonhoeffer Works*, edited by Clifford J. Green. Translated by Reinhard Krauss, Charles C. West, and Douglas W. Stott. Minneapolis: Fortress, 2005.

———. "Lectures on Christology." In *Berlin: 1921–33*. Vol. 12 of *Dietrich Bonhoeffer Works*, edited by Larry L. Rasmussen, 299–360. Translated by Isabel Best and David Higgins. Minneapolis: Fortress, 2009.

———. *Letters and Papers from Prison*, edited by Eberhard Bethge. The Enlarged Edition. New York: Macmillan, 1972.

———. *Life Together*. Vol. 5 of *Dietrich Bonhoeffer Works*, edited by Geffrey B. Kelly. Translated by Daniel W. Bloesch and James H. Burtness. Minneapolis: Fortress, 1996.

———. *No Rusty Swords: Letters, Lectures and Notes 1928–1936*, edited by Edwin H. Robertson. Translated by John Bowden and Eberhard Bethge. London: Collins, 1965.

———. *Sanctorum Communio: A Theological Study of the Sociology of the Church*. Vol. 1 of *Dietrich Bonhoeffer Works*, edited by Clifford J. Green. Translated by Reinhard Krauss and Nancy Lukens. Minneapolis: Fortress, 1998.

Calvin, John. *Institutes of the Christian Religion*. Translated by Henry Beveridge. Grand Rapids: Eerdmans, 1989.

Enns, Peter. *Inspiration and Incarnation: Evangelicals and the Problem of the Old Testament*. Grand Rapids: Baker Academic, 2015.

Erickson, Millard J. *Christian Theology*. Grand Rapids: Baker Academic, 1998.

Fowl, Stephen E. *Engaging Scripture: A Model for Theological Interpretation*. Oxford: Blackwell, 1998.

———. *Theological Interpretation of Scripture*. Eugene: Cascade, 2009.

———. *Two Horizons New Testament Commentary: Philippians*. Grand Rapids: Eerdmans, 2005.

Fowl, Stephen E., and Gregory Jones. *Reading in Communion. Scripture and Ethics in Christian Life*. Grand Rapids: Eerdmans, 1991.

Franklin, Patrick S. *Being Human, Being Church: The Significance of Theological Anthropology for Ecclesiology*. Milton Keynes: Paternoster, 2016.

———. "Bonhoeffer's Anti-Logos and its Challenge to Oppression." *Crux* 41.2 (2005) 2–9.

———. "Bonhoeffer's Missional Ecclesiology." *McMaster Journal of Theology and Ministry* 9 (2007–2008) 96–128.

———. "Francis Watson and Stephen E. Fowl as Theological Interpreters of Scripture." In *Prevailing Methods After 1980*, vol. 2 of *Pillars of Biblical Interpretation*, edited by Stanley E. Porter and Sean A. Adams, 458–77. McMaster Biblical Studies Series 2. Eugene, OR: Pickwick, 2016.

Gabler, Johann P. "An Oration on the Proper Distinction between Biblical and Dogmatic Theology and the Specific Objectives of Each." In *Old Testament Theology: Flowering and Future*, edited by Ben C. Ollenburger, 501–6. Winona Lake: Eisenbrauns, 2004.

Godsey, John. *The Theology of Dietrich Bonhoeffer*. London: SCM, 1960.

Gorman, Michael J. *Becoming the Gospel: Paul, Participation, and Mission*. Grand Rapids: Eerdmans, 2015.

Green, Clifford. "Human Sociality and Christian Community." In *The Cambridge Companion to Dietrich Bonhoeffer*, edited by John W. de Gruchy, 113–33. Cambridge: Cambridge University Press, 1999.

Gruchy, De, John W. "Editor's Introduction to the English Edition." In *Creation and Fall: A Theological Exposition of Genesis 1–3*, by Dietrich Bonhoeffer, 1–17, edited by John W. de Gruchy. Translated by Douglas Stephen Bax. Minneapolis: Fortress, 1997.

Hasel, Gerhard. "The Relationship between Biblical Theology and Systematic Theology." *Trinity Journal* 5.2 (1984) 113–27.

Kelsey, David H. *Eccentric Existence: A Theological Anthropology*. 2 vols. Louisville: Westminster John Knox, 2009.

Kierkegaard, Søren. *The Sickness Unto Death: A Christian Psychological Exposition for Edification and Awakening*. Translated by Alastair Hannay. London: Penguin, 1989.

Köstenberger, Andreas J., and Scott R. Swain. *Father, Son and Spirit: The Trinity and John's Gospel*. Downers Grove, IL: InterVarsity Press, 2008.

Marsh, Charles. *Strange Glory: A Life of Dietrich Bonhoeffer*. New York: Knopf, 2014.

Ngien, Dennis. *Gifted Response: The Triune God as the Causative Agent of our Responsive Worship*. Milton Keynes: Paternoster, 2008.

Pannenberg, Wolfhart. *Anthropology in Theological Perspective*. Translated by Matthew J. O'Connell. Edinburgh: T. & T. Clark, 1999.

Reno, R. R. "Series Preface." In *Brazos Theological Commentary on the Bible: Matthew*, by Stanley Hauerwas, 9–14. Grand Rapids: Brazos, 2006.

Ringma, Charles Richard. *Gadamer's Dialogical Hermeneutic: The Hermeneutics of Bultmann, of the New Testament Sociologists, and of the Social Theologians in Dialogue with Gadamer's Hermeneutic*. Heidelberg: Universitätsverlag C. Winter, 1999.

Schlingensiepen, Ferdinand. *Dietrich Bonhoeffer: 1906–1945: Martyr, Thinker, Man of Resistance*. Translated by Isabel Best. London: T. & T. Clark, 2010.

Shepherd, Victor. "'. . . That We May Perfectly Love Thee.' John Wesley and Sanctification." *Touchstone* (May 1988). Accessed online (Feb. 6, 2018). http://victorshepherd.ca/that-we-may-perfectly-love-thee-john-wesley-and-sanctification/

Root, Andrew. *Bonhoeffer as Youth Worker*. Grand Rapids: Baker, 2014.

Treier, Daniel J. *Introducing Theological Interpretation of Scripture: Recovering a Christian Practice*. Grand Rapids: Baker Academic, 2008.

Vanhoozer, Kevin J., Craig Bartholomew, and Daniel J. Treier. *Theological Interpretation of the Old Testament: A Book-by-Book Survey*. Grand Rapids: Baker Academic, 2008.

Vanhoozer, Kevin J., Daniel J. Treier, and N. T. Wright. *Theological Interpretation of the New Testament: A Book-by-Book Survey*. Grand Rapids: Baker Academic, 2008.

Volf, Miroslav. *Exclusion and Embrace: A Theological Exploration of Identity, Otherness, and Reconciliation*. Nashville: Abingdon, 1996.

Walton, John H. "Reading Genesis 1 as Ancient Cosmology." In *Reading Genesis 1–2: An Evangelical Conversation*, edited by J. Daryl Charles, 141–69. Peabody, MA: Hendrickson, 2013.

———. *NIV Application Commentary: Genesis*. Grand Rapids: Zondervan, 2001.

Watson, Francis. *Paul and the Hermeneutics of Faith*. London: T. & T. Clark, 2004.

———. *Text, Church and World: Biblical Interpretation in Theological Perspective* Grand Rapids: Eerdmans, 1994.

———. *Text and Truth: Redefining Biblical Theology*. Grand Rapids: Eerdmans, 1997.

Webster, John. *Holy Scripture: A Dogmatic Sketch*. Cambridge: Cambridge University Press, 2003.

———. *The Domain of the Word: Scripture and Theological Reason*. Bloomsbury T. & T. Clark, 2014.

Wenham, Gordon J. *Word Biblical Commentary: Genesis 1–15*. Waco: Word, 1987.

Wirzba, Norman. "The Art of Creaturely Life: A Question of Human Propriety." *Pro Ecclesia* XXII.1 (Winter 2013) 7–28.

Zimmermann, Jens. *Recovering Theological Hermeneutics: An Incarnational—Trinitarian Theory of Interpretation*. Eugene: Wipf and Stock, 2004.

Ancient Documents Index

OLD TESTAMENT

Genesis

1–11	64–65, 241n58
1–3	228–29, 232, 232n21, 234, 248
1	xvii, 217, 232n18, 234
1:2	98, 213
1:3	213
1:6	213
1:9	213
1:11	213
1:14	213
1:20	213
1:24	213
1:26	65, 213
1:28	65, 66, 213
1:29	213
2–3	240, 242, 242n63
2	236, 241
3	66, 243
3:17–19	66
3:20	244n66
3:22	242
3:23–24	66
4:11–12	66
5	65n15, 66
10:1–11:9	65n15
11	66
11:1–9	66
11:10–32	65n15
12–50	64
12–25	64
12:1–3	66
12:3	244n66
13:14–17	65
13:15–17	66
13:16	66
15:5	66
15:7–21	66
15:18–21	65, 66
31:24	237n39
36	84n37
41:45	68
49	64
50:19–20	243n66

Exodus

2:21	68
4:18	76
5:22	27
6:24	85
12:38	68, 72
20	214
25:30	153
25:34	151
25:38	154n29
26:7	166
26:12	166
32	51
34:10–26	214n2
34:28	204, 214n2
37:20	151
38:16	150, 151n19, 152
38:17	154

Leviticus

19:18	99
24:10–11	76

255

Leviticus (continued)

24:10 — 76

Numbers

4:25 — 166
11 — 33
11:17 — 37
11:24–25 — 214
11:25–26 — 33
11:25 — 37
11:29 — 37, 209
13 — 3
13:6 — 4
20 — 204
32:12 — 4
34:19 — 4

Deuteronomy

6:5 — 99
6:22 — 27
18:15–22 — 214
21:15–17 — 33n15
21:17 — 33
32 — 214
32:46–47 — 214
32:47 — 215

Joshua

1:7–8 — 215
1:8 — 216
6:26 — 215
7 — 3
8:14 — 39
8:19 — 39
8:21 — 40
14:6 — 4
14:14 — 4
15:17 — 5

Judges

1 — 8
1:1 — 3, 8
1:2 — 8
1:4–9 — 3
1:11 — 3
1:12 — 3
1:13 — 4
1:19 — 68
1:20 — 4
1:21 — 68
1:27–36 — 68
2:1–3 — 68, 72
2:10–19 — 6
2:11 — 19
2:18 — 6
3:5–6 — 5
3:7 — 19
3:9 — 4, 5
3:10 — 6, 25
3:12–14 — 17
3:12 — 19
3:15 — 18
3:18–26 — 10
3:27 — 10
3:28 — 10
4:1 — 19
4:5 — 10
4:6–9 — 10, 11
5 — 10
5:9 — 11
5:13–18 — 11
6:1 — 19
6:34 — 25
7:24 — 12
7:24–25 — 12
8:1 — 12
8:2–3 — 13
8:4 — 13
8:5–8 — 14
8:5 — 13
8:15–17 — 14
8:18–19 — 13
8:27–28 — 14
9 — 27–28
9:23 — 27
9:25 — 27
10:6 — 19
10:9 — 6n8
11:1 — 14
11:3 — 15
11:29 — 25, 26
11:30–31 — 25–26

Ancient Documents Index

11:32	25, 26	21:24	21
12:1	16	21:25	19, 21
12:3	16		
12:5	85n41	## Ruth	
12:6	16		
13:1	19	1:2	85
13:5	6	4	68
13:25	25, 26		
14:3	26	## 1 Samuel/1 Kingdoms	
14:4	7, 26		
14:6	25	1:1	85
14:9	26	2:18	85
14:19	25, 26	3:1–18	215
15:4–5	6	3:1	85
15:9	6	9:1	76
15:11	7	10:6	28–32
15:14	25	10:8	29
15:20	6	10:10	28–32
16	26	11	80
16:31	6	11:2	81
17–18	16n7	11:6	29, 32, 33
17:6	19	11:7–8	29
19–21	2, 16n7	11:9–11	29
19	8, 19	13	29
19:12	19	13:7–8	29
19:22	19	14:50	83
19:25–28	20	15:22–23	215
20	8, 9	16	86
20:2	7	16:10	84
20:11	8	16:13	28, 29, 32
20:12–15	20	16:14–23	29
20:12	10	16:14	28, 30, 32
20:16	17n18	16:15	30
20:18	8, 10	16:16	30–32
20:21	8	16:23	30–32, 38
20:22	10	17	29
20:23	8	17:12–14	84
20:28	9	17:12	76, 85
20:47	20	18:10–11	31
21:1–3	9	18:10	30–32
21:3	20	19	38
21:5	10	19:9	30, 32
21:8–14	20	19:20–24	30, 30n10
21:10	10	19:20	32
21:13	10	19:23	32
21:8–14	9	21:10–15	40
21:17–23	20	25	78n13
21:18–23	9	25:3	78n13

257

1 Samuel/1 Kingdoms (continued)

25:42	78n13
26:6	78n13

2 Samuel/2 Kingdoms

1:13	76
2:4	84
2:18	75
2:22	84
2:23	84
2:32	88n59
3	88
3:22–34	18n21
3:39	75, 88
8:13	87
10	81
10:2	81
11	88
13:3	83
13:32	83
16:10	75
17	89
17:25	74–75, 77, 78n13, 79–80, 83–84, 89
17:27	80, 80n25, 81
18	88
18:12	34
19:12–15	78
19:13	78, 87
19:22	75
20	88
20:8–10	18n21
21:17	83
21:21	83
23:1–7	215
23:2	29n10
23:8–39	87, 90
23:18	83n36, 87
23:24	84, 87
23:37	87n57
24:16	32

1 Kings/3 Kingdoms

2:5	76
7:35	150–51, 154
11:12	49
11:31	49
11:34–45	49
12	51
12:25–13:34	44n5
12:25–33	54
12:26–27	50n18
12:37–38	49
12:30	51
12:31	51
12:33	51
12:34	51
13	44, 44n5, 46, 48n14, 54–55
13:1	44, 47
13:2	44, 47
13:3	49
13:4	49, 50
13:5	44, 47, 49
13:6	50
13:9	47, 47–48n12, 50
13:10	50
13:12	50
13:16	50
13:17	47, 47–48n12, 50
13:18	45, 47, 50
13:19	50
13:20	47, 50
13:21–22	47, 47–48n12
13:22	45, 50
13:23	50
13:24	50
13:25	50
13:26	47, 50
13:28	50
13:29	50
13:30	45, 45n6
13:31	45n7
13:32	47
13:33	50
16:24	215
18:12	33
19:9–18	215
21:1	77
21:20–21	27
22	34, 36, 36n19, 54
22:10–12	29n10
22:6	34

Ancient Documents Index

22:7	34	1:4	62, 64
22:8	29n10	1:9–16	60
22:13	35	1:34	67
22:14	35	1:43–54	62
22:15	35	2–4	70
22:16	27	2	75
22:17	35	2:1–4	60
22:18	29n10, 35	2:1	63, 67
22:19–22	35	2:3	68, 72
22:20	35	2:7	67
22:21	35, 36n19	2:13–15	82n32
22:22	36, 36n19	2:15	84
22:23	35–37	2:16–17	79
22:24	35n18, 36	2:16	75
		2:17	62, 77
		2:35	68

2 Kings/4 Kingdoms

		3:10–16	70
2	33	3:10–15	60
2:9	33–34	3:15–24	60
2:14	34	3:24	85
2:15	33–34	4:4	85n41
2:16	34, 34n17	4:9–10	63
2:19–22	34	4:10	67
2:23–24	34	4:17	68
4:43–44	215	4:21	62
15:29	58	4:23	62
17	68	4:28	62
17:6	58, 113	5	68
17:7–23	68, 72	5:1	67
17:23	58	5:2	70
18–20	109, 110	5:3–10	62
18:11	113	5:3	67
19:7	37	5:11	62
20:12–19	109	5:17	67
21:11–12	27	5:19	62
22–23	215	5:25–26	63
23:15–16	49	5:26	62, 67
23:16–18	44n4	6	63, 70, 71
23:34	58	6:1–30	62
24:10–25:21	68, 72	6:11	86n46
24:14–16	58	6:12	86n46
25:11	58	6:19	86n46
		6:25–28	85
		6:31–46	62

1 Chronicles

		6:38	67
1–9	57–59, 61, 66–67	6:48–49	71
1:1	60, 63	6:49	67
1:4–27	62	6:54–81	62

259

Ancient Documents Index

1 Chronicles (continued)

6:64	67
7	68
7:9	62
7:12	68n20
7:29	67
9:1	67
9:2	67
11:1	69
11:4	69
11:6	88
11:8	88
11:10	69
11:20	87
12:24–37	69
11:26	87
12:38	69
13:5	69
13:8	69
15:3	69
18:12	87
19:11	87
19:13	88
19:15	87
19:17	69
21	38
21:6	88
21:15	88
22:17	69
23:2	69
25:1–8	86
27:1	87
27:7	87
28:1	69
28:4	86, 90
29:6	69
29:23	69

2 Chronicles

1:2	69
5:3	69
5:6	69
6:6	69
7:3	69
7:8	69
7:14	69
10	71
10:1	69
11:13–17	69
12:1	67n19
12:6	67n19
13	71
13:4–12	69
13:22	44
15:9	69
18	34
18:22	37
19:8	67n19
20:14	86
20:22	40
20:37	29n10
21:2	67n19
21:4	67n19
23:2	67n19
24:5	67n19
24:16	67n19
28:19	67n19
28:23	67n19
28:27	67n19
29:25	86
30:1	89
30:8–9	89
30:11	69
30:18	69
34:30	86
35:15	86
36:22–23	67

Ezra

1–2	58
1:1–3	59
2:59–60	61
2:61–63	61
2:64–65	61
3:2	217
3:4	217
4:1–5	59
7–8	58
7:6	217
7:10	64n14, 217
9–10	64n14
9:1–2	59
10	59

Ancient Documents Index

Nehemiah

1–2	59
5	64n14
8–9	217
8:13–18	64n14
9:5–37	217
9:20	37–38
13:4–9	64n14
13:15–22	64n14
13:23–29	59
13:23–28	64n14

Esther

2:5–7	58

Job

1–2	38, 39n23
1:1	96
4:7–8	98
6:24	99
7:20	99
15:7–9	242n63
15:40	242n63
19:6–12	97
20:8	160
42:7–8	100

Psalms

1:2	216
18:30	217
19	216
29	217, 217n6
33:4	217
33:6	217
33:9	217
37	185
37:11	173, 186
37:14	186
37:21–22	173
51:11	38
67:4	105n6
103:17	121
105:8–19	217
105:31	217
105:34	217
119	216
143:10	38

Proverbs

1:7	98, 242n63
15:1	7
29:6	27
30:1–4	242n63

Ecclesiastes/Qohelet

4:9–12	2
12:7	37

Isaiah

1–35	111
1:1	112
1:9	114
1:22	112
1:23	112
2	215
2:1	112
2:3–4	215
6:6–7	215
6:9–10	215
10:2	173, 174n13
11:11	113n24
13–27	120
13–23	105
13	105, 106, 112, 113n24, 119–20
13:1	111, 116, 118n39
13:2–22	115
13:2–16	116–18
13:2–8	118n39
13:2–3	117–18
13:2–5	116
13:3	117
13:4–5	116–17, 120
13:5	116
13:6–8	118
13:7–16	116
13:8	118
13:9–13	118, 120
13:9	116, 118–19
13:10	119
13:11	116, 119

261

Isaiah (continued)

13:12	118–19
13:13	118–19
13:14–16	118, 118n39
13:14	118
13:15–16	113n23
13:16	113n23
13:17–22	115, 117–18, 118n39
13:17–19	114
13:17–18	112, 113n23
13:17	114n26, 115–18
13:19	104, 112, 116
14	104n5, 105, 106, 112, 119
14:1–4	112
14:4–21	112
14:30	173
21	105, 106
21:2	113, 113n24
21:9	113n24
22:6	113n24
23:13	104
24–27	119–20
24	119
24:4	119
24:5–6	119
24:6	119
24:12	119
24:18	119
24:21–23	119
24:21	119
25:3–5	119
26:9	119
26:10	119
26:18	119
27:6	119
29:19	173
34:16–35:10	215
36–39	111
39	105, 109–11
40–66	111
40–55	118, 120
40–48	105, 106, 108, 109, 111, 120
40	215
40:6–8	220–21
40:8	215
40:9–10	215
41	108, 215
41:2–3	106
41:25	106, 108
42:1	37
42:5	37
42:9	215
43	108
43:14–15	105
43:14	104, 105, 107, 108
43:15	105
44:28	108
45	106
45:1–2	107, 115
45:1	107, 108
45:4	108
46	106n8
46:11	108
47	104n5, 106n8, 107
47:1	104, 106, 115
47:2–3	107
47:5	104, 107
48	106n8
48:14	104, 107, 108
48:15	108
48:20	104, 108
49–55	109n16
49:2	215, 221
49:14	173
50:4	216
52:7	216
52:11–12	109
52:13	109
55:1–2	216
55:10–11	216
61:1	172
63:10	38
63:11	38
66:2	172

Jeremiah

1:2	216
1:4	216
1:5	98
1:9–12	216
3:17	27
7:26	27
18:8–12	27
23:5	148
25:25	113

26:20	29n10	## Micah	
29:27	29n10		
42–44	58	4:1–4	216
50–51	106		
51:11	113	## Habakkuk	
51:28	113		
52	68	2:2	216
		2:18	216

Ezekiel

Zephaniah

2–3	216	1:12	31
5:16	27		
11:19	37	## Zechariah	
23:18	216		
23:22	216	1:8	145–46
23:29	216	3	38, 39n23
28:6	242n63	3:8	148
28:15–17	242n63	4	150
36:26	37	4:2–3	150–51
37:6	37	4:2	148, 152, 154
37:14	37	4:3	148–49
37:10	29n10	4:12	154–55, 155n30, 157
		6:3	145–46
## Daniel		6:7	145–46
		6:12	148
11:1	114n27	6:15	148
		7:7	216
## Hosea		7:11	162n47
		7:12	216
2:2	78	9:1	158
4:2	216	10:1	159
4:6	216	11:7	173, 174n13, 183
		11:10	164
## Joel		11:11	164, 173
		11:12	162, 164
1–2	117	11:14	164
3–4	117	11:16	164
		12:1	158
## Amos		13:4	165–66
		13:8	33n15
3:6	27		
8:11–12	216	## Malachi	
## Obadiah		1:1–6	64n14
		1:6–12	64n14
1:10–14	59	2:10–16	64n14
1:15	117	2:17–3:5	64n14
		3:5	64n14

Malachi (continued)

3:7–12	64n14
4:4	216

NEW TESTAMENT

Matthew

1–2	217
4	217
5:3–5	172
5:8	238
5:17–20	217
5:38–40	7
7:24–27	217, 235
8:26	218
9:1–8	218
13:18–23	218
15:24–26	247
21:19	218
22:37–40	99n10
25:31–46	4
26:15	164
26:56	217

Mark

2:2	218
4:14	218
4:33	218
13:11	218

Luke

1:2	218
1:37	218
1:79	202, 202n17
2:14	202, 202n17
2:29	202, 202n17
3:22	202
4:1–13	217
4:1	202
4:14	202
4:18–19	204
4:18	202, 204
4:32	218
4:36	218
5:1	218
6:27	205
7:7	218
7:50	202, 202n17
8:21	218
8:48	202, 202n17
9:24	206
9:51–10:24	202
10:5	202n17
10:6	202n17
10:25–37	4
10:39	218
11:21	202n17
11:28	218
12:1–12	207
12:51	202n17
14:32	202n17
18:35–19:44	202, 202n17
19:38	202
19:42	202n17
21:12–15	207
21:12	206
24:36	202n17
24:48	204

John

1:1–2	233
3:5–8	5
3:16	204
3:34	219
4:41	219
6:63	219
7:16–18	219
10:35	219
12:24–26	247
12:47–50	219
17:11	17
17:17	219

Acts

1:1	219
1:8	204
2	227
2:1–13	219
2:39	202
2:43	219
4	227

Ancient Documents Index

4:29	219	10:3–12	220
5:29	19	13:5	251
6:2	219		
6:4	219		
6:7	219	Galatians	
7:26	202n17	2:10	172
8:26	219	2:20	251
9:31	202n17		
10:36	202, 202n17	Ephesians	
11:1	219		
12:20	202n17	1:5	5
12:24	219	3:1–13	220
13:5	219	4:1–3	17
13:7	219	5:30–32	241
15:7	219	6:10–17	220
15:33	202n17		
16:6	219	Philippians	
16:32	219		
16:36	202n17	2:3	13, 14
17:11	219		
17:13	219	Colossians	
18:11	219		
19:10	219	1:6	220
19:20	219	1:27	220
20:32	219	2:2	220
24:2	202n17	3:16	222

Romans

1 Thessalonians

1:16	219	1:5	220
3:24	234n30	1:13	220
8:10	251		
12:17–18	19	1 Timothy	
13:1–2	19		
16:25–26	220	4:11–16	220

1 Corinthians

2 Timothy

1:18	219	2:9	220
2:6–16	220	3:16–17	220
4:17	220	4:2	220
15:1–2	219	6:17	220

2 Corinthians

Hebrews

2:17	220	1:2	220
4:7	220	3:7	220
5:19	220	3:15	220

Hebrews (continued)

4:7	220
4:12–13	220

James

1:18	220
1:13–15	242
1:21	220
1:22–25	220, 235

1 Peter

1:23–25	220–21
1:23	5

2 Peter

1:4	221
1:20–21	221
3:2	221
3:13	221
3:15–16	221

1 John

4:15	251
4:19	4

Revelation

1:2	221
1:16	221
11:4	155n30
17:17	221
19:11–16	221
19:15	221

DEAD SEA SCROLLS

1QHa

6:14–16	178
6:31	182
11:20–37	180
13:22–15:8	181
13:20–15:5	181n46
13:22–24	181, 183
13:27	182
23:13–16	172

1QM

11:9	173
11:13	173
13:14	173
14:7	173, 178

1QpHab

11:4–8	174n16
12:2–10	183

1QS

1:11–13	173
1:11–12	172
3:8	178
4:3	178
5:1–4	172

4Q161

8–10 3	173

4Q163

21 7	173
8–10 13	173
18–19 2	173

4Q171

1–10 ii 2 9–12	186
1–10 ii 9–25	174n16
1–10 ii 10	183
1–10 ii 18–20	174n16
1–10 iii 10	183, 186
1–10 iii 15–16	174n16

4Q176

1–2 ii 2	173

4Q416

2 ii 20–21	177
2 iii 2	176n24
2 iii 8	176n24
2 iii 12	176n24

4Q491

11 i 11	173

4QpPsa

1–10 ii 9–12	173
1–10 iii 8–11	173

CD

4:15–18	182
6:14–16	182
6:16	173, 174n13
13:11–12	174
14:12–17	182
19:9	173, 174n13, 182

ANCIENT JEWISH WRITERS

Josephus

Antiquities

8.9.1	44n4
12.11–118	128n3

Against Apion

2.45–47	128n3

Wars

2:122	172n7

Philo

Hypothetica

10:11–13	172n7

Prob.

84–88	172n7

Moses

2:26–44	128n3

RABBINIC WRITINGS

m. 'Abot

5.1	213

GRECO-ROMAN WRITINGS

Aristophenes

Clouds	146
Ecclesiazusae 5	155

Herodotus

Histories 2.86	155
Letter of Aristeas	128n3

EARLY CHRISTIAN WRITINGS

Basil the Great

Letter 210.6	161n41

Cyril of Alexandria

Commentary on Zechariah	161n42

Oecumenius

Commentarius in Apocalypsin 129.7	155n30

Authors Index

Abernathy, A. T., 103
Abernathy, D., 145
Ackroyd, P. R., 110
Adriaen, M., 146, 159, 163
Aejmelaeus, A., 74, 134
Aemelaeus, A., 134
Aitken, J. K., 134, 138
Alter, R., 75, 101
Angel, H., 52
Aufrecht, W. E., 61
Averbeck, R. E., 34

Bartlett, J. R., 84
Barton, J., 117
Bartusch, M. W., 7, 18
Begg, C. T., 104–5
Bendavid, A., 109
Berges, U., 106, 109, 111, 115, 117, 119
Berquist, J. L., 61
Billings, T. J., 229
Blass, F., 132
Blenkinsopp, J., 109
Block, D. I., 14–15, 22, 24, 27, 29, 31, 35–38, 40–41
Boda, M. J., xx, 3–4, 8, 12–13, 15, 17–18, 24–25, 27, 29, 31, 33, 35, 37, 39, 41, 53, 55, 86, 90, 126, 156
Boer, R., 46
Bonhoeffer, D., xx, 54, 206, 226–51
Bosshard-Nepustil, E., 117
Boyd-Taylor, C., 135
Braun, R., 59, 84–86, 88
Brouwer, C., 165
Bruce, F. F., 196

Calvin, J., 231, 247

Cassuto, U., 213, 242
Chalcraft, D. J., 7, 18
Chapman, S. B., 223
Chisholm, R. B., 34, 36
Cimos, M., 148
Clements, R. E., 111
Clines, D. J. A., 21, 190
Cohn, R. L., 50
Collings, J. J., 119
Collins, M. A., 187–88
Conway, M. L., xx, 1, 3–5, 7–9, 11, 13, 15, 17–19, 21, 25, 41
Cunha, W. de A., 119

Dandamayev, M., 115
Davies, G. I., 110
Dimant, D., 175
Deboys, D. G., 48
Deissmann, A., 132–34
Deist, F., 18
Dempster, M., 204
Dempster, S. G., 66
DeVries, S. J., 49, 53–54
Diakonoff, I. M., 113
Dimant, D., 175
Dorival, G., 128, 134
Douglas, M. C., 174
Doutreleau, L., 148–49, 154, 157–58, 162–64
Dozeman, T. B., 44
Du Cange, 147
Duhaime, J., 175
Duhm, B., 115
Dyck, J. E., 61

Eidevall, G., 116

Authors Index

Eissfeldt, O., 117
Elliger, K., 105
Enns, P., 233
Erickson, M. J., 237
Erlandsson, S., 114
Eslinger, L., 72
Evans, M., 80, 82
Evans, P. S., xx
Evans, T. V., 135
Ewald, H., 105
Exum, J. C., 25

Fabry, H. J., 171, 174, 178
Fee, G., 196-98
Finkelstein, J. J., 61
Flusser, D., 172, 174
Fowl, S. E., 229-31
Frame, G., 104
Franke, C., 104, 106
Franklin, P. S., 246, 248, 250
Frei, H., 223
Fretheim, T. E., 44
Fretz, M. J., 5

Gabler, J. P., 232
Gaebelein, F. E., 50
Geobey, R. A., 51
Godsey, J., 228
Goff, M. J., 175-77
Goldingay, J., 105-7
Gooding, D. W., 150-51, 153
Goodwin, W. W., 156
Gordon, R. P., 74, 85
Gorman, M. J., 251
Gosse, B., 118
Gray, G. B., 115
Green, C., 239-40
Gregory, B., 171
Gross, W., 44
Groves, J. W., 110
Gruchy, De, J. W., 229, 232, 236
Gulick, C. B., 156
Gundry, R., 218-19

Halpern, B., 17, 75, 77-78, 91
Halvorson-Taylor, M., 109
Hamori, E. J., 28, 32, 35, 40
Hanhart, R., 131, 157
Harl, M., 128, 134, 137

Hartman, T. C., 61
Hasel, G., 232
Hatch, E., 132
Hayes, J. H., 5, 114
Heater, H., 114
Hempel, C., 175
Hengel, M., 129, 137
Hermisson, H.-J., 107
Hertzberg, H. W., 75, 77, 79-80, 82-83
Heskett, R., 119
Hildebrandt, W., 40
Hill, A., 71
Hitzig, F., 105
Höffken, P., 118
Høgenhaven, J., 116
Holm-Nielsen, S., 174
Hom, M. K. Y. H., 114
Horrocks, G., 133
Horsley, G. H. R., 134
Horst, F., 153
Howard, D. M., 31
Howard, W. F., 133

Irvine, S. A., 114

Japhet, S., 5984-87
Jassen, A. P., 183-84
Jeppesen, K., 116
Jeremias, J., 117
Jobes, K. H., 96, 129-31, 135, 137-38
Johnson, D., xx
Johnson, L. T., 195, 199-200
Johnson, M. D., 60-61
Jokiranta, J., 171, 184-86
Jones, G., 231
Jonker, L. C., 61, 89

Kalluveettil, P., 81
Kaminski, C. M., 66
Kartveit, M., 106
Keck, L. E., 172-74
Kelsey, D. H., 237
Kierkegaard, S., 238, 247
Kim Harkins, A., 175
Kirkpatrick, S., 12
Kissane, E. J., 114
Klein, R. W., 84-87
Knoppers, G. N., 85

Authors Index

Konkel, A. H., xvii-xviii, 1, 41, 43, 46, 52–53, 57–58, 68, 74, 89–90, 93, 100–101, 103, 126–27, 144, 170, 209, 212, 228, 237, 241, 243
Köstenberger, A. J., 251
Koster, W. J. W., 147
Kratz, R. G., 107
Krause, A. F., 114
Kraybill, D., 208
Kuhrt, A., 113, 115
Kuntz, J. K., 5

Lambert, F., 7, 18
Lanier, G. R., 148
Leithart, P. J., 49, 51, 53, 54
Lee, J. A. L., 134
Levenson, J. D., 75, 77–78
Loader, J. A., 115
Lohfink, N., 177–78, 180
Lowe, W. H., 157

Malamat, A., 61
Markl, D., 171
Marti, K., 115, 117
Martin-Achard, R., 106
Marsh, C., 229
Marshall, I. H., 197
Matthews, V. H., 12
Mauchline, J., 82
Mead, J. K., 48, 51
Meisterhans, K., 154
Merrill, E. H., 26–27, 40
Metso, S., 175
Miller, D., 203
Miller, J. M., 5, 203
Mittelstadt, M. W., xx, 194, 201, 206
Moberly, R. W. L., 224
Montague, G. T., 40
Motyer, A., 215
Moulton, J. H., 132–33
Munnich, O., 128, 134
Muraoka, T., 135–37, 153, 162
Murphy, C., 174–77, 184, 188

Nelson, R. D., 52, 55
Newsom, C. A., 178–82
Niditch, S., 12
Ngien, D., 251

Oeming, M., 71
O'Reilly, L., 46
Oswalt, J. N., 114

Packer, J. I., 222
Panitz, R. I., 5, 22
Pannenberg, W., 240, 247
Parry, D. W., 172, 181
Payne, D., 105, 107
Pietersen, L. K., 188
Pietersma, A., 135–36
Polaski, D. C., 119
Polzin, R., 17–18, 59
Porter, S. E., xx, 130–31, 133–35, 139
Provan, I. W., 50, 54–55

Reis, P. T., 52
Reiter, G., 147
Reno, R. R., 232–33
Ringma, C. R., 233
Ristau, K. A., 87–88
Robertson, A. T., 196
Robinson, J., 44
Root, A., 227
Routledge, R. L., 38
Rudolph, W., 157, 160, 165

Sals, U., 104, 106–7, 119
Schleusner, J. F., 149, 154, 160
Schlingensiepen, F., 229
Schmid, K., 117, 119
Schniedewind, W. M., 188
Schofield, A., 175
Scholl, R., 119
Schuller, E. M., 172, 174–75
Schultz, B., 175
Seitz, C. R., 111, 119
Shepherd, V., 247
Sheppard, G., 216
Shipp, G. P., 147
Siedlecki, A., 62
Silva, M., 129–31, 134–35, 137–38
Smelik, K. A. D., 110
Smith, G. V., xx, 65, 114
Sparks, J. T., 60, 71
Stegemann, H., 172, 177
Stone, L. G., 12
Stromberg, J., 111
Stronstad, R., 195, 197–99

Authors Index

Stock, S. G., 132
Stuart, D., 196-97
Swain, S. R., 251
Swartley, W. M., 201, 204
Swete, H. B., 128, 130, 133

Thackeray, H. S. J., 130, 133
Thompson, D. W., 146
Thumb, A., 133
Tigchelaar, E., 176
Tino, J., 89
Tolini, G., 115
Tov, E., 77, 172, 181
Trebilco, P. R., 185, 187-88
Treier, D. J., 229

Unsok Ro, J., 177, 184

Vanderhooft, D. S., 106
Vanhoozer, K. J., 229
Vanier, J., 224
Van Winkle, D. W., 44, 48
Vermeylen, J., 116, 119
Voitila, A., 134
Volf, M., 247, 249

Wagner, J. R., 135
Walser, G., 134
Walsh, J. T., 51-53
Walton, J. H., 237, 242-43
Watson, F., 230-32
Watts, J. D. W., 115
Way, K. C., 52
Weaver-Zercher, D., 205-6
Webb, B. G., 18

Webster, J., 229-30
Wellhausen, J., 80, 82, 135
Wenham, G. J., 242
Whybray, R. N., 107
Wildberger, H., 109, 115-16
Williamson, H. G. M., xx, 59, 67, 89, 103
Wilson, R. R., 60-61, 86
Wirzba, N., 244-45
Wise, M. O., 173
Wiseman, D. J., 50
Wold, B. G., 171, 177
Wolters, A., xx, 144-45, 149, 151, 154, 156, 158, 160, 162, 164-66
Wong, G. T. K., 17-18
Wood, L. J., 40, 96
Wray Beal, L. M., 47, 53
Wright, B., 136, 174, 176
Wright, C. H. H., 161
Wright, C. J. H., 40
Wright, J. W., 88
Wright, N. T., 229

Yammamori, T., 203
Yoder, J. H., 195, 198-99
Yong, A., 201
Young, F., 224
Younger, K. L., 5

Zapff, B. M., 117-18, 120
Zanella, F., 171
Ziegler, J., 131, 145, 163
Zimmerman, J., 239

www.ingramcontent.com/pod-product-compliance
Lightning Source LLC
Chambersburg PA
CBHW061433300426
44114CB00014B/1661